M000190369

CLIMATE CHANGE AND THE VOICELESS

Future generations, wildlife, and natural resources – collectively referred to as "the voiceless" in this work – are the most vulnerable and least equipped populations to protect themselves from the impacts of global climate change. While domestic and international law protections are beginning to recognize rights and responsibilities that apply to the voiceless community, these legal developments have yet to be pursued in a collective manner and have not been considered together in the context of climate change and climate justice. In *Climate Change and the Voiceless*, Randall S. Abate identifies the common vulnerabilities of the voiceless in the Anthropocene era and demonstrates how the law, by incorporating principles of sustainable development, can evolve to protect their interests more effectively. This work should be read by anyone interested in how the law can be employed to mitigate the effects of climate change on those who stand to lose the most.

RANDALL S. ABATE is the inaugural Rechnitz Family and Urban Coast Institute Endowed Chair in Marine and Environmental Law and Policy, and Professor in the Department of Political Science and Sociology at Monmouth University. Professor Abate has taught at six US law schools over the course of twenty-four years. He also has taught international and comparative law courses – and delivered invited lectures – on environmental and animal law on six continents. He has published five books and thirty articles and book chapters on environmental and animal law topics.

Climate Change and the Voiceless

PROTECTING FUTURE GENERATIONS, WILDLIFE, AND NATURAL RESOURCES

RANDALL S. ABATE

Monmouth University

CAMBRIDGE
UNIVERSITY PRESS

University Printing House, Cambridge CB2 8BS, United Kingdom

One Liberty Plaza, 20th Floor, New York, NY 10006, USA

477 Williamstown Road, Port Melbourne, VIC 3207, Australia

314–321, 3rd Floor, Plot 3, Splendor Forum, Jasola District Centre, New Delhi – 110025, India

79 Anson Road, #06–04/06, Singapore 079906

Cambridge University Press is part of the University of Cambridge.

It furthers the University's mission by disseminating knowledge in the pursuit of education, learning, and research at the highest international levels of excellence.

www.cambridge.org
Information on this title: www.cambridge.org/9781108480116
DOI: 10.1017/9781108647076

© Randall S. Abate 2020

This publication is in copyright. Subject to statutory exception and to the provisions of relevant collective licensing agreements, no reproduction of any part may take place without the written permission of Cambridge University Press.

First published 2020

A catalogue record for this publication is available from the British Library.

Library of Congress Cataloging-in-Publication Data
NAMES: Abate, Randall, author.
TITLE: Climate change and the voiceless : protecting future generations, wildlife, and natural resources / Randall S. Abate, Monmouth University.
DESCRIPTION: Cambridge, United Kingdom ; New York, NY, USA : Cambridge University Press, 2020. | Includes index.
IDENTIFIERS: LCCN 2019017890 | ISBN 9781108480116 (hardback) | ISBN 9781108703222 (pbk.)
SUBJECTS: LCSH: Environmental law, International. | Climatic changes–Law and legislation.
CLASSIFICATION: LCC K3585 .A23 2020 | DDC 344.04/6–dc23
LC record available at https://lccn.loc.gov/2019017890

ISBN 978-1-108-48011-6 Hardback
ISBN 978-1-108-70322-2 Paperback

Cambridge University Press has no responsibility for the persistence or accuracy of URLs for external or third-party internet websites referred to in this publication and does not guarantee that any content on such websites is, or will remain, accurate or appropriate.

For my granddaughter, Vera, and the environmental stewards in her generation and in generations yet to come.

Contents

About the Author

Randall S. Abate is the inaugural Rechnitz Family and Urban Coast Institute Endowed Chair in Marine and Environmental Law and Policy and a tenured full professor in the Department of Political Science and Sociology at Monmouth University in West Long Brach, New Jersey. He joined the Monmouth University faculty in 2018 with twenty-four years of full-time law teaching experience at six US law schools, most recently as a tenured full professor at Florida A&M University College of Law in Orlando, where he also served as Associate Dean for Academic Affairs in 2017 and Director of the Center for International Law and Justice from 2012 to 2016.

Professor Abate teaches courses in domestic and international environmental law, constitutional law, and animal law. He has taught international and comparative law courses – and delivered lectures – on environmental and animal law topics in Argentina, Australia, Brazil, Canada, the Cayman Islands, China, Colombia, India, Kenya, Kyrgyzstan, the Netherlands, Serbia, South Africa, South Korea, Spain, Turkey, the United Kingdom, and Vanuatu. In April 2013, he taught a Climate Change Law and Justice course at the National Law Academy in Odessa, Ukraine on a Fulbright Specialist grant. From 2016 to 2018, he delivered invited lectures on climate justice and animal law topics at several of the top law schools in the world including Harvard University, University of Cambridge, University of Oxford, Yale University, the University of Pennsylvania, the University of Melbourne, the University of Sydney, King's College London, and Seoul National University.

Professor Abate has published more than thirty law journal articles and book chapters on environmental law topics, with a recent emphasis on climate change law and justice. He is the editor of *Climate Justice: Case Studies in Global and Regional Governance Challenges* (ELI Press, 2016), *What Can Animal Law Learn from Environmental Law?* (ELI Press, 2015), and *Climate Change Impacts on*

Ocean and Coastal Law: U.S. and International Perspectives (Oxford University Press, 2015), and coeditor of *Climate Change and Indigenous Peoples: The Search for Legal Remedies* (Edward Elgar, 2013). Early in his career, he handled environmental law matters at two law firms in Manhattan. He holds a BA from the University of Rochester and a JD and MSEL (Environmental Law and Policy) from Vermont Law School.

Preface

The voice of the inanimate object, therefore, should not be stilled. That does not mean that the judiciary takes over the managerial functions from the federal agency. It merely means that before these priceless bits of Americana (such as a valley, an alpine meadow, a river, or a lake) are forever lost or are so transformed as to be reduced to the eventual rubble of our urban environment, the voice of the existing beneficiaries of these environmental wonders should be heard.[1]

These famous words from Justice Douglas in his oft-quoted dissenting opinion in the US Supreme Court case, *Sierra Club* v. *Morton*, provided the foundation for the burgeoning field of environmental standing that unfolded in its wake and helped galvanize the ambitious and effective environmental protection movement in the United States in the 1970s. Nevertheless, despite decades of success in implementing and enforcing federal environmental laws in the United States, Justice Douglas's vision in this dissenting opinion for an ecocentric paradigm of environmental regulation (i.e., one that focuses on protecting the intrinsic value of nature rather than focusing on nature's value to humans) has not yet been realized. His message regarding the need for our legal system to recognize, amplify, and heed the interests of nature is more relevant and more necessary than ever today in the Anthropocene[2] era.

---

[1] Sierra Club v. Morton, 405 U.S. 727, 749–50 (1972) (Douglas, J., dissenting).
[2] The term "Anthropocene era" was coined as a reference point in environmental and geological history at approximately the turn of the twenty-first century to describe the time period in which humankind now finds itself. This is a time in the history of the planet during which human-kind has "caused mass extinction of plant and animal species through pollution and destruction of land, oceans, and the atmosphere" through our resource-intensive and consumption-driven lifestyles in the industrial and technological era of the past century. *See* Joseph Stromberg, *What Is the Anthropocene and Are We in It?* SMITHSONIAN.COM (Jan. 2013), https://www.smithsonianmag.com/science-nature/what-is-the-anthropocene-and-are-we-in-it-164801414/.

Climate change is the defining social, political, and legal issue of this century. Climate change regulation began with mitigation strategies, and these efforts remain an important and polarizing dimension of the climate change regulation debate. Within the past decade, however, climate change adaptation issues have posed daunting regulatory challenges from environmental and human rights perspectives. The need to implement effective climate change adaptation measures is an urgent political, economic, and legal concern in developed and developing nations alike. Climate adaptation challenges pose the gravest threat to climate justice communities throughout the world – those whose vulnerability causes them to be disproportionately affected by climate change impacts – such as low-lying island nations, indigenous communities in the Arctic, and low-income and minority communities that lack the resources and infrastructure to adapt effectively to climate change impacts.

In addition to the vulnerable climate justice communities that face climate adaptation challenges in the Anthropocene era, there are three populations in the global community that are most vulnerable and least equipped to protect themselves. These categories – collectively referred to as "the voiceless" in this book – include future generations,[3] wildlife, and natural resources. Domestic and international legal principles and initiatives are beginning to recognize rights and responsibilities that apply to the voiceless community; however, these protections have yet to be pursued across all three communities of the voiceless and have not been considered collectively in the context of climate change and climate justice. This book seeks to identify the common vulnerabilities of the voiceless and how the law can evolve to protect their interests more effectively in the face of climate change impacts.

Three themes apply to the collective protection of the voiceless in the Anthropocene era. First, these populations are similarly impacted by climate change in a manner that the law overlooks and that requires application of stewardship principles inherent in the public trust doctrine and in constitutional mandates in a growing number of countries. Second, their common vulnerability underscores the need for a new rights-based legal regime to respond to climate adaptation challenges. Third, recent developments in atmospheric trust litigation, rights-based litigation for protection of wildlife, and legislative initiatives conferring legal personhood rights to natural resources make the time right for this book. Each category has made progress in an independent yet piecemeal manner in limited contexts in recent years, but more coordinated and broad-scale efforts are necessary.

---

[3] For purposes of this book, the term "future generations" includes today's children and unborn children of the future. These populations share the common vulnerability of inheriting a planet plagued by the climate change crisis and relying on unsatisfactory existing regulatory strategies to protect themselves from environmental catastrophe.

This stewardship-focused and rights-based revolution will face significant challenges in the years ahead, primarily because it represents a departure from the successful but inflexible and outmoded command-and-control paradigm of environmental regulation that has been in place since the 1970s. Another challenge in ushering in this new regulatory model is striking a balance between anthropogenic stewardship and ecocentric legal personhood as mechanisms of legal protection. To achieve this balance, this book proposes a continuum of common but differentiated rights. Given how different categories of humans have different degrees of rights-based protections (individuals vs. corporations, adults vs. children, etc.), and how developed and developing countries bear different responsibilities to manage climate change impacts, a continuum of rights-based protections for future generations, wildlife, and natural resources can be implemented based on capacity for stewardship. In this regard, future generations of humans should have the most rights and responsibilities. They should have a positive right to inherit a stable climate as future climate stewards.[4] Positive rights are accompanied by responsibilities that only humans can bear. By contrast, wildlife and natural resources should have negative rights-based protections. For wildlife, this would entail the right to be free from abuse and unlawful confinement, and for natural resources (and some forms of wildlife), it would involve a right to be free from unsustainable use.

There are several reasons why this rights-based paradigm is necessary now. First, the failures of traditional international environmental governance are more apparent than ever. After more than a decade of efforts to incorporate human rights language into the international climate change treaty regime, the Paris Agreement and its limited reference to human rights in the preamble of the agreement underscores the urgency to bypass the gridlock of traditional international treaty diplomacy to create a rights-based approach outside of that framework. By contrast, domestic courts and legislatures have offered significant promise to advance a rights-based approach.

Second, the command-and-control paradigm of environmental regulation is not adequate to address the problem of climate change. That regulatory model was widely employed in the first two decades of climate regulation at the domestic and international levels with a focus on climate mitigation. When it became apparent that climate mitigation efforts would not be able to halt and reverse climate change impacts, the focus of climate change regulation shifted to adaptation. With the shift to adaptation, rights-based considerations emerged and the field of climate justice was born.

---

[4] This argument draws on the visionary language from the district court's decision in the *Juliana v. United States*. Drawing on the logic of the *Obergefell v. Hodges* that found constitutional protection for same-sex marriage, the court noted that a stable climate, like marriage, is an essential platform for the enjoyment of all other rights. This analysis will be explored in depth in Chapter 3 of the book.

The arsenal of federal environmental statutes in the 1970s in the United States was an effective regulatory system to address the domestic air, water, and land-based pollution crises. By contrast, climate change is a global problem with planetary implications that must draw on a more potent tool box of legal mechanisms. Recent legislative developments in legal personhood protections for natural resources, similar efforts in the courts for wildlife, and atmospheric trust litigation for future generations are important steps in this paradigm shift. Atmospheric trust litigation in the United States and abroad may be the tipping point for this legal revolution.

Third, the need for meaningful action is urgent. The sixth mass extinction that scientists predict may arrive this century is not just another episode of "the strong will survive and we will see who remains" transition, because it threatens the viability of humans as stewards of ecosystems. Climate change magnifies the natural and unnatural threats to ecosystems and puts the earth on a collision course with eco-catastrophe. Every crisis is an opportunity, however. Climate change threatens to decimate the earth and it threatens to do so quickly as a "threat multiplier" with critical "tipping points"[5] in the near future. Yet the urgency of this pending eco-catastrophe could be the impetus to transform our legal system to respond effectively with rights-based legal mechanisms for the voiceless.

Fourth, in promoting this paradigm shift toward enhanced stewardship duties and rights-based protections, this effort can capitalize on the momentum from recent legal victories in protecting the common vulnerability of marginalized climate justice communities. Climate change regulation is already starting to be perceived and applied as a human rights and justice issue, which has enabled marginalized climate justice populations like indigenous peoples to secure procedural and substantive protections in the climate change impacts context. Moreover, international human rights law has embraced the connection between climate change and human rights in UN resolutions and through the work of a special rapporteur on human rights and the environment. The progress made and lessons learned from protecting the *vulnerable* can serve as a valuable foundation on which to advance the effort to protect the *voiceless*. The voiceless community is just starting to see legal protections and advocates for their cause. Earlier calls for their protection were limited to academic discourse in foundational and groundbreaking works by Edith Brown Weiss,[6] Christopher Stone,[7] and Peter Singer.[8] The forward

---

[5] "Tipping points" in the scientific literature indicate that the international community's window of opportunity for meaningful action on global climate change is closing rapidly. The IPCC 1.5°C Assessment Report from October 2018 projected that the global community has approximately twelve years remaining to meet its targets from the Paris Agreement, after which all we can do is brace for climate change impacts and do our best to adapt.

[6] EDITH BROWN WEISS, IN FAIRNESS TO FUTURE GENERATIONS: INTERNATIONAL LAW, COMMON PATRIMONY, AND INTERGENERATIONAL EQUITY (1989).

[7] CHRISTOPHER D. STONE, SHOULD TREES HAVE STANDING? LAW, MORALITY, AND THE ENVIRONMENT (3d ed. 2010).

[8] PETER SINGER, ANIMAL LIBERATION (1975).

thinking on these issues from decades past now has an opportunity to take root as a response to the climate change crisis and as an extension of the law's effort to protect the vulnerable from climate change impacts. The time has come to implement those prescient visions for protection of the voiceless.

It is no longer a matter of whether this legal revolution will occur, but only a matter of when and how. The environmental management paradigm of the twentieth century is not sustainable. Striking examples of this reality are how the maximum sustainable yield model of fisheries management contributed to the collapse of global fisheries and the multiple use and sustained yield model of forest management similarly facilitated the demise of once-abundant forests in the United States. In both of these contexts, regulatory models are shifting to preservation-based strategies, such as marine and terrestrial protected areas to replace the (un)sustainable use model. These preservation-oriented approaches reflect the growing recognition of the intrinsic ecosystem value of these resources, irrespective of their value for human consumption.

Rights and responsibilities should offer a mix of benefits and burdens to those who hold them. The most common argument opposing the recognition of legal personhood rights for wildlife is that they are unable to bear human responsibilities. Yet those human responsibilities are not being fully engaged by humans in their relationship to wildlife and natural resources. Human responsibility means little if it is not exercised at least in part for the benefit of the vulnerable and voiceless. Unfortunately, human "responsibility" toward the voiceless has been to abuse the right to develop and seek economic gain in a manner that jeopardizes the sustainability of wildlife and natural resources. Efforts in the US in the past three decades to roll back the ambitious scope of protections for wildlife and natural resources under the Endangered Species Act (ESA) are a prime example of this clash between stewardship objectives and anthropocentric economic development values. The ESA is controversial by design because it is among the few environmental statutes that do not place human needs and objectives first. A new stewardship ethic of eco-responsibility is needed to protect all living entities' right to sustain themselves on the earth as a potent weapon in the struggle to endure in the face of the environmental and human rights impacts of the Anthropocene era.

The timing is right for this volume given the recent "perfect storm" of legal developments in these three voiceless communities. The Nonhuman Rights Project's legal personhood cases on behalf of primates and mammals have garnered national and international attention; legislative and judicial developments in legal personhood for natural resources in the United States and abroad have been in the headlines regularly in the past year; and the *Juliana* case, building on a longstanding tradition of protection of future generations, has been dubbed the "environmental trial of the century" as it works its way through multiple procedural challenges in US federal courts. These developments in the protection of the voiceless provide a valuable foundation on which to develop a stewardship-focused and rights-based approach to climate change adaptation.

This book seeks to make several unique contributions. First, it unites these three categories of the voiceless for the first time in a single legal analysis by highlighting and underscoring common and synergistic recent legal developments across these categories. Second, it uses climate change impacts and regulation as a unifying theme to protect the shared vulnerability that these communities face in the Anthropocene era. Third, it proposes enhanced governmental stewardship duties coupled with a rights-based framework for the protection of these communities in the Anthropocene era. Finally, this book offers valuable insights derived from interviews with lawyers working on some of the leading judicial developments on these topics in the United States and around the world.

The philosopher George Berkeley is famous (if not infamous) for his dialogue regarding perception of trees in a park[9]: "But, say you, surely there is nothing easier than for me to imagine trees, for instance, in a park ... and nobody by to perceive them."[10] To which Berkeley responds, "The objects of sense exist only when they are perceived ... the trees therefore are in the garden no longer than while there is someone by to perceive them."[11] This book's premise is a proposed emergency antidote to the anthropocentric perspective of nature reflected in Berkeley's dialogue. This view is the underlying cause of our global environmental crisis. Thinking of wildlife and nature as existing only through human perception objectifies these intrinsically valuable beings and resources as commodities for human consumption and development. This anthropocentric mindset has severed the ecosystem ties that unite us and has alienated us from our ancestors and successors in the human race. Failure to conserve wildlife and nature represents a failure to exercise our moral (and hopefully soon-to-be legal) duty to serve as stewards of the environment for the benefit of future generations.

[9] *See* GEORGE BERKELEY, A TREATISE CONCERNING THE PRINCIPLES OF HUMAN KNOWLEDGE (1734).
[10] *Id.* at Section 23.
[11] *Id.* at Section 45.

Acknowledgments

I was very fortunate to have indispensable research assistance on this book project from several loyal volunteers who generously devoted their time and outstanding services. The following individuals provided exceptionally high-quality assistance above and beyond the call of duty: Oshani Amaratunga; Jess Beaulieu, Esq; Ian Fisher, Esq.; Alexandra Horn; Zarije Kocic, LLM; Thea Philip, Esq.; Soraya Ridanovic, LLM; and Carita Skinner. Also providing valuable research assistance were Darly Bocanegra, Jennifer Gonzalez, Kaitlyn Groselle, Kelly Hanna, Avital Li, Julian Montoya, Alexis Nava-Martinez, Jackson Olsen, Kaela Sculthorpe, Bettina Tran, and Michael Wojnar.

I am also grateful to my colleagues who graciously hosted me for prepublication book talks during the 2018–19 academic year at the following law schools and universities: University of Cambridge, University of Strathclyde, King's College London, George Washington University Law School, University of Miami School of Law, Roger Williams University Law School, University of Detroit Mercy College of Law, and the New School for Social Research. I received valuable input and support from these audiences as I worked to refine my thesis in this book and complete the manuscript

Finally, I owe a deep debt of gratitude to my wife, Nigara, for her valuable proofreading, cover design input, and patience, love, and support through twenty-five years of marriage and innumerable publication deadlines.

1

An Anthropogenic Problem That Requires an Ecocentric Solution

The severity of the climate change crisis is caused exclusively by human action and inaction. First, for the past several decades, humans have been responsible for 100 percent of the greenhouse gases (GHGs) in the atmosphere that contribute to climate change.[1] Second, the failure of domestic and international climate change mitigation and adaptation efforts has exacerbated this crisis instead of managing it. This human-caused crisis cannot be addressed effectively by a human-centered, development-focused regulatory framework.

Recent developments in climate change diplomacy are just starting to implement legal protections for vulnerable and marginalized climate justice communities, but these efforts are too little and too late. After years of efforts to integrate human rights–based protections into the post-Kyoto climate change treaty regime, only lip service was secured in limited nonbinding and aspirational references to human rights dimensions of climate change in UN resolutions,[2] the Copenhagen

---

[1] JOSEPH ROMM, CLIMATE CHANGE: WHAT EVERYONE NEEDS TO KNOW 7 (2d ed. 2018) ("The latest science finds that *all* of the warming since 1970 is due to human causes.").

[2] Human Rights Council Res. 38/4, UN Doc. A/HRC/RES/38/4, ¶ 3 (July 16, 2018) ("*Calls upon* States to consider, among other aspects, human rights within the framework of the United Nations Framework Convention on Climate Change"); *see also* Human Rights Council Res. 35/20, UN Doc. A/HRC/RES/35/20, ¶ 4 (July 7, 2017); and Human Rights Council Res. 32/33, UN Doc. A/HRC/RES/32/33, ¶ 9 (July 18, 2016); Human Rights Council Res. 29/15, UN Doc. A/HRC/RES/29/15, ¶ 7 (July 22, 2015) ("*Encourages* relevant special procedures mandate holders to continue to consider the issue of climate change and human rights within their respective mandates" [emphasis added]); *see also* Human Rights Council Res. 26/27, UN Doc. A/HRC/RES/26/27, ¶ 8 (July 25, 2014); Human Rights Council Res. 18/22, UN Doc. A/HRC/RES/18/22, ¶¶ 2–4 (Oct. 17, 2011) (requesting the High Commissioner for Human Rights to organize a seminar and report on human rights and climate change); Human Rights Council Res. 10/4, UN Doc. A/HRC/RES/10/4, ¶¶ 1–2 (Mar. 25, 2009) (deciding to hold a panel discussion and prepare a summary on the relationship between climate change and human rights); Human Rights Council Res. 7/23, UN Doc. A/HRC/RES/7/23, ¶ 1 (Mar. 28, 2008) (expressing concern that climate change "poses an immediate and

Agreement,[3] the Cancun Agreements,[4] the Warsaw Loss and Damage Mechanism,[5] and the preamble of the Paris Agreement.[6] At this rate, it would take several decades to incorporate adequate protections for the voiceless into these instruments. A stewardship-focused, rights-based revolution is starting to percolate outside of the climate change context and it needs to be applied to inform a new approach to climate change regulation in order to address protections for the voiceless communities. An ecocentric paradigm is the only effective approach to regulate climate change.

This chapter first describes the deficiencies in the existing climate change regulatory regime at the international level and in the United States. It then addresses the constitutional, legislative, and common law mechanisms in the United States and in foreign domestic legal systems that have been used to promote a paradigm shift toward ecocentrism, primarily outside of the climate change context, which can be leveraged to help ensure protection of the voiceless in the Anthropocene era.

far-reaching threat to people and communities around the world" and requesting the Office of the High Commissioner for Refugees to prepare a study on the relationship between climate change and human rights).

[3] United Nations Framework Convention on Climate Change, *Copenhagen Accord*, UN Doc. FCCC/CP/2009/11/Add.1, Dec. 2/CP.15 (Mar. 30, 2010), https://unfccc.int/sites/default/files/resource/docs/2009/cop15/eng/11a01.pdf (providing a first step toward human rights recognition in the UNFCCC treaty regime by noting in para 1: "We recognize the critical impacts of climate change and the potential impacts of response measures on countries particularly vulnerable to its adverse effects and stress the need to establish a comprehensive adaptation programme including international support.").

[4] United Nations Framework Convention on Climate Change, The Cancun Agreements: Outcome of the work of the Ad Hoc Working Group on Long-Term Cooperative Action under the Convention, UN Doc. FCCC/CP/2010/7/Add.1, Dec. 1/CP.16, pmbl., ¶¶ 7–8, 72 (Mar. 15, 2011), https://unfccc.int/sites/default/files/resource/docs/2010/cop16/eng/07a01.pdf ("Recognizes the need to engage a broad range of stakeholders at the global, regional, national and local levels, be they government, including subnational and local government, private business or civil society, including youth and persons with disability, and that gender equality and the effective participation of women and indigenous peoples are important for effective action on all aspects of climate change.").

[5] United Nations Framework Convention on Climate Change, Warsaw international mechanism for loss and damage associated with climate change impacts, UN Doc. FCCC/CP/2013/10/Add.1, Dec. 2/CP.19, pmbl. (Jan. 31, 2014), https://unfccc.int/sites/default/files/resource/docs/2013/cop19/eng/10a01.pdf (noting that "climate change represents an urgent and potentially irreversible threat to human societies, future generations and the planet . . .").

[6] United Nations Framework Convention on Climate Change, *Adoption of the* Paris Agreement, UN Doc. FCCC/CP/2015/10/Add.1, Dec.1/CP.21, Annex, pmbl. (Jan. 29, 2016), https://unfccc.int/resource/docs/2015/cop21/eng/10a01.pdf ("*Acknowledging* that climate change is a common concern of humankind, Parties should, when taking action to address climate change, respect, promote and consider their respective obligations on human rights, the right to health, the rights of indigenous peoples, local communities, migrants, children, persons with disabilities and people in vulnerable situations and the right to development, as well as gender equality, empowerment of women and intergenerational equity" [emphasis added]).

I POLARIZING GRIDLOCK IN INTERNATIONAL AND US CLIMATE CHANGE REGULATION

The warning bells announcing the projected impacts of climate change have been ringing since the 1990s, and they have only grown louder and more frequent in the past decade. Building on the stern wake-up call regarding climate change projections contained in the IPCC First Assessment Report in 1990,[7] each subsequent report in seven-year increments has been progressively more grim and urgent than its predecessor. According to the IPCC's 1.5°C Report in October 2018,[8] the window of opportunity for the global community to have any meaningful impacts with mitigation efforts has narrowed further and is limited to little more than a decade from the time of this writing.[9] This prediction, and many other comparably disturbing and alarming projections, were contained in the IPCC's report.[10]

The urgency and severity of the climate crisis have not merely been conveyed on the pages of the IPCC's latest report. These realities have been on display for the world to witness in many manifestations, including the catastrophic wildfires in California in 2018 and devastating hurricanes such as Harvey and Irma in 2017 that caused extensive impacts to property, communities, and ecosystems. Hurricane Harvey triggered a flood of lawsuits against the federal government, local governments, and private-sector entities for failing to act or failing to act appropriately to protect citizens from the worst impacts of these storms.[11]

Impacts to the marine and coastal environment are not limited to the immediate damages to communities and property in the path of these hurricanes. Ocean acidification, invasive species, sea-level rise, coastal erosion, and saltwater intrusion are becoming increasingly more vexing threats from climate change. Climate change is also a potent public health threat in coastal areas and has been linked to an increase in waterborne and insect-borne diseases. Last but not least, scientists recently concluded that ocean warming is occurring 40 percent faster than

---

[7] UN Intergovernmental Panel on Climate Change, *Assessment Report 1: Impacts Assessment of Climate Change* (June 1990), https://archive.ipcc.ch/publications_and_data/publications_and_data_reports.shtml.

[8] UN Intergovernmental Panel on Climate Change, *Global Warming of 1.5°C* (Oct. 8, 2018), https://www.ipcc.ch/sr15/ (hereinafter "IPCC 1.5°C Report").

[9] *Id.*

[10] *Id.*

[11] *See, e.g.,* Kiah Collier, *Can Flooded-Out Houstonians Win Lawsuits against Army Corps?,* Texas Tribune (Sept. 28, 2017), https://www.texastribune.org/2017/09/28/will-flooded-out-hous tonians-prevail-lawsuits-against-army-corps/ (discussing inverse condemnation suits against US Army Corps of Engineers seeking damages for the avoidable flooding of property from Corps' "controlled releases" of water after the storm); Olivia Pulsinelli, *Riverstone Residents File Harvey-Related Lawsuit against Houston Engineering Firm,* HOUSTON BUS. J. (Apr. 8, 2018), https://www.bizjournals.com/houston/news/2018/04/06/riverstone-residents-file-harvey-related-lawsuit.html (describing a suit against an engineering firm, Costello Inc., alleging the defective design of a stormwater management system).

expected by the IPCC,[12] and that 2016, 2017, and 2018 were the warmest years on record for oceans.[13]

Climate change also is affecting both human rights and rights of the voiceless. Climate change is causing severe droughts, which have triggered food and water insecurity in many regions throughout the world. Sea-level rise is pushing many communities to face the imminent threat of forced migration, which in turn presents national and regional security issues. Climate change impacts destabilize marine and terrestrial ecosystems, compromising their natural resilience, which in turn causes a positive feedback loop to further destabilize these ecosystems and the wildlife that depend on them for sustenance and security. Climate change impacts threaten all of the earth's systems and leave future generations with a beleaguered planet fighting for its continued existence.

Much of the urgency and severity of the climate change crisis that the world now faces can be traced to two failures in political leadership: first, the intractable negotiations in three decades of Conferences of the Parties (COPs) at the international level, largely caused by uncompromising self-interest among some of the leading developed countries, and second, the failure of the United States to lead or even effectively participate in these negotiations and to implement federal climate and energy regulation at home. These two failures are related – they are rooted in shortsighted and unsustainable human consumption and overwhelming resistance to transitioning away from self-destructive habits that destroy our planet at an ever-accelerating pace.

International environmental diplomacy takes time, but in a few instances it was well worth the wait. For example, the United Nations Convention on the Law of the Sea[14] and the Montreal Protocol regime[15] are two international environmental treaty frameworks that have been highly successful in addressing daunting global environmental problems.[16] These two treaty regimes are nostalgic reference points for the positive results that the international community can realize when international environmental diplomacy devises effective international regulatory frameworks. Unfortunately, these examples of success in international environmental

---

[12] Chelsea Harvey, *Oceans Are Warming Faster than Predicted*, Sci. Am (Jan. 11, 2019), https://www.scientificamerican.com/article/oceans-are-warming-faster-than-predicted/.

[13] Doyle Rice, *Oceans Hottest on Record in 2018, Warming Faster than Previously Thought*, USA Today. com (Jan. 10, 2019), https://eu.usatoday.com/story/news/2019/01/10/global-warming-oceans-hottest-record-2018-heating-up-faster-pace/2539570002/.

[14] United Nations Convention on the Law of the Sea (Dec. 10, 1982), 1833 U.N.T.S. 397.

[15] Montreal Protocol on Substances that Deplete the Ozone Layer (Sept. 16, 1987), 1522 U.N.T.S. 3.

[16] *See* Joanna Mossop, *Can We Make the Oceans Greener? The Successes and Failures of UNCLOS as an Environmental Treaty*, 49 Vict. U. Wellington L. Rev. 573, 578–79 (2018); Melissa J. Durkee, *Persuasion Treaties*, 99 Va. L. Rev. 63, 104–10 (2013); Bryan A. Green, *Lessons from the Montreal Protocol: Guidance for the Next International Climate Change Agreement*, 39 Envtl. L. 253, 256–68 (2009); Cass R. Sunstein, *Of Montreal and Kyoto: A Tale of Two Protocols*, 31 Harv. Envtl. L. Rev. 1, 17–22, 22–35 (2007).

diplomacy did not penetrate the twenty-first century as the Anthropocene era ushered in a paralyzing impasse in responding to the most pressing political, environmental, and sociocultural issue of our time: climate change.

For a variety of reasons, the climate change treaty regime has been disappointingly different from these two global environmental success stories. From its auspicious beginnings at the United Nations Conference on Environment and Development in 1992, the United Nations Framework Convention on Climate Change (UNFCCC)[17] faced a daunting task in seeking to manage a global environmental problem that was larger and more rapidly progressing than most had anticipated.

In the early 1990s, climate change was perceived as a challenging global environmental problem that could be managed effectively through ambitious global GHG mitigation efforts. The UNFCCC laid a foundation that was painted with broad strokes, leaving the real challenges to be worked out in the details of the Kyoto Protocol[18] that followed shortly thereafter. If effectively implemented, the principles referenced in the UNFCCC – the precautionary principle, common but differentiated responsibility, common concern of humankind, and intergenerational equity – could be effective in regulating climate change. However, the ultimate approach to international climate change regulation belied the laudable objectives reflected in these principles. Instead of applying the precautionary principle to climate change threats, the global response has been muted by varying degrees of an unwarranted cost–benefit approach. Worse still, the most conservative and inexcusable cost–benefit approaches in favor of business-as-usual economic growth were implemented in some of the wealthiest and most developed countries that are also among the largest emitters of GHGs: the United States, Canada, and Australia.

Common but differentiated responsibility took various forms in the past three decades,[19] but it never adequately reflected the developed countries' moral and political responsibility to assist developing countries, even those with rapidly developing economies. The bedrock principle of international environmental diplomacy, the common concern of humankind, degraded into a shameful reality tantamount to "the economically and politically powerful will act in their self-interest with no consequences." Most tragically, the objective to act in a manner respectful of intergenerational equity was shamelessly overlooked in the climate change treaty framework. In fact, the most enduring legacy of climate change

[17] United Nations Framework Convention on Climate Change (UNFCCC) (May 9, 1992), 1771 U.N.T.S. 107 (entered into force Mar. 21, 1994).

[18] Kyoto Protocol to the United Nations Framework Convention on Climate Change, Dec. 10, 1997, 37 I.L.M. 22 (entered into force Feb. 16, 2005).

[19] See PATRICIA G. FERREIRA, *From Justice to Participation: The Paris Agreement's Pragmatic Approach to Differentiation*, in CLIMATE JUSTICE: CASE STUDIES IN GLOBAL AND REGIONAL GOVERNANCE CHALLENGES (Randall S. Abate ed., 2016) (discussing how the early form of common but differentiated responsibility in the UNFCCC treaty framework focused on justice considerations, whereas the form adopted in the Paris Agreement is grounded in pragmatism).

diplomacy will likely be the proliferation of climate justice litigation in the United States and in many countries across the globe seeking to hold governments and multinational corporations accountable with intergenerational equity-based lawsuits for these governments' and private actors' contributions to exacerbating the climate change crisis.[20] To help fill the void where politicians have failed to fulfill their responsibilities to present and future generations, the courts are now seizing the opportunity to reorient humanity's moral compass toward an ecocentric paradigm in regulating climate change before it is too late.

Was the Kyoto Protocol a success or failure? One statistic tells two stories. Global GHG emissions increased slightly during the Kyoto Protocol's implementation period from 1997 to 2012. While this statistic appears to be bad news, when one considers that the United States, China, and other major GHG-emitting countries did not participate in complying with the mandates of this regime, this outcome can be considered a success of near-global cooperation.[21] Ultimately, however, the fact that major GHG emitters were able to remain on the sidelines and refuse to participate in addressing this global crisis was a preview of the deepening dysfunction reflected in the Paris Agreement. The Kyoto Protocol's exclusive focus on mitigation also was perhaps misplaced in hindsight, but that was in part a function of the evolving clarity with which climate scientists conveyed the message that "all we can really do is brace for impacts" from climate change and promote effective adaptation strategies.

Adaptation quickly became the name of this new regulatory game. Notwithstanding the clear need for effective adaptation efforts, the integration of human rights considerations into the post-Kyoto regulatory efforts could not have been slower. Years of coordinated efforts from indigenous peoples and small island nations' organizations led to little or no progress in accounting for the human rights impacts of climate change. The ensuing agreements leading up to and including the post-Kyoto regime reflected in the Paris Agreement all failed miserably in properly acknowledging and implementing these principles. It was the failure of these international instruments that gave rise to a burgeoning and vocal climate justice movement in courts, negotiating rooms, legislatures, academia, and civil society.

International environmental diplomacy is always highly politicized and has featured many nearly irreconcilable impasses between developed and developing countries in many international environmental agreements. But the climate change treaty was different. Rather than striking effective compromises between developed and developing countries' interests (like the grace period for developing countries' compliance in the Montreal Protocol regime), the political clashes between the

---

[20] See *infra* Chapter 3 for a discussion of these lawsuits.
[21] See Duncan Clark, *Has the Kyoto Protocol Made Any Difference to Carbon Emissions?* THE GUARDIAN (Nov. 26, 2012), https://www.theguardian.com/environment/blog/2012/nov/26/kyoto-protocol-carbon-emissions.

developed and developing world in the climate change treaty regime only seemed to grow more strident and irreparable with every COP leading up to the Paris Agreement. Ultimately, the Paris Agreement reluctantly conceded that neither side would win that battle. Climate change treaty regime efforts have proceeded from that cracked foundation of the "new normal" of the developed and developing countries' failure to reach effective negotiated compromises on climate change regulation.

Last-minute deals, including efforts by the US delegation, saved the negotiations from collapsing with no agreement.[22] Heralded by some as a success,[23] the Paris Agreement features many compromises that only those with very low standards would consider a successful diplomatic outcome. Decades of dysfunction ultimately paved the way for cheers in welcoming this tepid diplomatic response to a burning global environmental problem. The mandate from Paris in oversimplified terms was

---

[22] Jonathan Chait, *The Paris Climate Deal Is President Obama's Biggest Accomplishment*, N.Y. MAGAZINE (Dec. 14, 2015), http://nymag.com/intelligencer/2015/12/climate-deal-is-obamas-big gest-accomplishment.html; Martin Pengelly, *Obama Praises Paris Climate Deal as "Tribute to American Leadership*," THE GUARDIAN (Dec. 12, 2015), https://www.theguardian.com/us-news/ 2015/dec/12/obama-speech-paris-climate-change-talks-deal-american-leadership; Justin Worland, *How the U.S. Became an Unlikely Hero at the Paris Climate Summit*, TIME (Dec. 9, 2015), http://time.com/4140684/obama-paris-climate-talks/.

[23] Commentators disagree on whether the Paris Agreement is a success, a failure, or an outcome with a mix of gains and setbacks. For articles praising the Paris Agreement as a success, *see generally* David G. Victor, *Why Paris Worked: A Different Approach to Climate Diplomacy*, YALE ENV'T 360 (Dec. 15, 2015), https://e360.yale.edu/features/why_paris_worked_a_different_ approach_to_climate_diplomacy (noting that flexible strategy and a willingness to accept nonbinding commitments helped the Paris Agreement secure a solid foundation to promote a carbon-free future); Radislav S. Dimitrov, *The Paris Agreement: Behind Closed Doors*, 16 GLOBAL ENVTL. POLITICS 1 (Aug. 2016) (contending that climate diplomacy succeeded in the Paris Agreement in part because of persuasive arguments the economic benefits of climate action altered preferences to support policy commitments at the national and international levels). For arguments characterizing the Paris Agreement as a failure, *see generally* Clive L. Spash, *This Changes Nothing: The Paris Agreement to Ignore Reality*, 13 GLOBALIZATIONS 928 (2016), https://www.clivespash.org/wp-content/uploads/2015/04/2016-Spash-This-Changes-Noth ing.pdf (expressing concern that the Paris Agreement reflects a commitment to sustained industrial growth, risk management over disaster prevention, and future innovations in technology as the preferred responses to the climate change crisis); Adam Frank, *Paris Climate Agreement: Success or Failure?*, NPR.ORG (Jan. 12, 2016), https://www.npr.org/sections/13.7/2016/ 01/12/462753762/paris-climate-agreement-success-or-failure (noting that the Paris Agreement's targets are too weak and the governance is too uncertain). For characterizations of the Paris Agreement as a mix of gains and setbacks, *see generally* Jeff Goodell, *Saving the Paris Agreement*, ROLLING STONE (Jan. 18, 2019), https://www.rollingstone.com/politics/politics-fea tures/saving-the-paris-agreement-780473/ ("imperfect, not ambitious enough, and failed to address the many inequities of climate-change impacts. But it was a platform from which a better, stronger agreement could be built"); Raymond Clemencon, *The Two Sides of the Paris Climate Agreement: Dismal Failure or Historic Breakthrough?*, 25 J. ENV'T & DEV'T 3 (2016), https://journals.sagepub.com/doi/full/10.1177/1070496516631362 (observing that the Paris Agreement is an aspirational global accord that will trigger and legitimize more climate action around the world; however it is unclear whether such efforts will happen quickly enough and at a sufficient scale to avoid disastrous warming of the planet).

that each country should do the best it can to reduce its GHGs – surely not a recipe to save the planet from ecological disaster.

And then the news got worse. The marginal agreement was insufficient to address what climate scientists were predicting. Groups and individuals sued their countries that had agreed to Paris Agreement targets, asserting that their countries had failed to fulfill those commitments[24] or needed to exceed those commitments based on the latest projections from climate scientists.[25] Most recently, the sobering 1.5°C IPCC Assessment Report in 2018[26] sent a wave of panic through the climate policy world. Incremental progress was achieved at COP 24 in Katowice, Poland, including the Katowice "Rulebook," which includes mandates for mitigation, adaptation, and finance to fulfill the Paris Agreement's goals.[27] Unfortunately, overall, the sense of urgency in the wake of the 1.5°C IPCC Report hit a brick wall at Katowice, where yet another climate change COP failed to command more aggressive global climate change regulation to respond to the evolving clarity and warnings from climate change science.[28]

Why has the climate change treaty regime failed so miserably? There are several reasons, but a discussion of most of them is beyond the scope of this book.[29] At the root of the failure is human nature. First, humans are very poor at regulating long-term, slow-onset crises.[30] We are much better at responding to disasters after they occur rather than preparing for the ones that are likely to occur in the future. Second, economic problems always take precedence over both real and perceived environmental threats, with no exceptions. Third, we prefer reactive, targeted interventions to address a problem rather than slowly evolving, cumulative, and proactive responses. Therefore, we have a history of waging war as the solution to a

---

[24] For more information on this theory of climate justice litigation, *see infra* Chapter 2 for a discussion of the *Leghari* case in Pakistan.

[25] For more information on this theory of climate justice litigation, *see infra* Chapter 2 for a discussion of the *Urgenda* case in the Netherlands.

[26] IPCC 1.5°C Report, *supra* note 8.

[27] For a comprehensive summary of the outcomes in Katowice, *see generally* Center for Climate and Energy Solutions, Outcomes of the UN Conference of Climate Change in Katowice (Dec. 2018), https://www.c2es.org/site/assets/uploads/2018/12/cop-24-katowice-summary.pdf.

[28] Prem Shankar Jha, *The Katowice Summit Has Been a Resounding Failure*, HINDUSTAN TIMES (Dec. 20, 2018), https://www.hindustantimes.com/analysis/the-katowice-summit-has-been-a-resounding-failure/story-A2BuBSYduWUvf2lNJFgpeK.html.

[29] The climate change crisis poses daunting challenges for many reasons beyond the scope of this book including human nature and the inherent reluctance to address long-term, slow-onset problems effectively; the economic implications of an aggressive response to the problem; the need to proceed in the face of persistent climate change denial efforts from politicians, civil society, and private sector funded scientists; the expansive scope of the problem across all sectors of society; and, the role of the United States and its failure to provide political leadership on this issue.

[30] George Monbiot, *Why Is Climate Change Denial So Seductive?*, CONSERVATION (Jan. 14, 2010), https://www.conservationmagazine.org/2010/01/why-is-climate-change-denial-so-seductive/.

diplomatic problem that was inconveniently protracted and difficult to address. We are now gearing up for the next global bombing campaign, but it has nothing to do with warfare. We are gearing up to "bomb" the atmosphere and other global commons resources in an effort to geoengineer our way out of the climate change crisis, or to at least extend our ability to survive as a species on this planet in the Anthropocene era.[31]

Another root problem in our regulatory efforts is that the climate change treaty regime – much like our air, water, and land-based pollution control and fisheries management regimes – is based on a flawed premise. They proceed from the assumption that resources are to be harnessed and consumed for human use. Therefore, the only "management" involved in this approach to natural resources is in regulating how much will be consumed and how soon. The discussion is hardly ever about a "no consumption" or "no development" option.

This pro-development, pro-consumption approach to environmental management is fundamentally unsustainable. Despite our blind assumptions about their inexhaustible supply, the planet's resources are finite and ecosystems have collapsed and continue to collapse under this exploitative pressure. The sustainable development paradigm that took hold in the late 1980s was the first step in rescuing humankind from its self-destructive practices. A long-overdue "look before you leap" mandate was imposed on development decisions, which asked whether a proposed development effort would be able to proceed in a manner that would ensure an adequate supply of resources for future generations. Regrettably, this "think before acting" mantra often was nothing more than lip service and a check mark on a form that enabled "business as usual" to proceed without interruption in most instances. Environmental consciousness became trendy, "greenwashing"[32] became the corporate sector's new way of conducting business, and our development-focused habits persisted.

The 1970s and 1980s revealed many global environmental crises that were caused by our development-focused relationship with the environment. Although many of the global environmental legal responses were effective in treating each of those "symptoms" of global environmental demise, the "disease" soon emerged. Regardless of how effective we were in addressing stratospheric ozone depletion, species extinction, ocean management, and wetlands conservation, the drivers underlying each of these problems had a cumulative effect on exacerbating the most significant

[31] For a discussion of the various forms, proposed uses, and risks of climate geoengineering techniques, *see generally* CLIMATE CHANGE GEOENGINEERING: PHILOSOPHICAL PERSPECTIVES, LEGAL ISSUES, AND GOVERNANCE FRAMEWORKS (Wil C. G. Burns & Andrew L. Strauss eds., 2013); Catriona McKinnon, *Time Is Running Out on Climate Change, but Geoengineering Has Dangers of Its Own*, THE CONVERSATION (Dec. 3, 2018), https://theconversation.com/time-is-running-out-on-climate-change-but-geoengineering-has-dangers-of-its-own-107732.

[32] "Greenwashing" refers to the practice of making unsubstantiated or misleading claims about the environmental benefits of a product or service. PETER N. GOLDER & DEBANJAN MITRA, HANDBOOK OF RESEARCH OF RESEARCH ON NEW PRODUCT DEVELOPMENT 234 (2018).

and multifaceted global environmental threat: climate change. Even with good intentions and good regulatory strategies – both of which we lacked, based on the earlier discussion – climate change was by far the most vexing global environmental threat because of its comprehensive scope and the financial commitment and political will that would be necessary to mobilize an effective response.

The calls for rights of future generations, wildlife, and nature came much later after efforts to engage common but differentiated responsibility under the UNFCCC regime did little to address the climate change crisis. Common but differentiated responsibility reflects a right to development, which deepened the climate change crisis. The ideal was to enable development in the developing world in a "clean" manner through mechanisms such as the Clean Development Mechanism (CDM). While the CDM made some progress toward this goal in economically advanced developing countries like China and India, it was not as effective in promoting clean development in the least developed countries, where traditional development continues unabated.[33]

The first step toward a paradigm shift in climate change regulation was realized in recognizing the plight of the vulnerable communities and nations, which shined a light on the human rights dimensions of climate change and laid a foundation for the climate justice movement to emerge. On the coattails of advocacy and some limited protections for the vulnerable, only recently have legal protections expanded to secure protection of the voiceless. Some of these developments are related to climate change impacts, while others are not.

Apart from inherent limitations of human nature, the elephant in the room of global climate change diplomacy dysfunction is the United States. The United States's failure to address climate change at the federal level spanned three frustrating decades and included worthwhile cap-and-trade and carbon tax bills that were resoundingly defeated. Even a significant victory in the courts – *Massachusetts v. EPA* – became embroiled in court challenges for a decade after the decision was handed down in 2007, only to be undone by the Trump administration and courts in the wake of the Obama administration's late and limited victory with the Clean Power Plan. Despite the federal government's inertia, state and local government regulatory measures and private sector initiatives have been encouraging and are better than nothing, but are also too little, too late.

---

[33] Marie Blévin, The Clean Development Mechanism and the Poverty Issue, 41 Envtl. L. 777, 783 (2011); Bharathi Pillai, *Moving Forward to 2012: An Evaluation of the Clean Development Mechanism*, 18 N.Y.U. Envtl. L.J. 357, 360, 383–402 (2010); Michael Wara, *Measuring the Clean Development Mechanism's Performance and Potential*, 55 UCLA L. Rev. 1759, 1763–64 (2008); *see generally* Stephan Hoch, *Governing Clean Development in LDCs: Do CDM rules promote renewable energy in Ethiopia?*, The Governance of Clean Development Working Paper Series (Jan. 2012), https://www.uea.ac.uk/documents/439774/5807661/GCD+Working+Paper+018+-+Hoch+2012.pdf/4b72ea9c-91f1-496f-9b01-0b392cb5e5a9.

II THE TRANSITION TO AN ECOCENTRIC PARADIGM:
WHAT, WHY, AND HOW

What will it take to move away from this conspicuous series of failures toward an ecocentric paradigm and address the climate change crisis more effectively? Action at the national level to promote increased government stewardship and rights-based protections enforced by the judiciary offer the most promise. Hints of a transition toward an ecocentric paradigm of regulation have started to surface in recent years in the United States and in several foreign domestic contexts. These developments have occurred within and outside the climate change context.

While many of these developments have occurred within the past decade, some of the opportunities for ecocentric regulation have been there for decades, their full potential yet to be realized. Two US environmental statutes – the National Environmental Policy Act[34] and the Endangered Species Act[35] – are marvelous exceptions to the development-focused paradigm and serve as a foundation for a shift from an anthropocentric to an ecocentric paradigm in the United States.[36] This book seeks to leverage and merge these seemingly unrelated mechanisms in a coordinated effort to promote ecocentric regulation to respond to the climate change crisis.

The anthropocentric paradigm under which the world currently operates is an approach under which "humans consider themselves the dominant and most important life form; non-humans are important only insofar as they are useful for maintaining the position of humans at the top of the social hierarchy."[37] The ecocentric approach, by contrast, embraces the inherent value of nature without regard for its value to humanity.[38] This approach is reflected in the rights of nature movement, most notably in Latin America, and most prominently reflected in the language in Ecuador's 2008 Constitution.[39]

There are several reasons why a transition toward an ecocentric paradigm is underway now. In the past decade, there has been a "perfect storm" of developments scientifically, politically, and culturally that have drawn increased attention to climate change and the need for more aggressive regulation. A growing awareness of major climate change impacts from hurricanes, record-setting heat, wildfires, and the urgent need to respond to and to regulate this crisis as reflected in the IPCC 1.5°C Report, has prompted increased dialogue and initiatives to develop more

---

[34] National Environmental Policy Act, 42 U.S.C. §§ 4321–47 (2018).
[35] The Endangered Species Act, 16 U.S.C. § 1531–40 (2018).
[36] *See infra* Chapter 6 for a discussion of how these statutes can facilitate the transition to an ecocentric paradigm.
[37] Paola Villavicenzio & Louis Kotze, *Living in Harmony with Nature? A Critical Appraisal of the Rights of Mother Earth in Bolivia*, 7 TRANSNAT'L ENVT'L L. 397, 398 (2018).
[38] *Id.* (internal citations omitted).
[39] *Id.* (internal citations omitted). For a discussion of the rights of nature movement in the US and in several foreign domestic contexts, *see infra* Chapter 5.

effective climate change regulation. Several ambitious and creative developments have occurred in recent years in the United States and abroad in the courts and in legislative arenas. The bold ambition of The Green New Deal[40] is a notable step in its proposal to transform the nature and scope of how the United States can address climate change by treating the issue as a societal problem with many social, political, and economic variables, rather than merely as an environmental problem.

Many significant legal developments offer promise to usher in a new era of potential protections for the vulnerable and voiceless in the near future. The rights of nature movement has secured impressive victories throughout the world in constitutional, legislative, and judicial developments that recognize the ability of natural resources to secure legal protections based on their intrinsic value and had the opportunity to vindicate these rights in court.[41] Another groundbreaking legal development to facilitate the transition to an ecocentric paradigm occurred in the Inter-American Court of Human Rights. On February 7, 2018, the Court published a landmark advisory opinion in response to a request to provide guidance on the interaction of international human rights law and international environmental law.[42]

The Court's opinion included three significant legal developments. First, the opinion recognized the existence of a fundamental right to a healthy environment, reflected in Article 26 of the American Convention and in member states' constitutions and international instruments.[43] Second, the Court articulated a new test to determine the Convention's extraterritorial application in cases involving environmental harm, clarifying the scope of the American Convention in environmental matters, which included the issue of whether the term "jurisdiction" in Article 1(1) of the American Convention could encompass extraterritorial obligations relating to environmental harm.[44] The Court determined that the term "jurisdiction" encompasses any situation in which a state exercises "authority" over a person or subjects the person to its "effective control," whether within or outside its territory, and explained that it can embrace activities within a state that cause cross-border effects, noting that states have a duty to prevent transboundary environmental

---

[40] H. Res., Recognizing the duty of the Federal Government to create a Green New Deal, 116th Cong., 1st Sess., (Feb. 7, 2019), https://ocasio-cortez.house.gov/sites/ocasio-cortez.house.gov/files/Resolution%20on%20a%20Green%20New%20Deal.pdf.

[41] For a discussion of these developments, *see infra* Chapter 5.

[42] Maria L. Banda, *Inter-American Court of Human Rights' Advisory Opinion on the Environment and Human Rights*, 22 ASIL Insights, Issue No. 6 (May 10, 2018), https://www.asil.org/insights/volume/22/issue/6/inter-american-court-human-rights-advisory-opinion-environment-and-human. Inter-American Court of Human Rights, *Advisory Opinion OC-23/17 on the Environment and Human Rights*, at 7 (Nov. 15, 2017).

[43] Inter-American Court of Human Rights, *Advisory Opinion OC-23/17 on the Environment and Human Rights*, 59 (Nov. 15, 2017); *see also* A. Papantoniou, *Advisory Opinion on the Environment and Human Rights*, 112 Am. J. Int'l L. 460 (2018).

[44] Inter-American Court of Human Rights, *Advisory Opinion OC-23/17 on the Environment and Human Rights*, 81.

damage that could impair the rights of persons outside their territory.[45] The Court essentially redefined the "effective control" test, now looking at the state's control over the domestic activities in question rather than control over a person or territory; further, it explained that the state has effective control over the activities that caused the damage and is in a position to prevent harm.[46]

Third, the Court clarified the duties, in the context of transboundary environmental harm, to respect and ensure the rights to life and personal integrity interpreted in light of international environmental law and provided guidance on their application in the Inter-American human rights system.[47] The Court emphasized the importance of (1) the duty to prevent environmental harm, (2) the precautionary principle, (3) the duty to cooperate with potentially affected states, and (4) procedural environmental rights.[48]

The Court reiterated that states have a duty to prevent "significant" harm to the environment of other States or the global commons, in that states must, at a minimum, regulate, supervise, and monitor activities under their jurisdiction that could cause significant harm to the environment.[49] Further, state responsibility is not limitless as the Court explained that international responsibility would attach if the state (a) knew, or should have known, that there was a real and immediate risk to protected rights and failed to take the necessary measures that would have been reasonably expected to prevent such risk, and (b) if there is a causal link between the significant harm to the environment and the human rights impacts.[50] The Court found sufficient evidence for states to act in accordance with the precautionary principle and adopt, even in the absence of scientific certainty, measures to prevent serious or irreversible damage to the environment.[51] Further, the Court also found that a duty to cooperate with potentially affected states in case of transboundary environmental harm is applicable under the American Convention and that states must cooperate to protect against environmental damage and rights of persons under their jurisdiction.[52]

The Court reaffirmed that procedural environmental rights are fundamental for the fulfillment of other rights in the American Convention, previously finding that Article 13 of the Convention requires states to grant access to information relating to activities that might harm the environment.[53] The Court recognized that states currently have a duty under Article 23(1)(a) to ensure the public's right to participate

---

[45] *Id.*
[46] *Id.*
[47] *Id.* at 101.
[48] *Id.* at 125.
[49] *Id.* at 145.
[50] *Id.* at 180.
[51] *Id.*
[52] *Id.*
[53] *Id.* at 210.

in decisions that might affect the environment, and a duty under Articles 8(1) and 25 to ensure public access to justice in environmental matters.[54]

The opinion will have significant implications including influencing how major infrastructure projects in the Americas are approved, monitored, and executed. The Court's new test for extraterritoriality is sufficiently broad so as to enable recovery for transboundary climate-related harms.[55] The opinion also could influence other human rights tribunals and national courts that have recognized the adverse impact of climate change on human rights.

Even more critical than meaningful legal developments seeking to facilitate a transition to an ecocentric paradigm, inspiration for reform must come from cultural and religious leaders to mobilize the masses. Pope Francis's encyclical letter, *Laudato Si'*, is a revolutionary text that discusses the deep connection between the earth and humanity.[56] It has already helped raise awareness of the need for urgent and effective responses to the climate change crisis.[57] Several passages in the letter address the need to provide protections and rights to future generations. Pope Francis notes, "We can no longer speak of sustainable development apart from intergenerational solidarity."[58] He discusses rampant consumerism and the disregard for what that lifestyle can bring for future generations. The Pope expresses concern regarding the lack of preparedness contemporary society faces in noting, "We have not yet managed to adopt a circular model of production capable of preserving resources for present and future generations, while limiting as much as possible the use of non-renewable resources, moderating their consumption, maximizing their efficient use, reusing and recycling them."[59] These words reflect the mandate of sustainable development, a goal that has been largely mere aspirational rhetoric since the term was coined in 1987. This book seeks to promote a transition to an ecocentric paradigm to protect the voiceless communities by building on the Pope's imploring message to take this sustainable development mandate far more seriously.

According to Pope Francis, the transition begins with humanity and our relationship to the earth. "There can be no renewal of our relationship with nature without a renewal of humanity itself."[60] In order to be proper stewards of the earth, society must reinvent its role and its relationship with nature. "[O]ur 'dominion' over

[54] *Id.*

[55] *Id. See also* Christopher Campbell-Duruflé & Sumudu Anopama Atapattu, *The Inter-American Court's Environment and Human Rights Advisory Opinion: Implications for International Climate Law*, 8 CLIMATE L. 321, 333–35 (2018).

[56] Pope Francis, *Laudato Si'* 118 (May 24, 2015), https://w2.vatican.va/content/dam/francesco/pdf/encyclicals/documents/papa-francesco_20150524_enciclica-laudato-si_en.pdf.

[57] Albert C. Lin, *Pope Francis' Encyclical on the Environment as Private Environmental Governance*, 9 GEO. WASH. J. ENERGY & ENVTL. L. 33, 44 (2018) ("'*Laudato Si'* advances discussion regarding what sustainable development should mean and why it matters to all of us, reminding us of the potentially critical role of religion in tackling environmental challenges.").

[58] *Laudato Si', supra* note 56, at 118.

[59] *Id.* at 22.

[60] *Id.* at 118.

the universe should be understood more properly in the sense of responsible stewardship."[61] Pope Francis stresses the principle of interconnectedness, which lies at the heart of ecocentrism. "Nature cannot be regarded as something separate from ourselves or as a mere setting in which we live. We are part of nature, included in it and thus in constant interaction with it."[62]

Despite these sources of hope, the anthropocentric lens through which humans view the environment is deeply ingrained in every aspect of society: philosophy, religion, science, and commerce. Humankind's dominion over nature and the bounty of resources that nature offers to fulfill human needs has inscribed a human signature on the widespread degradation of our planet over the past century, culminating in the climate change crisis. The unwavering focus on fulfilling human needs in the present has simultaneously betrayed future generations of humans and current generations of wildlife and natural resources. Examples of entities experiencing grave peril and possible extinction from human overconsumption in the present are the polar bear, the Great Barrier Reef, and our children and grandchildren. Their shared vulnerability has been underscored and accelerated due to climate change impacts, which threaten to push the planet and its inhabitants toward a state of irreversible environmental degradation. As the journey toward eco-annihilation has been accelerating with each passing year, so too must the efforts to force a paradigm shift in environmental governance. This paradigm shift will compel the long-overdue human perspective to perceive wildlife and nature as "subjects" rather "objects."

Unfortunately, the transition toward an ecocentric regulatory paradigm has moved at a glacial pace, which has been outpaced by the rate of glacial melting in the Anthropocene era. Since the 1970s, environmental protection measures have been perceived as Earth-friendly and exercising our stewardship responsibilities toward Mother Earth. "Recycling" is the best example of this "too little, too late" mentality. We manufacture products from natural resources, use those products, then use economic and environmental resources to recycle those products, and claim it as a victory for the environment. A victory for the environment would only occur if those resources were left intact in the first instance and we found a way to develop as a society without them.

Indigenous peoples have embraced and continue to embrace this ecocentric thinking through "traditional environmental knowledge." Rather than devise technologically advanced interventions to adapt to the climate, we stand to gain pearls of wisdom from the indigenous inhabitants of the earth who have lived in harmony with wildlife and nature for generations and have retained unsevered links to past and future generations. The devastation that climate change impacts have unleashed in indigenous communities is the first step toward protecting the

---

[61] *Id.* at 116 (internal citations omitted).
[62] *Id.* at 139.

voiceless communities. Understanding the perilous vulnerability under which many indigenous communities live in the face of climate change is the wake-up call that must be answered to focus on resilience-based legal responses that seek to promote true sustainable development and climate adaptation by fortifying the resilience of the voiceless communities.

Remarking on the enactment of important federal environmental legislation, President Nixon reflected: "I think that 1970 will be known as the year of the beginning, in which we really began to move on the problems of clean air and clean water and open spaces for the future generations of America." Sustainable development reflects the recognition and embrace of our duty to consider the needs of future generations in our environmental management decisions of today. Some scholars have suggested that sustainable development is on its way to becoming binding customary international law due to how commonly states throughout the world embrace it as if it were required by law to do so. This process takes time and sustainable development is already entering its fourth decade since its inception in 1987. The climate change crisis does not offer the luxury of time to allow this natural legal evolution to take its course. Urgent action is necessary now. The legal revolution toward embracing an ecocentric regulatory paradigm is the right thing at the right time to promote true sustainability on our planet.

2

Climate Change Litigation in Domestic Courts and Human Rights Commissions

The saddest aspect of life is that science gathers knowledge faster than society gathers wisdom.

–Isaac Asimov[1]

Creative climate change litigation has raised awareness of the human rights dimensions of climate change impacts and highlighted the deficiencies of the existing domestic and international regulatory regimes to address climate change. The Inuit petition, submitted to the Inter-American Commission on Human Rights (IACHR) in 2005, marked the beginning of this movement to hold public and private actors accountable for their contributions to climate change impacts and their failure to act (or at least to act adequately) to address the problem. A line of public nuisance cases was pending in US courts while the Inuit awaited the decision on its petition. This line of cases initially sought injunctive relief for climate change mitigation, but subsequently sought damages from private companies for their greenhouse gas emissions. The *Kivalina* case sparked the climate justice movement in this regard, where a small and remote Native Alaskan community sought damages under a public nuisance theory for the cost of relocation as a result of severe coastal erosion that caused its homeland to become imminently uninhabitable.

In an unrelated but highly significant and parallel development, the US Supreme Court in 2007 held that the state of Massachusetts had standing to sue the US Environmental Protection Agency for its failure to promulgate regulations for carbon dioxide emissions from new motor vehicles under the Clean Air Act. This notion of the state suing on behalf of its citizens was termed "special solicitude" and is a key concept for future climate litigation based on environmental stewardship duties.

---

[1]   ISAAC ASIMOV & JASON A. SHULMAN, ISAAC ASIMOV'S BOOK OF SCIENCE AND NATURE QUOTATIONS 281 (1988).

Outside the United States, a widely embraced positive development for climate litigation plaintiffs came in the *Urgenda* case. In this case, a district court and an appellate court in the Netherlands held that the government of the Netherlands has failed to do enough to regulate climate change even though it was in compliance with its commitment under the Paris Agreement. The plaintiffs argued that climate science required more ambitious greenhouse gas reduction goals, and supported its argument with references to domestic, regional, human rights, and climate change law. The government's appeal to the Supreme Court of the Netherlands was pending as of this writing in early 2019.

These cases transformed the landscape of climate change regulation in the United States and abroad in little more than a decade. Michael Burger, Director of the Sabin Center for Climate Change Law at Columbia Law School,[2] aptly made the following observation regarding this new role for litigation: "Litigation has arguably never been a more important tool to push policymakers and market participants to develop and implement effective means of climate change litigation and adaptation."[3]

This chapter discusses how these landmark cases ushered in a new era of using the courts to help change the paradigm for climate change regulation from government-oriented mitigation to rights-based stewardship and climate justice legal theories. These litigation theories are highly relevant for protection of the voiceless communities because they underscore how a creative and persistent movement can build momentum and achieve success quickly in a multipronged strategy, which is similar to the proposed coordination of efforts on behalf of the three voiceless communities considered in this book. These cases are also relevant to the protection of the voiceless in that the courts have shown receptivity to protecting vulnerable communities, such as future generations. These developments have the potential to help open the door for extending possible mechanisms for protection of voiceless communities in the Anthropocene era.

I US CASE STUDIES

In the Anthropocene era, the legislative branch's role in addressing climate change matters ground to a halt in the 1990s, and it has never recovered. *Massachusetts v. EPA* was at the center of a revolution to use the courts to compel the government to act to address climate change when it had failed to do so of its own volition. Climate change is a challenge that is most properly and effectively

---

[2] The Sabin Center has established a valuable clearinghouse of information on all forms of climate change litigation in the United States and foreign domestic jurisdictions. *See generally* Columbia Law School, Sabin Center for Climate Change Law (2019), http://columbiaclimate law.com/.

[3] UN Environment & Sabin Center for Climate Change Law, *The Status of Climate Change Litigation: A Global Review* (May 2017), http://columbiaclimatelaw.com/files/2017/05/Burger-Gundlach-2017-05-UN-Envt-CC-Litigation.pdf.

addressed as a matter for the executive and legislative branches. Ideally, the courts should simply play a referee role in enforcing mandates and objectives that these two branches have pledged to fulfill. But this balanced relationship among the three branches of the US government is not the reality in which the United States finds itself following the 1990s. The days in which the United States played a role as a leader in international environmental diplomacy under the Montreal Protocol regime and other multilateral environmental treaties are but a distant memory. Courts have had to take the lead in legislating from the bench to enable any progress in US climate change regulation. *Massachusetts* v. *EPA* was a significant and unexpected victory that launched a new direction in the United States of using the federal courts as a lawmaking proxy in the climate change regulation domain.

The case involved two significant legal victories: one with respect to standing and the other regarding the EPA's mandate to regulate carbon dioxide from new motor vehicles as a criteria air pollutant under the Clean Air Act. Joined by several other states, Massachusetts sued in its *parens patriae* capacity on behalf of its citizens, alleging injury based on the loss of coastal land in its state from sea level rise caused by climate change. In a landmark 5–4 opinion, Justice John Paul Stevens, writing for the majority, concluded that Massachusetts had standing by way of its "special solicitude" on behalf of its citizens, a concept that had been applied in cases involving suits by one state against another in the context of interstate pollution. While the special solicitude concept was relevant to the context in *Massachusetts* v. *EPA*, Justice John Roberts's dissenting opinion criticized the majority's use of this concept because the Court's environmental standing jurisprudence did not treat public and private litigants differently, and the Clean Air Act's authorization of states' capacity to sue under the Act did not confer this special status for states as plaintiffs.[4] Another criticism of the special solicitude reasoning was that it caused confusion in federal courts in the wake of *Massachusetts* v. *EPA* regarding whether the decision was limited to apply only to states as plaintiffs.[5]

Equally important, although perhaps less surprising, the Court also concluded that the EPA had the authority to require regulation of carbon dioxide as a criteria air pollutant for new motor vehicles under the Clean Air Act. The thrill of that victory soon dissipated, however, as the EPA's implementation of the mandate from the case was stalled in litigation for approximately a decade regarding challenges to EPA's "endangerment finding," which justified the agency's regulation of

---

[4] Massachusetts v. EPA, 549 U.S. 497, 536–37(2007) (Roberts, J., dissenting).

[5] For example, the native village of Kivalina was denied standing in *Native Village of Kivalina v. ExxonMobil Corp.* despite its status as a quasi-sovereign entity. For a discussion of the conflicting outcomes applying the special solicitude status to subsequent cases in the federal courts, *see generally* Randall S. Abate, *Massachusetts v. EPA and the Future of Environmental Litigation in Climate Change Litigation and Beyond*, 33 Wm. & Mary Envtl. L. & Pol'y Rev. 121 (2008).

greenhouse gases under the Clean Air Act as a threat to public health, and challenges to the applicability of the holding in *Massachusetts* v. *EPA* beyond the context in the case.[6]

Two tracks of climate change litigation emerged in the wake of *Massachusetts* v. *EPA*: suits against the government to compel action and suits against the private sector for damages. The latter line of cases marked the beginning of the climate justice movement, whereas the former was embraced as the foundation for atmospheric trust litigation. Within the government suit category, proceedings became further bifurcated to include those seeking enhanced government stewardship and those that sought enhanced rights-based protections. *Juliana* v. *United States* is unique in that it reflects both theories.[7]

Climate justice can be traced to the environmental justice movement, which began in the late 1980s. Employing a variety of legal theories, environmental justice suits sought injunctive relief or damages for the disproportionate impact of environmental pollution burdens on "environmental justice communities." These marginalized communities were exclusively African American communities initially, but later expanded to include other minority communities, indigenous communities, and low-income communities within the environmental justice tent.

At approximately the same time as *Massachusetts* v. *EPA*, a line of creative public nuisance climate change lawsuits was launched in US federal courts. These cases featured creative lawyering in two respects. First, they asserted that climate change constituted a public nuisance and, second, they relied on the rare and narrow federal common law doctrine of interstate pollution. This line of cases initially sued five major electric power companies, seeking to compel them to reduce their greenhouse gas emissions by 25 percent. One such case, *American Electric Power Company, Inc.* v. *Connecticut*,[8] reached the US Supreme Court, but was dismissed on federal displacement grounds. The Court concluded that because the Clean Air Act was available for potential regulation of climate change, claims for relief for climate change impacts should be pursued within the Clean Air Act framework and, therefore, federal common law claims outside of the framework should be dismissed.[9]

---

[6] *See* Beatrix Scolari, *EPA's Endangerment Finding Complicates Movement to Deregulate,* Environmental and Energy Study Institute (Oct. 13, 2017), https://www.eesi.org/articles/view/epas-endangerment-finding-complicates-movement-to-deregulate; Nick Sobczyk & Geof Koss, *Conservatives Warn Endangerment Finding Fight Is "Still Alive,"* E&E News (Aug. 22, 2018), https://www.eenews.net/stories/1060094933; Ross McKitrick, *Revisiting the EPA Endangerment Finding,* Cato Institute (Dec. 15, 2017), https://www.cato.org/publications/commentary/revisiting-epa-endangerment-finding; Coalition for Responsible Regulation, Inc. v. EPA, 684, 684 F.3d 102 (D.C. Cir. 2012); *but see* Utility Air Regulatory Group v. EPA, 573 U.S. 302 (2014) (holding that the decision in *Massachusetts* v. *EPA* does not require EPA to include greenhouse gas emissions every time the Clean Air Act refers to the term "air pollutant").
[7] For a full discussion of the *Juliana* case, *see infra* Chapter 3.
[8] 564 U.S. 410 (2011).
[9] *Id.* at 419.

The line of cases then shifted focus to suits for damages. The first in this progression was a suit that California filed against several leading automobile manufacturers seeking damages for these defendants' collective contribution to the public nuisance of climate change from the carbon dioxide emitted from the motor vehicles that they manufacture.[10] A subsequent case for damages, *Comer v. Murphy Oil USA, Inc.*,[11] involved a claim from victims of Hurricane Katrina who sued thirty-four energy companies for their collective contribution to global climate change, which in turn warmed the waters of the Gulf of Mexico, which in turn made Hurricane Katrina more intense, which in turn caused the plaintiffs to suffer extensive damages. The plaintiffs ultimately did not prevail before the US Circuit Court for the Fifth Circuit,[12] and their petition to the US Supreme Court for a writ of mandamus was denied.[13]

The line of cases culminated with the widely publicized *Kivalina* case.[14] A tiny Native Alaskan village of approximately four hundred residents faced certain inundation in the near future from severe coastal erosion due to sea level rise on their narrow strip of land in a remote location in the North Slope of Alaska.[15] The US Army Corps of Engineers estimated the cost of their relocation to be $400 million.[16] The Native Alaskan village sued the twenty-four largest multinational fossil fuel companies for the projected relocation costs.[17] The US District Court for the Northern District of California held that the plaintiffs lacked standing and that the court lacked jurisdiction to hear the case on political question doctrine grounds.[18] The plaintiffs appealed to the Ninth Circuit where the decision was affirmed on both grounds,[19] and the US Supreme Court denied certiorari.[20]

Although these cases may not appear to have made great strides in compelling climate change regulation in the United States, they are significant in many respects. First, these cases raised public awareness of climate change impacts in the United States in general and on vulnerable communities in particular. Second,

---

[10] California v. General Motors Corp., No. 07-16908 (June 24, 2009), http://blogs2.law.columbia .edu/climate-change-litigation/wp-content/uploads/sites/16/case-documents/2009/20090624_ docket-07-16908_order.pdf (granting motion for voluntary dismissal of case). For a discussion of this case and other climate change public nuisance cases, *see* Randall S. Abate, *Automobile Emissions and Climate Change Impacts: Employing Public Nuisance Doctrine as Part of a "Global Warming Solution" in California*, 40 CONN. L. REV. 591 (2008).

[11] 585 F.3d 855 (5th Cir. 2013) (dismissing the case on standing and political question doctrine grounds).

[12] *Id.* at 860 (dismissing the case on standing and political question doctrine grounds).

[13] 562 U.S. 1133 (2011).

[14] Native Village of Kivalina v. ExxonMobil Corp., 663 F. Supp. 2d 863 (N.D. Cal. 2009), *aff'd*, 696 F.3d 849 (9th Cir. 2012).

[15] Native Village of Kivalina v. ExxonMobil Corp., 696 F.3d 849, 853 (9th Cir. 2012).

[16] Native Village of Kivalina v. ExxonMobil Corp., 663 F. Supp. 2d 863, 869 (N.D. Cal. 2009).

[17] *Id.*

[18] *Id.* at 883.

[19] 696 F.3d 849 (9th Cir. 2012).

[20] 569 U.S. 1000 (2013).

they identified some possible legal theories through which the courts considered government and private sector entities' potential accountability for climate change impacts. The growing awareness of climate change as a threat to vulnerable communities has already opened the door for possible theories to protect the voiceless from climate change impacts, initially with lawsuits in the United States to compel federal and state climate change regulation to protect future generations, which can readily be extended to apply to the protection of wildlife and natural resources.

These encouraging developments are also significant in that they parallel developments in litigation and subsequent legislation regulating the tobacco industry after the scientific community conveyed its finding on the links between cigarette smoking and lung cancer, as well as the risks of secondhand smoke. The rapidly advancing field of climate change science, and the communication to the public regarding climate change impacts, is fueling similar efforts in the climate change litigation domain. As was the case in the tobacco context, climate change litigation efforts will be very challenging and largely unsuccessful until the proper claims and legal theories coalesce, as they did in the tobacco context. More promising still is that the court victories in the tobacco context not only yielded large damage settlements, but also prompted subsequent federal and state regulation of the tobacco industry.[21] A similar progression is likely with climate change litigation in the United States, but it will probably take a bit more time, which is why this battle needs to be waged on many fronts outside the judiciary and across many contexts.

II FOREIGN DOMESTIC CASE STUDIES

The climate change litigation developments over the past decade in foreign domestic courts are even more encouraging than those in the United States because the foreign domestic cases have produced substantial outcomes in compelling government action on climate change. This section summarizes two of the most significant successful cases in the Netherlands and Pakistan, and addresses two other notable cases from Switzerland and Norway that are pending as of this writing.

A *Netherlands:* Urgenda

A Dutch environmental group, the Urgenda Foundation,[22] and 882 Dutch citizens sued the Dutch government seeking to compel it to exceed the commitments it had

---

[21] *See generally* Michael Givel & Stanton A. Glantz, *The "Global Settlement" with the Tobacco Industry: 6 Years Later*, AM. J. PUB. HEALTH (Feb. 2004), https://www.ncbi.nlm.nih.gov/pmc/articles/PMC1448231/; Kristi Keck, *Big Tobacco: A History of Its Decline*, CNN POLITICS (June 19, 2009), http://edition.cnn.com/2009/POLITICS/06/19/tobacco.decline/; *Major Tobacco Control Litigation Victories*, TOBACCO CONTROL LAWS, https://www.tobaccocontrollaws.org/litigation/major_litigation_decisions.

[22] *See* Urgenda (2019), https://www.urgenda.nl/en/home-en/.

made pursuant to the Paris Agreement. Urgenda claimed that, as an Annex I country under the United Nations Framework Convention on Climate Change (UNFCCC), the state was neglecting its responsibility to take a national lead on fighting the global climate change crisis.[23] Urgenda further asserted that the "signing and ratification of the UN Climate Convention by the Netherlands should not be a mere formality."[24] It further argued that the state's current reduction goal of 20 percent by 2020 is not ambitious enough to prevent the adverse effects of climate change.[25] Urgenda alleged that if the state seeks to reduce its GHG emissions by 2020, it must commit to reduce its emission levels to 25–40 percent lower than it was in 1990.[26]

The court concluded that the state has a duty to take climate change mitigation measures due to the "severity of the consequences of climate change and the great risk of climate change occurring."[27] In reaching this conclusion, the court referenced Article 21 of the Dutch Constitution;[28] European Union (EU) emissions reduction targets;[29] principles under the European Convention on Human Rights (ECHR);[30] the "no harm" principle of international law;[31] the doctrine of hazardous negligence;[32] the principle of fairness,[33] the precautionary principle,[34] and the sustainability principle[35] embodied in the UN Framework Convention on Climate Change; and the principle of a high protection level,[36] the precautionary principle,[37] and the prevention principle,[38] each embodied in Art. 191 of the Treaty on the Functioning of the European Union.[39]

The Hague District Court found a violation of the Netherlands' duty of care, and required the government to limit its annual greenhouse gas emissions by at least 25 percent by the end of 2020 as compared to 1990 levels.[40] The District Court's

---

[23] *Id.* at ¶ 28.
[24] *Id.* at ¶ 28.
[25] *Id.* at ¶ 3.8.
[26] *Id.* at ¶ 11.
[27] Urgenda Foundation v. Kingdom of the Netherlands (District Court of the Hague, 2015), at ¶ 4.83.
[28] *Id.* at ¶ 4.52.
[29] *Id.*
[30] *Id.*
[31] *Id.*
[32] *Id.* at ¶ 4.53.
[33] *Id.* at ¶ 4.57.
[34] *Id.* at ¶ 4.58.
[35] *Id.* at ¶ 4.59.
[36] *Id.* at ¶ 4.61.
[37] *Id.*
[38] *Id.*
[39] The London School of Economics and Political Science, Urgenda Foundation v. Kingdom of the Netherlands (District Court of the Hague, 2015) (2019), www.lse.ac.uk/GranthamInstitute/litigation/urgenda-foundation-v-kingdom-of-the-netherlands-district-court-of-the-hague-2015/.
[40] Urgenda Foundation v. Kingdom of the Netherlands, *supra* note 27, at ¶ 5.1.

decision acknowledged that a safe temperature rise is 1.5°C rather than 2°C, a consensus that was also expressed in the Paris Agreement, in which it was argued that global warming should be limited to well below 2°C, with an aim for 1.5°C. The District Court ordered the Dutch government to limit its GHG emissions to 25 percent below 1990 levels by 2020,[41] concluding that the government's existing pledge to reduce emissions by 17 percent is insufficient to fulfill the state's participation in the Paris Agreement to keep global temperature increases within 2°C of preindustrial conditions.[42] The District Court's opinion was the first decision in the world to compel a state to limit GHG emissions for reasons other than statutory mandates.[43]

The Netherlands appealed in October 2015, arguing that the court could not issue decisions in this area of law. Although it agreed that action needs to be taken to reduce global GHG emissions, the Dutch government argued that its current reduction goal is adequate, as it aligns with the EU emissions commitment.[44] The state also argued that because the seriousness of climate change remains uncertain, so will the effectiveness of any proposed global solution.[45] Thus, any reduction in emissions the state may achieve will be minor in comparison to other countries because the "Netherlands cannot solve the global problem of climate change on its own."[46] In addition, the state argued that by upholding the District Court's ruling, the Court of Appeal would be interfering with the country's separation of powers system "because it is not up to the courts but to the democratically legitimised government"[47] to determine a climate change solution that is based on the nation's social, economic and political situation.[48]

The Hague Court of Appeal upheld the District Court's ruling ordering the Dutch government to reduce its cumulative greenhouse gas emissions by a minimum of 25 percent by the end of 2020.[49] The court concluded that the state's current GHG reduction goals were insufficient to provide its citizens protection from the "hazards of dangerous climate change."[50] Thus, by refusing to do more, the state had "fail[ed] to fulfill its duty of care" under Articles 2 and 8 of the ECHR.[51] The Court of Appeal also rejected the Dutch government's challenge to Urgenda's standing to bring the claim, concluding that Urgenda "acts on behalf of the interests of the current

---

[41] *Id.*
[42] The London School of Economics and Political Science, *supra* note 39.
[43] *Id.*
[44] *Id.* at ¶ 3.7.
[45] *Id.* at ¶ 30.
[46] *Id.*
[47] *Id.* at ¶ 67.
[48] *Id.* at ¶ 30.
[49] Urgenda Foundation v. The State of the Netherlands, C/09/456689/ HA ZA 13-1396 (HCA, Civil Law Division 2018) ¶ 76.
[50] *Id.* at ¶ 62.
[51] *Id.* at ¶ 73.

generation of Dutch nationals and individuals subject to the state's jurisdiction within the meaning of Article 1 ECHR." The Court of Appeal further recognized that:

> it is without a doubt plausible that the current generation of Dutch nationals, in particular but not limited to the younger individuals in this group, will have to deal with the adverse effects of climate change in their lifetime if global emissions of greenhouse gases are not adequately reduced. Therefore, the Court does not have to consider the questions raised by the State in this ground of appeal.[52]

In its decision, the Court of Appeal referred to several Intergovernmental Panel on Climate Change (IPCC) reports that state that the global community must work toward the stabilization of GHG emissions to 450 parts per million by 2100 to ensure that the global temperature stays below 2°C.[53] To achieve this goal, the Court of Appeal confirmed that an emissions reduction of 25–40 percent by 2020 is recognized as the standard target by UNFCCC's Conference of the Parties.[54] The court acknowledged that, as a country, the Netherlands has one of the highest per capita greenhouse gas emissions in the world[55] and, when compared to other EU member states, "Dutch reduction efforts are lagging far behind."[56] The court reasoned that by refusing to commit to a reduction target of at least 25 percent, the State has failed to comply with Articles 2 and 8 of the ECHR because it is willingly exposing Dutch citizens to a "real threat of dangerous climate change, resulting in the serious risk that the current generation of citizens will be confronted with a loss of life and/or a disruption of family life."[57] The Court of Appeal acknowledged that climate change is a global crisis and will not be solved by the sole actions of one country.[58] Nevertheless, the Court of Appeal concluded that "this does not release the State

---

[52] Urgenda Foundation v. Kingdom of the Netherlands, *supra* note 27, at ¶ 37.

[53] *Id.* at ¶ 12l; *see also* Josephine van Zeben, *Establishing a Governmental Duty of Care for Climate Change Mitigation: Will Urgenda Turn the Tide?* 4 Transnat'l Envtl. L. 339, 344 (2015) (stating that the Court accepted "'as fact' findings of the IPCC regarding dangerous anthropogenic climate change, and the link between climate change and GHG emissions.").

[54] *Id.* at ¶ 51; *see also* Patricia Ferreira, *"Common but Differentiated Responsibilities" in the National Courts: Lessons from Urgenda v. The Netherlands*, 5 Transnat'l Envtl. L. 329, 342 (2016) (noting that the court "decided that the government cannot ignore climate science and global climate politics in fulfilling its obligation to adopt effective national climate policies.").

[55] *Id.* at ¶ 66, 26. The court observed that CO2 emissions comprise 85 percent of the Netherlands' total GHG emissions and that these levels "have hardly dropped in the Netherlands since 1990."

[56] *Id.* at ¶ 56; *see also* Suryapratim Roy & Edwin Woerdman, *Situating Urgenda v. the Netherlands Within Comparative Climate Change Litigation*, 34 J. Energy & Nat. Resources L. 165, 180 (2016) (stating that "being a Member State of the EU does not take away the right of the Netherlands to adopt more stringent targets and measures.").

[57] *Id.* at ¶ 45.

[58] *Id.* at ¶ 62.

from its obligations to take measures in its territory"[59] and confirmed that the state must take precautionary action to fight the adverse effects of climate change.[60]

This landmark decision[61] is recognized as "the first time any court in the world [has] ordered its own government to strengthen its response to the climate change crisis."[62] Moreover, it is also the first successful climate change challenge to rely on human rights law.[63] Consequently, *Urgenda* has potential to lay the foundation for a "broader recognition of the application of human rights norms to the global climate change crisis."[64]

B *Pakistan:* Leghari

The plaintiff, a farmer, filed this lawsuit alleging violation of his fundamental rights in relation to the Pakistani government's "inaction, delay and lack of seriousness."[65] The plaintiff asserted that there was a lack of progress in the government's efforts in the National Climate Change Policy (2012) and the Framework for Implementation of Climate Change Policy (2014–2030).[66] The plaintiff maintained that "climate change is a serious threat to [the] water, food and energy security of Pakistan."[67] He invoked Article 9 of the Constitution – the right to life, and Article 14 – the right to dignity, as well as the public trust doctrine and several international environmental principles including sustainable development, the precautionary principle, and intergenerational equity.[68]

---

[59] *Id.; see generally* Ferreira, *supra* note 54 (examining the principle of "common but differentiated responsibilities and capabilities" and analyzing how the Court utilized this principle as an "interpretative aid" in its decision making).

[60] *See generally* Eleanor Stein & Alex Geert Castermans, *Urgenda v. the State of the Netherlands: The Reflex Effect – Climate Change, Human Rights, and the Expanding Definitions of the Duty of Care*, 13 McGILL J. SUST. DEV. L. 303 (2017) (discussing the precautionary principle and how it can play an important role in determining a state's "duty of care" in climate change obligations); Roy & Woerdman, *supra* note 56 (examining the role of the precautionary principle and analyzing the principle's procedural and substantive elements).

[61] *See* Roy & Woerdman, *supra* note 56, at 166 (acknowledging that this decision was informally translated into English immediately after it was made. Given that this is not common practice in the Netherlands, Roy and Woerdman concluded that this was intended to set a "global precedent.").

[62] Stein & Castermans, *supra* note 60, at 305; *accord* Ferreira, *supra* note 54, at 331.

[63] *Id.* at 317.

[64] Following the District Court's decision in *Urgenda*, other courts such as *Juliana v. US* and *Leghari v. Pakistan* have reached comparably favorable conclusions. *Id.* at 318; *see also* Jacqueline Peel & Hari M. Osofsky, *A Rights Turn in Climate Change Litigation?* 7 TRANSNAT'L ENVTL. L. 37 (2017) (examining post-Urgenda climate change challenges in Philippines, Austria, South Africa, and the United States).

[65] Leghari v. Federation of Pakistan (W.P. No. 25501/2015), Lahore High Court Green Bench, Order of Sept. 4, 2015, https://elaw.org/pk_Leghari [Leghari], at 2, ¶ 1.

[66] *Id.*

[67] *Id.*

[68] *Id.* at 4, ¶ 4.

The Joint Secretary from the Federal Ministry of Climate Change submitted that under the Climate Change Framework, there are 734 action points, 232 of which are priority items, which must be completed by 2016.[69] He argued that the Ministry for Climate Change was established in 2015, and as of the first meeting in April 2015, reminders were sent to the various governmental departments to send progress reports, which reflected that much work remained to be completed.[70]

In September 2015, the Lahore High Court held that the Federal Government and the Government of Punjab had violated fundamental rights due to "the delay and lethargy of the State in implementing the Framework [for Implementation of Climate Change Policy (2014–2030)]."[71] In its order, the Court directed that the Ministries, Departments, and Authorities mentioned in the case (1) "shall nominate a CLIMATE CHANGE *FOCAL PERSON* within their institution to closely work with the Ministry of Climate Change to ensure the implementation of the Framework and also assist the Court in the instant petition";[72] and (2) "shall present a list of adaptation action points (out of the priority items of the Framework) that can be achieved by 31st December, 2015."[73] Furthermore, the order mandated creation of a Climate Change Commission comprised of representatives of the key ministries/departments, NGOs, and technical experts[74] to assist the court in monitoring the progress in implementing the Framework for the December 31, 2015 deadline. In the September 14, 2015 order, the Court recognized that "climate change is no longer a distant threat – we are already feeling and experiencing its impacts across the country and the region ... with far reaching consequences and real economic costs."[75]

As a result of the Court's order, the Commission issued a report on January 16, 2016 in response to which the Court commended the Commission's work and the progress that has been made. On February 24, 2017 and January 24, 2018, the Commission submitted supplemental reports indicating that 66 percent of the priority items were completed and that the Government should be responsible for the continued implementation of the Framework.[76] On January 25, 2018, the Court suspended the Commission and appointed a Standing Committee in its place.[77]

---

[69] *Id.* at 3, ¶ 2.
[70] *Id.* at 4, ¶ 3.
[71] *Id.* at 6, ¶ 8.
[72] *Id.* at 6–7, ¶ 8 (i).
[73] *Id.* at 7, ¶ 8 (ii).
[74] *Id.* at 7, ¶ 8(iii)
[75] Order of Sept. 14, 2015, at 3, ¶ 3.
[76] Hon. Justice Brian J. Preston, "Using environmental rights to address climate change," SC Chief Judge of the Land and Environment Court of NSW. Law Council of Australia, Future of Environmental Law Symposium, 10 (Apr. 19, 2018).
[77] *Id.* at 11.

With regard to the alleged human rights violations in this case, the court stated:

Fundamental rights, like the right to life (article 9) which includes the right to a healthy and clean environment and right to human dignity (article 14) read with constitutional principles of democracy, equality, social, economic and political justice include within their ambit and commitment, the international environmental principles of sustainable development, precautionary principle, environmental impact assessment, inter and intra-generational equity and public trust doctrine. Environment and its protection has taken a center stage in the scheme of our constitutional rights. It appears that we have to move on. The existing environmental jurisprudence has to be fashioned to meet the needs of something more urgent and overpowering i.e., Climate Change. From Environmental Justice, which was largely localized and limited to our own ecosystems and biodiversity, we need to move to Climate Change Justice. Fundamental rights lay at the foundation of these two overlapping justice systems.[78]

The *Leghari* case has had significant influence on international environmental law and climate change litigation, due to its rights-based approach, which serves "as a model for future rights-based, adaptation-focused litigation."[79] It reflects a plurality of legal issues and "polycentricity."[80]

C *Switzerland*: KlimaSeniorinnen

On November 25, 2016, KlimaSeniorinnen ("Climate Seniors") – a group of older Swiss women seeking more ambitious climate change action – filed a petition to the Federal Council, the Federal Department of the Environment, Transport, Energy, and Communication (FDETEC), the Federal Office of Environment, and the Federal Office of Energy.[81] The group claimed a unique health-based vulnerability to climate change–induced heat waves. In the extremely hot summer of 2003, seventy thousand additional deaths were recorded in Europe, compared to any

---

[78] *Id.* at 5–6, ¶ 7.

[79] Peel & Osofsky, *supra* note 64, at 52; *see also* Sam Adelman & Bridget Lewis, Symposium Foreword: Rights-Based Approaches to Climate Change, 7 TRANSNAT'L ENVTL. L. 15 (2018) (discussing whether landmark cases such as *Urgenda* in the Netherlands and *Leghari* in Pakistan herald the emergence of a trend for petitioners to employ rights-based claims in climate change lawsuits despite the failure of previous claimants to successfully deploy such claims).

[80] Basil Ugochukwu, *Litigating the Impacts of Climate Change: The Challenge of Legal Polycentricity*, 7 GLOBAL J. COMP. L. 91,102 (2018) (noting that "Polycentricity in this case showed up in its novelty and uncertainty, the sheer range of government functions and institutions that it implicated, and the court's approach in making it amenable to some form of adjudication").

[81] Swiss Senior Women for Climate Protection v. Swiss Federal Council et al., filed Oct. 25, 2016, English translation, [3], http://klimaseniorinnen.ch/wp-content/uploads/2017/05/request_Klima Seniorinnen.pdf.

previous summer. In Switzerland, these impacts yielded a death toll that was 6.9 percent higher than average. This was not randomly distributed among the population, but had a disproportionate impact on persons aged 75–85.[82] The group also asserted that women were more affected than men, and that older women with respiratory diseases suffered the most. While heat waves in Switzerland placed populations such as infants and children at significant risk of heat-related health impacts, current research indicates that older women suffer the highest rate of mortality in periods of extreme temperatures.[83] The causal link between climate change and premature death is growing stronger, especially in this particularly vulnerable group.

The Climate Seniors challenged the adequacy of the Swiss government's climate policies and mitigation measures. The group asserted that Swiss authorities failed to offer them protection under Swiss constitutional law, the ECHR, and the Paris Agreement. They alleged a breach of the right to life from the Swiss Constitution and the ECHR, as well as the ECHR right to private and family life.[84]

The Climate Seniors also sought to compel the Swiss government to improve its climate change mitigation standards to a 25 percent emission reduction by 2020, which parallels what the District Court ordered the Dutch government to do in the *Urgenda* case. The group sued four government authorities in Switzerland to ensure that greenhouse gas emission reduction targets and measures are at least as strict as what the Paris Agreement requires. The Climate Seniors asserted that Switzerland is failing to comply with the Paris Agreement's mandate of "dangerous interference with the climate system" insofar as the average global warming of the earth's atmosphere compared to preindustrial times should be kept "well below 2°C."[85]

On April 26, 2017, the FDETEC rejected the Climate Seniors' petition for lack of standing, concluding that the applicants failed to establish that their rights had been affected under Article 25a of the Swiss Administrative Procedure Act.[86] In May 2017, the Climate Seniors appealed to the Federal Administrative Court, but the Court dismissed the appeal in July 2018. On January 21, 2019, the Climate Seniors appealed the case to the Federal Supreme Court, which is pending as of this writing.[87] This case confirms that governments should expect more cases

---

[82] *Id.*

[83] *Id.*

[84] Art. 25(a) APA; Art. 6 Ziff. 1; ECHR Art. 13.

[85] Pl. Pet. at § 60. (Paris Agreement, art. 2, ¶ 1(a)).

[86] *Unofficial Translation of the Juridical Relevant Part of the Order the KlimaSeniorinnen Received the 26th of April 2017 by the Federal Department of the Environment, Transport, Energy and Communications,* https://klimaseniorinnen.ch/wp-content/uploads/2017/11/Verfue gung_UVEK_Abschnitt_C_English.pdf (cited in https://www.elgaronline.com/view/journals/jhrc/9-2/jhrc.2018.02.04.xml#bib-079).

[87] Greenpeace International, *Climate Case Brought by 1000 Swiss Seniors May Not Be Over Yet* (Dec. 7, 2018), https://www.greenpeace.org/international/press-release/19848/climate-case-brought-by-1000-swiss-seniors-may-not-be-over-yet/; Greenpeace International, *Swiss Seniors Appeal Climate Case in Federal Supreme Court* (Jan. 21, 2019), https://www.greenpeace.org/

addressing government actions or omissions as potentially violating international law and constitutional law mandates to ensure that actions are taken to prevent dangerous climate change.

D *Norway:* People *v.* Arctic Oil

On October 1, 2016, just six months after Norway signed the Paris Agreement, Greenpeace and Natur Og Ungdomf, a youth association, sued the Norwegian government – represented by the Ministry of Petroleum and Energy – for granting licenses to thirteen corporations for oil and gas drilling in the Barents Sea.[88] The plaintiffs argued that opening up this area for oil drilling constituted a violation of the government's duties arising from environmental protection mandates in the Norwegian Constitution. The plaintiffs relied on Article 112 of the Norwegian Constitution: "Everyone has the right to an environment that safeguards their health and to nature where production ability and diversity are preserved. Natural resources must be managed from a long-term and versatile consideration which also upholds this right for future generations." This case was the first time that this provision of the Norwegian Constitution was used in a high-level court case.[89] The plaintiffs further asserted that these production licenses constituted a breach of the government's human rights protection obligations and that they would result in increased GHG emissions, in violation of Norway's commitments under the Paris Agreement.

In January 2018, the Oslo District Court rejected the plaintiffs' claims. While the Court concluded, like the *Urgenda* case, that Norway has a duty to protect its citizens and future citizens and provide a healthy environment, the Court reasoned that the oil that would be extracted from the Barents Sea would be exported and used outside of Norwegian borders. The Court further stated that Article 112 does not apply abroad, and given that carbon dioxide emissions will come from exported oil and gas, Article 112 does not apply to these government-granted licenses. "The Court cannot see that the duty to assess impacts includes climate consequences of emissions from oil and gas exported abroad or therefore the costs of such emissions."[90] On February 5, 2018, the plaintiffs appealed the judgment, which is pending as of this writing.

international/press-release/20343/swiss-seniors-appeal-climate-case-in-federal-supreme-court/; for a thorough analysis of the KlimaSeniorinnen case, *see generally* Cordelia Christiane Bahr et al., *KlimaSeniorinnen: Lessons from the Swiss Senior Women's Case for Future Climate Litigation*, 9 J. HUMAN RIGHTS & ENV'T 194 (2018), https://www.elgaronline.com/view/journals/jhre/9-2/jhre.2018.02.04.xml.

[88] People v. Arctic Oil, https://ejatlas.org/conflict/the-people-versus-arctic-oil.

[89] *Id.*

[90] People v. Arctic Oil, Case No. 16-166674TVI-OTIR/06 (Oslo Dist. Ct. Jan. 4, 2018), 45, https://secured-static.greenpeace.org/norway/Global/norway/Arktis/Dokumenter/2018/Judgement%20-%204.%20jan%202017%20-%20Oslo%20District%20Court%20stamped%20version.pdf.

III HUMAN RIGHTS COMMISSION CASE STUDIES

Climate change impacts present serious threats to human rights. These threats are wide-ranging and include food and water insecurity, loss of shelter, and the threat of climate change–induced displacement. Once again, creative use of courts and tribunals has helped advance the goal to draw attention to these human rights impacts and seek legal mechanisms to address them. The Inuit petition is the leading example of a human rights petition filed against a governmental entity, whereas the "Carbon Majors" petition seeks to promote awareness and recovery for alleged human rights violations associated with multinational corporations' significant global GHG emissions.

A *The Inuit Petition*

In another effort to expose and hold the US government accountable for its failure to act on climate change, the Inuit petition before the IACHR proceeded on a parallel track at about the same time as *Massachusetts v. EPA*. The Inuit are a large indigenous community located throughout the Arctic in the United States, Canada, Greenland, and Russia.[91] Their culture, spirituality, and sustenance are tied to the frozen environment in the Arctic, and that frozen habitat is melting at alarming rates. The IPCC's initial projection for the loss of summer sea ice was 2050, which was subsequently revised to as soon as 2020 after additional study.[92] Thawing permafrost is another significant problem for the Inuit because the integrity of their housing is destabilized and elders' hunting and fishing efforts cause injury and death because of the perilous conditions of the melting permafrost.[93] The situation is so dire that the suicide rate among Inuit teenagers skyrocketed in a short period of time while these impacts manifested in their culture – they felt an overwhelming sense of despair in their inability to see any hope for the future for their people.[94]

Undaunted by their dire circumstances, Shelia Watt-Cloutier, then-Chair of the Inuit Circumpolar Conference, filed a petition[95] in 2005 with the IACHR entitled

---

[91] Leanna Ellsworth & Annmaree O'Keeffe, *Circumpolar Inuit Health Systems*, 72 Int'l J. Circumpolar Health 1, 1 (2013), www.ncbi.nlm.nih.gov/pmc/articles/PMC3753164/.

[92] *See* Carl Franzen, *Arctic Will Be Basically Ice-Free by 2050, NOAA Study Says*, The Verge (Apr. 12, 2013), www.theverge.com/2013/4/12/4217786/arctic-ice-free-summer-2050-noaa-study/; James E. Overland & Muyin Wang, *When Will the Summer Arctic Be Nearly Sea Ice Free?*, 40 Geophysical Res. Lett. 2097 (2013). https://agupubs.onlinelibrary.wiley.com/doi/full/10.1002/grl.50316.

[93] Paul Brown, *Global Warming Is Killing Us, Too*, The Guardian (Dec. 10, 2003), https://www.theguardian.com/environment/2003/dec/11/weather.climatechange.

[94] Helen Branswell, *Death, Suicide Rates Among Inuit Kids Soar Over Rest of Canada*, The Globe and Mail (July 18, 2012), https://www.theglobeandmail.com/news/national/death-suicide-rates-among-inuit-kids-soar-over-rest-of-canada/article4426600/.

[95] Petition to the Inter-American Commission on Human Rights Seeking Relief from Violations Resulting from Global Warming Caused by Acts and Omissions of the United States (Dec. 7,

"Violations Resulting from Global Warming Caused by the United States" on behalf of herself, sixty-two named petitioners, and "all other Inuit of the arctic regions of the United States of America and Canada who have been affected by the impacts of climate change described in this petition."[96] The petition claimed that the IACHR was obligated to address climate change regulation issues because, as reflected in the circumstances of the Inuit people, "global warming directly impedes human rights by disrupting a culture."[97] The petition included a list of alleged human rights violations associated with the United States' refusal to join the Kyoto Protocol and fulfill its responsibility to the global community to reduce its greenhouse gas emissions pursuant to the terms of that regime. The alleged violations of human rights protected under the Inter-American Human Rights System included the right to enjoy the benefits of their culture; the right to use and enjoy lands that they have traditionally occupied; the right to use and enjoy their personal property; the right to the preservation of health; the right to life, physical integrity, and security; the right to their own means of subsistence; and the rights to residence, movement, and inviolability of the home.[98] According to Shelia Watt-Cloutier, these human rights violations collectively amounted to a violation of the Inuit's "right to be cold."[99]

After much anticipation, the IACHR's two-paragraph response to the petition[100] was very disappointing for the Inuit, as well as the climate change and human rights community. Although unsuccessful in the legal system, the Inuit petition was perhaps the most successful effort to advance awareness of the connection between climate change impacts and human rights violations. It inspired an international movement to pursue legal protections for these human rights concerns in international climate change treaty negotiations and in domestic and international courts and tribunals.[101]

2005), http://blogs2.law.columbia.edu/climate-change-litigation/wp-content/uploads/sites/16/non-us-case-documents/2005/20051208_na_petition.pdf.

[96] *Id.* at 1.

[97] *Id.*

[98] *Id.* at 74–95.

[99] For a powerful account of the Inuit culture's struggle to survive in the face of climate change and other threats to the sustainability of her people, *see generally* SHEILA WATT-CLOUTIER, THE RIGHT TO BE COLD (2015).

[100] Letter from the Organization of American States to Sheila Watt-Cloutier et al. regarding Petition No. P-1413-05 (Nov. 16, 2006), http://blogs2.law.columbia.edu/climate-change-litigation/wp-content/uploads/sites/16/non-us-case-documents/2006/20061116_na_decision.pdf (concluding that "the information provided does not enable us to determine whether the alleged facts would tend to characterize a violation of rights protected by the American Declaration.").

[101] Elizabeth Ann Kronk Warner & Randall S. Abate, *International and Domestic Law Dimensions of Climate Justice for Arctic Indigenous Peoples*, 43 U. OTTAWA L. REV. 113, 139 (2013) ("An interesting postscript to the ICC's petition, however, is that the international community's awareness of the relationship between climate change and human rights has developed considerably in the years following the petition."). For a discussion of the Inuit petition and its implications for climate justice litigation, *see generally* HARI M. OSOFSKY, *Complexities of*

B *The "Carbon Majors" Petition*

In September 2015, ten years after the Inuit petition, Greenpeace Southeast Asia, Filipino human rights groups, and Filipino citizens petitioned the Commission on Human Rights of the Philippines (CHR) to investigate the responsibility of forty-seven oil, gas, coal, and cement companies for human rights violations or threats resulting from the impacts of climate change. Known as the "Carbon Majors" petition, this action alleges that these multinational corporations knowingly contributed to the root causes of climate change and thus violated the human rights of Filipinos.[102] The petition asserts that the Filipino Constitution empowers the CHR to investigate alleged human rights violations and to recommend to the executive and legislative branches appropriate responses to identified harms.[103]

Greenpeace Southeast Asia characterized the theory underlying the petition in a provocative manner:

> This case exposes the crime of corporations continuing to fuel climate change whilst deriving huge profits from it. Climate change is fueling extreme weather events such as ferocious typhoons and severe droughts that batter vulnerable nations like the Philippines, discussed in this case. As a test case for remedies using the human rights framework, the complaint highlights the failure of the current corporate accountability system to ensure extraterritorial accountability for human rights implications of climate change and the lack of access to remedy for its victims.[104]

The petition makes three requests: (1) conduct an investigation and, following the investigation, issue a finding on the responsibility of the investor-owned Carbon Majors for human rights threats and/or violations in the Philippines, resulting from climate change and ocean acidification; (2) monitor people and communities

---

Addressing the Impacts of Climate Change on Indigenous Peoples through International Law Petitions: A Case Study of the Inuit Petition to the Inter-American Commission on Human Rights, in CLIMATE CHANGE AND INDIGENOUS PEOPLES: THE SEARCH FOR LEGAL REMEDIES 313 (Randall S. Abate & Elizabeth Ann Kronk Warner eds., 2013).

[102] Tracy Bach, *Human Rights in a Climate Changed World: The Impact of COP21, Nationally Determined Contributions, and National Courts*, 40 VT. L. REV. 561, 591 (2016).

[103] *Id.* For a discussion of various aspects of the Carbon Majors petition, *see generally* Isabella Kaminski, *Can Fossil Fuel Companies Be Held Responsible for Human Rights?*, CLIMATE LIABILITY NEWS (Nov. 8, 2018), https://www.climateliabilitynews.org/2018/11/08/human-rights-philippines-commission-fossil-fuel/; Desiree Llanos Dee, *Four Reasons Why Communities Are Beating Corporate Climate Polluters*, Greenpeace Philippines Blog (Aug. 31, 2018), https://www.greenpeace.org/seasia/ph/News/greenpeace-philippine-blog/four-reasons-why-communities-are-beating-corp/blog/61830/; Richmund Sta. Lucia, Update on the Carbon Majors Petition: Role of the Philippines Human Rights Commission, Climate Law Blog (Mar. 8, 2018), http://blogs.law.columbia.edu/climatechange/2018/03/08/update-on-the-carbon-majors-petition-the-role-of-the-philippine-commission-on-human-rights/.

[104] Greenpeace, *Carbon Majors: People vs. Big Polluters* (2017), https://www.greenpeace.ch/wp-content/uploads/2016/06/Carbon-Majors.pdf.

acutely vulnerable to the impacts of climate change; and (3) require policymakers and legislators to develop and adopt clear and implementable objective standards for corporate reporting of human rights issues in relation to the environment, with special regard for current and future climate change impacts and GHGs associated with fossil fuel products.[105]

The petition's basis is the individual human rights affected by climate change as listed in UN Human Rights Council resolutions,[106] and that the Carbon Majors violated the human rights of Filipinos through their extensive GHG emissions, which caused climate change impacts with human rights implications in the Philippines. The petition also relies on international recognition of the intersection of human rights and climate change, using Human Rights Council resolutions, the Special Procedures Joint Letter, and the Climate Vulnerable Forum reports developed as part of the campaign to include human rights obligations in the Paris Agreement.[107] The specific violations, or threats of violation, of Filipino rights are outlined in the petition as the rights to: (a) life; (b) the highest attainable standard of physical and mental health; (c) food; (d) water; (e) sanitation; (f) adequate housing; (g) self-determination; (h) the rights of those particularly likely to be affected by climate change, including women, children, persons with disabilities, those living in extreme poverty, indigenous peoples, displaced persons, and workers; and (i) the right of Filipinos to development.[108]

The petition requests that the CHR adopt an approach patterned on market-share liability used in products liability cases when multiple parties contribute to a problem over time.[109] The petition relies on GHG emissions data that calculates responsibility for climate change in gigatons of carbon dioxide–equivalent emissions since industrialization. The Carbon Majors Database on which the petition relies was originally published in 2013 and approximates that almost 65 percent of emissions can be attributed to specific emitters.[110] In July 2017, an updated Carbon Majors Report found that just one hundred active fossil fuel producers, including

---

[105] Petition to the Commission on Human Rights of the Philippines Requesting for Investigation of the Responsibility of the Carbon Majors for Human Rights Violations or Threats of Violations Resulting from the Impacts of Climate Change, 31 (Sept. 22. 2015), http://www.greenpeace.org/seasia/ph/PageFiles/105904/Climate-Change-and-Human-Rights-Complaint.pdf.

[106] Human Rights Council, Resolution 7/23, A/HRC/7/78, Mar. 29, 2008; Human Rights Council, Resolution 10/4, A/HRC/RES/10/4, Mar. 25, 2009; Human Rights Council, Resolution 18/22, A/HRC/RES/18/22, Oct. 17, 2011; and Human Rights Council Resolution 26/27, A/HRC/RES/26/27, July 15, 2014.

[107] Bach, *supra* note 102, at 592.

[108] Sara L. Seck, *Revisiting Transnational Corporations and Extractive Industries: Climate Justice, Feminism, and State Sovereignty*, 26 TRANSNAT'L L. & CONTEMP. PROBS. 383, 396 (2017) (citing *Philippines Climate Petition*, 31).

[109] Bach, *supra* note 102, at 592.

[110] *Id.*

those listed in the petition such as ExxonMobil and Shell, are linked to 71 percent of industrial greenhouse gas emissions since 1988.[111]

The petition further requests that the CHR investigate "the human rights implications of climate change and ocean acidification" and specific violations of these rights by investor-owned Carbon Majors, located in the Philippines. The petition does not seek injunctive or compensatory relief, but instead seeks to channel the CHR's work into legislative action on climate change.[112]

In December 2017, CHR exercised its jurisdiction to investigate the petition and announced several fact-finding missions and public hearings to be held in 2018, both within the Philippines and internationally.[113] Some respondents challenged the CHR's jurisdiction to hear the petition, arguing that a state's jurisdiction is limited "only to the confines of its physical boundaries."[114] However, as long as CHR's investigation falls within one of the established principles of jurisdiction, it will be in accordance with international law. The most relevant principles for the purposes of the petition are the territorial and protective principles.[115]

The territorial principle provides that "any state may impose liabilities, even upon persons not within its allegiance, for conduct outside its borders that has consequences within its borders, which the state reprehends."[116] While there is significant recognition of the links between states' obligations under human rights and climate change law, there has been little climate change litigation argued on human rights grounds. Consequently, such litigation will face substantial challenges. The suitability of human rights law to address harm caused by climate change turns on whether a victim can substantiate a claim that a duty bearer has contributed to climate change in such a way as to amount to a human rights violation.[117] As scientific knowledge improves, tracing causal connections between particular emissions and resulting harms is becoming less difficult.[118]

---

[111] Paul Griffin, CDP Carbon Majors Report 2017 8 (July 2017).

[112] Bach, *supra* note 102, at 593.

[113] Annalisa Savaresi, Ioana Cismas, & Jacques Hartmann, *The Philippines Human Rights Commission and the "Carbon Majors" Petition*, EUROPEAN J. INT'L LAW: TALK! (Dec. 22, 2017), https://www.ejiltalk.org/the-philippines-human-rights-commission-and-the-carbon-majors-petition/.

[114] *Id.*

[115] ANNALISA SAVARESI, IOANA CISMAS, & JACQUES HARTMANN, AMICUS BRIEF – HUMAN RIGHTS AND CLIMATE CHANGE 8 (May 2017) (Submission in Support of Petitioners, Asia Pacific Forum of National Human Rights Institutions and Global Alliance of National Human Rights Institutions), https://www.asiapacificforum.net/media/resource_file/APF_Paper_Amicus_Brief_HR_Climate_Change.pdf; Savaresi, Cismas, & Hartmann, *supra* note 113.

[116] US v. Aluminum Co. of Am., 148 F. 2d 416, 443 (2d Cir. 1945).

[117] Savaresi, Cismas, & Hartmann, *supra* note 115, at 12.

[118] John Knox, *Report of the Special Rapporteur on the Issue of Human RightsOobligations Relating to the Enjoyment of a Safe, Clean, Healthy and Sustainable Environment*, UN GAOR, 32nd session, Agenda Item 3, UN Doc. A/HRC/31/52 (Feb. 1, 2016) para 36.

The protective principle empowers states to protect themselves by regulating and adjudicating conduct carried out abroad that may damage their essential security interests. The principle applies regardless of the place of commission or of the conduct or the nationality of the alleged offender or victim. Initially, this principle only applied in the context of criminal law, but since the 1980s, several states have applied it to other areas of law. Under the protective principle, it is irrelevant whether any of the Carbon Majors do business in the Philippines, so long as the effects of their activities may be regarded as a threat to essential or vital interests of the Philippines.[119]

The Environmental Law Alliance Worldwide (ELAW) drafted a memo commending the Philippine Commission for opening an investigation into the Carbon Majors.[120] The ELAW memo concluded that the right to life enshrined in the 1987 Philippine Constitution encompasses the economic, social, and cultural rights listed in the Carbon Major petition that have been affected by climate change.[121]

Under the UN Guiding Principles on Business and Human Rights, businesses have an obligation to respect human rights.[122] The UN Office of the High Commissioner for Human Rights also supports the idea that "[i]t is not only States that must be held accountable for their contributions to climate change but also businesses which have the responsibility *to respect* human rights and do no harm in the course of their activities."[123] The ELAW memo sets forth international jurisprudence to support the argument that a business' obligation to respect human rights, including the right to life, encompasses the economic, social, and cultural rights affected by a business' contribution to adverse environmental changes.

The right to life includes the right to enjoyment of clean water and air, as found by the Supreme Court of India,[124] the Supreme Court of Pakistan,[125] and the Supreme Court of Bangladesh.[126] In particular, the Supreme Court of Bangladesh has held that the right to life, as included in Articles 31 and 32 of its Constitution, "encompasses within its ambit, *the protection and preservation of the environment*, ecological

---

[119] Savaresi, Cismas, & Hartmann, *supra* note 115, at 10.

[120] Memo to the Philippine Commission on Human Rights (Nov. 7, 2016), https://elaw.org/system/files/ELAW.submission.pdf.

[121] *Id.* at 13.

[122] *Guiding Principles on Business and Human Rights*, UNITED NATIONS, 14–17 (2011), https://www.ohchr.org/Documents/Publications/GuidingPrinciplesBusinessHR_EN.pdf.

[123] Environmental Law Alliance Worldwide, Letter from Chairman José Luis C. Gascon 15 (2016), https://elaw.org/system/files/ELAW.submission.pdf; *Understanding Climate Change and Human Rights*, http://www.ohchr.org/Documents/Issues/ClimateChange/COP21.pdf (emphasis added).

[124] Environmental Law Alliance Worldwide, *supra* note 123, at 6; Subhash Kumar v. State of Bihar, 1991 A.I.R. SC 420, ¶ 7, http://elaw.org/india.subhash.kumar.1991.

[125] Environmental Law Alliance Worldwide, *supra* note 123, at 8; West Pakistan Salt Miners Labour Union v. Industries & Mineral Development, 1994 S.C.M.R. 2061, https://www.elaw.org/system/files/SC-1994-Salt-Miners-v.-Director-Industries-and- Mineral-Development.pdf (stating "the right to have water free pollution and contamination is [a] right to life itself . . .").

[126] Environmental Law Alliance Worldwide, *supra* note 123, at 9; Farooque v. Bangladesh (1997) 17 B.L.D. (A.D.) 1, https://elaw.org/bd.farooque.FAP.1996.

balance free from pollution of air and water, and sanitation without which life can hardly be enjoyed. Any act or omission contrary thereto will be violative of the said right to life."[127] Similarly, the Supreme Court of Pakistan has held that the right to life, enshrined in Article 9 of its Constitution, entitles individuals to freedom from the environmental effects of "electromagnetic fields or any other such hazards which may be due to installation and construction."[128] In Nigeria, Shell Petroleum was found to have violated the right to a healthy environment, and therefore the right to life, for gas flares caused by oil exploration.[129] Furthermore, in a case regarding residential houses being built in an area designated for recreation, the Supreme Court of India found that the construction was contrary to the right to life.[130] The Court issued a writ of mandamus to halt construction, reasoning that "[t]he *slow poisoning by the polluted atmosphere* caused by environmental pollution and spoliation should also be regarded as amounting to a violation of Art. 21 of the Constitution."[131]

In addition to a business's obligation to respect human rights, states have an obligation to protect human rights. The UN Human Rights Committee 2015 General Comment specified that a state's positive obligations to protect the right to life include the duty "to protect the environment against life threatening pollution."[132] Human rights institutions, such as the African Commission on Human and Peoples' Rights (ACPHR) and the IACHR, interpret the right to life to include positive duties for the states to protect against the third parties, including an obligation to take "preventive steps to preserve and protect the natural environment."[133]

Commencing in March 2018, the CHR of the Philippines conducted a series of hearings to gather information on the allegations in the Carbon Majors petition. The hearings sought to foster a non-adversarial "global dialogue" on whether oil companies have violated human rights by causing climate change through

---

[127] Farooque v. Bangladesh, *supra* note 126 (emphasis added).

[128] Environmental Law Alliance Worldwide, *supra* note 123, at 8–9; Shehla Zia v. WAPDA, P.L.D. 1994 S.C. 693, ¶ 12, http://elaw.org/pk.shehla.zia.1994.

[129] Environmental Law Alliance Worldwide, *supra* note 123, at 9–10; Gbemre v. Shell Petroleum Dev. Co. Nigeria Ltd., (2005) AHRLR 151, ¶ 5.4, https://www.informea.org/sites/default/files/court-decisions/COU10156302.pdf.

[130] Environmental Law Alliance Worldwide, *supra* note 123, at 7; T. Damodhar Rao v. Municipal Corp. of Hyderabad, 1987 A.I.R (AP) 171, https://indiankanoon.org/doc/205063/.

[131] T. Damodhar Rao v. Municipal Corp. of Hyderabad, *supra* note 130, at 24–25 (emphasis added).

[132] Environmental Law Alliance Worldwide, *supra* note 123, at 10; HRC Draft General Comment No. 36, ¶ 28, http://www.ohchr.org/EN/HRBodies/CCPR/Pages/GC36-Article6Righttolife.aspx (under the section entitled "Outcome").

[133] Environmental Law Alliance Worldwide, *supra* note 123, at 11–12; African Charter of Human and Peoples' Rights. General Comment No. 3 on the African Charter of Human and Peoples' Rights (General Comment No. 3, paras. 41–43), http://www.achpr.org/files/instruments/general-comments-right-tolife/general_comment_no_3_english.pdf.

carbon emissions.[134] Commissioner Roberto Eugenio Cadiz, Chairman of the Commission on Human Rights of the Philippines, made the following remark regarding the hearings: "At the end of the day, what will carry will be the credibility of our findings, our inclusivity, our adherence to due process and that our recommendations will be based on clear scientific evidence."[135]

In the hearings held in New York in September 2018,[136] Commissioner Cadiz stated that he hoped the Commission's findings led to the establishment of an international treaty regarding businesses respecting human rights in relation to climate change.[137] "We want to come up with the process to address human rights issues for climate change and the reporting requirements for business, and legal remedies for climate change victims." He also noted that the respondent companies "haven't stepped up."[138] Not one of the Carbon Majors companies participated or sent a representative to these hearings.[139] Experts did not testify that holding the Carbon Majors/respondents accountable would completely solve the problem of climate change but agreed "it will play an important role."[140] The Commission is expected to issue recommendations under the petition in June 2019.[141]

Survivors of climate change–related disasters in the Philippines and the United States (such as Typhoon Haiyan and Hurricane Sandy, respectively) testified

---

[134] Dana Drugmand, *Courts Will Play Key Role in Addressing Climate Crisis, Experts Say*, CLIMATE LIABILITY NEWS (Sept. 27, 2018), https://www.climateliabilitynews.org/2018/09/27/climate-crisis-litigation-columbia/.

[135] *Id.*

[136] Cyrus R. Vance Center for International Justice, *Vance Center Hosts Philippines Commission on Human Rights for Dialogue on Climate Chane and Human Rights* (Oct. 2018), https://www.vancecenter.org/vance-center-hosts-philippines-commission-on-human-rights-for-dialogue-on-climate-change-and-human-rights/.

[137] Sebastien Malo, *Seeking Global Attention, Philippines Moves Human Rights Probe to New York*, REUTERS (Sept. 27, 2018), https://www.reuters.com/article/us-phillipines-usa-climatechange/seeking-global-attention-philippines-moves-human-rights-probe-to-new-york-idUSKCN1M72Vo.

[138] Ucilia Wang, *Human Rights Hearing: Emotional Testimony, No Oil Industry Response*, CLIMATE LIABILITY NEWS (Sept. 28, 2018), https://www.climateliabilitynews.org/2018/09/28/human-rights-hearing-philippines-new-york/.

[139] Malo, *supra* note 137.

[140] Drugmand, *supra* note 134.

[141] Cyrus R. Vance Center for International Justice, *supra* note 136; *see also* Sophie Marjanac, *Why Climate Activists Are Turning to the Law to Take on Fossil Fuel Companies*, AMNESTY INT'L (Oct. 3, 2018), https://www.amnesty.org/en/latest/news/2018/10/why-climate-activists-are-turning-to-the-law-to-take-on-fossil-fuel-companies/ (discussing the "missed opportunity" of companies to participate after none of the respondents participated in the Commission's hearings in the Philippines, calling it a demonstration of "misunderstanding of the responsibility of multinational corporations . . . to respect human rights, as expressed under the United Nations Guiding Principles on Business and Human Rights." Amnesty International further explains that it believes companies can preventively address their effects on climate change "by changing their business models in alignment with the goals of the Paris Agreement," an act that should not be "complex" because companies "already publically (sic) support the Paris Agreement's goals" and already are under pressure from shareholders and activists to conform.).

regarding the impacts of these events on their communities and livelihoods,[142] as did prominent scientific and legal experts. Brenda Ekwurzel, Senior Climate Scientist and Director of Climate Science for the Climate and Energy Program of the Union of Concerned Scientists,[143] testified regarding the effects of major carbon producers on "global atmospheric carbon dioxide, surface temperature, and sea level."[144] She confirmed that current science helps scientists attribute "the frequency and intensity of weather events to the emissions of specific industries."[145] Sharon Y. Eubanks, Former Director at US Department of Justice Tobacco Litigation Team that handled the famous Phillip Morris litigation, testified regarding respondents' knowledge of the effects of greenhouse gas emissions as far back as the 1980s.[146]

John Knox, Former UN Special Rapporteur on Human Rights and the Environment, presented the 2018 Framework Principles on Human Rights and the Environment, published by the UN Office of the High Commissioner for Human Rights.[147] He also testified on the obligations of business and states under the Framework Principles and UN Guiding Principles on Business and Human Rights.[148] He noted that the world is "moving into unchartered territory" when it comes to climate change and that "[t]he Philippines is already experiencing this future through Haiyan and other events."[149] Commissioner Cadiz asked Mr. Knox whether the respondents should be compelled under the Framework Principles to appear at the hearing. Mr. Knox responded that "[t]his is an extremely important opportunity for corporations to *show good faith and concerns about human rights* by cooperating with you."[150]

Another set of hearings was held in London in November 2018 at the London School of Economics.[151] As was the case at the hearings in Manila and New York, none of the respondent companies testified or participated.[152] The London School

---

[142] Drugmand, *supra* note 134; Cyrus R. Vance Center for International Justice, *supra* note 136.

[143] Union of Concerned Scientists, *Brenda Ekwurzel* (2019), https://www.ucsusa.org/about/staff/staff/brenda-ekwurzel.html#.W-mtVvZFxPY.

[144] *Id.*; *see also* Brenda Ekwurzel, et al., *The Rise in Global Atmospheric CO2, Surface Temperature, and Sea Level from Emissions Traced to Major Carbon Producers.* 144 CLIMATIC CHANGE 579 (2017), https://link.springer.com/article/10.1007%2Fs10584-017-1978-0.

[145] Cyrus R. Vance Center for International Justice, *supra* note 136.

[146] Center for International Environmental Law, *Sharon Y. Eubanks* (2015), https://www.ciel.org/about-us/environmental-law-board-of-trustees/sharon-y-eubanks/.

[147] *See* United Nations Office of the High Commissioner for Human Rights, Framework Principles on Human Rights and the Environment (2018), https://www.ohchr.org/EN/Issues/Environment/SREnvironment/Pages/FrameworkPrinciplesReport.aspx. The Framework Principles are comprised of sixteen principles that "relat[e] to human rights and the environment that are based on existing work of human rights system." *Id.*

[148] *Guiding Principles on Business and Human Rights, supra* note 122; Cyrus R. Vance Center for International Justice, *supra* note 136.

[149] Wang, *supra* note 138.

[150] *Id.* (emphasis added).

[151] The London School of Economics and Political Science, *Human Rights and Climate Change* (Nov. 8, 2018), http://www.lse.ac.uk/Events/2018/11/20181108t1830vHKT/Human-Rights-and-Climate-Change.

[152] Kaminski, *supra* note 103.

of Economics noted that the impact of the Commission potentially attributing responsibility to the Carbon Majors for climate change could "spark a domino effect, similar to that witnessed in relation to litigation for harm caused by tobacco: once a sufficient causal link is established, it may be only a matter of time before courts start to award damages to victims."[153]

Several experts offered a wide range of testimony. Dr. Dylan Tanner,[154] Executive Director of Influence Map, a climate policy lobbying organization, testified about how the Carbon Majors are undermining global progress on climate change, not necessarily by denying global science but through "egregious lobbying." Dr. Roda Verheyen, an environmental lawyer,[155] testified that courts do not generally interfere or attribute responsibility for human rights to corporations unless the courts are interpreting contracts, or nuisance or tort provisions in statutes and common law rules.[156] She acknowledged that the CHR for the Philippines inquiry is "novel," but that it "could help to shape law internationally."[157] Dr. Jaap Spier, Professor of Law and Global Challenges at the University of Amsterdam,[158] testified that there are many laws that hold companies accountable for complying with human rights law.[159] He testified that it is "quite clear that the harms done by climate change violate human rights" because climate stability is essential for civilized society.[160]

The final round of hearings on the Carbon Majors petition was held at the Philippine CHR in December 2018 in Quezon City, Philippines. Kumi Naidoo, Secretary General of Amnesty International,[161] testified at the hearings.[162] Naidoo asserted that the CHR's investigation:

> should act as a warning signal to fossil fuel companies everywhere that they need to quickly shift to clean energy. What these brave Filipino women and men have proved by bringing this case is that people refuse to be victims. They don't plan to sit idly by as their future is taken from them ... [k]nowing what we know about

---

[153] The London School of Economics and Political Science, *The Carbon Majors Inquiry Comes to London* (Oct. 30, 2018), http://www.lse.ac.uk/GranthamInstitute/news/the-carbon-majors-inquiry-comes-to-london/.

[154] YouTube, *National Inquiry on Climate Change, Commission on Human Rights of the Philippines London Hearing – 2* (Nov. 7, 2018), https://www.youtube.com/watch?v=-Zn62FUggbE.

[155] Lawyers Gunther, *Dr. Roda Verheyen* (2019), https://rae-guenther.de/anwaelte/dr-roda-verheyen/.

[156] Kaminski, *supra* note 152.

[157] *Id.*

[158] YouTube, *GranthamResearch Live Stream* (Nov. 6, 2018), https://www.youtube.com/watch?v=U3cOypvLu98.

[159] Kaminski, *supra* note 152.

[160] *Id.*

[161] Originally from South Africa, Kumi Naidoo previously served as the International Executive Director for Greenpeace from November 2009–December 2015. More information about Naidoo can be found here: https://www.amnesty.org/en/profiles/kumi-naidoo.

[162] Amnesty International, *Landmark Human Rights and Climate Change Investigation Could Help Millions Worldwide* (Dec. 11, 2018), https://www.amnesty.org/en/latest/news/2018/12/landmark-human-rights-and-climate-change-investigation-could-help-millions-worldwide/.

climate change, it is not hard to see that the business model of fossil fuel companies is literally putting our lives and rights in danger. It is time for a reckoning.[163]

His testimony also included Oxfam's recommendation that companies be required to "measure and disclose climate risks and climate related impacts in line with the taskforce on Climate Financial disclosure and publish their GHG emissions and formulate reduction targets in line with the Paris Agreement."[164] He advocated for a "rights-based approach to climate action" that: (1) would give locals/individuals access to participate in the process; (2) was nondiscriminatory; (3) was transparent and accountable; and (4) was sustainability- and evidence-based.[165]

Naidoo further commented about why climate change is, undoubtedly, a human rights issue. He noted that the obligation lies with both the states to protect those human rights and with corporations to respect those human rights:[166]

> In this moment, we need everybody to live up to their responsibilities to act on climate change and protect human rights. This CHR has now the opportunity to play its part. By positively responding to the petitioners' first prayer and recognizing the legal responsibility of the respondent carbon majors for human rights abuses resulting from climate change, the CHR would take an historical step in meaningfully ensuring the right to remedy to all those who have suffered as the result of the actions of these companies, but also in ensuring that a different future is written for the people in the Philippines and for humanity as a whole.[167]

In his remarks to close the proceedings, Commissioner Roberto Cadiz[168] recognized that climate change is a human rights issue, a global issue, and an existential issue.[169] He discussed the momentum leading up to the Carbon Majors petition, including a reference to the Inuit petition in 2005 that "attempted to establish a

---

[163] *Id.*

[164] YouTube, *Commission on Human Rights' National Inquiry on Climate Change Dec. 11, 2018* (Dec. 11, 2018), https://www.youtube.com/watch?v=3H7vrxT5d4o.

[165] YouTube, *Commission on Human Rights' National Inquiry on Climate Change Dec. 12, 2018* (Dec. 12, 2018), https://www.youtube.com/watch?v=I_nQ8KGoym8.

[166] YouTube, *Commission on Human Rights' National Inquiry on Climate Change Dec. 12, 2018 PM Session* (Dec. 12, 2018), https://www.youtube.com/watch?v=wUDHv_cqTgY. Naidoo's full testimony transcript can also be found at https://www.amnesty.org/en/latest/news/2018/12/kumi-naidoo-testimony-at-philippines-human-rights-commission-investigation-into-carbon-majors-climate-change/.

[167] Kumi Naidoo, *Kumi Naidoo: Carbon Majors Cannot Put their Interests Before Humanity's Survival,* AMNESTY INTERNATIONAL (Dec. 12, 2018), https://www.amnesty.org/en/latest/news/2018/12/kumi-naidoo-testimony-at-philippines-human-rights-commission-investigation-into-carbon-majors-climate-change/.

[168] The Commission on Human Rights also released a statement summarizing Commissioner Cadiz's closing remarks, http://chr.gov.ph/chr-concluded-landmark-inquiry-on-the-effects-of-climate-change-to-human-rights-expects-to-set-the-precedent-in-seeking-climate-justice/.

[169] Commission on Human Rights, *CHR Concluded Landmark Inquiry on the Effects of Climate Change to Human Rights; Expects to Set the Precedent in Seeking Climate Justice* (Dec. 13, 2018), http://chr.gov.ph/chr-concluded-landmark-inquiry-on-the-effects-of-climate-change-to-human-rights-expects-to-set-the-precedent-in-seeking-climate-justice/.

nexus between climate change and human rights." The CHR noted, however, that the Inter-American Commission refused to review the Inuit petition because "[the] information provided by the [Inuits] does not enable [the Commission] to determine whether the alleged facts would tend to characterize a violation of rights protected by the American Declaration."[170] Thus, the Carbon Majors petition was considered to be "the second attempt to cast climate change as a human rights issue."[171]

When the CHR accepted the petition, it lacked legal precedent and resources to handle such a large case. Further, because the IACHR had declined the Inuit's petition, it could have just dismissed the petition and "nobody would have questioned [the CHR]."[172] Commissioner Cadiz noted the respondents' lack of participation in the proceedings[173] and confirmed the unique role of the CHR: "[U]nlike courts which are largely governed by precedents, the challenge to National Human Rights Institutions is to test boundaries and create new paths; to be bold and creative, instead of timid and docile; to be more idealistic, and less pragmatic; to promote soft laws into becoming hard laws; to be able to see beyond legal technicalities and establish guiding principles that can later become binding treaties. In sum, to set the bar of human rights protection to higher standards."[174] The findings and recommendations from the Carbon Majors petition are expected to be released in June 2019.[175]

---

[170] *Id.*
[171] *Id.*
[172] *Id.*
[173] Commissioner Cadiz noted in the final hearing that "[respondents] boycotted the process, but regardless of their participation, we went on with our proceedings because climate change is a life and death issue, and its effects can be irreversible." Llanesca T. Panti, *Oil Firms Boycott CHR Probe on Rights Abuses from Climate Change*, GMA NEWS ONLINE (Dec. 13, 2018), https://www.gmanetwork.com/news/news/nation/678058/oil-firms-boycott-chr-probe-on-rights-abuses-from-climate-change/story/.
[174] Commission on Human Rights, *supra* note 169.
[175] *Id.*

3

Protection of Future Generations

Prior to and during the Anthropocene Era

We do not inherit the Earth from our ancestors; we borrow it from our children.[1]

Building on Chapter 2's focus on the use of the courts to advance the foundations of the climate justice movement in the United States and at the foreign domestic and international levels, Chapter 3 discusses the "future generations" component of the voiceless community and how the common law has been a valuable tool to protect it on environmental matters. The stewardship-oriented focus on the protection of future generations began with protection of environmental resources generally and then adjusted its focus to the protection of the climate system in the Anthropocene era through stewardship-focused and rights-based theories.

Chapter 3 first addresses varying conceptions of intergenerational equity in the scholarly literature and in climate justice litigation. It then reviews foundations for the protection of future generations in international human rights law, international environmental law, and international climate change law, and the role of intergenerational equity in foreign domestic law and administrative bodies charged with the protection of future generations' interests.

The chapter also examines the *Minors Oposa* v. *Factoran* case in the Philippines from the early 1990s as the first important step in this legal theory in the courts. It explores the nature of the legal theory that prevailed in that case and how it laid a foundation for protection of future generations that subsequently took hold in international environmental law generally and climate change regulation more specifically, through the stewardship-based principle of intergenerational equity. Twenty-five years later, the focus on protection of future generations has taken center stage once again, this time in the context of climate justice litigation.

---

[1] Secretary James Baker, Current Policy No. 1254, US Dept. of State, Bureau of Public Affairs Office of Communication (Feb. 1990), https://catalog.hathitrust.org/Record/100798576 (crediting Ralph Waldo Emerson for the quote).

The chapter concludes with a discussion of protection of future generations' interests through atmospheric trust litigation in the landmark *Juliana* v. *United States* case. It also reviews how variations of this theory have been pursued in several other countries, with an especially promising outcome in Colombia.

I WHAT IS INTERGENERATIONAL EQUITY?

A *A Definitional Quandary*

The term "future generations" is difficult to define. It could refer to all future people, some future people, all future generations (focusing on the generation as such, not on its members), some future generations (e.g., temporally closer future generations), certain future age groups or birth cohorts, future groups (e.g., future generations of Romanians), future members of a certain future group, or types of future people.[2] It remains to be determined which of these groups should be the holder of the legal rights ascribed to "future generations." Some aspects of intergenerational equity may be relevant to all members of future generations, such as a shared interest in a sustainable ecosystem. Under international human rights law, there is a similar focus on what is owed to all future people and on the corresponding universal rights that all legal systems should provide. Future people, however, will most likely be a diverse collection of individuals of different and even conflicting interests, which in turn may impose different demands on current generations. Accordingly, the use of the term "future generations" is much more versatile, potentially referring to a variety of different future groups and types of people.[3]

The protection of future generations under domestic and international law can mean many things, and protections can take many forms.[4] While the idea of current generations acting as stewards of the earth can be found in many traditions and cultures, Edith Brown Weiss is widely regarded for giving contemporary expression to the concept in her 1989 book addressing the protection of future generations.[5] Professor Edith Brown Weiss, of Georgetown University Law Center, has proposed three basic principles of intergenerational equity in her book *In Fairness to Future Generations: International Law, Common Patrimony, and Intergenerational Equity*:[6]

---

[2]   Ori J. Herstein, *The Identity and (Legal) Rights of Future Generations*, 77 Geo. Wash. L. Rev. 1173, 1174–75 (2009).

[3]   *Id.* at 1182–83.

[4]   The climate justice plaintiffs' strategies discussed in Part I, section B of this chapter reflect some of these varying conceptions through a wide range of legal mechanisms and requested remedies.

[5]   Edith Brown Weiss, In Fairness to Future Generations: International Law, Common Patrimony, and Intergenerational Equity (1989).

[6]   *Id.* at 38.

- "Conservation of Options": each generation shall conserve the diversity of the natural and cultural resource base;[7]
- "Conservation of Quality": each generation shall maintain the quality of the planet so that subsequent generations are entitled to a comparable level of that enjoyed by previous generations;[8]
- "Conservation of Access": each generation shall provide its members with equitable rights of access to the legacy of past generations and conserve such access for future generations.[9]

While many acknowledge that humankind has a responsibility to take account of its actions for the future,[10] this moral imperative has found only limited recognition in law.[11] The idea of taking into account the needs of future generations appears in some national laws, constitutions, international law instruments, preambles of multilateral environmental agreements, and, most notably, the operative provisions of the United Nations Framework Convention on Climate Change (UNFCCC).[12] Recognition of intergenerational equity in these instruments, discussed later in the chapter, is a positive step forward, albeit a small and inadequate one. This recognition needs to be combined with a procedural mechanism that provides a voice for future generations whose ability to inherit a habitable planet is imperiled.[13] Customary international law can help move this doctrine in this direction, and it would be ignoring its basic responsibilities if it did not.[14]

---

[7] *Id.*

[8] *Id.*

[9] *Id. See also* Burns H. Weston & Tracy Bach, *Recalibrating the Law of Humans with the Laws of Nature: Climate Change, Human Rights, and Intergenerational Justice* 19 (Aug. 3, 2009). Vermont Law School Research Paper No. #10–06, https://ssrn.com/abstract=1443243 (discussing Weiss's three principles on intergenerational equity).

[10] WILFRED BECKERMAN, *The Impossibility of a Theory of Intergenerational Justice, in* HANDBOOK OF INTERGENERATIONAL JUSTICE 53, 64 (Joerg Chet Tremmel ed., 2006).

[11] Jane Anstee-Wedderburn, *Giving a Voice to Future Generations: Intergenerational Equity, Representatives of Generations to Come, and the Challenge of Planetary Rights*, 1 AUST. J. ENVI'L L. 37, 38–39 (2014); *see also* Daniel Farber, *Does the Future Have Standing?* LEGAL PLANET (Feb. 7, 2019), http://legal-planet.org/2019/02/07/does-the-future-have-standing/ (recognizing precedent from property law for appointing a legal representative for future generations); Neil H. Buchanan, *What Do We Owe Future Generations?* 77 GEO. WASH. L. REV. 1237 (2009).

[12] United Nations Framework Convention on Climate Change, art. 3, 1771 U.N.T.S. 107 (entered into force Mar. 21, 1994) [hereinafter "UNFCCC"].

[13] For a proposal on substantive and procedural dimensions of accountability for future generations, *see infra* Chapter 6.

[14] Judge C. G. Weeramantry, *Commentary on Securing the Rights of Future Generations in International Law*, 2 (2008), http://futureroundtable.org/documents/2238847/0/Judge+C.+G .+Weeramantry.pdf.

B *Conceptions of Future Generations in Climate Justice Litigation*

Climate justice litigation has exploded in the past decade to promote protection of "future generations" and their interest in inheriting a habitable planet. The organization, Our Children's Trust,[15] has been leading this charge with many cases in state courts throughout the United States and in the highly regarded "environmental trial of the century" proceeding against the federal government in *Juliana v. United States*. Similar cases that were focused on climate justice and intergenerational equity have already been successful in the Netherlands, Pakistan, and Colombia. This section briefly reviews the nature of the future generations at issue in each case, the types of claims filed, and the relief sought in each case.

In *Juliana*, the youth plaintiffs contend that the US government's failure to regulate climate change violates "their substantive due process rights to life, liberty, and property, and that the federal government has violated its obligation to hold certain natural resources in trust for the people and for future generations."[16] The complaint alleges that "[t]he present level of CO_2 and its warming, both realized and latent, are already in the zone of danger."[17] Lead plaintiff Kelsey Juliana asserts that algae blooms contaminate the water she drinks, and drought-induced low water levels kill the wild salmon she eats.[18] Plaintiff Xiuhtezcatl Roske-Martinez alleges increased wildfires and extreme flooding endanger his personal safety.[19] Plaintiff Alexander Loznak maintains that record setting temperatures impact the health of the hazelnut orchard on his family farm, which is an important source of food and income for him and his family.[20] Plaintiff Jacob Lebel asserts that drought conditions required installation of an irrigation system on his family's farm.[21] Plaintiff Zealand B. alleges that decreased snowpack has prevented him from skiing during the winter.[22] Plaintiff Sahara V. alleges that the hot and dry conditions from forest fires aggravate her asthma.[23] The youth plaintiffs each allege harm that is ongoing and likely to continue in the future.[24]

In *Urgenda Foundation v. State of the Netherlands*, the plaintiffs relied in part on Article 3 of the UN Climate Change Convention: "The Parties should protect the

---

[15] For a description of Our Children's Trust's future generations–focused cases filed by youth plaintiffs in state and federal courts, *see* https://www.ourchildrenstrust.org/.

[16] *Juliana v. United States*, 217 F.Supp.3d 1224, 1233 (D. Or. 2016).

[17] *Id.* at 1244.

[18] *Id.* at 1242.

[19] *Id.*

[20] *Id.*

[21] *Id.*

[22] *Id.*

[23] *Id.*

[24] *Id.* at 1244; *see, e.g., id.* ("alleging current harm" and "harm '[i]n the coming decades' from ocean acidification and rising sea levels" and "alleging damage to freshwater resources now and in the future 'if immediate action is not taken' to reduce CO_2 emissions'").

climate system for the benefit of present and future generations of humankind, on the basis of equity and in accordance with their common but differentiated responsibilities and respective capabilities."[25] The District Court observed that "[t]he principle of fairness means that the policy should not only start from what is most beneficial to the current generation at this moment, but also what this means for future generations, so that future generations are not exclusively and disproportionately burdened with the consequences of climate change."[26] In compelling language, the District Court concluded that "the possibility of damages for those whose interests Urgenda represents, including current and future generations of Dutch nationals, is so great and concrete that, given its duty of care, the state must make an adequate contribution – greater than its current contribution – to prevent hazardous climate change."[27] In upholding the District Court's decision, the Appellate Court in *Urgenda* confirmed the strong future generations foundation in the case in noting: "it is without a doubt plausible that the current generation of Dutch nationals, in particular but not limited to the younger individuals in this group, will have to deal with the adverse effects of climate change in their lifetime if global emissions of greenhouse gases are not adequately reduced.[28] Therefore, the Court does not have to consider the questions raised by the State in this ground of appeal."[29]

In the youth climate justice suit in Colombia,[30] a group of twenty-five children, adolescents, and young adults ranging from seven to twenty-five years of age who live in Colombian cities most at risk from climate change impacts[31] sought to compel the government to address deforestation in the Colombian Amazon to regulate climate change impacts in the country more effectively. The plaintiffs asserted that deforestation in the Amazon causes "short, medium, and long term imminent and serious damage to the children, adolescents and adults who filed this lawsuit ... including both present and future generations, as it leads to rampant emissions of carbon dioxide (CO_2) into the atmosphere ... which in turn transforms and fragments ecosystems, altering water sources and the water supply for population centers and land degradation."[32] They further contended that "natural resources are shared by all inhabitants of Planet Earth, and by their descendants or future

[25] Urgenda Foundation v. The State of the Netherlands, 200.178.245, ¶ 2.38 (Apr. 18, 2017).
[26] Urgenda Foundation v. The State of the Netherlands, C/09/456689/HA ZA 13–1396, ¶ 4.57 (June 24, 2015).
[27] *Id.* at ¶ 4.89.
[28] Urgenda Foundation v. The State of the Netherlands, 200.178.245/01, ¶ 37 (Oct. 9, 2018).
[29] *Id.*
[30] Dejusticia v. Colombia, STC4360–2018, https://claw.org/system/files/attachments/publicre source/Colombia%202018%20Sentencia%20Amazonas%20cambio%20climatico.pdf (original Spanish); *see also* Dejusticia v. Colombia, STC4360–2018, https://www.dejusticia.org/wp-con tent/uploads/2018/04/Tutela-English-Excerpts-1.pdf (English translation of the decision).
[31] *Id.* at ¶ 2.1.
[32] *Id.* at ¶ 34.

generations who do not yet have a physical hold of them, but who are tributaries, recipients, and owners of them … Thus, without an equitable and prudent approach to consumption, the future of humankind may be compromised due to the scarcity of essential life resources."[33]

The theory of the Colombian case involved a balance of enhanced government stewardship and increased environmental rights for future generations. The plaintiffs maintained that the government's failure to act effectively on this critical issue constitutes an omission that "translates into a limitation to the freedom of action of present generations, while simultaneously implicitly demanding new burdens of environmental commitments, to the extent that they take on the care and steward-ship of natural resources and the future world."[34]

The momentum from these successful cases has inspired additional promising climate justice cases seeking protection of future generations. In the People's Climate Case in the European Union brought by various plaintiffs throughout the EU, the plaintiffs assert that "unless drastic action is taken now, today's children will face environmental conditions in their future lives that are far worse than those enjoyed by present day adults."[35] In addition to noting the future generations protection mandate in Article 3(1) of the UNFCCC, the plaintiffs also referred to the UN International Law Commission's 2017 Draft Guidelines on Protection of the Atmosphere, which provide that "the interests of future generations of human-kind in the long-term conservation of the atmosphere should be fully taken into account."[36]

The theory of the case in the People's Climate Case draws on two compelling observations that underscore the vulnerability of future generations to climate change impacts. "First, as … catalogued by UNICEF and other bodies, children are more susceptible than adults to risks from the higher incidence of disease, malnutrition, fires, floods and displacement that may result from climate change. Second, climate change will progressively worsen over time, affecting children and the succeeding generations with increasing severity. A failure to abate climate change therefore violates equality of treatment based on age."[37]

In other promising pending climate justice litigation seeking protection of future generations, two young girls in Pakistan and India have filed claims against their respective governments demanding enhanced action on climate change regulation. In the Pakistan case, a seven-year-old girl sued on behalf of herself, the people of

---

[33] *Id.* at ¶ 20.
[34] *Id.* at ¶ 21.
[35] People's Climate Case, Case T-##/18. Application for Annulment and Application/Claim for Non-Contractual Liability and Application for Measures of Inquiry, ¶ 192 (2018), https://peoplesclimatecase.caneurope.org/wp-content/uploads/2018/05/application-delivered-to-european-general-court.pdf.
[36] *Id.* at ¶ 194.
[37] *Id.* at ¶ 251.

Pakistan, and future generations "for the protection of her and the people of Pakistan's Fundamental Rights, as guaranteed by the Constitution."[38] She alleged that continuing to burn fossil fuels will further destabilize the climate system on which present and future generations depend for their well-being and survival.[39] The impacts associated with the emissions of CO_2 today will be mostly borne by children and future generations.[40]

In compelling and dramatic language, the young Pakistani further asserted: "By choosing to develop coal as an energy source instead of renewable, nonfossil fuel resources, the Respondents are ignoring the long-term adverse consequences they are bringing upon both current and future generations of Pakistanis, in violation of their fundamental rights."[41] The intergenerational equity mandate is quite clear as she further alleged that the "cumulative effects of CO_2 emissions from the continued burning of fossil fuels will make life inhospitable and unsafe, for those alive now and for future generations, who will have to endure the inherited Environment degraded by the choices made by current generations as the adverse impacts of climate change increase in severity and frequency."[42] She implored the court to follow the globally accepted precautionary principle in an effort to protect future generations from the irreversible harm threatened by climate change.[43]

Similarly, in an action against the Government of India, nine-year-old Ridhima Pandey maintained that children of today and the future will disproportionately suffer the dangers and catastrophic impacts of climate destabilization and ocean acidification.[44] The applicant's theory of the case is rooted in a combination of the government's environmental duties on behalf of future generations and rights-based protections for these vulnerable populations: "It is submitted that the State and its machinery is a trustee of vital natural resources on which human survival and welfare depend, bound by a fiduciary duty under the Public Trust Doctrine to mitigate climate change so as to protect such resources for the benefit of current and future generations."[45] The applicant asserts that she "as well as the entire class of children and future generations have the right to a healthy environment under the principle of intergenerational equity," and that the applicant "is part of a class that amongst all Indians, is most vulnerable to changes in climate in India and yet are not part of the decision-making process."[46]

---

[38] Ali v. Federation of Pakistan, No. / 1 of 2016, 4 (Apr. 2016).

[39] *Id.* at ¶ 6.

[40] *Id.* at ¶ 7.

[41] *Id.* at ¶ 31.

[42] *Id.* at 29.

[43] *Id.* at 36.

[44] Pandey v. Union of India, National Green Tribunal, Original Application No: ___ of 2017, 2–3, https://static1.squarespace.com/static/571d109b04426270152febe0/t/58dd45319f74568a83fd7977/1490896178123/13.03.22.ClimateChangePetition.pdf.

[45] *Id.* at ¶ 2.

[46] *Id.* at 25.

II INTERGENERATIONAL EQUITY IN INTERNATIONAL
LAW INSTRUMENTS

International law is replete with references to intergenerational equity. Part II addresses how these references originated in international human rights law and instruments and then proliferated in international environmental law scholarship and binding and nonbinding instruments. Part II concludes with a summary of how international climate change law also embraces intergenerational equity in nonbinding measures, and how the lack of binding mandates in these instruments has laid a foundation for courts and tribunals to lead the way in fashioning governmental duties with respect to protection of future generations' interests in inheriting a stable climate system.

A *International Human Rights Law*

International human rights law predates international environmental law by three decades. It was established in the 1940s in response to the human rights atrocities of World War II and has been very effective in galvanizing global political will to provide legal frameworks and remedies for human rights violations. International environmental law traces its roots to the 1970s with several instruments addressing transboundary global environmental challenges. A tense and reluctant relationship between these two fields has emerged in the past two decades that reflects the wide variety of ways in which global environmental problems present human rights implications, with a recent focus on the area of climate change impacts.[47]

In January 2009, The Office of the UN High Commissioner for Human Rights (OHCHR) prepared a report on the effects of climate change on the full enjoyment of human rights.[48] The report concluded that climate change had a "range of implications for the effective enjoyment of human rights," including "direct" effects, such as extreme weather events posing a threat to the right to life, but also "indirect

---

[47] The challenge of managing climate refugees (also referred to in the literature as "climate displaced peoples" and "climate migrants") lies at the heart of this uneasy and dysfunctional relationship between international environmental law and international human rights law. The two fields need to cooperate more effectively and devote more attention to this crisis, which is already occurring and promises to become much worse in the coming decades. For a discussion of the challenge of responding to the climate refugees crisis and some proposed solutions, *see generally* NAFEES AHMAD & STELLINA JOLLY, CLIMATE REFUGEES IN SOUTH ASIA: PROTECTION UNDER INTERNATIONAL LEGAL STANDARDS AND STATE PRACTICES IN SOUTH ASIA (2019); Thea Philip, *Climate Change Displacement and Migration: An Analysis of the Current International Legal Regime's Deficiency, Proposed Solutions and a Way Forward*, 19 MELB. J. INT'L L. 639 (2019); Marissa Knodel, *Wet Feet Marching: Climate Justice and Sustainable Development for Climate Displaced Nations in the South Pacific*, 14 VT. J. ENVTL. L. 127 (2011).

[48] Report of the Office of the United Nations High Commissioner for Human Rights on the relationship between climate change and human rights, A/HRC/10/61 (Jan. 15, 2009), https://undocs.org/A/HRC/10/61 [hereinafter "OHCHR Report"].

and gradual" effects on human rights, such as increasing stress on health systems.[49] The report recognized that existing human rights instruments contain rights that would be infringed by governments' failure to address climate change, including the right to a standard of living adequate for health and well-being, the right to the highest attainable standard of health, the human right to life, and the right to subsistence.[50] In March 2009, in response to the report, the Human Rights Council adopted Resolution 10/4, explaining that climate change related impacts have a range of direct and indirect implications for the effective enjoyment of human rights.[51]

International human rights law imposes duties on states to cooperate in order to avoid the "foreseeable destruction of the human rights of substantial numbers of people by, for example, allowing global warming to continue at levels that would inundate small island states"; however, this approach as a benchmark is considered too vague.[52] Appropriate mitigation targets within national or international instruments can be devised by combining science, economics, and human rights, with human rights serving as a reference point to provide the minimum benchmarks that should be protected by the mitigation target.[53]

Human rights should be used as the basis to develop the mitigation targets and efforts necessary to protect each specific right such as the human right to subsistence; however, human rights are limited in that they cannot resolve the distributional issues involved in crafting mitigation targets such as how to balance current and future generations' interests.[54] Efforts are underway to enhance how human rights law can address future generations' needs. For example, the UN Educational, Scientific and Cultural Organization's Declaration on the Responsibilities of the Present Generations Towards Future Generations contains twelve articles defining issues regarded as relevant to protect for future generations, including non-environmental goals such as education, peace, common heritage, and cultural diversity.[55] In addition, Human Rights for Future Generations (HRFG) is an interdisciplinary research program funded by the Oxford Martin School.[56] The HRFG investigates the existing institutional human rights frameworks to advance contributions to academic and policy thinking regarding twenty-first-century issues

[49] *Id.* at 29 ¶ 92.
[50] *Id.* at 8–15 ¶¶ 20–41, 24 ¶ 74.
[51] Human Rights Council Res. 10/4, U.N. Doc. A/HRC/RES/10/4, ¶¶ 1–2 (Mar. 25, 2009), https://ap.ohchr.org/documents/E/HRC/resolutions/A_HRC_RES_10_4.pdf.
[52] Peter Lawrence, Justice for Future Generations: Climate Change and International Law 136 (2014).
[53] *Id.*
[54] *Id.* at 137–38.
[55] United Nations Educational, Scientific and Cultural Organization, Declaration on the Responsibilities of the Present Generations Towards Future Generations (Nov. 12, 1997).
[56] The Oxford Martin Programme on Human Rights for Future Generations, https://www.law.ox.ac.uk/research-and-subject-groups/oxford-martin-programme-human-rights-future-generations (last accessed Jan. 8, 2019).

such as poverty, armed conflict, and environmental changes.[57] The project seeks to advance a new framework built on ethical, legal, and political dimensions that will help translate theory into real legal and policy solutions on these issues; lead and promote high-level research on human rights; and contribute to a better understanding of the contemporary challenges.[58]

B *International Environmental Law*

The UN Sustainable Development Goals (SDGs) contain a few references to "future generations." In a section on "Planet," the States expressed their commitment "to protect the planet from degradation ... so that it can support the needs of the present and future generations."[59] Even though the title of this section suggests that it is the interest of the planet itself that is at stake, it is fair to infer that the protection of the planet from degradation is pursued in the interest of today's and tomorrow's people. In other paragraphs, the SDGs more explicitly refer to the present and future generations – and not nature itself – as the beneficiaries: "We will implement the [Sustainable Development] Agenda for the full benefit of all, for today's generation and for future generations."[60] Calls to act sustainably and save the planet "for future generations" or "for our children and grandchildren" appear almost interchangeably.[61]

The UN Convention on Biological Diversity (1992), the Convention to Combat Desertification (1994), and the Joint Convention on the Safety of Spent Fuel Management and on the Safety of Radioactive Waste Management (1997) stand out in highlighting the needs of future generations. The UNESCO Declaration on the Responsibilities of the Present Generations Towards Future Generations (1997) directly addresses the issue. Other declarations and UN General Assembly Resolution 37/7 on a World Charter for Nature (1982) also address the need to protect future generations.[62]

---

[57] *Id.*

[58] *Id.*

[59] United Nations General Assembly, *Transforming Our World: The 2030 Agenda for Sustainable Development*, Resolution 70/1, 2 (adopted Sept. 25, 2015).

[60] *Id.* at art. 18; Otto Spijkers, *Intergenerational Equity and the Sustainable Development Goals*, 10 SUSTAINABILITY 3836 (2018), https://www.mdpi.com/2071-1050/10/11/3836/htm.

[61] Report of the Secretary-General, United Nations General Assembly, *Intergenerational Solidarity and the Needs of Future Generations*, 9 (2013). Defining the moral status of future persons raises unique and extraordinary moral and metaethical problems, to which conventional moral and political theories are unable to provide an adequate response. *See also* STEPHEN A. GARDINER, A PERFECT MORAL STORM: THE ETHICAL TRAGEDY OF CLIMATE CHANGE (2011).

[62] Report of the Secretary-General, UN General Assembly, *supra* note 61, at 23. Other international agreements and declarations that make references to future generations and common heritage include: the International Convention for the Regulation of Whaling (1946), Convention on International Trade in Endangered Species of Wild Fauna and Flora (CITES) (1975), African Convention on the Conservation of Nature and Natural Resources (1968), Convention

The number of instruments demonstrate that concern for future generations has developed as a guiding principle in international norms. The references to future generations in these instruments also demonstrate that, at least to a certain extent, states are not only willing to make, but also have already made, international commitments for the sake of future generations. However, these references to future generations remain, for the most part, in preambles and not in the operative text of the instruments. There are no legally binding international law instruments specifically committing states to the protection of future generations.[63]

As there is debate over whether future generations have rights, it is necessary to determine if present generations have an obligation to preserve, protect, and use the natural environment in a sustainable manner. Present generations cannot be named "trustees" of the environment for the benefit of future generations if the environment is not entitled to protection in the present.[64] International law has not explicitly established a human right to a healthy environment;[65] however, several nonbinding instruments have recognized an entitlement to a healthy environment.[66]

Notwithstanding the lack of express recognition of rights of future generations to environmental protection, several international environmental law instruments address the need to protect resources for the benefit of future generations. The 1946 International Whaling Convention is the earliest example of an international environmental treaty addressing intergenerational equity, though it does so

---

on the Prohibition of Military or any Other Hostile Use of Environmental Modification Techniques (1976), Bonn Convention on the Conservation of Migratory Species of Wild Animals (1979), Convention on the Conservation of European Wildlife and Natural Habitats (1979), Council of Europe Convention for the Protection of the Architectural Heritage of Europe (1985), ASEAN Agreement on the Conservation of Nature and Natural Resources (1985), Paris Convention for the Protection of the Marine Environment of the North-East Atlantic (1992), Convention on the Transboundary Effects of Industrial Accidents (1992), UNECE Convention on the Protection and Use of Transboundary, Watercourses and International Lakes (1992), North American Agreement on Environmental Cooperation (1993), UNECE Aarhus Convention on Access to Information, Public Participation in Decision-making and Access to Justice in Environmental Matters (1998), Charter of Fundamental Rights of the European Union (2000), Stockholm Convention on Persistent Organic Pollutants (2001), WHO Framework Convention on Tobacco Control (2003), Vienna Declaration and Programme of Action, World Conference on Human Rights (1993), UNESCO Universal Declaration on Bioethics and Human Rights (2005), Antarctic Treaty (1959), Agreement Governing the Activities of States on the Moon and Other Celestial Bodies (1979), United Nations Convention on the Law of the Sea (1982), and UNESCO Universal Declaration on the Human Genome and Human Rights (1997).

[63] Report of the Secretary-General, UN General Assembly, *supra* note 61, at 24.

[64] CLEMENT YOW MULALAP, *"To Preserve the Heritage of the Past, and to Protect the Promise of the Future": Intergenerational Equity Challenges from Climate Change in the Federated States of Micronesia, in* CLIMATE JUSTICE: CASE STUDIES IN GLOBAL AND REGIONAL GOVERNANCE CHALLENGES 337 (Randall S. Abate ed., 2016).

[65] *Id.*

[66] *Id.*

from the perspective of maintaining whales as a sustainable resource to harvest: "Recognizing the interest of the nations of the world in safeguarding for future generations the great natural resources represented by the whale stocks...."[67] The treaty would later embrace an environmental conservation focus in the 1980s with the moratorium on commercial whaling.

Three more recent examples are the 1973 Convention on International Trade in Endangered Species of Wild Fauna and Flora (CITES), the Convention on Biological Diversity (CBD) in 1992, and a 1994 United Nations convention that addresses drought. CITES recognizes that "wild flora and fauna in their many beautiful and varied forms are an irreplaceable part of the natural systems of the earth which must be protected for this and the generations to come."[68] Similarly, the 1992 CBD provides that parties must "conserve and sustainably use biological diversity for the benefit of present and future generations."[69] Finally, the 1994 United Nations Convention to Combat Desertification in Countries Experiencing Serious Drought and/or Desertification, Particularly in Africa provides that parties shall "take appropriate action in combating desertification and mitigating the effects of drought for the benefit of present and future generations."[70]

International environmental law instruments that cover intergenerational equity do not speak directly to *how* rights of future generations should be protected. As such, much work remains in seeking to provide viable legal protections under international law for future generations.[71]

Judicial opinions in international law addressing consideration of future generations include *Denmark* v. *Norway* (1993), where the judge identified various examples of equitable principles based on global jurisprudence that emerge from traditional societies, including "the sacrosanct nature of earth resources, harmony of human activity with the environment, respect for the rights of future generations and the custody of earth resources with the standard of due diligence expected of a trustee."[72] In the dissenting opinion for the International Court of Justice's (ICJ) advisory opinion on the legality of the threat or use of nuclear weapons, Judge Christopher Weeramantry insisted that the ICJ, as the principal judicial organ of the United Nations, must give due regard to the rights of future generations.[73]

International environmental soft law is replete with references to future generations across three decades. For example, Principle 2 of the 1972 Stockholm Declaration on the Human Environment provides: "The natural resources of the earth

---

[67] 161 U.N.T.S. 72, 10 U.S.T. 952.

[68] Mulalap, *supra* note 64, at 334 (internal citations omitted).

[69] *Id.* (internal citations omitted).

[70] 1954 U.N.T.S. 3, Secretariat home page, www.unccd.int.

[71] One promising step forward on this path is a draft UN resolution, *"Towards the sustainable development of the Caribbean Sea for present and future generations,"* G.A. Draft Res. A/C.2/73/L.27/Rev.1 (Nov. 23, 2018), https://undocs.org/A/C.2/73/L.27/Rev.1.

[72] Mulalap, *supra* note 64, at 335.

[73] *Id.* at 336.

including the air, water, land, flora and fauna and especially representative samples of natural ecosystems must be safeguarded for the benefit of present and future generations through careful planning or management as appropriate."[74] The 1982 World Charter for Nature similarly provides that "man must acquire the knowledge to maintain and enhance his ability to use natural resources ... which ensures the preservation of the species and ecosystems for the benefit of present and future generations."[75] Finally, Principle 4 of the 1992 Rio Declaration on Environment and Development provides: "The right to development must be fulfilled so as to equitably meet developmental and environmental needs of present and future generations."[76] Though not exclusively focused on the environment, the 2007 United Nations Declaration on the Rights of Indigenous People provides in Principle 25: "the right to maintain and strengthen their distinctive spiritual relationship with their traditionally owned or otherwise occupied and used lands, territories, waters and coastal seas and other resources and to uphold their responsibilities to future generations in this regard."[77]

The principle of sustainable development institutionalized the recognition of future generations' interests to inherit a clean and healthy environment. The 1987 "Report of the World Commission on Environment and Development: Our Common Future" (commonly referred to as the "Brundtland Report")[78] addressed sustainable development and arguably shaped subsequent international law as it deals with sustainable development and intergenerational equity with the following powerful language:

> 25. Many present efforts to guard and maintain human progress, to meet human needs, and to realize human ambitions are simply unsustainable – in both the rich and poor nations. They draw too heavily, too quickly, on already overdrawn environmental resource accounts to be affordable far into the future without bankrupting those accounts. They may show profit on the balance sheets of our generation, but our children will inherit the losses. We borrow environmental capital from future generations with no intention or prospect of repaying. They may damn us for our spendthrift ways, but they can never collect on our debt to them. We act as we do because we can get away with it: future generations do not vote; they have no political or financial power; they cannot challenge our decisions.[79]

---

[74] *Id.*

[75] World Charter on Nature, U.N.G.A. Res 37/7, 22 I.L.M. 455 (1983).

[76] Rio Declaration on Environment and Development, Pr. 4, U.N. Doc. A/CONF.151/26, 31 I.L.M. 874 (1992).

[77] United Nations Declaration on the Rights of Indigenous Peoples, G.A. Res. 61/295, U.N. Doc. A/RES/61/295 (Sept. 13, 2007), 46 I.L.M. 1013 (2007), https://www.un.org/development/desa/indigenouspeoples/wpcontent/uploads/sites/19/2018/11/UNDRIP_E_web.pdf.

[78] Report of the World Commission on Environment and Development: Our Common Future (1987), http://www.un-documents.net/our-common-future.pdf.

[79] World Commission on Environment and Development, http://www.un-documents.net/our-common-future.pdf.

Agenda 21 followed in 1992 with its ambitious and comprehensive blueprint for sustainable development.[80] Chapter 25 of Agenda 21, which addresses "Children and Youth in Sustainable Development," reflects concern regarding environmental protection for future generations.[81] Ten years later, the 2002 Johannesburg Declaration of Sustainable Development confirmed a strong focus on intergenerational equity that sought "to ensure that through our actions they [the children of the world] will inherit a world free of the indignity and indecency occasioned by poverty, environmental degradation and patterns of unsustainable development."[82]

The concept of protecting a resource for future generations was addressed more than 125 years ago in the 1893 Seal Fur Arbitration; however, the international tribunal rejected the argument.[83] Since then, decisions from international law courts and tribunals have increasingly recognized the importance of intergenerational equity. In the ICJ's advisory opinion on the *Legality of the Threat or Use of Nuclear Weapons*, the Court recognized that the environment is under daily threat and that the use of nuclear weapons could constitute a catastrophe for the environment. The Court also recognized that the environment is not an abstraction but represents the living space, the quality of life, and the health of humans, including generations unborn.[84] Further, the use of nuclear weapons would be a serious danger to future generations. Ionizing radiation has the potential to damage the future environment, food, and marine ecosystem, and to cause genetic defects and illness in future generations. As such, in order to apply the Charter law on the use of force and the law applicable in armed conflict, in particular humanitarian law, it is imperative for the Court to take account of the unique characteristics of nuclear weapons, and in particular their destructive capacity, their capacity to cause untold human suffering, and their ability to cause damage to generations to come.[85]

---

[80] Agenda 21, UN Conference on Environment and Development. Rio de Janeiro (June 3–14, 1992), https://sustainabledevelopment.un.org/content/documents/Agenda21.pdf.

[81] *Id.* Ch. 25, ¶ 12, www.un-documents.net/a21-25.htm ("The specific interests of children need to be taken fully into account in the participatory process on environment and development in order to safeguard the future sustainability of any actions taken to improve the sustainability of the environment.").

[82] Johannesburg Declaration on Sustainable Development, ¶ 3, https://unhabitat.org/wp-content/uploads/2014/07/A_CONF.199_20-Johannesburg-Declaration-on-Sustainable-Development-2002.pdf. For additional discussion of future generations' protection in the environmental context, *see generally* LAURA WESTRA, ENVIRONMENTAL JUSTICE AND THE RIGHTS OF THE UNBORN AND FUTURE GENERATIONS: LAW, ENVIRONMENTAL HARM AND THE RIGHT TO HEALTH (2006); Lynda M. Collins, *The Doctrine of Intergenerational Equity in Global Environmental Governance*, 30 DALHOUSIE L.J. 79 (2007).

[83] PHILIPPE SANDS, JACQUELINE PEEL, ADRIANA FABRA & RUTH MACKENZIE, PRINCIPLES OF INTERNATIONAL ENVIRONMENTAL LAW (4th ed. 2018).

[84] Legality of the Threat or Use of Nuclear Weapons, Advisory Opinion, I.C.J. Reports 1996, 226, 241, https://www.refworld.org/cases,ICJ,4b2913d62.html.

[85] *Id.* at art. 35.

C *International Climate Change Law*

Although there are obstacles in establishing an obligation of intergenerational equity under contemporary international law, this concept has begun to play an important role in the reasoning of international laws, particularly as an integral part of sustainable development.[86]

Breaking the term down into its two components, "intergenerational" is the notion that there are links between the present generation and the future generations of humankind.[87] The present generation encompasses all generations currently living.[88] "Equity" in international law is defined as fairness or justice, with procedural and substantive dimensions to ensure that individuals and entities are able to access international legal processes and receive judgments on the merits that are fair and reasonable.[89] The main issue with intergenerational equity is whether the present generation has an obligation to preserve, protect, and use the natural environment in a sustainable manner for the sake of future generations.[90] Such a duty would allow future generations to enjoy the natural environment to at least the same degree as the present generation.[91]

Building on the OHCHR report,[92] there has been a gradual introduction of human rights language in the UNFCCC process, including the preamble to the Cancun Agreement, which recognized the need to consult with a wide range of stakeholders and that the gender equality and the effective participation of women and indigenous peoples are important for effective action on all aspects of climate change.[93] However, after the Cancun Agreement, there has been no explicit mention of human rights. For example there was no mention or reference at the Durban Conference, or at Doha 2012, and while 2012 Rio+20 reaffirmed the importance of human rights, it did not affirm a human right to the environment or a right to climatic stability, and the section of the final report on climate change did not use any human rights language.[94]

The 1992 UNFCCC committed its States parties "to protect the climate system for the benefit of present and future generations of humankind."[95] The UNFCCC is rooted in the principle of common but differentiated responsibility.[96] It recognizes that while all states should do their part to address climate change, certain States

---

[86] LAWRENCE, *supra* note 52, at 118.
[87] Mulalap, *supra* note 64, at 332.
[88] *Id.*
[89] *Id.*
[90] *Id.* at 337.
[91] *Id.*
[92] *See* OHCHR Report, *supra* note 48.
[93] LAWRENCE, *supra* note 52, at 134–35.
[94] *Id.* at 135.
[95] *Id.*
[96] Mulalap, *supra* note 64, at 341.

have historically been high emitters of GHGs and should therefore take the lead in addressing climate change.[97] It provides that the parties should protect the climate system for the benefit of present and future generations, on the basis of equity and in accordance with their common but differentiated responsibilities and respective capabilities.[98] Accordingly, the developed countries should take the lead in combating climate change and the adverse effects thereof.[99] Additionally, the parties have a right to and should promote sustainable development, policies, and measures to protect the climate system against human-induced change.[100]

In response to the international concerns surrounding the effects of global climate change, the Kyoto Protocol to the UNFCCC was drafted in 1997.[101] Implemented pursuant to the UNFCCC with 192 parties, the Kyoto Protocol sought to reduce emissions of greenhouse gases into the atmosphere through a series of varying targets and timetables depending on whether the party was a developed or developing country.[102] Intergenerational equity was not mentioned within the Kyoto Protocol. Despite the widespread global consensus and action to reduce greenhouse gas emissions under the Kyoto Protocol, global GHG emissions increased slightly during its implementation due largely to the refusal of leading emitters like the United States and China to participate in its reduction mandates.[103]

Intergenerational equity is not mentioned in the Cancun Agreement, which was adopted by the UNFCCC in 2010.[104] The agreement places substantial emphasis on developing and disseminating technology through private markets.[105] The agreement also contemplates transferring public and private funds from developed countries to developing countries of at least one hundred billion per year by 2020.[106] The

---

[97] *Id.*

[98] United Nations Framework Convention on Climate Change (1992), https://unfccc.int/resource/docs/convkp/conveng.pdf.

[99] *Id.*

[100] *Id.*

[101] Kyoto Protocol to the United Nations Framework Convention on Climate Change (Dec. 10, 1997), U.N. Doc. FCCC/CP/1997/7/Add.1, 37 I.L.M. 22 (1998); *see also* Sikina Jinnah, *Emissions Trading under the Kyoto Protocol: NAFTA and WTO Concerns*, 15 Geo. Int'l Envtl. L. Rev. 709, 710 (2002).

[102] *Id.*

[103] Commentators disagree in assessing whether the Kyoto Protocol was a success. *Compare* Duncan Clark, *Has the Kyoto Protocol Made Any Difference to Carbon Emissions?*, The Guardian (Nov. 26, 2012), https://www.theguardian.com/environment/blog/2012/nov/26/kyoto-protocol-carbon-emissions ("Overall, the result is that global emissions have showed no sign of slowing down ... [i]n that sense, the Kyoto protocol is a failure.") *with* Eric Johnston, *20 Years after Kyoto Protocol, Where Does World Stand on Climate Change?*, Japan Times (Dec. 4, 2017), https://www.japantimes.co.jp/news/2017/12/04/reference/20-years-kyoto-protocol-world-stand-climate ("total emissions by advanced countries had dropped 22.6 percent compared with 1990 levels by 2012").

[104] Joshua D. Sarnoff, *The Patent System and Climate Change*, 16 Va. J. L. & Tech. 301, 303 (2011).

[105] *Id.*

[106] *Id.*

agreement references the Green Climate Fund (GCF), which provides funding to countries for dealing with the adverse effects of climate change.[107] It seeks to promote a paradigm shift to low-emission and climate-resilient development, taking into account the needs of nations that are particularly vulnerable to climate change impacts.[108] The GCF also does not mention intergenerational equity.

The Warsaw International Mechanism for Loss and Damage was established to address climate change-associated loss and damage.[109] There are three primary functions: (1) enhancing knowledge and understating of comprehensive risk management approaches to address loss and damage, (2) strengthening dialogue, coordination, coherence, and synergies among relevant stakeholders, and (3) enhancing action and support, including finance, technology and capacity building.[110] Although there is no mention of intergenerational equity, migration due to climate change is referenced, which is perhaps the most significant human rights impact from climate change worldwide. It developed a two-year work plan related to forced migration in 2016, which includes an "Action Area" focused on how the impacts of climate change are affecting patterns of migration, displacement, and human mobility.[111]

Despite persistent and intractable differences, the parties involved in the Paris Agreement harnessed the political will necessary to arrive at an agreement that strikes a careful balance between ambition and differentiation.[112] The Paris Agreement acknowledges that climate change is a common concern of humankind.[113] It mentions that parties when taking action to address climate change should respect, promote, and consider their respective obligations on human rights, the right to health, the right of indigenous peoples, local communities, migrants, children, persons with disabilities, people in vulnerable situations, gender equality, and the empowerment of women and intergenerational equity.[114] Although the Paris Agreement does not define intergenerational equity, it recognizes that it needs to be

---

[107] The Green Climate Fund, *About the Fund*, https://www.greenclimate.fund/who-we-are/about-the-fund (last accessed July 16, 2018).

[108] *Id.*

[109] United Nations Framework Convention on Climate Change, Warsaw international mechanism for loss and damage associated with climate change impacts, UN Doc. FCCC/CP/2013/10/Add.1, Dec. 2/CP.19 (Jan. 31, 2014), https://unfccc.int/sites/default/files/resource/docs/2013/cop19/eng/10a01.pdf; *see* Wil Burns, *Loss and Damage and the 21st Conference of the Parties to the United Nations Framework Convention on Climate Change*, 22 ILSA J. INT'L & COMP. L. 415, 421 (2016).

[110] *Id.*

[111] Jullee Kim, *Reframing Humans (Homo Sapiens) in International Biodiversity Law to Frame Protections for Climate Refugees*, 42 WM. & MARY ENVTL. L. & POL'Y REV. 805, 811 (2018).

[112] *See* Lavanya Rajamani, *Ambition and Differentiation in the 2015 Paris Agreement: Interpretative Possibilities and Underlying Politics*, 65 INT'L & COMP. L. Q. 493 (2016).

[113] Paris Agreement, pmbl. (Dec. 12, 2015, entered into force Nov. 4, 2016), https://unfccc.int/sites/default/files/english_paris_agreement.pdf.

[114] *Id.*

referenced in the Agreement.[115] It also recognizes that parties may be affected not only by climate change, but also by the impacts of the measures taken in response to it.[116]

The UNFCCC mentions current and future generations without using the term intergenerational equity. The Kyoto Protocol, Cancun Agreement, and the Warsaw International Mechanism for Loss and Damage do not directly distinguish the importance of generational concerns. The Paris Agreement is the only international climate change law instrument that mentions intergenerational equity, but it does not provide a definition of the term. Given the concept's ambiguous nature, intergenerational equity can be interpreted in many ways, which perhaps explains the absence of the term in many of the aforementioned instruments.

III INTERGENERATIONAL EQUITY IN FOREIGN DOMESTIC CHARTERS AND CONSTITUTIONS

The Charter of Fundamental Rights of the European Union, whose preamble states that the rights ensured by the Charter include duties concerning future generations, was the first foundational legal instrument to refer to future generations explicitly.[117] The Charter became legally binding with the adoption of the 2008 Lisbon Treaty. References to intergenerational justice also can be found in various constitutions of member states. Thirteen constitutions contain explicit references to future generations (Belgium, Bolivia, the Czech Republic, Ecuador, Estonia, France, Germany, Kenya, Luxemburg, Norway, Poland, South Africa, and Sweden), and five constitutions make indirect reference to future generations via the concept of heritage (Finland, Italy, Portugal, Slovakia, and Slovenia).[118]

The constitution of Bolivia provides that among the purpose and functions of the state are the responsible use of natural resources, the promotion of industrialization, and the conservation of the environment for the welfare of current and future generations.[119] The constitution of Ecuador provides in article 317 that in the management of nonrenewable resources "the State shall give priority to responsibility between generations, the conservation of nature, the charging of royalties or other non-tax contributions and corporate shares...."[120]

---

[115] *Id.*

[116] *Id.*

[117] Charter of Fundamental Rights of the European Union pmbl., Dec. 18, 2000, 2000 O.J. (C 364) 1, https://eur-lex.europa.eu/legal-content/EN/TXT/PDF/?uri=CELEX:32000X1218(01).

[118] *Id.* at 5. For a discussion of these explicit and implicit references to protection of future generations, *see generally* Maja Göpel & Malte Arhelger, *How to Protect Future Generations' Rights in European Governance*, 10 INTERGENERATIONAL JUSTICE REV. 4 (2010).

[119] CONST. OF BOLIVIA, art. 9(6), http://pdba.georgetown.edu/Constitutions/Bolivia/bolivia09.html.

[120] CONST. OF ECUADOR, art. 317, http://pdba.georgetown.edu/Constitutions/Ecuador/english08.html.

Article 110(b) of the Norwegian constitution provides that every person has a right to an environment that is conducive to health and that: "Natural resources should be managed on the basis of comprehensive long-term considerations whereby this right will be safeguarded for future generations as well." Article 20a of German Basic Law (the German constitution) states that: "[t]he state takes responsibility for protecting the natural foundations of life and animals in the interest of future generations." The phrase "foundations of life" "embraces all components of the environment which are necessary for the maintenance of life over long periods." Thus, the provision places responsibility for protection of the natural environment on the state. The South African constitution states that everyone has the right to "have the environment protected, for the benefit of present and future generations, through reasonable legislative and other measures ..." "Similarly, the Kenyan constitution provides for the right to a 'clean and healthy environment', which includes the right to have the environment 'protected for the benefit of present and future generations through legislative and other measures....'"[121] Several countries also either have or had administrative bodies charged with stewardship responsibilities for future generations.[122]

IV ENVIRONMENTAL PROTECTION FOR FUTURE GENERATIONS IN THE COURTS: THE *MINORS OPOSA* CASE IN THE PHILIPPINES

The plaintiffs in *Minors Oposa* v. *Factoran* were Antonio Oposa, a noted environmentalist and lawyer, his children, other children and their parents, unnamed children of the future, and the Philippine Ecological Network Inc., a nonprofit organization established for the purposes of protecting the environment and natural resources on the Philippines. The original defendant was Fulgencio S. Factoran, then-Secretary of the Department of Environmental and Natural Resources (DENR). The original complaint was filed as a taxpayers' class action to compel the defendant to cancel all existing timber license agreements (TLAs) and to cease and desist from granting new applications, in order to stop excessive deforestation and environmental degradation in the Philippines. The Regional Trial Court dismissed the case for failure to state a cause of action against the defendant and that granting the relief requested would result in the impairment of contracts, which is prohibited by the Constitution. The plaintiffs then petitioned the Supreme Court to reverse the original ruling on the ground that the trial court gravely abused its discretion in dismissing the complaint. The Supreme Court ruled unanimously in favor of the petitioners.[123]

---

[121] Report of the Secretary-General, UN General Assembly, *supra* note 61, at 26 (quoting CONSTITUTION art. 42 (2010) (Kenya).
[122] For a discussion of these administrative bodies, *see infra* Chapter 6.
[123] Minors Oposa v. Factoran, G.R. No. 10 1083, July 30, 1993, *reprinted in* 33 I.L.M. 173 (1994).

The complaint was filed as a taxpayers' class action and alleged that the plaintiffs are citizens of the Republic of the Philippines and are "entitled to the full benefit, use and enjoyment of . . . the country's virgin tropical forests."[124] The suit was filed on the basis that the plaintiffs have a clear constitutional right to a balanced and healthful ecology under Section 16, Article II of the Constitution and are entitled to protection from the state in its capacity as *parens patriae*.[125] The plaintiffs argued that the defendant's continued failure and refusal to cancel the TLAs violated the rights of plaintiffs, especially plaintiff minors who may ultimately find themselves in a country that is devoid of the beautiful flora, fauna, and indigenous cultures that the Philippines has been fortunate to enjoy.[126] In support of this argument, the plaintiffs contended that twenty-five years prior to the suit, the Philippines had forty million acres of rain forests, which comprised approximately 53 percent of the country's landmass. Satellite images taken in 1987 revealed that only 4 percent of the country's land area remained covered by rain forest.[127] The plaintiffs asserted that the defendant's continued authorization of TLA holders to deforest the Philippines will cause substantial damage and irreparable injury to the plaintiffs – particularly to minors and their successors – who may never see, use, benefit from, and enjoy this rare natural resource treasure.[128]

The Supreme Court held that the Petitioners had standing to bring a class action on the grounds that "[t]he subject matter of the complaint is of common and general interest not just to several, but to all citizens of the Philippines. Consequently, since the parties are so numerous, it becomes impracticable, if not totally impossible, to bring all of them before the court."[129]

The Supreme Court also found that the parents, on behalf of the petitioner children, correctly asserted that the children represented their generation as well as generations yet unborn.[130] However, the Court commented that "[t]heir personality to sue on behalf of the succeeding generations can only be based on the concept of intergenerational responsibility insofar as the right to a balanced and healthful ecology is concerned."[131]

The Supreme Court held that the petitioners had a sufficient cause of action, stating: "The complaint focuses on one specific fundamental right, the right to a balanced and healthful ecology which, for the first time in our nation's constitutional history, is solemnly incorporated in the fundamental law."[132] Section 15,

---

[124] *Id.* at 176.
[125] *Id.* at 181
[126] *Id.* at 180.
[127] *Id.* at 179.
[128] *Id.*
[129] *Id.* at 184.
[130] *Id.*
[131] *Id.* at 185.
[132] *Id.* at 187.

Article II, which requires the state to "protect and promote the right to health of the people and instill health consciousness among them,"[133] was also cited.

The Supreme Court also recognized the primacy of the right to ecological security and health among the many rights assured by the Constitution. In now-famous language, the Court provided the following compelling reasoning that is even more relevant today than it was at the time of the decision:

> While the right to a balanced and healthful ecology is to be found under the declaration of Principles and State Policies and not under the Bill of Rights, it does not follow that it is less important than any of the civil and political rights enumerated in the latter. Such a right belongs to a different category of rights altogether, for it concerns nothing less than self-preservation of self-perpetuation – the advancement of which may even be said to predate all governments and constitutions. As a matter of fact, these basic rights need not even be written in the Constitution for they are assumed to exist from the inception of mankind. If they are now explicitly mentioned in the fundamental charter, it is because of the well-founded fear of its framers that unless the rights to a balanced and healthful ecology and to health are mandated as state policies by the Constitution itself, thereby highlighting a solemn obligation to preserve the first and protect and advance the second, the day would not be too far when all else would be lost not only for the present generation, but also for those to come – generations which stand to inherit nothing but parched earth incapable of sustaining life.[134]

The Court further stated that the right to a balanced and healthful ecology, or a sound environment, is a self-executory constitutional policy and that the right itself is actionable.[135] As such, the right is actionable against the DENR Secretary as the institutional body responsible for implementing the state's constitutional mandate to control and supervise the exploration, development, utilization, and conservation of natural resources in the Philippines.[136]

Finally, the Supreme Court held that this determination was a proper exercise of the Court's discretion to decide whether a legally enforceable right was at stake, rather than the determination of a political issue. The Court cited Article VIII, Section 1 of the Constitution, which states that judicial power includes: "[T]he duty of the courts of justice to settle actual controversies involving rights which are legally demandable and enforceable, and to determine whether or not there has been a grave abuse of discretion amounting to lack or excess of jurisdiction on the part of any branch or instrumentality of the Government."[137]

---

[133] *Id.* (quoting CONST. (1987), art. II § 15 [Phil.]).

[134] *Id.* at 188.

[135] Antonio G. M. La Viña, *The Right to a Sound Environment in the Philippines: The Significance of the Minors Oposa Case*, 3 REV. EUROPEAN, COMP. & INT'L ENVT'L L. 246, 248 (1994).

[136] *Id.*

[137] *Id.*

Minors Oposa is significant because it was the first case to expressly interpret the constitutional right to a balanced and healthful ecology under the 1987 Philippine Constitution. The Court held that Section 16, Article II can alone be invoked to question acts or omissions by branches of government, to litigate, and also to grant the substantive right to protection.[138] The Court determined that Section 16, Article II is as self-implementing as the right to free speech and other rights enumerated in the Bill of Rights.[139] The principles of environmental protection embraced by the Court in *Minors Oposa* were so fundamental that they were "assumed to exist from the inception of mankind."[140]

Minors Oposa is also significant in its broadening of standing in Philippine environmental cases. In the Philippines, all actions must be prosecuted and defended in the name of the real party in interest, who has traditionally been restricted to "the party who stands to be benefitted or injured by the judgment or the party entitled to the avails of the suit. 'Interest' within the meaning of the rule means material interest, an interest in issue and to be affected by the decree, as distinguished from mere interest in the question involved, or a mere incidental interest."[141] The Supreme Court extended this concept of who are "proper parties" to include the present generation. Accepting the principle of intergenerational responsibility and equity in the Philippines, the present generation now has standing to represent future generations, since each generation has a responsibility to future generations to preserve nature.[142] Notably, standing in *Minors Oposa* reaches beyond US environmental jurisprudence, which requires that specific, material injury must still be alleged before an action can be filed.[143]

More than a decade after the judgment, Professor Oliver Houck wrote on the circumstances surrounding *Minors Oposa*, the judgement itself, and its impact on the Philippine environmental landscape.[144] In assessing the case's impact, Houck notes that during the proceedings, Secretary Factoran issued an administrative order that prohibited new logging concessions on the remaining virgin stands. Significantly, there were 142 TLAs in the mid-1980s when the issue came to Oposa's attention, 92 when he filed suit, 41 when the case was decided, and 19 remaining in 2001. By early 2006, there were only three TLAs still in effect, one inactive, and one under review, all set to expire within the following five years. The annual rate of

---

[138] Oliver A. Houck, *Light from the Trees: The Stories of Minors Oposa and the Russian Forest Cases*, 19 GEO. INT'L ENVTL. L. REV. 321, 336 (2007).

[139] La Viña, *supra* note 135, at 248.

[140] Houck, *supra* note 138, at 336.

[141] La Viña, *supra* note 135, at 249.

[142] Tina Hunter, *Equality for the Earth – The Role of Intergenerational Equity and Customary International Law*, 17 NAT'L LEGAL EAGLE 19, 20 (2011).

[143] La Viña, *supra* note 135, at 249.

[144] *See* Houck, *supra* note 138.

deforestation had fallen to 2.1 percent.[145] Unfortunately, illegal logging boomed in the wake of the expiration of TLAs.[146] Nevertheless, *Minors Oposa* continues to operate in support of environmentally protective decisions. As Houck notes, "[t]he recognition of future generations as stakeholders cast issues in an entirely new light. It challenges a multitude of assumptions concerning national wealth, the value of future interests, and whether sustainable development is a nice idea or a legal command."[147]

V PROTECTION OF FUTURE GENERATIONS IN THE ANTHROPOCENE

Part V addresses protection of future generations in climate justice litigation in the United States and in several foreign domestic jurisdictions. It first reviews the theory and progress in the *Juliana* case in the United States and then addresses successful, unsuccessful, and promising pending cases in foreign domestic contexts.

A *United States: The* Juliana *Case*

With the advent of atmospheric trust litigation, the pendulum swung back in favor of suits for injunctive relief.[148] Atmospheric trust litigation (ATL)[149] began slowly with scattered modest victories at the state level[150] preceding and following a disappointing defeat in federal court in the *Alec L. v. Jackson*[151] case. Thanks to the perseverance of the attorneys on the Our Children's Trust team, youth plaintiffs filed the *Juliana* case, which was similar to the *Alec L.* case in that it relied on atmospheric trust theory, but this time it also asserted violations of constitutionally protected rights, including the Due Process and Equal Protection Clauses. The *Juliana* case was initially filed against the Obama administration and is pending as of this writing against the Trump administration.

---

[145] Houck, *supra* note 138, at 339.

[146] *Id.* at 340.

[147] *Id.* at 341. For a critical evaluation of the effect of the *Minors Oposa* case as intergenerational equity precedent for future cases, *compare* Dante B. Gatmaytan, *The Illusion of Intergenerational Equity: Oposa v. Factoran as Pyrrhic Victory*, 15 GEO. INT'L ENVTL. L. REV. 457 (2003) *with* Ma. Socorro Z. Manguiat & Vicente Paolo B. Yu III, *Maximizing the Value of* Oposa v. Factoran, 15 GEO. INT'L ENVTL. L. REV. 487 (2003).

[148] For a discussion of the progression of theories and stages of climate justice litigation leading up to atmospheric trust litigation and the *Juliana* case, *see generally* RANDALL S. ABATE, *Atmospheric Trust Litigation in the United States: Pipe Dream or Pipeline to Justice for Future Generations?* in CLIMATE JUSTICE: CASE STUDIES IN GLOBAL AND REGIONAL GOVERNANCE CHALLENGES 543–69 (Randall S. Abate ed., 2016).

[149] Atmospheric trust litigation is a strategy pioneered by Professor Mary Wood of the University of Oregon School of Law. For a detailed discussion of the conceptual foundations of this theory, *see generally* MARY CHRISTINA WOOD, NATURE'S TRUST: ENVIRONMENTAL LAW FOR A NEW ECOLOGICAL AGE (2013).

[150] *Id.* at 553–58.

[151] 863 F. Supp. 2d 11 (D.D.C. 2012).

In a landmark decision, Judge Aiken concluded that the federal government's motion to dismiss should be denied because the youth plaintiffs alleged facts that merited a trial on standing and on the atmospheric trust and Due Process Clause claims. Judge Aiken's reasoning in *Juliana* provides fertile opportunities for the ATL theory in this case to open the door for possible Due Process Clause protection of the right to a stable climate system. Her decision laid a valuable foundation for extending fundamental rights jurisprudence under the Due Process Clause to environmental rights. In concluding that the case could proceed to trial, Judge Aiken noted that, "[f]ederal courts too often have been cautious and overly deferential in the arena of environmental law, and the world has suffered for it."[152]

Judge Aiken stated that the identification and protection of fundamental rights "has not been reduced to any formula."[153] She concluded that the plaintiffs had adequately alleged infringement of a fundamental right, explaining that "[t]o hold otherwise would be to say that the Constitution affords no protection against a government's knowing decision to poison the air its citizens breathe or the water its citizens drink."[154] She then explained that courts should "exercise reasoned judgment in identifying interests of the person so fundamental that the State must accord them its respect."

Judge Aiken then turned to the *Obergefell* v. *Hodges* decision, which recognized "marriage as a right underlying and supporting other liberties" and as "a keystone of our social order."[155] Relying on Justice Kennedy's reasoning in his majority opinion in *Obergefell*, Judge Aiken connected the reasoning on same-sex marriage to the stable climate context in *Juliana*. In "[e]xercising [her] 'reasoned judgment,'" Judge Aiken had "no doubt that the right to a climate system capable of sustaining human life is fundamental to a free and ordered society.'[156] Just as marriage is the 'foundation of the family,' a stable climate system is quite literally the foundation 'of society, without which there would be neither civilization nor progress.'"[157] Accepting as true plaintiffs' allegations that the government "played a unique and central role in the creation of our current climate crisis; that they contributed to the crisis with full knowledge of the significant and unreasonable risks posed by climate change; and that the Due Process Clause therefore imposes a special duty on defendants to use their statutory and regulatory authority to reduce greenhouse gas emissions," Judge

---

[152] *Juliana*, 217 F. Supp. 3d at 1262.

[153] *Id.* at 1249.

[154] *Id.* at 1250.

[155] *Id.*

[156] *Id.*

[157] *Id.* The plaintiffs asserted that if the government's actions that contributed to climate change were to continue unchecked, such actions would "permanently and irreversibly damage plaintiffs' property, their economic livelihood, their recreational opportunities, their health, and ultimately their (and their children's) ability to live long, healthy lives."

Aiken held that the plaintiffs adequately alleged their claim and may proceed to trial on the due process issues.[158]

The youth plaintiffs also made public trust claims. These claims arose from the application of the public trust doctrine to essential natural resources.[159] The plaintiffs stated that with respect to these essential resources, the sovereign's public trust obligations prevent it from "depriving a future legislature of the natural resources necessary to provide for the well-being and survival of its citizens."[160]

Judge Aiken recognized that, "the government, as trustee, has a fiduciary duty to protect the trust assets from damage so that current and future trust beneficiaries will be able to enjoy the benefits of the trust."[161] She concluded that plaintiffs had adequately alleged harm to public trust assets because "[t]he federal government holds title to the submerged lands between three and twelve miles from the coastlines of the United States" and "a number of plaintiffs' injuries relate to the effects of ocean acidification and rising ocean temperatures."[162] Judge Aiken also stated that plaintiffs' federal public trust claims are recognized in federal court and that "the federal government, like the states, holds public assets – at a minimum, the territorial seas – in trust for the people."[163] Judge Aiken added that "[a]lthough the public trust predates the Constitution, plaintiffs' right of action to enforce the government's obligations as trustee arises from the Constitution."[164]

Judge Aiken further observed that this action is of a different order than the typical environmental case. It alleges that [the government's] actions and inactions – regardless of whether they violate any specific statutory duty – have so profoundly damaged our home planet that they threaten plaintiffs' fundamental constitutional rights to life and liberty.[165] In addition, "[e]ven when a case implicates hotly contested political issues, the judiciary must not shrink from its role as a coequal branch of government."[166]

Judge Aiken's decision could secure a historic victory for environmental rights in the US federal court system, but it has a long way to go. The outcome in *Obergefell* appeared to be similarly improbable just five years ago as it was working its way through the federal courts, and yet the right to same-sex marriage is now constitutionally enshrined under the Due Process Clause. In the meantime, the ATL movement will continue to be propelled forward by favorable tail winds in the

---

[158] *Id.* at 1251–52.
[159] *Id.* at 1253.
[160] *Id.*
[161] *Id.* at 1254.
[162] *Id.* at 1255–56.
[163] *Id.* at 1257, 1259.
[164] *Id.* at 1261.
[165] *Id.*
[166] *Id.* at 1263.

United States and abroad as it seeks to secure recognition of a constitutional right to a stable climate system under the Due Process Clause of the US Constitution.[167]

In the wake of the Judge Aiken's groundbreaking decision, the *Juliana* case has generated global enthusiasm and anticipation tempered by frustration resulting from the federal government's relentless efforts to have the case dismissed. The following discussion summarizes the multiple steps in this lengthy postponement of the trial in the case.

On November 10, 2016, US District Court Judge Ann Aiken adopted the report and recommendation of Magistrate Judge Thomas Coffin and denied the federal defendants' and industry intervenor defendants' motions to dismiss.[168] For more than two years after that decision, the federal defendants employed a wide range of desperate strategies to stop the case from moving forward, focusing primarily on the novelty of the plaintiffs' claims, asserted errors in the district court's legal analyses, and discovery and trial burdens. On March 24, 2019, the Ninth Circuit scheduled oral arguments for June 4, 2019 in Portland, Oregon on the federal government's motion for preliminary injunction and interlocutory appeal.

On March 7, 2017, the federal defendants asked the district court for certification to bring an interlocutory appeal of the order denying the motions to dismiss and moved to stay the litigation until the Ninth Circuit issued a decision.[169] On April 7, 2017, Magistrate Judge Coffin denied the motion to stay the case.[170] Magistrate Judge Coffin then referred Findings and Recommendations denying the motions to certify appeal on May 1, 2017.[171]

---

[167] The momentum from the *Juliana* litigation has inspired additional promising ATL cases in US state courts. For example, in Reynolds v. Florida, youth plaintiffs sued Governor Rick Scott for failing to act on climate change and, in many ways, taking actions to deepen the crisis. South Florida is one of the most vulnerable areas in the world to sea level rise, with the number of high tide floods in Miami Beach increasing by 400 percent since 2006. The suit alleges that the state government has violated: (1) youth plaintiffs' rights to due process by violating their rights to life, liberty, and property; and (2) the public trust doctrine as reflected in the ATL theory by allowing and sometimes facilitating fossil fuel companies in their carbon-intensive fossil fuel extraction and production activities, including supporting offshore drilling and imposing strict regulations on solar energy development. *See* Complaint, Reynolds v. Florida, No. 18-CA-000819, Apr. 16, 2018, https://static1.squarespace.com/static/571d109b04426270152febeo/t/5ad6274f575d1f452d0e0015/1523984211940/2018.04.15.FL. Complaint.FINAL.pdf; *see also* Our Children's Trust, press release, *Constitutional Climate Lawsuit Brought by Young Alaskans Heard in Anchorage* (Apr. 30, 2018), https://static1.squarespace. com/static/571d109b04426270152febeo/t/5ae7f3f770a6ad3043d94eec/1525150712298/2018.04.30+Sin nok+v.+Alaska+hearing+press+release.pdf.

[168] Juliana v. US, 217 F. Supp. 3d at 1224.

[169] Fed. Defs.' Mot. to Certify Order for Interlocutory Appeal, Juliana v. US, No. 6:15-cv-01517-TC (D. Or. Mar. 7, 2017), ECF No. 120; Fed. Defs.' Mot. to Stay Litig., Juliana v. US, No. 6:15-cv-01517-TC (D. Or. Mar. 7, 2017), ECF No. 121.

[170] Mins. of Proceedings: Tel. Status Conference, Juliana v. US, No. 6:15-cv-01517-TC (D. Or. Mar. 10, 2017), ECF No. 137.

[171] Juliana v. US, No. 6:15-cv-1517-TC, 2017 WL 9249531 (D. Or. May 1, 2017).

Magistrate Judge Coffin explained that to appeal a nonfinal order, defendants bear the burden of establishing:

(1) the order involves a "controlling issue of law";
(2) the controlling issue of law is one to which there is a "substantial ground for difference of opinion"; and
(3) "an immediate appeal from the order may materially advance the ultimate termination of the litigation."[172]

Magistrate Judge Coffin concluded that development of the record through litigation rather than certifying a hypothetical question would better decide the issues defendants want to raise on appeal.[173] On June 8, 2017, District Court Judge Aiken adopted those Findings and Recommendations, concluded that certification for interlocutory appeal is not warranted, and denied the motions to certify the appeal over defendant and defendant intervenors' objections.[174]

On the following day, defendants notified the district court, and filed with the Ninth Circuit, a Petition for a Writ of Mandamus seeking a stay of the district court proceedings.[175] With that petition pending, Magistrate Judge Coffin granted intervenor defendants' motion to withdraw on June 28, 2017.[176]

On July 28, 2017, the Ninth Circuit temporarily stayed the district court proceedings.[177] The court then concluded the petition raised issues that warrant an answer, ordering the real parties in interest to address the status of discovery requests, pending discovery deadlines, discovery disputes, jurisdiction to resolve a particular constitutional challenge, as well as other issues the parties wish to address.[178]

On March 7, 2018, the Ninth Circuit concluded that the federal defendants had not met the high bar to grant mandamus relief at that time, and that the issues they raised are better addressed through the ordinary course of litigation.[179] The court found federal defendants' request premature: they were not challenging a specific discovery order and they would have ample remedies to seek protection from the district court in the event of discovery disputes.[180] With regard to the federal defendants' burden from litigation, the court explained that Congress had not exempted the federal government from the normal rules of appellate litigation and any asserted errors on the merits are correctable through the ordinary course of

---

[172] *Id.* at *2 (quoting 28 U.S.C. § 1292(b)).
[173] *Id.* at *3–*8.
[174] Juliana v. US, No. 6:15-cv-01517-TC, 2017 WL 2483705 (D. Or. June 8, 2017).
[175] Pet. for Writ of Mandamus, *In re* U.S., No. 17–71692 (9th Cir. June 9, 2017), ECF No. 1; Notice of Filing Pet. for Writ of Mandamus, Juliana v. US, No. 6:15-cv-01517-TC (D. Or. June 9, 2017), ECF No. 177.
[176] Order, Juliana v. US, No. 6:15-cv-01517-TC (D. Or. June 28, 2017), ECF No. 182.
[177] Order, *In re* U.S., No. 17–71692 (9th Cir. July 25, 2017), ECF No. 7.
[178] Order, *In re* U.S., No. 17–71692 (9th Cir. July 28, 2017), ECF No. 8.
[179] *In re* U.S., 884 F.3d 830 (9th Cir. 2018).
[180] *Id.* at 834–35.

litigation.[181] The court declined to find the district court's order clearly erroneous as a matter of law or an oft repeated error in the absence of controlling precedent.[182] Finally, although the court agreed the legal theories raise issues of first impression, it explained that the order denying a motion to dismiss on the pleadings does not present the possibility that those issues will evade appellate review.[183] The court signaled the possibility for future relief.[184]

Back in the district court in the week after the Ninth Circuit decision, on March 19, 2018, plaintiffs moved for a status conference,[185] which the court set for March 26, 2018.[186] At that conference, the court ordered the parties to meet and confer and set deadlines for expert witness statements and trial memoranda.[187] At an April 12 status conference, the court set the case for trial on October 29, 2018.[188]

On May 9, the federal defendants moved for judgment on the pleadings, a protective order, and a stay of all discovery.[189] With plaintiffs' response and a decision pending, on May 22, defendants also moved for summary judgment.[190]

On May 25, Magistrate Judge Coffin denied the federal defendants' Motion for a Protective Order, explaining that plaintiffs' complaint does not contain, and is not required to be based on, an Administrative Procedure Act claim (which would limit their entitlement to discovery).[191] Magistrate Judge Coffin also rejected defendants' argument that the separation of powers doctrine and the potential implication of privilege justifies the stay as overbroad.[192] Defendants objected to Magistrate Judge Coffin's order and moved for a stay of discovery pending resolution of objections.[193]

On June 14, Judge Aiken denied defendants' motion to stay discovery pending resolution of objections, reasoning that defendants had not shown irreparable harm

---

[181] *Id.* at 836.

[182] *Id.* at 837.

[183] *Id.*

[184] *Id.* at 838 ("The issues pertaining to the merits of this case can be resolved by the district court, in a future appeal, or, if extraordinary circumstances later present themselves, by mandamus relief.").

[185] Mot. for Hr'g Status Conference, Juliana v. US, No. 6:15-cv-01517-TC (D. Or. Mar. 16, 2018), ECF No. 185.

[186] Scheduling Order, Juliana v. US, No. 6:15-cv-01517-TC (D. Or. Mar. 21, 2018), ECF No. 188.

[187] Mins. of Proceedings: Tel. Status Conference, Juliana v. US, No. 6:15-cv-01517-TC (D. Or. Mar. 26, 2018), ECF No. 189.

[188] Mins. of Proceedings: Tel. Status Conference, Juliana v. US, No. 6:15-cv-01517-TC (D. Or. Apr. 12, 2018), ECF No. 192.

[189] Defs.' Mot. for J. on the Pleadings, Juliana v. US, No. 6:15-cv-01517-TC (D. Or. May 9, 2018), ECF No. 195; Defs.' Mot. for Protective Order and Stay of Disc., Juliana v. US, No. 6:15-cv-01517-TC (D. Or. May 9, 2018), ECF No. 196.

[190] Defs.' Mot. for Summ. J., Juliana v. US, No. 6:15-cv-01517-TC (D. Or. May 22, 2018), ECF No. 207.

[191] Order, Juliana v. US, No. 6:15-cv-01517-TC, at 1–2 (D. Or. May 25, 2018), ECF No. 212.

[192] *Id.* at 3.

[193] Defs.' Objs. to Order Den. Mot. for a Protective Order and Stay of Disc., Juliana v. US, No. 6:15-cv-01517-TC (D. Or. June 1, 2018), ECF No. 215; Defs.' Mot. to Stay Disc. Pending Resolution of Objs., Juliana v. US, No. 6:15-cv-01517-TC (D. Or. June 1, 2018), ECF No. 216.

likely under the circumstances and defendants' concerns would be better addressed to specific discovery requests rather than a blanket stay of all discovery.[194] On June 29, Judge Aiken affirmed Magistrate Judge Coffin's order denying defendants' motion for protective order and stay of discovery, concluding it was not clearly erroneous or contrary to law.[195] The court also declined to certify the decision for interlocutory appeal.[196]

On July 5, defendants again petitioned the Ninth Circuit for a Writ of Mandamus with an emergency motion to stay discovery and trial,[197] and asked the district court to stay pending the petition.[198] On July 16, the Ninth Circuit denied the emergency motion for stay, noting that it would hear the petition for writ of mandamus on an expedited basis.[199]

On July 17, defendants applied to the Supreme Court for a stay of proceedings pending the Ninth Circuit's consideration of the mandamus petition.[200] Alternatively, defendants suggested the Supreme Court could construe its application as a petition for a writ of mandamus or petition for writ of certiorari from the Ninth Circuit's March decision denying mandamus.[201] That same day the district court denied defendants' motion to stay pending the petition for writ of mandamus.[202] Then, on July 20, the Ninth Circuit declined to grant mandamus relief, concluding no new circumstances justify the second petition.[203] The court reasoned that the government still can challenge any discovery order that is unduly burdensome or violates the separation of powers and the government has not shown it would be meaningfully prejudiced by engaging in discovery or trial.[204] And on July 30 the Supreme Court denied defendants' application without prejudice, reasoning that it was premature.[205] The Court expressed discomfort with the case though, stating:

> The breadth of respondents' claims is striking, however, and the justiciability of those claims presents substantial grounds for difference of opinion. The District Court should take these concerns into account in assessing the burdens of discovery and trial, as well as the desirability of a prompt ruling on the Government's pending dispositive motions.[206]

[194] Order, Juliana v. US, No. 6:15-cv-01517-TC (D. Or. June 14, 2018), ECF No. 238.
[195] Order, Juliana v. US, No. 6:15-cv-01517-TC (D. Or. June 29, 2018), ECF No. 300.
[196] *Id.*
[197] Notice of Filing Pet. for Writ of Mandamus, Juliana v. US, No. 6:15-cv-01517-TC (D. Or. July 5, 2018), ECF No. 308.
[198] Defs.' Mot. for a Stay Pending Pet. for Writ of Mandamus, Juliana v. US, No. 6:15-cv-01517-TC (D. Or. July 5, 2018), ECF No. 307.
[199] Order, *In re* U.S., No. 18–71928 (9th Cir. July 16, 2018), ECF No. 9.
[200] Appl., *In re* U.S., No. 18A65 (US July 17, 2018).
[201] *Id.*
[202] Order, Juliana v. US, No. 6:15-cv-01517-TC (D. Or. July 17, 2018), ECF No. 324.
[203] *In re* U.S., 895 F.3d 1101 (9th Cir. 2018).
[204] *Id.* at 1104–06.
[205] *In re* U.S., No. 18A65, 2018 WL 3615551 (US July 30, 2018).
[206] *Id.* at *1.

With the October 29 trial date approaching, on October 5 and 12, defendants again asked the district court for a stay and then filed another petition for a writ of mandamus with the Ninth Circuit requesting a stay of the district court proceedings pending Supreme Court review.[207] Defendants stated that they will file a petition for writ of mandamus or, in the alternative, certiorari in the Supreme Court.[208]

On October 15, the district court decided defendants' motions for judgment on the pleadings and summary judgment.[209] The court granted defendants' request to dismiss the claims against President Trump (without prejudice) based on respect for separation of powers because, the court explained, it appeared likely plaintiffs' injuries could be redressed through relief against other defendants.[210] The court again rejected defendants' arguments that the Administrative Procedure Act was the exclusive avenue for plaintiffs' claims.[211] The court further concluded that nothing has changed to warrant revisiting its earlier rulings on separation of powers and subject matter jurisdiction.[212]

With respect to defendants' motion for summary judgment, the court, relying on plaintiffs' and their experts' declarations, defendants' admissions, and evidence of defendants' actions, found plaintiffs have standing.[213] The court also rejected defendants' Administrative Procedure Act and separation of powers arguments for the same reasons as it did so with respect to the motion for judgment on the pleadings.[214] And the court recognized the plaintiffs' due process claim presented complicated and novel questions but plaintiffs presented enough evidence to survive summary judgment.[215]

The court refused to recognize plaintiffs' proposed suspect class – minors and future generations – but concluded that the claimed violation of a fundamental right still should be evaluated using strict scrutiny and would be aided by further factual development.[216] The court granted defendants' summary judgment on plaintiffs' Ninth Amendment claim, finding it has never been

---

[207] Defs.' Mot. to Stay Disc. and Trial Pending Supreme Ct. Review, Juliana v. US, No. 6:15-cv-01517-TC (D. Or. Oct. 5, 2018), ECF No. 361; Notice of Filing Pet. for Writ of Mandamus Requesting a Stay of Dist. Ct. Proceedings Pending Supreme Ct. Review, Juliana v. US, No. 6:15-cv-01517-TC (D. Or. Oct. 12, 2018), ECF No. 365.

[208] Defs.' Mot. to Stay Disc. and Trial Pending Supreme Ct. Review, Juliana v. U.S., No. 6:15-cv-01517-TC (D. Or. Oct. 5, 2018), ECF No. 361; Notice of Filing Pet. for Writ of Mandamus Requesting a Stay of Dist. Court Proceedings Pending Supreme Ct. Review, Juliana v. US, No. 6:15-cv-01517-TC (D. Or. Oct. 12, 2018), ECF No. 365.

[209] Juliana v. US, No. 6:15-CV-01517-AA, 2018 WL 4997032 (D. Or. Oct. 15, 2018).

[210] *Id.* at *7–*11.

[211] *Id.* at *11–*14.

[212] *Id.* at *14–*16.

[213] *Id.* at *17–*25.

[214] *Id.* at *25–*26.

[215] *Id.* at *26–*30.

[216] *Id.* at *31–*32.

recognized as independently securing a constitutional right for purposes of pursuing a civil rights claim.[217] At the same time, the court denied defendants' requests to certify the opinion for interlocutory appeal, concluding that some claims present mixed questions of law and fact that would benefit from further record development, and even if there is substantial ground for difference of opinion on some claims, certification of those would not materially advance the litigation.[218]

That same day the court denied defendants' motion to stay discovery and trial, concluding that it had previously considered similar arguments and that defendants had not shown a likelihood of success on the merits or irreparable injury to justify a stay.[219] Both parties also filed trial briefs on October 15.[220]

On October 18, defendants applied to the Supreme Court for a stay pending disposition of a petition for a writ of mandamus and requested an administrative stay.[221] On October 19, the Supreme Court, through Chief Justice Roberts as the Justice overseeing the Ninth Circuit at that time, ordered that discovery and trial stayed pending receipt of a response.[222]

Based on that stay, the Ninth Circuit denied defendants' motion for a stay as moot on November 2, noting that defendants' filing before that court was not a substantive petition for mandamus.[223] But later that day, the Supreme Court denied the defendants' application for a stay and vacated the order entered by Chief Justice Roberts.[224] The Court concluded the defendants' petition for a writ of mandamus does not have a fair prospect of success at that level because adequate relief may be available in the Ninth Circuit. The Court reasoned that the Ninth Circuit's earlier denials rested in large part on the early stage of litigation and other reasons that are no longer pertinent.[225]

Plaintiffs then requested an immediate status conference at the district court,[226] which the court set for November 8.[227] Before that could happen, on November 5, defendants moved for a stay in the district court and filed a petition for a writ of

---

[217] *Id.* at *31.

[218] *Id.* at *32–*33.

[219] Order, Juliana v. US, No. 6:15-cv-01517-TC (D. Or. Oct. 15, 2018), ECF No. 374.

[220] *See* Trial Mem., Juliana v. US, No. 6:15-cv-01517-TC (D. Or. Oct. 15, 2018), ECF No. 378; Trial Br., Juliana v. US, No. 6:15-cv-01517-TC (D. Or. Oct. 15, 2018), ECF No. 384.

[221] Notice of Filing of Pet. for a Writ of Mandamus, Juliana v. US, No. 6:15-cv-01517-TC (D. Or. Oct. 18, 2018), ECF No. 390; Notice of Filing of Appl. to the Supreme Ct. for a Stay, Juliana v. US, No. 6:15-cv-01517-TC (D. Or. Oct. 18, 2018), ECF No. 391.

[222] Order, *In re* U.S., No. 18A410 (US Oct. 19, 2018).

[223] Order, *In re* U.S., No. 18–72776 (9th Cir. Nov. 2, 2018), ECF No. 5.

[224] Order in Pending Case, *In re* U.S., No. 18A410 (US Nov. 2, 2018).

[225] *Id.*

[226] Req. for Immediate Status Conference, Juliana v. US, No. 6:15-cv-01517-TC (D. Or. Nov. 2, 2018), ECF No. 405.

[227] Scheduling Order, Juliana v. US, No. 6:15-cv-01517-TC (D. Or. Nov. 5, 2018), ECF No. 417.

mandamus in the Ninth Circuit.[228] Pointing to the Supreme Court's language, defendants also asked the district court to reconsider its denial of the requests to certify the orders denying the motions to dismiss and denying the motions for judgment on the pleadings and summary judgment for interlocutory appeal.[229]

On November 8, the Ninth Circuit stayed the trial pending its consideration of the petition.[230] Similar to the first petition, the court stated that the petition raises issues that warrant an answer and requested the real parties in interest respond within 15 days.[231] The Ninth Circuit also requested that the district court promptly resolve defendants' motion to reconsider the denial of the request to certify orders for interlocutory review, pointing to the Supreme Court's dicta that the case presented "substantial grounds for difference of opinion."[232]

B *Foreign Domestic Developments*

This section addresses three categories of foreign domestic developments in climate justice litigation filed by youth plaintiffs seeking to compel government regulation of climate change to enhance the protection of future generations. It first addresses the successful effort in securing a judicial order to compel the reduction of deforestation in the Colombian Amazon to zero. It then considers an unsuccessful effort in the "Share the Road" petition in the Philippines. The section concludes with a discussion of promising pending litigation in the EU, Canada, Pakistan, and India.

1 Successful: Colombia

Home to 10 percent of the world's flora and fauna species,[233] and more than forty-nine million people,[234] Colombia is developing creative regulatory tools to harmonize human activities and nature. The Colombian Constitution does not recognize nature as a direct subject of rights, but it provides extensive constitutional protections and legal tools to enforce these rights. In 1991, the Constitution established an obligation on the state and on individuals to protect the cultural and natural assets

---

[228] Mot. for Stay of Litig., Juliana v. US, No. 6:15-cv-01517-TC (D. Or. Nov. 5, 2018), ECF No. 419; Notice of Filing Pet. For Writ of Mandamus, Juliana v. US, No. 6:15-cv-01517-TC (D. Or. Nov. 5, 2018), ECF No. 420.

[229] Defs.' Mot. to Reconsider Denial of Reqs. to Certify Orders for Interlocutory Review, Juliana v. US, No. 6:15-cv-01517-TC (D. Or. Nov. 5, 2018), ECF No. 418.

[230] Order, *In re U.S.*, No. 18-73014 (9th Cir. Nov. 8, 2018), ECF No. 3.

[231] *Id.*

[232] *Id.* (citing Order, *In re U.S.*, No. 18-065 (US July 30, 2018); Order, *In re U.S.*, No. 18-410 (US Nov. 2, 2018). More information on these proceedings in the *Juliana* case is available on the Our Children's Trust website: https://www.ourchildrenstrust.org/federal-proceedings/.

[233] Costas Christ, *This Country is a Haven for Biodiversity*, NAT'L GEOGRAPHIC (Sept. 27, 2017), http://www.nationalgeographic.com.au/nature/this-country-is-a-haven-for-biodiversity.aspx.

[234] Colombia Population, WORLD METERS, http://www.worldometers.info/world-population/colombia-population/.

of the nation.[235] The Constitution imposes a duty on the government "to protect the diversity and integrity of the environment, to conserve the areas of special ecological importance, and to foster education for the achievement of these ends."[236]

The most relevant law that protects nature is codified in Law 281 of 1994.[237] The Code of Natural Resources embraces the idea that the environment is common heritage and expresses that nature has a legal right to be protected and preserved.[238] This Code inspired a sustainable development model in the Colombian legal system, which promotes "permanent availability" of natural resources for present and future generations.[239]

Currently, there is a referendum project to include in the Constitution an article in which the country recognizes and guarantees the rights to nature as a living being.[240] In addition, on July 1, 2018, the Serrania of Chiribiquete National Natural Park, located in the Colombian Amazon, was included on the list of World Heritage Sites by UNESCO,[241] a significant step in safeguarding this natural resource treasure for future generations. Meanwhile, the judicial branch has taken steps in protecting the rights of nature in decisions that affirm the duty of the state to protect nature and recognizing personhood and legal rights in the Atrato River[242] and the Amazon forest.[243]

In a decision that has revolutionized and energized climate justice and intergenerational equity litigation around the world, Colombia's highest court has ordered the government to take urgent action to protect its Amazon forests from the increasing rate of deforestation. If properly implemented, this groundbreaking ruling will likely help conserve and counter both deforestation and climate change.[244]

---

[235] Colombian Constitution of 1991, art 8, https://www.constituteproject.org/constitution/Colombia_2005.pdf.

[236] Id.

[237] National Code of Renewable Natural Resources and of Protection of the Environment, Law 2811 (1974).

[238] Law 2811 of 1974, Art. 1.

[239] Law 2811 of 1974, Art. 2.

[240] Referendum for the Rights of Nature, Ati Quigua, http://derechosdelanaturaleza.co/ (last accessed July 14, 2018) (recognizing Mother Nature as a living source of life food, education with inherent and inalienable rights).

[241] Parque de la Serranía de Chiribiquete is now a World Heritage Site. See Josh Gabbatiss, Colombian National Park Becomes Largest Protected Rainforest and New World Heritage Site, Independent (July 3, 2018), https://www.independent.co.uk/environment/colombia-rainforest-national-park-world-heritage-site-serrania-del-chiribiquete-a8428371.html.

[242] For a discussion of the landmark decision conferring legal personhood to the Atrato River in Colombia, see infra Chapter 5.

[243] United Nations, Harmony with Nature U.N. Rights of Nature Law and Policy/Colombia Court Decisions (2019), http://www.harmonywithnatureun.org/rightsOfNature/.

[244] Anastasia Moloney, Colombia's Top Court Orders Government to Protect Amazon Forest in Landmark Case, Reuters (Apr. 6, 2018), https://www.reuters.com/article/us-colombia-deforestation-amazon/colombias-top-court-orders-government-to-protect-amazon-forest-in-landmark-case-idUSKCN1HD21Y. For an excellent description of key components of the Court's decision and reasoning, see generally Dejusticia, Climate Change and Future Generations Lawsuit in

The case came before the court after twenty-five youth plaintiffs and the organization Dejusticia filed suit against the government demanding that the court order the government to protect their right to a healthy environment. Using a "tutela"[245] cause of action, the plaintiffs claimed that the government's failure to prevent the rising rates of deforestation jeopardizes their futures and violates their constitutional right to a healthy environment, life, food and water.[246]

The Colombian Amazon rain forests experienced a 44-percent increased rate of deforestation from 2015 to 2016. The Supreme Court concluded that Colombia had not efficiently addressed the deforestation problem in the Amazon, despite having signed numerous international agreements and despite ample national laws and jurisprudence addressing the issue.[247] Ultimately, the court ordered the environmental and agricultural ministries, the national park service, several local municipalities, and the national government to create an action plan to combat deforestation of the Amazon within four to five months of the decision. A presidential directive implements the decision.[248]

The court explained that deforestation is a main source of GHG emissions that accelerate climate change. The court noted that the rising rate of deforestation in the Amazon is due to agriculture and grazing, illegal mining and logging, as well as illegal cocaine production.[249] In addition, the Court explained that the alarming rate of deforestation causes "imminent and serious damage" to the plaintiffs, "and in general, to all the inhabitants of the national territory, both for present and future generations, because it uncontrollably releases carbon dioxide into the atmosphere, producing the greenhouse effect, which transforms and fragments ecosystems, altering water resources and thus the water supply of populated areas and soil degradation."[250]

Echoing Colombia's Constitution, the court declared that the "Colombian Amazon is recognized as an entity, a subject of rights," which includes the right

---

Colombia: Key Excerpts from the Supreme Court's Decision, https://www.dejusticia.org/en/cli mate-change-and-future-generations-lawsuit-in-colombia-key-excerpts-from-the-supreme-courts-decision/.

[245] A "tutela" action is a constitutional mechanism that addresses protection of fundamental rights.

[246] Moloney, *supra* note 244.

[247] Claudia Fonsecaln, *Corte Supreme Ordena Proteccion Imediata de la Amazonia Colombiana,* CORTE SUPREMA DE JUSTICIA, http://www.cortesuprema.gov.co/corte/index.php/2018/04/05/corte-suprema-ordena-proteccion-inmediata-de-la-amazonia-colombiana/.

[248] Presidential Directive No. 5, Institutional Articulation for the Compliance of the Orders Given by the Supreme Court of Justice by the Sentence 4360–2018 on April 5, 2018, Concerning the Deforestation of the Amazon, Republic of Colombia (Aug. 6, 2018), http://es.presidencia.gov .co/normativa/normativa/DIRECTIVA%20PRESIDENCIAL%20N%C2%B0%2005%20DEL %2006%20DE.%20AGOSTO%20DE%202018.pdf (Spanish Original).

[249] Peter Stubley, *Colombian Government Ordered to Protect Amazon Rainforest in Historic Legal Ruling,* INDEPENDENT (Apr. 6, 2018), https://www.independent.co.uk/news/world/americas/amazon-rainforest-colombia-protect-deforestation-environment-logging-supreme-court-legal-rights-a8292671.html.

[250] Louisa Wright, *Colombia's Top Court Orders Government to Protect Amazon for Future Generations,* DEUTSCHE WELLE, https://www.dw.com/en/colombias-top-court-orders-govern ment-to-protect-amazon-for-future-generations/a-43288343.

to "legal protection, preservation, conservation, maintenance, and restoration."[251] This decision builds on the legal precedent set forth in the Atrato River case in November of 2016, when Colombia's Constitutional Court ruled that the Atrato River possessed legal rights to "protection, conservation, maintenance, and restoration."[252]

The court cited the Constitutional Court's 2016 opinion, which stated that it was "necessary to take a step forward in jurisprudence" to change the relationship of humankind with nature before it is too late or the damage is irreversible."[253] The court ruled that the state had not sufficiently addressed deforestation of the Amazons and ordered the government to adopt a plan with short, medium, and long-term goals to protect the region.[254]

The plaintiffs argued that deforestation and the increase of the average temperature in Colombia jeopardizes their fundamental constitutional rights. The Supreme Court agreed and found that there was a causal link between the adverse impacts on their rights and the GHG emissions from the progressive reduction of forest caused by the unprecedented rate of deforestation.[255] In its ruling, the court ordered that an "Intergenerational Pact for the Life of the Colombian Amazon" be developed within five months by government bodies, affected communities, scientific organizations, and environmental groups. This order is like the Atrato River case, where the Court ordered the government to appoint a representative for the Atrato River, as it is now considered a legal entity. The court here, however, mandated the reduction of deforestation and GHG emissions to zero.[256]

Thus, the Supreme Court declared the Colombian Amazon to be an entity subject to rights, just like the Constitutional Court did with the Atrato River in 2016. The Colombian state has a duty to protect, conserve, maintain, and restore the Amazon. The Supreme Court ordered the municipalities with jurisdiction and competence to update their land management plans and develop an action plan within five months of the Court's decision to reduce deforestation to zero.[257]

The Director of Dejusticia, Cesar Rodriquez, stated that "[a]t the national level, it categorically recognizes that future generations are subject to rights, and it orders the government to take concrete actions to protect the country and planet in which they live."[258] Moreover, Rodriquez noted that the ruling also sets a legal precedent for

---

[251] Mari Margil, *Colombia Supreme Court Rules That Amazon Region Is Subject of Rights*, COMMUNITY ENVTL. LEGAL DEFENSE FUND, https://celdf.org/2018/04/press-release-colombia-supreme-court-rules-that-amazon-region-is-subject-of-rights/.

[252] *Id.* For a detailed discussion of the 2016 decision regarding the Atrato River in Colombia's Constitutional Court, *see infra* Chapter 5.

[253] Margil, *supra* note 251.

[254] Wright, *supra* note 250.

[255] *Id.*

[256] *Id.*

[257] *Id.*

[258] *Id.*

other climate change lawsuits.[259] "The ruling is a fundamental step in the direction that other courts have been taking worldwide, ordering governments to fulfill and increase their commitments to address climate change," Rodriquez said. This case follows a global phenomenon of atmospheric trust litigation and climate change litigation that seeks to compel government action or claim damages for climate change impacts.

The Supreme Court's decision makes Colombia the first country in South America to recognize that a portion of the Amazon is a legal "person."[260] Unlike the Atrato River decision, the Supreme Court based its ruling on both nature and future generations. The CEO of the Center for International Environmental Law, Carrol Muffet, stated that this case is "not about [legal] personhood for the forest itself"; instead, the case "is so powerful and remarkable" because it joins a growing body of atmospheric trust litigation using future generations as a legal argument.[261] The Supreme Court ruled that the "fundamental rights of life, health, liberty, and human dignity are determined by the environment and ecosystems. Without a clean environment the plaintiffs and human beings, in general, can't survive, much less protect those rights for the children of future generations. The existence of family can't be guaranteed, either, neither from society or [sic] the state itself."[262]

The youth plaintiffs explained that the national government took on national and international commitments through the Paris Agreement and Law 1753 of 2015, which implements the Paris Agreement and mandates reductions in deforestation and greenhouse gases.[263] In particular, the plaintiffs refer to Colombia's pledge to reach zero emissions of greenhouse gases in the Amazon by the year 2020.[264]

The plaintiffs asserted "the Amazon is the region ... with 66.2% of the total [amount of deforestation]. ..."[265] The plaintiffs denounced the causes of deforestation, which include "land grabbing (60–65%), illegal drug cultivation (20–22%), illegal mining (7–8%), agricultural industries and illegal logging. ..."[266] The plaintiffs argued that "deforestation in the Amazon has consequences not only for that region but also for the ecosystems from outside" the nation's territory.[267] Yet, the plaintiffs here predicted that they will be part of "the future generation that faces the effects of climate change during the period between 2041–2070 and 2071–2100. ..."[268]

---

[259] *Id.*

[260] Yessenia Funes, *The Colombian Amazon is Now a Person, and You Can Thank Actual People*, EARTHER (Apr. 9, 2018), https://earther.com/the-colombian-amazon-is-now-a-person-and-you-can-thank-1825059357.

[261] *Id.*

[262] *Id.*

[263] Dejusticia v. Colombia, *supra* note 30 (Spanish Original).

[264] *Id.*

[265] *Id.* at 2.

[266] *Id.* at 3.

[267] *Id.*

[268] *Id.*

The court began with the criteria for a "tutela" action. The court stated that a tutela generally may not proceed for the protection of collective rights and interests. In unusual circumstances, however, constitutional jurisprudence has established safeguards when the impairment of group interests violates individual rights.[269] Under such circumstances, a tutela action must establish:

(1) the connection between the violation of collective rights and the violation of a fundamental and individual right;

(2) the individuals asserting alleged violation of individual fundamental rights must be directly affected;

(3) the impairment of the fundamental right should not be hypothetical because Article 86 of the Constitution requires that the alleged individual fundamental right must be violated or threatened by the act or omission of any public authority; and

(4) the judicial order would remedy the alleged violations of individual fundamental rights.[270]

The Court observed that "the fundamental rights of life, health, liberty, and human dignity are linked substantially and determined by the environment and the ecosystem. Without a healthy environment. . . . we cannot survive, much less safeguard these rights, for our children nor for the future generations. Neither would we be able to guarantee the existence of the family, society, or the State."[271] Thus, in this case, the Court concluded that the tutela was appropriate because the youth plaintiffs are seeking to defend their prerogatives and interests and do not represent a third party.[272]

The Court recognized the growing awareness to protect the environment within the notion of sustainable development, to reach "an equilibrium among economic growth, social welfare, and environmental protection," with the understanding that present actions should sustain future use of those resources.[273] The Court further recognized that environmental rights of future generations are grounded in (1) the ethical duty of solidarity of the human species and (2) in the intrinsic value of nature.[274] The Court explained that natural resources are shared by all the inhabitants of the earth, and by all the descendants or future generations who, despite the fact that they do not have the resources in a material sense, they are tributaries, destined and entitled to those limited natural resources that are becoming

---

[269] *Id.* at 10–12.
[270] *Id.* at 11.
[271] *Id.* at 13.
[272] *Id.* at 15.
[273] *Id.* (internal citations omitted).
[274] *Id.*

increasingly diminished.[275] Without equitable criteria and prudent consumption, the human species may be endangered in the future by the shortage of resources essential for life.[276]

The Court also relied on the ecocentric paradigm, which is grounded in the concept of the intrinsic value of nature. It discussed the interconnection between respecting the integrity of nature and ensuring the protection of future generations.[277] The Court noted several binding and aspirational international laws and norms that form a global public-ecological order and serve as an example for domestic legislatures to resolve citizens' complaints over destruction of habitat, to protect present and future generations.[278] It referenced Article 12 of the International Covenant on Economic Social and Cultural Rights (ICESCR), which provides that everyone has the right to enjoy the highest attainable standard of physical and mental health.[279] In addition, the Court noted that the Geneva Convention and the Additional Protocols prohibit unjustified attacks to nature under Articles 35 and 55.[280] The Court also referenced the Stockholm Declaration of 1972 and the Rio Declaration of 1992, both of which enshrined important international environmental law principles.[281]

The Court also determined that the Paris Agreement provides strong support for the plaintiffs' case.[282] The Court referenced Colombia's pledges and commitments to the Paris Agreement, which include the pledge to (1) improve the administration, vigilance, and control of forests for its sustainable use; (2) promote land use planning and green infrastructure, as well as green fuel; (3) halt agricultural expansion; (4) finance protection of the forests; and (5) monitor forests with precision.[283]

Next, the Court concluded that many articles of the 1991 Colombian Constitution, as well as other domestic rules, support the plaintiffs' position.[284] It explained that the Constitutional Court has a line of cases that welcomed the emerging concepts and progress on this theme.[285] In this sense, the Court has analyzed the constitutional issues from a "green" perspective, characterizing the Colombian Constitution as an "ecological constitution" that elevates the environment to the fundamental rights category.[286] The Court also noted that Articles 79 and 80 of the

---

[275] *Id.* at 20.
[276] *Id.*
[277] *Id.*
[278] *Id.* at 22.
[279] *Id.*
[280] *Id.* at 22–23.
[281] *Id.* at 24–25.
[282] *Id.* at 25.
[283] *Id.* at 32.
[284] *Id.* at 26 (citing arts. 49, 58, 63, 67, 79–80, 88, 95–98, 215, 226, 268, 277, 289, 300, 311).
[285] *Id.* at 27.
[286] *Id.*

Colombian Constitution create a constitutional collective right and a right to environment.[287] The Court explained that the conservation of the Amazon is both a national and global obligation, since the region is known as the "world's lungs."[288]

The Court also concluded that a causal nexus exists between climate change generated by the progressive reduction of forest cover, which is further caused by the expansion of agriculture, narcotics cultivation, illegal mining and logging, and the negative effects on the well-being of people in Colombia.[289] The Court determined that the main causes of deforestation are illegal land grabs, illegal cultivation, and illegal mining.[290] These factors directly contributed to the deforestation in the Amazon, which created a short-, medium-, and long-term serious and imminent harm to the youth plaintiffs in this case, and to all the inhabitants of the nation's territory, and for future generations of Colombians.[291] These negative effects transform and fragment ecosystems, alter the water cycle, deplete bodies of water, and cause soil degradation.[292]

The Court relied on three environmental principles to support its reasoning: (1) the precautionary principle, (2) intergenerational equity, and (3) solidarity. The Court noted the consequences of deforestation and how it causes the fragmentation and destruction of connectivity of ecosystems that will likely cause the extinction or threat of extinction for many species inhabiting the region further generating "damages to the ecological integrity."[293] Likewise, the GHG emissions caused by deforestation will cause additional negative consequences. The Court considered the irreversibility of the damages and the scientific certainty, which are the two components of the precautionary principle, to conclude that the GHG emissions from the current rate of deforestation pose a grave danger and require immediate action.[294]

The Court further explained that the intergenerational equity elements are violated when science predicts with certainty that the increase of average temperatures in Colombia for the year of 2041 will be 1.6 degrees Celsius hotter and up to 2.14 degrees Celsius hotter in 2071, yet the future generations are the ones at risk unless deforestation is reduced to zero.[295] It also relied on the principle of solidarity, which refers to the duty and responsibility of the Colombian state to halt the causes that increase GHG emissions, which are further caused by the rapid rate of

---

[287] *Id.* at 29.
[288] *Id.* at 30.
[289] *Id.* at 33.
[290] *Id.* at 34.
[291] *Id.*
[292] *Id.* at 35.
[293] *Id.* at 36.
[294] *Id.* at 36–37.
[295] *Id.* at 37.

deforestation within the Amazon.[296] The Court explained that the alarming rate of deforestation in the Amazon is a primary reason why the government must immediately adopt measures to mitigate the harms and protect the plaintiffs and all the people that live and share the Amazon, which includes not only Colombian nationals but also the entire global population, including ecosystems and human beings.[297]

The Court then addressed how the Colombian state has not fulfilled its promise to reduce deforestation of the Colombian Amazon, which required a reduction to zero deforestation policy by the year 2020.[298] The Court stated that the regional autonomous corporations (CARs) must adopt an immediate plan to (1) halt the expansion of illegal cultivation and illegal mining that destroys the Amazon rain forest, (2) fill the void left by FARC and the paramilitary to create an active presence of the Colombian state for the conservation of the Amazon territory, and (3) prevent and mitigate growing wildfires, deforestation, and agricultural expansion.[299]

Finally, the Supreme Court relied on the Atrato River case to support its ruling that the Amazon is an authentic subject of rights.[300] The Court concluded that despite all of the governing international and domestic law on the topic, the Colombian state has not sufficiently confronted the problem of deforestation in the Amazon, which includes the three CARs with jurisdiction in the Amazon region, the three national parks within the National Natural Park System, and the departments and municipalities with jurisdiction in the Amazon territory.[301]

Thus, just like the Constitutional Court declared the Atrato River a subject of rights, entitled to the protection, conservation, maintenance, and restoration by the state, the Supreme Court declared the Amazon region is equally important to protect Colombia's vital ecosystems.[302] The Court ordered the national government to create an action plan and an Intergenerational Pact for the Life of the Colombian Amazon (PIVAC).[303] Likewise, the court ordered the Amazon municipalities and the CARs located in the Amazon to create their own action plans.[304]

The author interviewed Gabriela Eslava, lawyer with Dejusticia, in Bogotá on September 19, 2018 to solicit her thoughts on the strategy underlying this ground-breaking case and its connection to this book.

[296] *Id.*
[297] *Id.*
[298] *Id.* at 38.
[299] *Id.*
[300] *Id.* at 39–41.
[301] *Id.* at 41–44.
[302] *Id.* at 45.
[303] *Id.* at 45–46
[304] *Id.* at 46–47.

ABATE: What problems in Colombia's environmental governance regime
            prompted Dejusticia's creative climate justice litigation to protect
            future generations? Has the protection of future generations been a
            focus in other environmental litigation in Colombia prior to
            this case?

ESLAVA: The main problem that prompted Dejusticia's lawsuit is deforestation
            in the Amazon Rain Forest and the omissions from the Colombian
            government in protecting this ecosystem. At the 2015 climate
            change negotiations, Colombia reaffirmed its commitment to reach
            zero-net deforestation in the Colombian Amazon by year 2020.
            Two years before the deadline, the government has yet to develop
            significant and effective actions to stop deforestation. Deforestation
            emits more carbon dioxide (CO_2) than any other activity in
            Colombia, which is the main GHG causing climate change.
            In 2016, deforestation in Colombia increased by 44 percent,
            meaning that a total of 178,597 hectares were deforested. On its
            own, deforestation is contributing 36 percent of the country's total
            greenhouse gas emissions. The problem is that cutting down the
            rain forest not only contributes to climate change–related impacts
            such as melting of glaciers, temperature increase, and the spread of
            vector-borne diseases, but also alters the water cycle. This in turn
            generates a serious threat of floods, droughts, landslides, food
            shortages, crop loss, and affects rainfall patterns. Deforestation in
            the most biodiverse region in the world violates the right of
            Colombian children and youth to enjoy a healthy environment.
            Given that all ecosystems are interconnected, deforestation in the
            Amazon not only affects those living in the region, but also
            elsewhere in Colombia. In turn, the violation of the right to enjoy a
            healthy environment threatens the rights to life, health, food, and
            water of the ones who are young today and who will face as adults
            the future climate change scenarios predicted by the Institute of
            Hydrology, Meteorology and Environmental Studies (IDEAM):
            current research indicates that between 2041–2070, the average
            temperature in Colombia will increase 1.6°C.

ABATE: Has the protection of future generations been a focus in other
            environmental litigation in Colombia prior to this case?

ESLAVA: No, this is the first time that a case focuses on climate change and
            future generations in Colombia.

ABATE: Was Dejusticia's case filed on behalf of the youth plaintiffs inspired
            by atmospheric trust litigation in the United States, particularly the

renowned *Juliana* case? In what ways is this case different from the *Juliana* case?

ESLAVA: While we were researching we found the Sabin Center Climate Change Litigation Database and read about other climate change cases around the world such as the *Urgenda* case in The Netherlands and the *Juliana* case in the United States. It was inspiring for us that in both cases the plaintiffs were common people and we thought that something similar would be possible in Colombia. There was one element that inspired us the most in the *Juliana* case, and it was how they got to individualize the threats that climate change poses on each of the plaintiffs.

ABATE: In the *Juliana* case and other atmospheric trust cases in the United States, two of the greatest barriers to the plaintiffs' success are securing standing to sue and overcoming the political question doctrine to secure the court's jurisdiction to hear the case. What are the greatest obstacles under Colombian law for cases like this one to succeed?

ESLAVA: There were at least two great obstacles in our case. The first is the same as in the *Juliana* case: plaintiffs had to prove they had legal standing. The second is related to having enough evidence to prove causality. We had to prove that something that is happening in the south region of the country (in the Amazon rain forest) is a threat not only for the plaintiffs who live in the Amazon rain forest but for the whole group of plaintiffs who live in seventeen different cities and municipalities of Colombia. To prove that there is a deep relation between ecosystems we use, mostly, official information provided by the Colombian government.

ABATE: Did the success in the Atrato River case inspire Dejusticia to pursue this case? Did the success in that case make success in this case more likely?

ESLAVA: Although the decisions are similar, the cases are very different. In the Atrato case there was no special focus on climate change or future generations' rights. In our case, those two subjects were our main focus. In a sense we got inspired by the Atrato River case: that case succeeded at showing a difficult environmental case to a judge and get a structural decision.

ABATE: In its ruling in this case, the court ordered that an Intergenerational Pact for the Life of the Colombian Amazon be developed within five months by government bodies, affected communities, scientific organizations, and environmental groups. This order appears to be much stronger than the remedy in the Atrato River case, where the Court ordered the government to appoint a representative for the River Atrato, as it is now considered a legal entity. The court order here seeks to reduce deforestation and GHG emissions to zero. What is the status of the implementation of this ambitious order? Are you optimistic that it will be fulfilled?

ESLAVA: Once the Supreme Court's decision was released, the Colombian government, especially the Ministry of Environment, called five meetings in five different cities of the Amazon. The government called communities, indigenous peoples, local government, and the plaintiffs to join those meetings. The main purpose of those meetings was to collect ideas for the creation of two of the orders of the Supreme Court; one of those was the creation of the Intergenerational Pact for the Life of the Colombian Amazon (PIVAC). Although there is enough information to create the pact it was not possible for the government to develop it within five months. We have to take into account that the government changed during the implementation process and that has an effect on the timing. Nevertheless, we are optimistic about the creation of the PIVAC as it is a tool to get communities and young people involved not only in the protection of the Amazon rain forest but also as the ones who are going to be in charge of holding the government accountable in regards to its environmental commitments.

ABATE: *Climate Change and the Voiceless* seeks to bring together the protection of animals, natural resources, and future generations in the climate change era. Do you see any parallels and synergies between your work on animal rights and your work on climate justice and/or natural resource protection cases in Colombia?

ESLAVA: I think the most important synergy between climate justice, future generations' rights, and the defense of animal rights is that all those subjects involve thinking there is a new paradigm possible. By this I mean that fighting for the protection of animals, of future generations, or for nature as a subject of rights involves being aware that anthropocentrism is no longer an option for our planet and that we have to change to a new ecocentric paradigm in which humans recognize that they are only one part of the planet and that we share the Earth with sentient beings that should not be understood as resources.

Dejusticia's successful youth climate case against the government of Colombia stands out as a leading global example of how the court system can be used creatively and effectively to compel government action to promote climate justice. The challenge that remains in the wake of this remarkable victory in Colombia is the enforcement of the ambitious terms of the Court's order to achieve the prescribed zero deforestation in such a short period.

2 Unsuccessful: Philippines ("Share the Road" Petition)

In *Segovia v. Climate Change Comm'n*, the Supreme Court of the Philippines rejected a "Share the Road" petition that sought to compel the government to dedicate half of its roadways for the use of bicycles, walkers, and nonmotorized vehicles.[305] Originating under the Presidential Task Force on Climate Change (PTFCC,) the Road Sharing Principle is contained in Section 9(a) of Executive Order 774 (EO 774.)[306] EO 774 mandated the creation of a task force under the Department of Transportation and Communications (DTC) to help reduce the consumption of fossil fuels.[307]

The Road Sharing Principle provides that "the new paradigm in the movement of men and things must follow a simple principle: 'Those who have less in wheels must have more in road." For this purpose, the system shall favor nonmotorized locomotion and collective transportation system (walking, bicycling, and the man-powered mini-train)."[308] This principle is also found in AO 254, a similar mandate to EO 774, for the DTC to "[r]eform the transport sector to reduce the consumption of fossil fuels."[309] In 2009, the Climate Change Commission created by Congress absorbed the duties of the PTFCC.[310]

As a result of the Road Sharing Principle and other environmental laws, *Segovia v. Climate Change Comm'n* was filed on behalf of "the carless people of the Philippines," Filipino children, future Filipino children, and "car-owners who would rather not have cars if good public transportation were safe, convenient, accessible and reliable."[311] Several government agencies were listed as respondents,

---

[305] Segovia v. Climate Change Comm'n, G.R. 211010, (S.C., Mar. 7, 2017) (Phil.), http://sc.judiciary.gov.ph/pdf/web/viewer.html?file=/jurisprudence/2017/march2017/211010.pdf. For a discussion of the background of the Share the Road movement, *see* Brook Meakins, *Share the Road Movement in the Philippines*, HUFFINGTON POST (Aug. 10, 2013), https://www.huffingtonpost.com/brook-meakins/share-the-road-movement-i_b_3417124.html.
[306] *Id.* at 3–4.
[307] *Id.*
[308] *Id.* at 4.
[309] *Id.*
[310] *Id.*
[311] *Id.* at 1.

including the Climate Change Commission, the DTC, and the Department of Environment and Natural Resources.[312]

The petition alleged that the respondents had violated rights, including the right to a balanced ecology,[313] by failing to implement the Road Sharing Principle and other laws intended to reduce fossil fuel consumption and protect the atmosphere and air quality of the Philippines.[314] The petitioners alleged unequal protection of the law on the basis that only 2 percent of Filipinos own cars, but the majority of road space and national budget is allotted for cars rather than "sidewalks, bike lanes and nonmotorized transportation systems."[315]

The petition was filed on behalf of a movement of people collectively known as "Share the Road,"[316] with the petitioners consisting of: (1) the carless people of the Philippines; (2) those with cars who would prefer public transportation; (3) Filipino youths; and (4) future generations of Filipinos.[317] The movement was created out of concern regarding the increased air pollution around the Philippines, particularly in the Manila metro area, and the effects of the pollution "of such magnitude as to prejudice the life, health and property of all Filipinos."[318] The petitioners initially wrote the respondents requested reformation of the transportation system in accordance with the Road Sharing Principle.[319]

After no response was received, a petition for a writ of *kalikasan* and a writ of continuing mandamus was filed with the Supreme Court.[320] The petitioners alleged that the respondents: violated the atmospheric trust created under Article XI, Section 1 of the Constitution; failed to reduce personal and official fossil fuel consumption; failed to implement the Road Sharing Principle; failed to create more sustainable urban farming spaces; failed to reduce air pollutant emissions; and failed to make the road users' tax available.[321] For these reasons, the petitioners asked the Court to compel the government to rectify these violations and implement the laws by: dividing the roads in half to create more sidewalks and road space for bicycles and nonmotorized transportation; compelling the president and government officials to reduce fossil fuel consumption by 50 percent and increase their use

---

[312] *Id.* at 1–2.
[313] The "right to a balanced ecology" was first recognized in the landmark decision in the *Minors Oposa* case discussed in Part IV of this chapter.
[314] *Id.* at 5.
[315] *Id.* at 6.
[316] For a discussion of the background of the Share the Road movement, *see* Meakins, *supra* note 305.
[317] Segovia v. Climate Change Comm'n, G.R. 211010, (Phil), at 1.
[318] *Id.* at 5, 9.
[319] *Id.* at 4.
[320] *Id.* at 3–4.
[321] *Id.* at 4.

of public transportation by the same; and compelling the release of funds from the road users' tax to finance the bifurcation of the roads.[322]

On March 7, 2017, in a unanimous opinion written by Associate Justice Alfredo Benjamin S. Caguioa, on behalf of the other twelve justices of the Court, the Court dismissed the petition.[323] The Court held that the petitioners did not sufficiently support their allegations of an actual or threatened violation of their right to a balanced and healthful ecology as a result of the respondent's acts, omissions, or neglect.[324]

The Court first held that the petitioners had standing.[325] Citing the relaxed rules of standing, which resulted from *Minors Oposa*, the Court concluded that standing was valid because the suit was filed as a citizen's suit "for the enforcement of rights and obligations under environmental laws."[326] The Court also held that the petitioners did not violate the hierarchy of the courts in this petition.[327] The Court determined that a writ of *kalikasan* may be sought directly from the Supreme Court for environmental cases when such potential environmental danger could "prejudice the life, health or property of inhabitants in two or more cities or provinces."[328] The Court has the discretion to accept petitions that have not adhered to the doctrine of hierarchy of the courts.[329]

On the merits, the Court first held that the petitioners were not entitled to the issuance of a writ of *kalikasan*.[330] The Court held that the petitioners did not show the respondents had violated or neglected any rights.[331] Nor did they establish a "causal link or reasonable connection" between the government's actions and the environmental damage and air pollution alleged.[332] The respondents were able to show that they did not unlawfully violate the laws or refuse to implement the laws.[333] They provided evidence of several government-sponsored projects that were designed to implement the laws and "tak[e] concrete steps to improve national air quality."[334]

Regarding the writ of continuing mandamus, the Court held that the petitioners failed to prove a direct or personal injury, even in light of the relaxed

---

[322] *Id.* at 3.
[323] *Id.* at 1, 13–14.
[324] *Id.* at 13.
[325] *Id.* at 8.
[326] *Id.*
[327] *Id.*
[328] *Id.*
[329] *Id.*
[330] *Id.*
[331] *Id.* at 9.
[332] *Id.*
[333] *Id.* at 10.
[334] *Id.*

standing requirement in environmental cases.[335] The Court noted that the Road Sharing Principle is just that – a principle – and consequently "cannot be considered an absolute imposition"[336] that the Court may compel. Given that a writ of mandamus is used to compel the performance of ministerial duties, and nothing in EO 774 or AO 254 required a specific course of implementation, such as the bifurcation of the roads, the government cannot be "enjoined by law"[337] to fulfill such a duty. In sum, the Court stated that "what the Petitioners are seeking to compel is not the performance of a ministerial act, but a discretionary act."[338]

The Court also dismissed the petitioner's request for the court to compel the release of the road users' tax to fund the implementation of the Road Sharing Principle, finding the demand is not supported by law and the executive issuances that created the Road Sharing Principle cannot serve as the basis for the release of taxpayer funds.

Although ultimately unsuccessful, the petition is noteworthy for its creative attempt to hold the Filipino government accountable for the laws addressing climate change. The obstacle in this case appears to be the lack of causation. Even though the petitioners provided air pollution evidence, the causal connection between any action, omission, or neglect of the government and such air pollution was not sufficiently established. Furthermore, the petition relied too heavily on a discretionary principle that did not contain compellable ministerial duties.[339]

The outcome in the Share the Road petition case appears to be at odds with MMDA v. *Residents of Manila Bay*, a 2008 case that Antonio Oposa filed, which succeeded in applying a writ of continuing mandamus against government agencies to clean up and preserve Manila Bay.[340] Justice Velasco, who had concurred in part and dissented in part with the majority in the Share the Road petition regarding the implementation of the Road Sharing Principle, drafted the opinion.[341] The agencies had been responsible for public services such as waste management, and the waste management systems and agencies' indifference were deemed the

---

[335] *Id.*
[336] *Id.* at 11–12.
[337] *Id.*
[338] *Id.*
[339] For a helpful discussion of the Supreme Court's analysis in the Share the Road petition case, see *Supreme Court Junks Road Sharing Petition*, RAPPLER (Mar. 7, 2017), https://www.rappler .com/nation/163498-supreme-court-junks-road-sharing-petition.
[340] MMDA v. Residents of Manila Bay, G.R. 171947–48 (S.C., Dec. 18, 2008) (Phil.), http://sc .judiciary.gov.ph/jurisprudence/2008/december2008/171947–48.htm. For a helpful discussion of the Residents of Manila Bay case, see generally Juan de Castro, *Cleaning Up Manila Bay: Mandamus as a Tool for Environmental Protection*, 37 ECOLOGY L. Q. 797 (2010).
[341] *Id.*

cause of the pollution and degradation of Manila Bay.[342] In *Residents of Manila Bay*, the Court defined a ministerial duty as "one that requires neither the exercise of official discretion nor judgment."[343] The government argued that the duty of creating waste systems was discretionary.[344] The residents of Manila Bay argued that creating waste management systems was a "clear mandate of the law [that] does not require the exercise of discretion."[345] The Court agreed with the residents of Manila Bay, stating that "[w]hile the implementation of the MMDA mandated tasks may entail a decision-making process, the enforcement of the law or the very act of doing what the law exacts to be done is ministerial in nature and may be compelled by mandamus."[346]

The Court relied on *Minors Oposa* in support of the state's obligation to protect the right to a balanced and healthful ecology, stating that:

> Even assuming the absence of [a] categorical legal provision specifically prodding petitioners to clean up the bay, they and the men and women representing them cannot escape their obligation to future generations of Filipinos to keep the waters of the Manila Bay clean and clear as humanly possible. Anything less would be a betrayal of the trust reposed in them.[347]

Thus, the Court issued a writ of mandamus in *Residents of Manila Bay* even when there was an "absence of [a] categorical legal provision"[348] and some degree of governmental discretion in how the mandate was implemented because it found the *obligation to perform the duty* was ministerial and could be compelled by mandamus.[349]

This reasoning regarding compelling ministerial and discretionary duties by mandamus was seemingly not applied to the Share the Road petition opinion. Similarities can be drawn between the governmental duties in *MMDA* and the governmental duties under the Road Sharing Principle, including the fact that the Court noted the Road Sharing Principle was part of a mandate that did not have a categorical provision outlining its implementation. Therefore, the missing thread in the *Segovia* petition is likely causation. Comparing the two petitions and outcomes, the Court appears to be receptive to issuing writs of continuing mandamus – even if the legal provision provides some governmental discretion – so long as there is a sufficient causal connection between the harm being caused and the government action or inaction.

The *Segovia* petition reflects the continuing interest of younger Filipino generations in learning from successful environmental attorneys and continuing to hold

---

[342] *Id.* at 4, 8–16.
[343] *Id.* at 7.
[344] *Id.*
[345] *Id.*
[346] *Id.* at 8.
[347] *Id.* at 24.
[348] *Id.*
[349] *Id.* at 8.

the Filipino government accountable for climate change and environmental issues. Like the *Minors Oposa* and *Residents of Manila Bay* cases, the Share the Road movement is also championed in part by Antonio Oposa.[350]

3 Pending: European Union, Canada, India, and Pakistan

Several creative and potentially groundbreaking climate justice lawsuits premised on intergenerational equity theories are pending throughout the world as of this writing. This section briefly summarizes the parties and legal theories involved in these pending actions.

In the People's Climate Case in the European Union, the plaintiffs are children and their parents who work in agriculture and tourism in the EU and abroad and who are increasingly adversely affected by climate change such as droughts, flooding, heat waves, sea level rise, and the disappearance of cold seasons. They assert violations of rights to life, health, occupation, and property. Among the applicants in the case, Sweden's indigenous Sami community has found that global warming has impacted their livelihood, namely reindeer herding. France and Portugal have suffered as a result of heat waves, which impacted local farmers and villages.[351] Maurice Feschet of France brought his claims before the Court to protect the future generations of his family.

On May 23, 2018, the applicants in the People's Climate Case requested the annulment of the GHG Emission Acts because the Acts allow GHG emissions between 2021 and 2030 in an amount corresponding to 90 percent of the 1990 emissions in 2021, and decrease to 60 percent of the 1990 emissions in 2030. The GHG Emissions Acts include: (1) Directive 2003/87/EC (the Emissions Trading System or ETS Directive);[352] (2) Regulation (EU) 2018/842 (the Effort Sharing Regulation);[353] and (3) Regulation (EU) 2018/841 (the LULUCF Regulation).

The plaintiffs argue that this tripartite legislation, which is the EU's principal legal response to achieve its 2030 climate targets, has been set too low to comply with the 2015 Paris Agreement. This case is modeled after the *Urgenda* case, where the Dutch court ruled that the Dutch government must protect its citizens from the

---

[350] Meakins, *supra* note 305.

[351] Josh Gabbatiss, *EU Taken to Court by Families in "People's Climate Case" Over Inadequate 2030 Emissions Target*, INDEPENDENT (May 24, 2018), https://www.independent.co.uk/news/world/europe/eu-emissions-targets-peoples-climate-case-change-european-parliament-global-warming-a8367146.html.

[352] Directive (EU) 2018/410 of the European Parliament and of the Council of March 14, 2018 amending Directive 2003/87/EC to enhance cost-effective emission reductions and low-carbon investments, and Decision (EU) 2015/1814, OJ L 76/3.

[353] Regulation (EU) 2018/842 of the European Parliament and of the Council on binding annual greenhouse gas emission reductions by Member States from 2021 to 2030 contributing to climate action to meet commitments under the Paris Agreement and amending Regulation (EU) No 525/2013, OJ L 156/26.

consequences of climate change and needs to reduce its GHG emissions by at least 25 percent from its 1990 emissions.

The Court of Justice of the European Union accepted the case on August 13, 2018. Although the People's Climate Case against the European Union is still at an early stage, the fact that the Court accepted the case is a significant development. There is positive interplay between environmental law and human rights law, such as using human rights to protect the environment. Examples include: right to life (ICCPR), right to health (ICESCR) (interpreted as requiring states to take measures to protect the environment), and a right to a healthy environment.[354]

Canada also has an intergenerational equity climate justice lawsuit on its docket. On November 26, 2018, following widespread protests demanding climate action in Quebec,[355] the nonprofit ENvironnement JEUnesse filed a class action lawsuit against the Government of Canada for its failure to act on climate change.[356] Acting pro bono on behalf of the nonprofit group, a law firm filed this action with the Quebec Superior Court.[357] The plaintiffs' argument is that the failure of the Canadian government to take adequate action to mitigate the impacts of climate change constitutes a violation of Quebec youth's rights to life, equality, and security of person as delineated in the Canadian Charter of Rights and Freedoms.[358] Notably, they argue that the brunt of the impacts will be borne by young Quebec residents under the age of thirty-five and their children, who in turn will have little to no capacity to reverse the course of these impacts.[359] Beyond failing to enact adequate measures to combat climate change, which they argue represents negligence so extreme that it constitutes an intentional harm,[360] the plaintiffs accuse the Canadian government of pursuing actions that will continue and even increase

---

[354] For additional information on the People's Climate Case in the EU, *see generally* http://www .caneurope.org/publications/press-releases/1671-european-parliament-calls-for-stepping-up-eu-cli mate-action; https://www.clientearth.org/peoples-climate-case-highlights-lack-of-access-to-the-eu-courts.

[355] Cecilia Keating, *Quebecers Mobilize to Demand Climate Action*, NAT'L OBSERVER (Nov. 22, 2019), https://www.nationalobserver.com/2018/11/22/news/quebecers-mobilize-demand-climate-action.

[356] Ingrid Peritz, *Quebec Group Sues Federal Government over Climate Change*, THE GLOBE AND MAIL (Nov. 27, 2018), https://www.theglobeandmail.com/canada/article-quebec-group-sues-fed eral-government-over-climate-change.

[357] Megan Darby, *Quebec Youth Launch Climate Lawsuit against the Canadian Government*, CLIMATE HOME NEWS (Nov. 27, 2018), http://www.climatechangenews.com/2018/11/27/quebec-youth-launch-climate-lawsuit-canadian-government.

[358] Allison Hanes, *Young Quebecers Are Suing for Climate Negligence*, MONTREAL GAZETTE (Nov. 26, 2018), https://montrealgazette.com/opinion/columnists/allison-hanes-young-quebec ers-are-suing-for-climate-negligence.

[359] The Canadian Press, *In Quebec, Teenaged Activists Launch Climate Change Lawsuit against Ottawa*, THE STAR (Nov. 26, 2018), https://www.thestar.com/news/canada/2018/11/26/quebec-environmentalists-launch-climate-change-lawsuit-against-ottawa.html.

[360] ENvironnement JEUnesse v. Procureur Général Du Canada (2018) http://tjl.quebec/wp-con tent/uploads/2018/11/2018-11-26-Demande-autorisation-ENJEU-c.-Canada.pdf.

Canada's emissions in years to come, such as ramping up the development of Alberta's tar sands.[361]

The suit seeks punitive damages, a declaratory judgment, and a court order that would require the government to take action to uphold young peoples' rights.[362] The Authorization Demand itself includes specific examples demonstrating Canada's recognition of the anthropogenic causes of climate change and its impacts on the health of Canadians as well as Canada's previous commitments to reduce its contributions to climate change.[363] According to Anne-Julie Asselin, a lawyer at the firm, it should take approximately one year to certify the class action after which the trial process may take around two to three years.[364] The case has been compared to other citizen and youth-led cases around the world in which courts are tasked with cases seeking to compel governments to take robust action to mitigate climate change, including *Urgenda*,[365] *Juliana*,[366] and *Dejusticia v. Colombia*.[367]

India and Pakistan secured headlines in climate justice intergenerational equity litigation developments when one young girl in each country sued their respective government to compel action on climate change. In March 2017, nine-year-old Ridhima Pandey filed a petition, through her legal guardian, against the Indian Government asserting that the Indian government has failed in its duties to mitigate climate change.[368] The petition was filed in the National Green Tribunal (NGT),

---

[361] *Ongoing Class Actions*, TRUDEL JOHNSTON & LESPÉRANCE, http://tjl.quebec/en/class-action/climate-change/.

[362] ENVironnement JEUnesse v. Canada, Climate Case Chart, Sabin Center for Climate Change Law, http://climatecasechart.com/non-us-case/environnement-jeunesse-v-canadian-government/; *see also* Dana Drugman, *Canada Faces Latest Youth-Led Climate Lawsuit*, CLIMATE LIABILITY NEWS (Nov. 27, 2018), https://www.climateliabilitynews.org/2018/11/27/canada-youth-climate-lawsuit/.

[363] Summary of the Case: ENvironnement JEUnesse v. Attorney General of Canada, Environnement Jeunesse, https://enjeu.qc.ca/wp-content/uploads/2018/11/Case-summary_EN.docx.

[364] Carl Meyer, *Quebec Youth Apply to Sue Canada to Get Tougher Carbon Pollution Targets*, NAT'L OBSERVER (Nov. 26, 2018), https://www.nationalobserver.com/2018/11/26/news/quebec-youth-apply-sue-canada-get-tougher-carbon-pollution-targets.

[365] Urgenda, The Urgenda Climate Case against the Dutch Government, https://www.urgenda.nl/en/themas/climate-case/.

[366] Juliana v. United States, Climate Case Chart, Sabin Center for Climate Change Law, http://climatecasechart.com/case/juliana-v-united-states/.

[367] *In Historic Ruling, Colombian Court Protects Youth Suing the National Government for Failing to Curb Deforestation*, DEJUSTICIA (Apr. 5, 2018), https://www.dejusticia.org/en/en-fallo-historico-corte-suprema-concede-tutela-de-cambio-climatico-y-generaciones-futuras/. For additional discussion of this case, *see generally* Summary of the Case: ENvironnement JEUnesse v. Attorney General of Canada, ENvironnement JEUnesse, https://enjeu.qc.ca/wp-content/uploads/2018/11/Case-summary_EN.docx [download]; *Ongoing Class Actions*, Trudel Johnston & Lespérance, http://tjl.quebec/en/class-action/climate-change/; Drugman, *supra* note 362; Carl Meyer, *Even in Canada, Kids Are Suing the Government over Climate Change*, MOTHER JONES (Nov. 27, 2018), https://www.motherjones.com/environment/2018/11/even-in-canada-kids-are-suing-the-government-over-climate-change/.

[368] Pandey v. India – NGT Climate Change Petition, http://climatecasechart.com/non-us-case/pandey-v-india/.

a specialized court that hears only environmental cases. The respondents in the case, against whom the lawsuit was filed, were the Ministry of Environment, Forest & Climate Change, and the Central Pollution Control.

In her petition, Ridhima contends that she is directly affected by the adverse impacts of climate change in her state of Uttarakhand and is part of a class that among all Indians is most vulnerable to changes in climate in India, yet not part of the decision-making process.[369] Ridhima alleges that India – the third-largest greenhouse gas emitter in the world – is failing to meet its emissions reduction policies, the standards it has set for itself and its obligations of following a low carbon path to progress under the Paris Agreement.[370] The petition also alleges that the non-implementation of four environmental laws – Forest (Conservation) Act, Air (Prevention and Control of Pollution) Act, Environmental (Protection) Act, 1986 and Biological Diversity Act – dating as far back as 1980, has contributed to adverse climate change impacts in India.[371]

The petition outlines the "eight national missions" of the National Action Plan on Climate Change (NAPCC), put forth by the prime minister's Council on Climate Change, and failure to meet some of its targets. For instance, in scaling up use of renewable energy sources under the National Action Plan on Climate Change (NAPCC), the Central Government had failed to meet its targets for raising renewable energy sources to 8 percent of the national energy mix for electricity by 2012–2013 and 9 percent by 2013–2014. As per the audit report, the national achievement for purchase of electricity from renewable energy sources in those two years was only 4.28 percent and 4.51 percent, respectively, the petition stated.[372]

In her petition, Ridhima directs the government to prepare a carbon budget for the total amount of CO_2 emissions that can be released, prepare an inventory of every substantial source of GHG emissions in India, and prepare a national climate recovery plan that includes mitigation actions.[373] In addition to a low carbon path, Ridhima also seeks to compel the government to protect grasslands, forests, soil, and mangroves. She further seeks to compel to engage in massive reforestation and improve agricultural and forestry practices to enhance natural carbon sequestration,

---

[369] Our Children's Trust, press release, *Global Legal Action, India,* https://www.ourchildrenstrust .org/india.

[370] Pandey v. India, National Green Tribunal, Original Application No: _____ of 2017, 3–4, https://static1.squarespace.com/static/571d109b04426270152febeo/t/58dd45319f74568a83fd7977/ 1490896178123/13.03.22.ClimateChangePetition.pdf.

[371] Our Children's Trust, press release, *Youth Files Climate Case with India's Environmental Court* (Mar. 2017), https://static1.squarespace.com/static/571d109b04426270152febeo/t/58dd78f5f7c0a be149e9fb35/1490909429734/2017.03.30+India+Climate+Case+PR.pdf.

[372] *9-Yr-Old Moves NGT on Issue of Adverse Impact of Climate Change,* HINDUSTAN TIMES (Mar. 29, 2017), https://www.hindustantimes.com/india-news/9-yr-old-moves-ngt-on-issue-of- adverse-impact-of-climate-change/story-exdiQrbGGAdsz5vUmAeK9J.html.

[373] Pandey v. Union of India, National Green Tribunal, Original Application No: _____ of 2017, 50, https://static1.squarespace.com/static/571d109b04426270152febeo/t/58dd45319f74568a83fd7977/ 1490896178123/13.03.22.ClimateChangePetition.pdf.

and protect previously stored carbon.[374] Our Children's Trust is currently assisting Ridhima Pandey and her legal team, working on the legal challenges surrounding this case. As of this writing, the case has not yet been scheduled for trial.[375]

On April 5, 2016, then seven-year-old Rabab Ali, through her father and environmental attorney Qazi Ali Athar, filed a petition with the Supreme Court of Pakistan. The Petition alleges that, through the exploitation and continued promotion of fossil fuels – in particular, dirty coal through the Thar Engro Coal Mine Project – the governments of Pakistan and Sindh violate constitutionally protected fundamental rights, the Public Trust Doctrine as it relates to Pakistan's atmosphere and climate, and rights relating to environmental degradation expected to result from burning coal to generate electricity.[376] Rabab Ali hopes that through this petition, the Pakistan government will create a plan that will allow her and future generations a safe environment in which to grow up.[377] Aside from the environmental degradation in water and air quality impacts, the petition also notes that the people living in the region, who even now face caste-based discrimination, will also be displaced from their homes and lose their local livelihoods with the development and opening of the coal reserve.[378]

The Thar coalfield reserve is in Sindh's remote Tharparkar district, in the lower Indus basin of Pakistan, a mere twenty-five kilometers away from the town of Islamkot. Estimates by the Pakistan Geological Survey put the coalfield reserves at approximately 175 billion tons, making it one of the largest lignite coal reserves in the world.[379] The development is anticipated to increase coal production from 4.5 to 60 million tons per year, with commensurate increase in greenhouse gases.

The development of Thar coal reserves is conducted through a public–private partnership. The Sindh Engro Coal Mining Company (SECMC) was formed as a joint venture between Government of Sindh and Engro Corporation in October 2009.[380] The source of the funding is from the China–Pakistan Economic Corridor, investing $1.2 billion for coalfield development and multiple coal-fired power plant

---

[374] *Id.*

[375] Katy Scott, *Can "Climate Kids" Take on Governments and Win?*, CNN (July 25, 2018), https://edition.cnn.com/2018/07/24/health/youth-climate-march/index.html.

[376] Ali v. Federation of Pakistan – Climate Change Litigation, http://climatecasechart.com/non-us-case/ali-v-federation-of-pakistan-2/.

[377] Our Children's Trust, press release, *Global Legal Action, Pakistan*, https://www.ourchildrenstrust.org/pakistan/.

[378] *Seven Year Old Sues Pakistan Government over Climate Change*, https://www.thethirdpole.net/en/2016/07/05/seven-year-old-sues-pakistan-government-over-climate-change/.

[379] Thar Coal Mining Project, Engro, https://www.engro.com/our-stories/thar-coal-mining-project-addressing-pakistans-rising-energy-needs/.

[380] Aslam Shah, *JIT Asks SINDH Govt to Provide Details of Development Projects*, PAKISTAN DAILY TIMES (Nov. 4, 2018), https://dailytimes.com.pk/318237/jit-asks-sindh-govt-to-provide-details-of-development-projects/.

developments. Construction of the coal power plant began in 2014, scheduled for completion in 2019.[381] It is projected to produce 660 megawatts in Phase-I.

Pakistan has an electricity crisis: supply does not meet demand. Although 70 percent of households are connected to the national grid, few get uninterrupted power supply. Peak production is approximately 16,500 MW; however, demand can reach up to 21,200 MW. In the past, Pakistan has relied on imported coal to bridge the gap. The overall objective of developing the Thar coal deposits is to reduce Pakistan's dependence on imported coal to meet electricity needs. Electricity production from the coal mined by SECMC is projected to have the potential to provide 100,000 MW of power – enough for the next two hundred years.[382]

Qazi Ali Athar (Rabab Ali's father) asserts that Pakistan is rich in renewable energy resources such as solar and wind, which is more than enough to meet current and future energy needs, and that funding and resources should be directed to institutions such as the Alternative Energy Development Board, committed to the design and production of alternative and renewable energy.[383] In the petition, he directs the Pakistan government to "take immediate steps to transition power in Pakistan to non-CO_2 emitting sources such as wind and solar." Our Children's Trust is currently assisting Rabab Ali and her legal team. As of this writing, the case has not yet proceeded to trial.[384]

---

[381] Hanif Samoon, *Thar Coal Project to start Production by Mid-February, Says CM*, Dawn News (Dec. 7, 2018), https://www.dawn.com/news/1449853.

[382] Zofeen T. Ebrahim, *Seven Year Old Sues Pakistan Government over Climate Change*, THE THIRDPOLE.NET (July 5, 2016), https://www.thethirdpole.net/en/2016/07/05/seven-year-old-sues-pakistan-government-over-climate-change/.

[383] Our Children's Trust, press release, *Global Legal Action, Pakistan*, https://www.ourchildrenstrust.org/pakistan/.

[384] Scott, *supra* note 377.

4

Legal Personhood for Wildlife

US and Foreign Domestic Judicial Developments

Just as we now look back on the past 40 years with some bewilderment – and embarrassment – that we were so slow to recognize the human rights of indigenous people, children, people with a disability, older people, and others – it is intriguing to wonder whether our children will look back in 40 years and wonder how we possibly failed for so long to take animal rights seriously.[1]

This chapter considers the role of the courts in addressing recent efforts to protect wildlife, the second category of the voiceless. It examines several case studies in the United States and in foreign domestic jurisdictions in which the Nonhuman Rights Project (NhRP) has filed habeas corpus petitions seeking to establish rights for primates and higher mammals to be free from unlawful confinement and abuse. The chapter underscores how persistent and creative efforts to use the common law can be a tool to raise awareness of important changes that need to occur at the constitutional and legislative levels. Animal protection organizations such as NhRP, People for the Ethical Treatment of Animals (PETA), and the Animal Legal Defense Fund (ALDF) have filed cases addressing what qualities wildlife must possess to be entitled to stewardship and guardianship protection in our legal system. If corporations, ships, and natural resources have legal personhood protections, it follows that at least some, if not all, forms of wildlife should enjoy similar protections. Animals are treated as property under US law and in most foreign domestic jurisdictions, and historically have been used as a means to an end to fulfill human needs for food, companionship, and entertainment. This property-based model facilitates exploitation and interferes with the implementation of the legal protections necessary to help ensure ecosystem integrity and protection of wildlife populations in the face of climate change impacts.

---

[1]   David Weisbrot, Comment, 91 AUST. L. REFORM COMM'N REFORM J. 1 (2007), http://classic
.austlii.edu.au/au/journals/ALRCRefJl/2007/1.html.

I US JUDICIAL DEVELOPMENTS

All living beings deserve the right to live autonomously and free from torture and confinement. Human beings, no matter their legal status, cannot be deprived of life and liberty notwithstanding past precedents.[2] American law has historically viewed nonhuman animals as the property of humans. Although litigation strategies based on animal rights theories have captured public attention, they have gained little traction in the courts.[3] Legal developments have lagged behind public opinion, failing to provide even basic protections to many animals.[4] Based on a Gallup poll survey, one-third of Americans believe that animals should have the same protection from harm and exploitation as people,[5] yet a growing body of jurisprudence rejects progressive advances to improve the legal status of animals.[6]

[2] *See generally* Obergefell v. Hodges, 135 S. Ct. 2584 (2015) (holding that the denial of marriage licenses to same-sex couples violated the Fourteenth Amendment, notwithstanding centuries of historical evidence reflecting the fact that marriage was always understood to be between a man and a women).

[3] *See* Charles Siebert, *Should a Chimp Be Able to Sue Its Owner?*, N.Y. TIMES MAG. (Apr. 23, 2014), https://www.nytimes.com/2014/04/27/magazine/the- rights-of-man-and-beast.html; Nonhuman Rights Project, Inc. *ex rel.* Tommy v. Lavery, 54 N.Y.S.3d 392 (App. Div. 2017) (denying habeas corpus relief for two adult male chimpanzees); Nonhuman Rights Project, Inc. *ex rel.* Kiko v. Presti, 999 N.Y.S.2d 652 (App. Div. 2015), *appeal denied* 3 N.Y.S.3d 698 (App. Div. 2015) (same); People *ex rel.* Nonhuman Rights Project, Inc. v. Lavery, 998 N.Y.S.2d 248 (App. Div. 2014), *leave to appeal denied*, 38 N.E.3d 828 (Sup. Ct. 2015); Nonhuman Rights Project, Inc. *ex rel.* Hercules v. Stanley, 16 N.Y.S.3d 898 (Sup. Ct. 2015) (declining to sign an order to show cause for a habeas petition seeking release of two chimpanzees confined for research purposes).

[4] Only 3 percent of Americans believe that animals need little protection from harm "since they are just animals." Rebecca Riffkin, *In U.S., More Say Animals Should Have Same Rights as People*, GALLUP NEWS (May 18, 2015), http://www.gallup.com/poll/183275/say-animals-rights-people.aspx; Justin F. Marceau, *Killing for Your Dog*, 83 GEO. WASH. L. REV. 943, 952–59 (2015) (noting the discord between social attitudes of pets as family members and the legal status of pets); Elizabeth Paek, *Fido Seeks Full Membership in the Family: Dismantling the Property Classification of Companion Animals by Statute*, 25 U. HAW. L. REV. 481, 483 (2003) ("[T]he law fails to reflect the special relationships shared between animal guardians and their companion animals [because the] animals are legally classified as property.").

[5] Riffkin, *supra* note 4 (reporting Gallup poll result that one-third of Americans want animals to have the same protection from harm and exploitation as people). The poll was conducted by Gallup Poll Social Series and consisted of a random sample of 1,024 US adults via telephone from May 6–10, 2015.

[6] *See* Cetacean Cmty. v. Bush, 386 F.3d 1169 (9th Cir. 2004); Tilikum *ex rel.* People for the Ethical Treatment of Animals v. Sea World Parks & Entm't Inc., 842 F. Supp. 2d 1259 (S.D. Cal. 2012). *But see* Palila v. Haw. Dep't Land & Nat. Resources, 852 F.2d 1106, 1107 (9th Cir. 1988) (in a suit brought by environmental groups on behalf of an endangered bird species, the court acknowledged the personhood of the bird; "as an endangered species under the Endangered Species Act . . . the bird . . . also has legal status and wings its way into federal court as a plaintiff in its own right. The Palila [which has earned the right to be capitalized since it is a party to this proceeding . . .]").

Animal law is a burgeoning practice area with rapidly increasing inclusion in law schools' curricula.[7] The field is at a critical juncture in its development in light of recent efforts to secure legal personhood protections with the help of NhRP. The organization has been pursuing multiyear litigation in several state courts to advance larger objectives that benefit wildlife.[8] The courts are now confronting the issue of whether habeas corpus can apply to wildlife[9] with NhRP spearheading the movement seeking to establish legal personhood protections for wildlife through writ of habeas corpus petitions under the common law.[10]

A *Habeas Corpus: Teaching an Old Dog a New Trick*

Lawyers have relied on a wide range of legal theories to support legal protection for wildlife.[11] One of the most recent and creative theories involves seeking common law habeas corpus relief. Habeas corpus, Latin for "you have the body," is defined by *Black's Law Dictionary* as "a writ employed to bring a person before a court, most frequently to ensure that the person's imprisonment or detention is not illegal."[12]

The writ of habeas corpus in American law is considered "a vital instrument for the protection of individual liberty …"[13] The Supreme Court has explained that the purpose of the writ is to "provide a prompt and efficacious remedy for whatever society deems to be intolerable restraints."[14] State courts have similarly held that the "[t]he great purpose of the writ of habeas corpus is the immediate delivery of the party deprived of personal liberty."[15] Prior to the

---

[7]   In 2000, only nine law schools in the United States offered a course in animal law; today more than 150 do. *Where Should You Go to Law School*, ANIMAL LEGAL DEF. FUND, https://aldf.org/article/where-should-you-go-to-law-school/ (last accessed Jan. 21, 2019).

[8]   *See* NONHUMAN RIGHTS PROJECT, https://www.nonhumanrights.org (last accessed Jan. 27, 2018).

[9]   *See* People *ex rel.* Nonhuman Rights Project, Inc. v. Lavery, 998 N.Y.S.2d 248 (App. Div. 2014); Nonhuman Rights Project, Inc., *ex rel.* Kiko v. Presti, 999 N.Y.S.2d 652 (App. Div. 2015); Nonhuman Rights Project, Inc. *ex rel.* Hercules v. Stanley, 16 N.Y.S.3d 898 (Sup. Ct. 2015).

[10] Randall S. Abate & Jonathan Crowe, *From Inside the Cage to Outside the Box: Natural Resources as a Platform for Nonhuman Animal Personhood in the U.S. and Australia*, 5 GLOBAL J. ANIMAL L. 54, 56 (2017), https://ojs.abo.fi/ojs/index.php/gjal/article/view/1588.

[11] *See, e.g., Tilikum*, 842 F. Supp. 2d 1259 (S.D. Cal. 2012) (alleging a violation of Thirteen Amendment's prohibition of slavery for orcas' confinement at SeaWorld); Complaint – Personal Injury (Negligence Per Se), Justice v. Vercher (Ore. Cir. Ct. May 1, 2018) (Justice, a neglected and emaciated horse, sues ex-owner for abuse), http://media.oregonlive.com/washingtoncounty_impact/other/horse%20lawsuit.pdf.

[12] Habeas Corpus, BLACK'S LAW DICTIONARY (10th ed. 2014).

[13] Boumediene v. Bush, 553 U.S. 723, 743 (2008).

[14] Harris v. Nelson, 394 U.S. 286, 291 (1969) (internal quotations omitted) (citation omitted).

[15] *See* Sheriff of Suffolk Cty. v. Pires, 777 N.E.2d 1231, 1234 (Mass. 2002) (citation omitted); *see also* Murray v. Regier, 872 So. 2d 217, 222 (Fla. 2002) ("[T]he traditional purpose of the writ of habeas corpus is to furnish a *speedy* hearing and remedy to one whose liberty is unlawfully restrained."); State *ex rel.* O'Leary v. Smith, 37 N.E.2d 60, 60 (Ind. 1941) ("The purpose of the

Civil War, slaves were considered property, not persons, and were not capable of seeking habeas relief.[16]

Steven M. Wise is the founder and president of NhRP, which identifies itself as "the only civil rights organization in the United States working through litigation, public policy advocacy, and education to secure legally recognized fundamental rights for nonhuman animals."[17] NhRP not only seeks to secure court judgments for select intelligent and social animals who are being mistreated, but also strives to change the legal status of nonhuman animals in US and foreign domestic courts. In the United States, NhRP cases initially focused on writ of habeas corpus petitions as a mechanism to secure chimpanzees' release from confinement,[18] but have recently expanded to include elephants as the initial strategy in this process.

B NhRP Seeks to "Unlock the Cage"[19] in Habeas Corpus Proceedings to Secure Legal Personhood Protections for Wildlife

1 Chimpanzees

NhRP filed a series of cases on behalf of chimpanzees Tommy,[20] Kiko,[21] and Hercules and Leo,[22] seeking relief through the common law writ of habeas corpus to secure their release. These cases collectively involve four chimpanzees: two of whom were kept by private individuals in New York State, and two of whom were kept until recently at Stony Brook University for research on the evolution of bipedalism.

In the first case, *Nonhuman Rights Project, Inc. v. Lavery*,[23] NhRP filed a habeas corpus petition on behalf of Tommy and Kiko, two captive chimpanzees. NhRP filed suit after discovering that the owners had confined the adult chimpanzees in small cages in a warehouse and a cement storefront in a crowded residential area.[24] NhRP appealed from an order of the Appellate Division, First Department affirming two judgments of the Supreme Court in which the Court declined to sign show cause orders that would have required justification for the chimpanzees' confinement.[25]

---

writ of habeas corpus is to bring the person in custody before the court for inquiry into the cause of restraint.").

[16] *See* Dred Scott v. Sandford, 60 U.S. 393 (1856).

[17] Marc Gunther, *This Lawyer Isn't Monkeying Around*, NONPROFIT CHRON. (June 6, 2017), https://nonprofitchronicles.com/2017/06/06/this-lawyer-isnt-monkeying-around/.

[18] Abate & Crowe, *supra* note 10.

[19] In 2016, NhRP released the documentary, *Unlocking the Cage* (Pennebaker Hegedus Films & HBO Documentary Films, 2016), which details NhRP's work on these habeas corpus cases. *Unlocking the Cage*, https://www.unlockingthecagethefilm.com/ (last accessed Jan. 27, 2019).

[20] Nonhuman Rights Project, Inc. *ex rel.* Tommy v. Lavery, 54 N.Y.S.3d 392 (App. Div. 2017).

[21] Nonhuman Rights Project, Inc., *ex rel.* Kiko v. Presti, 999 N.Y.S.2d 652 (App. Div. 2015).

[22] Nonhuman Rights Project, Inc. *ex rel.* Hercules v. Stanley, 16 N.Y.S.3d 898 (Sup. Ct. 2015).

[23] *Tommy*, 54 N.Y.S.3d at 393.

[24] *Id.* at 394.

[25] *Id.* at 393–94.

The pertinent question is not whether chimpanzees possess anything that could be characterized as a sense of responsibility and duty, but rather whether they possess limited legal rights to be free from confinement and torture under the human legal system. The appellate court held that a "chimpanzee is not a 'person' [within New York Civil Practice Law and Rules (C.P.L.R.) article 70] entitled to the rights and protections afforded by the writ of habeas corpus."[26] The court explained that the word "person" was purposely left undefined by the legislature to ensure that it did not "change the instances in which the writ was available, which has been determined by the slow process of decisional accretion."[27] The court began its analysis by highlighting the historical fact that animals have never been considered eligible for habeas corpus relief nor have they ever been considered capable of asserting rights for the purposes of state or federal law.[28]

The court acknowledged that because there is a lack of precedent for treating animals as persons for habeas corpus purposes, the writ's "great flexibility and vague scope" necessitates that the issue be considered in full.[29] The court emphasized that unlike human beings, chimpanzees are incapable of bearing legal duties, carrying social responsibility, and being held legally accountable for their actions.[30] In denying the habeas corpus petition for Tommy, the court reasoned that a "person" must have the ability to engage in the "social contract."[31]

Yet even humans who lack the capacity for duties or responsibilities to choose, understand, or make a reasoned decision about medical treatment possess common law autonomy and dignity equal to the competent.[32] For example, infants and the

---

[26] People ex rel. Nonhuman Rights Project, Inc. v. Lavery, 998 N.Y.S.2d 248 (App. Div. 2014), *appeal denied*, 38 N.E.3d 828 (N.Y. 2015); *see generally* N.Y.C.P.L.R. § 7002(a) (McKinney 2018) ("A person illegally imprisoned or otherwise restrained in his liberty within the state, or one acting on his behalf or a party in a child abuse proceeding subsequent to an order of the family court, may petition without notice for a writ of habeas corpus to inquire into the cause of such detention and for deliverance. A judge authorized to issue writs of habeas corpus having evidence, in a judicial proceeding before him, that any person is so detained shall, on his own initiative, issue a writ of habeas corpus for the relief of that person.").

[27] *Tommy*, 998 N.Y.S.2d at 249 (quoting People ex rel. Keitt v. McMann, 220 N.E.2d 653, 655 (N.Y. 1966) (internal quotation omitted).

[28] *Id.* at 249–50. ("Petitioner does not cite any precedent – and there appears to be none – in state law, or under English common law, that an animal could be considered a 'person' for the purposes of common law habeas corpus relief. In fact, habeas corpus relief has never been provided to any nonhuman entity.").

[29] *Id.* at 250 (citation omitted) (internal quotation omitted).

[30] *Id.* at 251. See DANIEL A. DOMBROWSKI, BABIES AND BEASTS: THE ARGUMENT FROM MARGINAL CASES 26 (1997) (citing Tom Regan, *The Moral Basis of Vegetarianism*, 5 CAN. J. PHIL. 191, 193 (1975)).

[31] *Id.* at 250.

[32] *See, e.g.*, *in re* M.B., 846 N.E.2d 794, 797–98 (N.Y. 2006); Rivers v. Katz, 495 N.E.2d 337, 341 (N.Y. 1986) (citing Superintendent of Belchertown State Sch. v. Saikewicz, 370 N.E.2d 417, 425 (Mass. 1977)); *in re* Storar, 420 N.E.2d 64, 72–73 (N.Y. 1981).

mentally ill cannot comprehend that they owe duties or responsibilities, and a comatose person lacks sentience, yet they all have legal rights.[33] Thus, NhRP argued that the ability to acknowledge a legal duty or legal responsibility should not be determinative of entitlement to habeas relief.[34] The First Department's entire response, without providing any justification, was that NhRP "ignores the fact that these are still human beings, members of the human community."[35]

Similarly, NhRP contends that the word "person" is simply a legal term of art and is without merit since inanimate objects, such as corporations, have been deemed legal persons for purposes of the Fourteenth Amendment, and, thus, its property cannot be taxed differently from the property of individuals.[36] The appellate court explained the underlying reasoning was that the corporation's property was just the property of the individual shareholders who owned the corporation and therefore should be protected in the same manner.[37] This reasoning acknowledges that such laws pertain to humans or individuals in a human community. Essentially, it is the capabilities of the human beings who control the corporation that constitute the personhood of the corporation. Without a natural person to make decisions and act on behalf of the corporation, the corporation would not be a legal person at all.[38]

On May 8, 2018, the New York Court of Appeals in *Lavery* denied NhRP's motion for leave to appeal. New York Court of Appeals Judge Eugene M. Fahey issued a concurring opinion in which he lamented that the Court's failure to grapple with the issues the NhRP raised "amounts to a refusal to confront a manifest injustice."[39] Judge Fahey concluded with an affirmation of the animal rights community's concern for the appropriate treatment of animals. "To treat a chimpanzee as if he or she had no right to liberty protected by habeas corpus is to regard the chimpanzee as entirely lacking independent worth, as a mere resource for human use, a thing the value of which consists exclusively in its usefulness to others."[40] Judge Fahey explained that the court should instead consider whether a chimpanzee is an individual with inherent value who has the right to be treated with respect.[41] Judge Fahey concluded his opinion with a noteworthy personal reflection:

---

[33] *Tommy*, 54 N.Y.S.3d at 396.

[34] *Id.* at 396–97.

[35] *Id.* at 396.

[36] *Id.*

[37] *Id.*

[38] *See generally* Lewis A. Kornhauser & W. Bentley MacLeod, *Contracts between Legal Persons*, INST. FOR THE STUD. OF LAB., No. 53525, Dec. 2010, at 4, https://www.econstor.eu/bitstream/10419/51588/1/670033332.pdf (emphasizing the necessity of natural persons for interaction with the legal system: "Legal persons act through natural persons. When the legal person is simply a natural person, both action and identification of which acts are attributable to her is relatively straightforward. Many legal persons, however, are complex; they are constituted by and encompass large numbers of other legal persons, both natural and artificial.").

[39] Nonhuman Rights Project, Inc. *ex rel.* Tommy v. Lavery, 100 N.E.3d 846, 848 (N.Y. 2018).

[40] *Id.*

[41] *Id.*

In the interval since we first denied leave to the Nonhuman Rights Project, I have struggled with whether this was the right decision. Although I concur in the Court's decision to deny leave to appeal now, I continue to question whether the Court was right to deny leave in the first instance. The issue whether a nonhuman animal has a fundamental right to liberty protected by the writ of habeas corpus is profound and far-reaching. It speaks to our relationship with all the life around us. Ultimately, we will not be able to ignore it. While it may be arguable that a chimpanzee is not a "person," there is no doubt that it is not merely a thing.[42]

Shortly after the trial court's dismissal of the *Lavery* case in January 2016, NhRP filed another lawsuit, *Nonhuman Rights Project, Inc. ex rel. Kiko v. Presti*.[43] This case involved a single chimpanzee, Kiko, who was kept in New York State by private owners, Carmen and Christie Presti.[44] Kiko is partially deaf as a result of physical abuse suffered on the set of a Tarzan movie in which he was featured.[45] Carmen and Christie Presti kept him in a cage with a steel chain and padlock around his neck.[46]

In June 2017, the Appellate Division of the Supreme Court of New York, First Department, issued its *Lavery* decision rejecting both the *Lavery* and *Presti* appeals.[47] The reasoning, however, was not based on whether Kiko was a "person" capable of asserting habeas corpus rights, but that NhRP was not seeking Kiko's immediate release.[48] The NhRP sought to have Kiko transferred from his current location, which was alleged to be illegal due to its unsuitable conditions, to a facility selected by The North American Primate Sanctuary Alliance.[49] The court dismissed the NhRP's claim, stating that a habeas corpus claim can only lie where the petitioner is entitled to immediate release from confinement, not a transfer from one confinement to another.[50]

In this case, the NhRP did not seek Kiko's immediate release, nor did it allege that Kiko's continued detention is unlawful, but instead sought to have Kiko placed in a different facility that the NhRP deemed more appropriate.[51] The only appropriate remedy, the court reasoned, would be the immediate release of the chimpanzee – a

---

[42] *Id.* at 849.

[43] 999 N.Y.S.2d 652 (App. Div. 2015).

[44] *Client, Kiko (Chimpanzee): A Former Animal "Actor," Partially Deaf from Past Physical Abuse*, NONHUMAN RTS. PROJECT, https://www.nonhumanrights.org/client-kiko/ (last accessed Jan. 21, 2019).

[45] *Id.* According to the Prestis, "[Kiko] bit an actor and was punished by having two trainers hold him while a third struck him on the head with a blunt instrument" while on the set of *Tarzan in Manhattan*.

[46] *Id.*

[47] Nonhuman Rights Project, Inc. *ex rel.* Tommy v. Lavery, 54 N.Y.S.3d 392, 394 (App. Div. 2017).

[48] *Id.* at 397.

[49] Nonhuman Rights Project, Inc. *ex rel.* Kiko v. Presti, 999 N.Y.S.2d 652, 653 (App. Div. 2015).

[50] *Id.*

[51] *Id.*

result NhRP did not seek.[52] The court concluded that even if it had agreed with the NhRP that Kiko should have been deemed a person, the matter was governed by "the line of cases standing for the proposition that habeas corpus does not lie where a petitioner seeks only to change the conditions of confinement rather than the confinement itself."[53]

The final case in this chimpanzee trilogy, *Nonhuman Rights Project, Inc. ex rel. Hercules and Leo* v. *Stanley*,[54] concerned two young adult chimpanzees, Hercules and Leo, who had been held at Stony Brook University since November 2010.[55] The two were used as research subjects in the study of locomotion of chimpanzees and other primates.[56] The NhRP sought habeas corpus relief for their release and transfer to a sanctuary in Florida.[57] NhRP did not challenge the conditions of their confinement, nor did they allege that Stanley violated any state or federal law.[58] Instead, NhRP offered evidence from a variety of experts who had conducted "in-depth research into the behavior, personality, cognition, intelligence, communication, and language skills of chimpanzees and other nonhuman primates" all of whom attested to the "complex cognitive abilities of chimpanzees."[59] NhRP submitted this evidence to support its assertion that the chimpanzees were being unlawfully detained and denied their basic legal rights to liberty.[60] In denying NhRP's petition for a writ of habeas corpus, the court focused its analysis on the issue of whether chimpanzees can be considered a "person" and whether it was bound by the Third Department's decision in *Lavery*.[61]

The court first acknowledged that the term "legal personhood" is not defined nor is it synonymous with being a human being.[62] The court also noted the increasing recognition of nonhuman animals, specifically pets, as more than just property, if not quite as persons, by courts and legislatures.[63] While the court thoughtfully discussed both primary and secondary sources for and against the extension of legal personhood status for nonhuman animals, it ultimately declined to make its own determination on the issue.[64] The Court denied the petition for a writ of habeas

[52] *Id.*

[53] *Id.* at 654.

[54] 16 N.Y.S.3d 898 (Sup. Ct. 2015).

[55] *Id.* at 900.

[56] *Id.*

[57] *Id.*

[58] *Id.* at 901.

[59] *Id.*

[60] *Id.* at 902.

[61] *Id.* at 911–18.

[62] *Id.* at 911.

[63] *Id.* at 912 ("[P]ets and companion animals are gradually being treated as more than property, if not quite as persons, in part because legislatures and courts recognize the close relationships that exist between people and their pets, who are often viewed and treated by their owners as family members.").

[64] *Id.* at 912–15.

corpus and dismissed the case.[65] Justice Jaffe ultimately affirmed the property status of nonhuman animals, noting that "[t]he past mistreatment of humans" who were once classified as property – "whether slaves, women, indigenous people or others" – does not "serve as a legal predicate or appropriate analogy for extending to nonhumans the status of legal personhood."[66]

The court then analyzed New York's *stare decisis* jurisprudence and found that the Third Department's decision was controlling absent a controlling decision by the Court of Appeals or Appellate Division within its judicial department.[67] Justice Jaffe relied on the "social contract and the common law in determining that chimpanzees are disqualified from receiving the status of legal personhood,"[68] the *Lavery* decision,[69] and *Black's Law Dictionary*'s definition of "person."[70] The court added, in dicta, that even if it were not bound by the Third Department in *Lavery*, the issue of a chimpanzee's right to invoke the writ of habeas corpus is best decided by the Court of Appeals, given its role in setting state policy.[71] While this line of NhRP cases has yet to produce a favorable outcome, Judge Jaffe observed that "[e]fforts to extend legal rights to chimpanzees are ··· understandable; some day they may even succeed."[72] Even though Judge Jaffe ultimately decided not to grant habeas corpus in *Hercules & Leo*, she acknowledged the empathy inspired by chimpanzees' similarities to humans, describing herself as bound by the *Tommy* precedent only "for now."[73]

2 Elephants

Undaunted by the failure to secure the release of its clients in the trilogy of chimpanzee cases, NhRP turned its attention to filing habeas corpus petitions on behalf of elephants in captivity. In *Nonhuman Rights Project, Inc. ex rel Beulah, Minnie & Karen v. R. W. Commerford & Sons, Inc.*, NhRP filed a habeas corpus

---

[65] *Id.* at 918.

[66] *Id.* at 912.

[67] *Id.* at 916–17.

[68] *Id.* at 914.

[69] *Id.* at 916–17; *see also* People *ex rel.* Nonhuman Rights Project, Inc. v. Lavery, 998 N.Y.S.2d 248 (App. Div. 2014), *appeal denied*, 38 N.E.3d 828 (N.Y. 2015) (finding that conferring the status of legal personhood to chimpanzees is inappropriate as they are incapable of bearing any legal responsibilities and societal duties).

[70] "Person" includes "human being," or "natural person," and "[a]n entity (such as a corporation) that is recognized by law as having most of the rights and duties of a human being," also described as an "artificial person." BLACK'S LAW DICTIONARY (10th ed. 2014).

[71] Nonhuman Rights Project, Inc. *ex rel.* Hercules v. Stanley, 16 N.Y.S.3d 898, 917 (Sup. Ct. 2015).

[72] *Id.*

[73] *Id.* at 918. For a compelling discussion of philosophical arguments supporting legal personhood for chimpanzees, which was prepared by several prominent animal rights philosophers in support of this line of NhRP cases, *see generally* CHIMPANZEE RIGHTS: THE PHILOSOPHERS' BRIEF (2019).

petition on behalf of Beulah, Karen, and Minnie, elephants owned by R. W. Commerford & Sons, Inc. a/k/a Commerford Zoo, and William R. Commerford, as president of R. W. Commerford & Sons, Inc.[74] These elephants are forced to give rides at the Commerford Zoo, which also frequently uses them in circuses and fairs.[75] NhRP petitioned for recognition of Beulah's, Karen's, and Minnie's legal personhood and fundamental right to bodily liberty and their release to a sanctuary.[76] The sole issue in this case was whether the court should grant the habeas corpus petition based on the elephants' status as "persons" entitled to liberty and equality for purposes of habeas corpus.[77]

On December 26, 2017, the court denied the petition on the grounds that (1) the petitioner lacked standing, and (2) the petition is wholly frivolous on its face in legal terms.[78] The court began by noting that "a petitioner deemed to be a 'next friend' of a detainee has standing to bring a petition for writ of habeas on the detainee's behalf."[79] Parties seeking recognition as "next friend" must "by the very nature of the proceeding … have no specific personal and legal interest in the matter."[80] Consistent with the US Supreme Court's approach in *Whitmore*,[81] the court cautioned that "not just anyone who expresses an interest in the subject matter of a suit is eligible to be the plaintiff's next friend."[82]

The court then offered this important framework governing next friend standing:

> Decisions applying the habeas corpus statute have adhered to at least two firmly rooted prerequisites for next friend standing. First, a next friend must provide an adequate explanation – such as inaccessibility, mental incompetence, or other disability – why the real party in interest cannot appear on his own behalf to prosecute the action … Second, the next friend must be truly dedicated to the best interests of the person on whose behalf he seeks to litigate … and it has been further suggested that a next friend must have some significant relationship with the real party in interest.[83]

---

[74] No. LLICV175009822S, 2017 Conn. Super. LEXIS 5181 (Super. Ct. Dec. 26, 2017).
[75] *Clients, Beulah, Karen, Minnie (Elephants): Torn from Their Families and Forced to Perform for Humans for Decades*, NONHUMAN RTS. PROJECT, https://www.nonhumanrights.org/clients-beulah-karen-minnie/ (last accessed Jan. 27, 2019) [hereinafter "Nonhuman Rights Project (Beulah, Karen, Minnie)"].
[76] *Beulah*, 2017 Conn. Super. LEXIS 5181, at **1–2.
[77] *Id.* at *1.
[78] *Id.*
[79] *Id.* at *7 (citing State v. Ross, 863 A.2d 654, 655 (2005)).
[80] *Id.*
[81] Whitmore v. Arkansas, 495 U.S. 149, 163–64 (1990). Connecticut courts have not adopted *Whitmore's* second prong or its dicta regarding the need for a "significant relationship."
[82] *Beulah*, at *9 (citing T.W. v. Brophy, 124 F.3d 893, 897 [7th Cir. 1997]).
[83] *Id.* at **7–8 (citing *Ross*, 863 A.2d at 666) (internal quotation omitted).

Judge Bentivegna stated that the main issue in this case was whether the petitioner is "truly dedicated to the best interests of the [elephants] and whether it has some significant relationship with the [elephants]."[84] He ultimately concluded the petitioner "failed to allege that it possesses *any* relationship with the elephants."[85] Thus, the petitioner lacked standing under the first prong, so the court did not need to consider the second prong.[86]

On January 16, 2018, NhRP filed a motion to reargue with the Connecticut Superior Court, asking the court to reverse its dismissal. In this court's memorandum of decision denying the petition, the court concluded that the petitioner lacked standing because it failed to allege that it had a significant relationship with the elephants.[87] The court noted that such failure may be overcome when the confined person has no significant relationships but that the petitioner failed to allege this in its petition as well.[88] Judge Bentivegna explained that NhRP "includes as an exhibit to this motion a blacklined proposed amended petition where it appears as though the original petition alleged that the elephants lacked any significant relationships and provided supporting law."[89] He further stated that the original petition "did not contain any of the language that is crossed out on these pages."[90] NhRP requested leave to amend to address these flaws.[91] The court denied NhRP's motion to reargue and refused to allow NhRP to amend its petition.[92]

Judge Bentivegna explained that "even if the court were to grant the petitioner leave to amend, its proposed amendments do not change the outcome."[93] He continued by stating, "[d]enial of the petition did not rest exclusively on the petitioner's lack of standing, but also on the legal conclusion that the basis for the petition is not a constitutionally protected liberty, which is required in order to issue a writ of habeas corpus."[94] On March 16, 2018, NhRP filed a notice of appeal of both the denial of its petition and the denial of its motion to reargue.[95] A month later, the NhRP filed a Motion for Articulation with the Connecticut Appellate Court, seeking clarification of the legal and factual basis for

---

[84] *Id.* at *11.

[85] *Id.*

[86] *Id.*

[87] Nonhuman Rights Project, Inc. *ex rel.* Beulah. R. W. Commerford & Sons, Inc., No. LLICV175009822S, 2018 Conn. Super. LEXIS 554 (Super. Ct. Feb. 27, 2018).

[88] *Id.* at **2–3.

[89] *Id.* at *4 n.1.

[90] *Id.*

[91] *Id.* at *3.

[92] *Id.* at *1.

[93] *Id.* at *4.

[94] *Id.*

[95] Appeal E-File Confirmation, Nonhuman Rights Project, Inc. *ex rel.* Beulah. R. W. Commerford & Sons, Inc., (Mar. 16, 2018) (No. LLI-CV-17-5009822-S), https://www.nonhumanrights.org/content/uploads/2018-03-16-Appeal-FILED.pdf.

Connecticut Superior Court Judge James Bentivegna's December 26, 2017 and February 27, 2018 decisions.[96]

In *Nonhuman Rights Project, Inc. v. R. W. Commerford & Sons, Inc.*, Judge Bentivegna granted just one of the NhRP's sixteen requests for articulation.[97] It addressed only the request to clarify the basis of its determination that the petition is wholly frivolous on its face in legal terms.[98] The court found the nonbinding legal authority in judicial decisions outside the US and the nonlegal authority that the petitioner cited to be unpersuasive.[99] The court concluded that "the NhRP was unable to point to any authority demonstrating a possibility or probability of victory for its theory that an elephant is a legal person for the purpose of issuing a writ of habeas corpus."[100] The court reasoned that "the NhRP failed to show that the issues presented are debatable among jurists of reason, that a court could resolve the issues in a different manner, or that the questions presented are adequate to deserve encouragement to proceed further and failed to show that the petition merits a legal victory."[101]

In a second habeas corpus petition proceeding on behalf of an elephant, NhRP sought to protect Happy, a forty-seven-year-old Asian elephant, who was captured as a calf in the 1970s along with six others.[102] In 1977, she was sold to the Bronx Zoo

---

[96] Motion for Articulation, Nonhuman Rights Project, Inc. *ex rel.* Beulah. R. W. Commerford & Sons, Inc., (Apr. 18, 2018) (No. LLI-CV-17-5009822-S), https://www.nonhumanrights.org/content/uploads/2018-04-18-Motion-for-Articulation.pdf.

[97] *Beulah*, 2018 Conn. Super. LEXIS 1065, at *1.

[98] *Id.* at *2.

[99] *Id.* at *4; *see also NhRP to Seek Review of Connecticut Superior Court Decision in Elephant Rights Case*, NONHUMAN RTS. PROJECT (May 31, 2018), https://www.nonhumanrights.org/blog/decision-on-motion-for-articulation ("The judge dismissed the relevance of nonhuman rights cases from outside Connecticut that demonstrate the willingness of other judges to address the novel and important legal questions that NhRP and others are putting before the courts. These cases include the well-known cases of chimpanzees Hercules and Leo in New York and chimpanzee Cecilia in Argentina, the latter of whom was recognized in 2016 as a 'non-human legal person' with 'inherent rights' and transferred to a sanctuary").

[100] *Id.*

[101] *Id.* On June 11, 2018, the NhRP filed a second habeas corpus petition in Tolland County because of that court's extensive experience and expertise with habeas corpus petitions. *Nonhuman Rights Project (Beulah, Karen, Minnie)*, supra note 75. On Sept. 25, 2018, NhRP filed a brief in the Appellate Court of Connecticut, seeking review of the lower court's dismissal of its first petition. Id.; *see also Brief for Plaintiff-Appellant*, Nonhuman Rights Project, Inc. *ex rel.* Beulah. R. W. Commerford & Sons, Inc., (Sept. 24, 2018) (No. AC41464), https://www.nonhumanrights.org/content/uploads/2018-09-24-Brief.pdf. In its appellate brief, NhRP argued: (1) the trial court erred in dismissing the habeas petition on the ground that plaintiff lacked standing, (2) in deciding plaintiff lacked standing, the trial court erred in denying plaintiff's motion to amend the petition to add the allegation that the plaintiff either had a significant relationship with the elephants or that the elephants had no significant relationships, and (3) the trial court erred in dismissing the habeas petition on the alternative ground that it was "wholly frivolous." *Id.*

[102] *Client, Happy (Elephant): First Elephant to Pass Mirror Self-Recognition Test; Held Alone at the Bronx Zoo*, NONHUMAN RTS. PROJECT, https://www.nonhumanrights.org/client-happy/ (last accessed Jan. 7, 2019).

where she was displayed as part of an Asia exhibit.[103] Happy was forced to give rides to guests, participate in tug-of-war contests, and perform other tricks.[104] In 2005, Happy became the first elephant to pass the mirror self-recognition test, meaning that she exhibited a level of self-awareness.[105] Other highly complex animals such as great apes and dolphins have also demonstrated this ability to distinguish themselves from others.[106] After both of Happy's elephant companions were euthanized (for health complications), she became the sole occupant of her 1.15-acre exhibit.[107] It is considered inhumane to have an exhibit with a single elephant because they are highly social creatures.[108]

On October 2, 2018, NhRP announced that it would file a petition for a writ of habeas corpus demanding recognition of both Happy's legal personhood and her fundamental right to bodily liberty, and requesting her immediate transfer to an animal sanctuary.[109] In the petition, NhRP opens with a statement from the Honorable Eugene Fahey, hinting at regret in denying Tommy (chimpanzee) a writ of habeas corpus.[110] The last sentence reads, "[w]hile it may be arguable that a chimpanzee is not a 'person,' there is no doubt that it is not merely a thing."[111] The petition then states that Happy, "The Bronx Zoo's Loneliest Elephant," as recognized by the *New York Times*, is being unlawfully imprisoned at the Bronx Zoo.[112] NhRP argues that autonomous nonhuman animals like Happy should have the "right to liberty protected by Habeas Corpus."[113]

The issue in this case is whether Happy, an "extraordinarily cognitively complex and autonomous nonhuman being," should be recognized as a legal person with the right to bodily liberty.[114] Specifically, the petition requests that the Court:

---

[103] *Id.*

[104] *Id.*

[105] *Id.*

[106] *Elephants Have a Concept of Self, Study Suggests*, NAT'L PUBLIC RADIO (Oct. 31, 2006), https://www.npr.org/templates/story/story.php?storyId=6412620.

[107] NONHUMAN RTS. PROJECT, *supra* note 102.

[108] *Id.*

[109] *Id.*

[110] *Petition for Writ of Habeas Corpus and Order to Show Cause*, Nonhuman Rights Project, Inc. *ex rel.* Happy v. Breheny, 1 (Oct. 2, 2018), https://www.nonhumanrights.org/content/uploads/Happy-Petition-10.1.18.pdf [hereinafter "Petition for Happy"].

[111] *Id.* (citing Nonhuman Rights Project, Inc. *ex rel.* Tommy v. Lavery, 100 N.E.3d 846, 849 [N.Y. 2018] [Fahey, J., concurring]).

[112] *Id.* at 2 (citing Tracy Tullis, *The Bronx Zoo's Loneliest Elephant*, N.Y. TIMES (June 26, 2015), https://www.nytimes.com/2015/06/28/nyregion/the-bronx-zoos-loneliest-elephant.html).

[113] *Id.* (citing *Tommy*, 100 N.E.3d at 847). NhRP supports its position by analogy in arguing that all human beings in New York should be granted habeas corpus protection regardless of whether they have the ability to choose, understand, or make reasoned decisions. *See* Id. at 8; *see also Tommy*, 100 N.E.3d at 847 ("[N]o one would suppose that it is improper to seek a writ of habeas corpus on behalf of one's infant child … or a parent suffering from dementia") (Fahey, J., concurring) (citations omitted).

[114] *Petition for Happy*, *supra* note 110, at 35.

a) issue the requested Order to Show Cause requiring Respondents to justify their imprisonment of Happy; b) after the return, determine that Happy possesses the common law right to bodily liberty, thereby rendering unlawful Respondents' imprisonment and deprivation of that bodily liberty; c) order Happy's immediate release from Respondents' unlawful imprisonment; and d) decide where Happy should thereafter be placed, which NhRP suggests is the Performing Animal Welfare Society ("PAWS") near Sacramento, California.[115]

The term "person" is not exclusively reserved for human beings.[116] The current and historical recognition of animals is as "rightless legal things."[117] However, the New York Supreme Court Appellate Division, Fourth Department, recently held in *People* v. *Graves* that "it is common knowledge that personhood can and sometimes does attach to nonhuman entities like ... animals."[118] The court further stated that "personhood is 'not a question of biological or natural' correspondence."[119] NhRP also attached expert scientific affidavits to the petition. The report by Joyce Poole provides:

> Elephants have evolved to move. Holding them captive and confined prevents them from engaging in normal, autonomous behavior and can result in the development of arthritis, osteoarthritis, osteomyelitis, boredom and stereotypical behavior. Held in isolation elephants become bored, depressed, aggressive, catatonic and fail to thrive. Human caregivers are no substitute for the numerous, complex social relationships and the rich gestural and vocal communication exchanges that occur between free-living elephants.[120]

NhRP asserts that writs of habeas corpus have been granted to animals in Argentina, India, and Colombia,[121] and were also issued to human slaves before they were considered legal "persons."[122] According to a joint affidavit by Lucy Bates and Richard Byrne, "African and Asian elephants share numerous complex cognitive abilities with humans, such as self-awareness, empathy, awareness of death, intentional communication, learning, memory, and categorization abilities."[123] The affidavit also explains how elephants have the largest brain of any land mammal and unpacks the scientific implications of this trait, such as their heightened cognitive abilities, long-lasting memory, and emotional complexities.[124]

---

[115] *Id.* at 4.

[116] *See* People v. Graves, 78 N.Y.S.3d 613, 617 (App. Div. 2018).

[117] *Petition for Happy, supra* note 110, at 5.

[118] *Graves,* 78 N.Y.S.3d at 617.

[119] *Id.* (quoting Byrn v. New York City Health & Hospitals Corp., 286 N.E.2d 887, 889 (N.Y. 1972).

[120] *Petition for Happy, supra* note 110, at 7.

[121] *Id.* at 10–11.

[122] *Id.* at 11.

[123] *Id.* at 27 (citing the supplemental joint affidavit of Lucy Bates, PhD and Richard Byrne, PhD, and the supplemental affidavits of Karen McComb, PhD, Joyce Poole, PhD, and Cynthia Moss; all are considered experts on the cognitive abilities of elephants).

[124] *Id.* at 27–47.

The NhRP argues that it has standing to file the petition on behalf of Happy. Pursuant to CPLR section 7002(a), a petition may be brought by "one acting on . . . behalf" of "[a] person illegally imprisoned or otherwise restrained in his liberty within the state."[125]

In an unprecedented development, on November 16, 2018, the Honorable Tracey A. Bannister of the New York Supreme Court, Orleans County issued an Order to Show Cause.[126] Judge Bannister set December 14, 2018, as the date for oral arguments to determine whether Happy should be released.[127] If the judge orders that Happy should be removed from the Bronx Zoo, she will become the first nonhuman granted personhood in the United States.[128] As of this writing, Happy's case has been transferred to Bronx County.[129]

C Monkey See, Monkey Sues for Selfie Copyright Infringement

"A monkey, an animal-rights organization and a primatologist walk into federal court to sue for infringement of the monkey's claimed copyright."[130] This section addresses the case of *Naruto v. Slater*.[131] In 2011, British photographer David Slater traveled to an Indonesian forest where he spent three days photographing a troop of crested black macaques.[132] During one of his photoshoots, Slater set up his camera on its tripod for the monkeys' use, and a number of photographs were taken by a macaque named Naruto.[133] The series of pictures Naruto took of himself were

---

[125] *Id.* at 15–16.
[126] Lauren Choplin, *World's First Habeas Corpus Order Issued on Behalf of an Elephant*, NONHU-MAN RTS. BLOG (Nov. 19, 2018), https://www.nonhumanrights.org/blog/first-habeas-corpus-order-happy/; *see also Order to Show Cause*, NONHUMAN RTS. BLOG (Nov. 16, 2018), https://www.nonhumanrights.org/content/uploads/Order-to-Show-Cause-Happy.pdf.
[127] Choplin, *supra* note 126.
[128] Andrea Morris, *Judge to Rule on Historic Case of Whether an Elephant Is a Person*, FORBES (Nov. 19, 2018), https://www.forbes.com/sites/andreamorris/2018/11/19/judge-grants-historic-case-on-whether-an-elephant-is-a-person/.
[129] Lauren Choplin, *Nonhuman Rights Project Argues for Elephant Personhood, Rights in New York Supreme Court*, NONHUMAN RTS. BLOG (Dec. 14, 2018), https://www.nonhumanrights.org/blog/happy-habeas-hearing-albion/; *Client, Happy (Elephant): First Elephant to Pass Mirror Self-Recognition Test; Held Alone at the Bronx Zoo*, client profile, NONHUMAN RTS. PROJECT, https://www.nonhumanrights.org/client-happy/.
[130] Mike McPhate, *Monkey Has No Rights to Its Selfie, Federal Judge Says*, N.Y. TIMES (Jan. 8, 2016), https://www.nytimes.com/2016/01/09/business/media/monkey-has-no-rights-to-its-selfie-federal-judge-says.html (quoting some of the mocking language in the motion to dismiss from the lawyers for the photographer in this case).
[131] No. 15-cv-04324-WHO, 2016 U.S. Dist. LEXIS 11041 (N.D. Cal. Jan. 28, 106), *aff'd*, 888 F.3d 418 (9th Cir. 2018).
[132] Louise Stewart, *Wikimedia Says When a Monkey Takes a Selfie, No One Owns It*, NEWSWEEK (Aug. 21, 2014), https://www.newsweek.com/lawyers-dispute-wikimedias-claims-about-monkey-selfie-copyright-265961 (last accessed Jan. 7, 2019).
[133] *Id.*

published by Slater.[134] The self-portraits have since been referred to as the first ever "monkey selfies."[135] The photos went viral and caused Slater to face two legal battles over the monkey selfies. The first, and still ongoing, battle is for the photographer's own copyright of the photo against Wikimedia.[136] The second is a case brought by Naruto against Slater. For purposes of this discussion, only the latter is relevant.

PETA brought a claim in the US District Court for the Northern District of California on behalf of Naruto against Slater for copyright infringement. PETA claimed that as the author of the works in question, Naruto owned the copyright to the images and that all proceeds gained from their use, therefore, belonged to him, and should be used for the preservation of his species and their habitat.[137] PETA relied on "next friend" status to represent Naruto's interests in this case.[138] The case was dismissed by the Northern District of California as unsupported by precedent.[139] The court also held that "animals like Naruto" lack standing under the federal Copyright Act.[140]

US District Judge William Orrick explained that although the Copyright Act[141] does not define "works of authorship" nor "author," the Act does not "plainly" extend the concept of authorship or statutory standing to animals.[142] The court further noted that "there is no mention of animals anywhere in the Act. The Supreme Court and Ninth Circuit have repeatedly referred to 'persons' or 'human beings' when analyzing authorship under the Act."[143] The court could not find a "single case that expands the definition of authors to include animals."[144]

After oral arguments before the Ninth Circuit in September 2017, the parties agreed to a settlement that provided that "25 percent of any proceeds from Slater's sale of the photos would be donated to charities working to protect the dwindling habitat of crested macaques in Indonesia."[145] In addition, both parties sought to have

---

[134] *Id.*

[135] *Id.*

[136] *Id.*

[137] *Naruto*, 2016 U.S. Dist. LEXIS 11041, at *4.

[138] Nicole Pallotta, *En Banc Review Requested in "Monkey Selfie" Copyright Case*, ANIMAL LEGAL DEFENSE FUND ANIMAL L. UPDATE (Aug. 7, 2018), https://aldf.org/article/en-banc-review-requested-in-monkey-selfie-copyright-case/ (last accessed Jan. 7, 2019).

[139] *See Naruto*, 2016 U.S. Dist. LEXIS 11041.

[140] *Id.* at *2.

[141] The Copyright Act protects "original works of authorship fixed in any tangible medium of expression, now known or later developed, from which they can be perceived, reproduced, or otherwise communicated, either directly or with the aid of a machine or device." 17 U.S.C. § 102(a) (2018). The "fixing" of the work in the tangible medium of expression must be done "by or under the authority of the author." 17 U.S.C. § 101 (2018).

[142] *Naruto*, 2016 U.S. Dist. LEXIS 11041, at **7–8.

[143] *Id.* at *8.

[144] *Id.* at *9.

[145] Pallotta, *supra* note 138.

the appeal dismissed, and the District Court decision vacated.[146] The Ninth Circuit denied both components of that joint motion.[147]

On April 23, 2018, a three-judge panel for the Ninth Circuit Court of Appeals issued a ruling that Naruto's claim had Article III standing under the US Constitution but that he ("and all animals, since they are not human") lacked statutory standing under the federal Copyright Act.[148] The Ninth Circuit based Naruto's Article III standing on *Cetacean Community* v. *Bush*,[149] where it held that a group of cetaceans could demonstrate Article III standing. The Ninth Circuit panel acknowledged *Cetacean Community* as binding precedent but made clear that it believed the case was incorrectly decided.[150]

In an interesting twist, on May 25, 2018, the monkey selfie case swung back into action when a Ninth Circuit judge sought a vote to determine whether en banc review of the District Court's decision would be appropriate.[151] The court requested briefs on whether the appeal should be reheard en banc.[152] However, on August 31, 2018, the Ninth Circuit denied en banc review.[153]

D A Horse with a Name: Seeking Justice for "Justice"

On May 1, 2018, the Animal Legal Defense Fund (ALDF) brought a claim on behalf of an abused horse named Justice against his former owner, Gwendolyn Vercher, who previously pled guilty to misdemeanor animal neglect.[154] Justice is an eight-year-old horse who suffered "extreme pain, distress, and permanent injury due to the criminal neglect of Vercher."[155] The complaint further alleged:

[146] Naruto v. Slater, No. 16-15469, 2018 U.S. App. LEXIS 9477 (9th Cir. Apr. 13, 2018).

[147] *Id.* The Ninth Circuit noted in its latest order that the court does not have to dismiss a case when all of the parties agree to dismiss it. The order lists a number of reasons not to dismiss the case, and also notes that because PETA made a point of stating in its motion to dismiss that "Naruto is not a party to the settlement agreement," the settlement agreement would not bar "attempt[s]" at filing an action on Naruto's behalf in the future.)

[148] Naruto v. Slater, 888 F.3d 418 (9th Cir. 2018).

[149] 386 F.3d 1169, 1171–72 (9th Cir. 2004).

[150] *Naruto*, 888 F.3d at 425, n.7 ("While we believe *Cetacean* was incorrectly decided, it is binding circuit precedent that nonhuman animals enjoy constitutional standing to pursue claims in federal court.").

[151] Naruto v. Slater, No. 16-15469, 2018 U.S. App. LEXIS 24925 (9th Cir. Aug. 31, 2018); Pallotta, *supra* note 138.

[152] *Naruto*, 2018 U.S. App. LEXIS 24925, at **1–2.

[153] *Id.*

[154] In the case brought by Justice's caretakers, Vercher pled guilty to first degree animal neglect on July 2017. She received no jail time but agreed to pay restitution. Vercher is only obligated to pay the caretakers the cost of Justice's care prior to her July 6, 2017 conviction. She was ordered to pay about $3,700 in past expenses for the equine. Aimee Green, *Groundbreaking Case of Horse Suing Ex-owner for Abuse Now in Judge's Hands*, OREGONIAN (Sept. 14, 2018), https://www.oregonlive.com/washingtoncounty/index.ssf/2018/09/udge_ponders_landmark_decision.html.

[155] Complaint – Personal Injury (Negligence Per Se), *supra* note 11, at 1.

Vercher denied Justice food and shelter for months, abandoning him to starve and freeze.[156] As a result of this neglect, Justice was left debilitated and emaciated.[157] He continues to suffer from this neglect, including a prolapsed penis from frostbite as a result of his exposure to the cold that was left untreated for months.[158] These injuries will require special and expensive medical care for the remainder of his life.[159]

Justice brought a negligence per se[160] claim based on Oregon's anti-cruelty statute.[161] This claim integrated two longstanding criminal law principles: "first, that animals are properly considered the victims of animal cruelty crimes and second, that victims of crimes have a right to sue their abusers in civil court for damages for injuries caused by the defendant."[162] Oregon law recognizes sentient beings as victims of a crime.[163] The argument is that Justice, although not a person, has a right to legal personhood. Legal "personhood" does not require one to be human. For example, corporations, ships, and rivers in India and New Zealand have been granted legal personhood.[164] Similar to legal personhood protection for these entities, assigning legal personhood to animals would merely require that someone be appointed to advocate for their interests and to vindicate the rights the law recognizes for the animals, which may mean a minimum standard of care and protection in this instance.[165]

Unfortunately, on September 17, 2018, the Oregon court dismissed Justice's case for lack of standing. The court offered the following reasoning:

> The court finds that a non-human animal such as Justice lacks the legal status or qualifications necessary for the assertion of legal rights and duties in a court of

---

[156] *Id.*

[157] *Id.* On March 16, 2017, a medical examination of Justice revealed that he was lethargic, had significant difficulty walking, and was three hundred pounds underweight. He had a Henneke horse body condition score (BCS) of 1 out of 9. A healthy horse has a BCS between 4 and 6. *See* Complaint – Personal Injury (Negligence Per Se), *supra* note 11, at 1.

[158] ALDF's Director of Litigation, Matthew Liebman, stated that Vercher had no poverty or mental health issues, and that he does not know why she treated her horse this way. Mariann Sullivan, *Animal Law Podcast #40: The Case of Justice for Justice*, OUR HEN HOUSE (Sept. 27, 2018), https://www.ourhenhouse.org/2018/09/animal-law-podcast-40-the-case-of-justice-for-justice/.

[159] The lawsuit seeks damages for Justice's care from the July 2017 restitution cutoff date. Damages awarded from the lawsuit will be placed in a trust account for Justice's future care. *Justice the Horse Sues Abuser*, ANIMAL LEGAL DEF. FUND https://aldf.org/case/justice-the-horse-sues-abuser/ (last accessed Jan. 26, 2019).

[160] Negligence per se requires four elements: (1) was there a statute that defendant violated; (2) did violation of that statute cause plaintiff's injuries; (3) is the plaintiff a member of the class of persons for whose benefit the legislature enacted the statute; and (4) is the plaintiff's injury within the class of injuries that the legislature intended to prevent in passing that statute. *See* Buoy v. Soo Hee Kim, 221 P.3d 771, 779 (Or. Ct. App. 2008).

[161] Complaint – Personal Injury (Negligence Per Se), *supra* note 11.

[162] Nicole Pallotta, *Advocating for Justice in Oregon: Neglected Horse Sues Former Owner*, ANIMAL LEGAL DEF. FUND ANIMAL L. UPDATE (Sept. 13, 2018), https://aldf.org/article/advocating-for-justice-in-oregon-neglected-horse-sues-former-owner/.

[163] *See* Or. Rev. Stat. §§ 167.305, 167.325(1).

[164] Pallotta, *supra* note 162.

[165] *Id.*

law . . . . There are profound implications of a judicial finding that a horse, or any non-human animal for that matter, is a legal entity that has the legal right to assert a claim in a court of law . . . . Perhaps an appellate court would come to a different conclusion if it wades into this public policy debate involving the evolution of animal rights . . . . This court, however, is unable to take that leap.[166]

Thanks to the persistence of the attorneys working on this case, Justice is not a "one trick pony." As of this writing, attorneys for ALDF are appealing the matter.[167]

II FOREIGN DOMESTIC JUDICIAL DEVELOPMENTS

Although NhRP has provided assistance to other groups around the world, as of this writing, the organization has not filed any cases outside of the United States. Nevertheless, several animal protection organizations outside the US have made progress in actions that seek legal personhood protection for wildlife.

A *Argentina: Cecilia the Chimpanzee*

Cecilia the chimpanzee is a widely reported case due to her landmark judicial release from a zoo in Argentina on November 3, 2016, through a habeas corpus proceeding.[168] For the past several years, Cecilia was without a companion following the deaths of the two chimps who once shared the small space with her.[169] The barren confines in which she lived, as well as the psychological toll taken by her solitude, drove her into a deep depression.[170] The Association of Professional Lawyers for Animal Rights (AFADA) filed the case of Cecilia the chimpanzee to the court in Mendoza, arguing her confinement without companionship was

---

[166] *Id.*

[167] *Id.* For a helpful discussion of Justice's case in the broader context of recent developments in animal rights litigation discussed in this chapter, *see* Karen Brulliard, *Seeking Justice for Justice the Horse: Can a Neglected Animal Sue?*, WASH. POST (Aug. 13, 2018), https://www.washingtonpost .com/news/national/wp/2018/08/13/feature/a-horse-was-neglected-by-its-owner-now-the-horse- is-suing.

[168] Presentacion Efectuada Por A.F.A.D.A. Respecto del Chimpace "Cecilia" Sujeto No Humano, File No. P-72.254/15 (Tercer Juzgado de Garantias Poder Judicial Medoza (Nov. 3, 2016), https:// www.nonhumanrights.org/content/uploads/2016/12/Sentencia-de-Habeas-Corpus-de-Cecilia .pdf [hereinafter "Cecilia Decision in Spanish"]. For the English translation, *see* https://www .nonhumanrights.org/content/uploads/2016/12/Chimpanzee-Cecilia_translation-FINAL-for-web site.pdf [hereinafter "Cecilia Case (English Translation)"]; *see also* Gabriel Samuels, *Chimpanzees Have Rights, Says Argentine Judge as She Orders Cecilia Be Released from Zoo*, INDEPENDENT (Nov. 7, 2016), http://www.independent.co.uk/news/ world/americas/argentina-judge-says-chim panzee-poor-conditions-has-rights-and-should-be- freed-from-zoo-a7402606.html.

[169] AFP, *Love Beckons for Recovering Monkey in Chimp Refuge*, TIMES LIVE (Aug. 22, 2017), https://www.timeslive.co.za/news/sci-tech/2017-08-22-love-beckons-for-recovering-monkey-in- chimp-refuge/.

[170] *Id.*

"unlawful" and had a detrimental impact on her health.[171] A judge in Argentina, in the absence of applicable legislation, granted a writ of habeas corpus to the chimpanzee held in captivity, ordering that it be released.[172] Judge Mauricio explained:

> [We] [] recogniz[e] and confirm[] that primates are non-human legal persons and they possess fundamental rights . . . . This is not about granting them the same rights humans have, it is about accepting and understanding once and for all that they are living sentient beings, with legal personhood and that among other rights; they are assisted by the fundamental right to be born, to live, grow and die in the proper environment for their species.[173]

Cecilia was declared a "non-human legal person" with "inherent rights" and transferred to the Sorocaba Sanctuary in the Republic of Brazil.[174] Although Cecilia's successful Argentina case was modeled after NhRP's habeas petitions,[175] the United States has yet to replicate a result in which a nonhuman animal is entitled to release from confinement through the writ of habeas corpus.

B Colombia: Chucho the Bear

Chucho, a twenty-two-year-old spectacled bear born and raised in semi-captivity,[176] lived for eighteen years in a natural reserve in Manizales, Colombia with his female companion, Clama.[177] After Clama died, Chucho became depressed, made attempts to escape from his enclosure, and "started to deteriorate from malnutrition and a lack of both a suitable habitat and contact with animals of his own species."[178] As a result, the environmental authorities thought that it would be in Chucho's best

---

[171] Samuels, *supra* note 168.

[172] *Cecilia Case (English Translation)*, *supra* note 168, at 32.

[173] *Id.* at 26–27.

[174] Nicole Pallotta, *Though Denied by New York Court of Appeals, Habeas Corpus Claim for Chimpanzees Prompts Reflection*, ANIMAL LEGAL DEF. FUND ANIMAL L. UPDATE (Sept. 7, 2018), https://aldf.org/article/though-denied-by-new-york-court-of-appeals-habeas-corpus-claim-for-chimpanzees-prompts-reflection/; *see also* Lauren Choplin, *Chimpanzee Cecilia Finds Sanctuary: An Interview with GAP Brazil*, NONHUMAN RTS. BLOG (Apr. 20, 2017), https://www.nonhumanrights.org/blog/chimpanzee-cecilia/.

[175] *See* Shirley Shtiegman, *Building an International Nonhuman Rights Movement*, NONHUMAN RTS. BLOG (July 5, 2017), https://www.nonhumanrights.org/blog/international-work/.

[176] MICH. ST. U.: ANIMAL LEGAL & HIST. CTR., https://www.animallaw.info/case/decision-ahc4806−2017 (last accessed Jan. 27, 2019). For the original version of the ruling in Spanish, *see* http://static.iris.net.co/semana/upload/documents/radicado-n-17001-22-13-000-2017-00468-02.pdf; for the translated version in English, *see* https://www.nonhumanrights.org/content/uploads/Translation-Chucho-Decision-Translation-Javier-Salcedo.pdf [hereinafter "Chucho Decision (English Translation)"].

[177] *Id.*

[178] Carmen Mandel, *Chucho, the Spectacled Bear, Triumphs in the Supreme Court of Justice*, SEMANA (July 30, 2019), https://www.nonhumanrights.org/content/uploads/Chucho-Semana-news-translation-Carmen-Mandel.pdf.

interest to relocate him to a zoo in northern Colombia.[179] However, Chucho's living conditions were diminished as he went from living in semi-captivity to living in a smaller area.[180]

On July 13, 2017, attorney and law professor at the Universidad Manuela Beltrán, Luis Domingo Maldonado, filed a habeas corpus petition on behalf of the bear that the Civil Chamber of the Superior Tribunal of Manizales denied.[181] The court determined that "both custodianship and habeas corpus are mechanisms inherent to human beings; therefore, they cannot protect an animal on behalf of whom administrative or popular actions are requested."[182] Citing precedents from Brazil and Argentina involving an orangutan and a chimpanzee, respectively, who were granted habeas corpus, Attorney Maldonado requested that the court order Chucho be released to La Planada, a nature reserve located in the Department of Nariño.[183]

On July 26, 2017, the Supreme Court of Justice ruled in favor of Chucho, granting him the habeas corpus petition after the bear's attorney challenged the lower court's decision denying it.[184] The Court reversed the decision and ordered that Chucho be relocated from the zoo in Barranquilla to a location comparable to the semi-captivity conditions in which he was originally located.[185] The Court reasoned that "animals are entitled to rights as sentient beings, not as humans, and that the idea is to insert a morality of respect to counter a global ecological public order where the tendency of men is to destroy the habitat."[186]

The court concluded that "it is necessary to modify the concept of 'subject of rights' in relation with nature, understanding that who is the subject of rights is not necessarily correlatively bound to have duties ... If fictitious legal entities [such as corporations] are subjects of rights ... for what reason should those who are alive or are 'sentient beings' not be so?"[187]

Unfortunately, in August 2017, the Colombian Supreme Court reversed the decision. The Court held that "the writ of habeas corpus is inappropriate in the present case, because it was designed for persons, rational animals, not for nonhuman or irrational Animals, and the foundations of such a decision [i.e., granting a writ of habeas corpus to Chucho] are incompatible with the purpose

---

[179] MICH. ST. U.: ANIMAL LEGAL & HIST. CTR, *supra* note 176.
[180] *Id.*
[181] *Chucho Decision (English Translation), supra* note 176, at 1. Attorney Maldonado argued that Chucho's living conditions in the zoo violated his fundamental rights of mental and physical well-being. *See* Laura Choplin, *Nonhuman Rights in Colombia: An Interview with Luis Gomez Domingo Maldonado,* NONHUMAN RTS. BLOG (Nov. 10, 2017), https://www.nonhumanrights .org/blog/nonhuman-rights-colombia-interview/.
[182] Mandel, *supra* note 178.
[183] *Id.*
[184] *Id.* at 17.
[185] *Id.*
[186] MICH. ST. U.: ANIMAL LEGAL & HIST. CTR, *supra* note 176; *see also Chucho Decision (English Translation), supra* note 176, at 7.
[187] *Chucho Decision (English translation), supra* note 176, at 6.

for which the writ was created."[188] Attorney Maldonado is currently appealing this decision.[189] Regardless of the reversal, the granting of a habeas corpus writ for a bear is no small feat and shows a shift in the way many people, including judges, are viewing animals and their rights to bodily integrity.

C India: Groundbreaking Legal Personhood Developments for Wildlife

The question of legal personhood received worldwide attention in 2013 when India seemingly attributed legal personhood to dolphins.[190] In response to activism against the cruelty of dolphin shows in India, the Indian Central Animal Authority stated that dolphins should be "seen as 'nonhuman persons' and as such should have their own specific rights."[191] Policymakers were motivated by the cruel and harsh conditions in which dolphins were kept. That evidence, in conjunction with scientific research to support the dolphins' high level of emotional and practical intelligence,[192] prompted activists and legislators to seek a way to protect dolphins. Legal personhood is the ultimate protection.

However, dolphins were never officially declared as persons.[193] In a policy statement, the minister of India's Ministry of Environment and Forests indicated that dolphins should be *seen* as "non-human persons,"[194] which falls short of a formal legal declaration of dolphins as persons.[195] Being *seen* as "non-human persons" is far different from *possessing* the rights and protections of a non-human person.

Nevertheless, India banned the use of dolphins in aquatic theme parks, advising state governments to reject any proposal to establish a dolphinarium "by any person/persons, organizations, government agencies, private or public enterprises that involves import, capture of cetacean species to establish for commercial

---

[188] Choplin, *supra* note 181.

[189] *Id.*

[190] *See, e.g.,* Timothy Bancroft-Hinchey, *India: Dolphins Declared Non-Human Persons,* PRAVDA (Aug. 5, 2013), http://english.pravda.ru/science/earth/05-08-2013/125310-dolphins-india-0/.

[191] Laura Bridgeman, *What India's Decision to Ban Dolphin Captivity Means,* EARTH ISLAND J. (June 12, 2013), http://www.earthisland.org/journal/index.php/articles/entry/what_indias_decision_to_ban_dolphin_captivity_means.

[192] *See* MINISTRY OF ENVIRONMENT, FOREST & CLIMATE CHANGE: GOV'T OF INDIA (May 17, 2013), http://www.moef.nic.in/assets/ban%20on%20dolphanariums.pdf ("[V]arious scientists who have researched dolphin behavior have suggested that the unusually high intelligence . . . means that dolphin should be seen as 'non-human persons' and as such should have their own specific rights and is morally unacceptable to keep them captive for entertainment purpose.").

[193] George Dvorsky, *No, India Did Not Just Grant Dolphins the Status of Humans,* GIZMODO I09 (Aug. 15, 2013), https://i09.gizmodo.com/no-india-did-not-just-grant-dolphins-the-status-of-hum-1149482273.

[194] *India Bans Captive Dolphin Shows as "Morally Unacceptable,"* ENVTL. NEWS SERV. (May 20, 2013), http://ens-newswire.com/2013/05/20/india-bans-captive-dolphin-shows-as-morally-unacceptable/.

[195] Alexis Dyschkant, Note, *Legal Personhood: How We Are Getting It Wrong,* 2015 U. ILL. L. REV. 2075, 2100 (2015).

entertainment, private or public exhibition and interaction purposes whatsoever."[196] India is also the fourth country in the world to ban the capture and import of cetaceans for the purpose of commercial entertainment, joining Costa Rica, Hungary, and Chile.[197]

On July 4, 2018, in *Bhatt* v. *Union of India & Others*,[198] the Uttarakhand High Court effectively conferred legal personhood in its judgment in the case to "the entire animal kingdom including avian and aquatic," with the citizens in the State of Uttarakhand being declared "persons in loco parentis as the human face for the welfare/protection of animals."[199] The Court noted that "the freedoms of animals included the freedom from hunger, fear and distress, physical and thermal discomfort, freedom from pain and injury and freedom to express normal behavior patterns, all of which must be read into the Prevention of Cruelty to Animals Act."[200] In its decision, the court referenced Justice Douglas's dissenting opinion in *Sierra Club* v. *Morton*,[201] noting that "animals including avian and aquatics have a right to life and bodily integrity, honor and dignity. Animals cannot be treated merely as property."[202]

---

[196] *Id.*

[197] Saroja Coelho, *Dolphins Gain Unprecedented Protection in India*, DEUTSCHE WELLE (May 24, 2013), https://www.dw.com/en/dolphins-gain-unprecedented-protection-in-india/a-16834519 (last accessed Nov. 3, 2018).

[198] Writ Petition (PIL) No. 43 of 2014, Bhatt v. Union of India (Apr. 7, 2018), https://drive.google .com/file/d/1wIdRJoQybhoGfP8YVeJFSKroaHUzQuDs/view.

[199] *Id.* at 50; Mrinalini Shinde, *Here's the Problem with Declaring Animals as Legal Beings in India*, QUINT (July 11, 2018), https://www.thequint.com/voices/opinion/uttarakhand-high-court-declares-animals-legal-beings-questions.

[200] Shinde, *supra* note 199. *See also Terrestrial Animal Health Code*, WORLD ORG. FOR ANIMAL HEALTH, 289 (2011), https://www.oie.int/doc/ged/D10905.pdf (outlining the guiding principles for animal welfare under Article 7.1.2, including the "internationally recognized 'five freedoms'," and how those freedoms provide guidance on the "critical relationship between animal health and *animal welfare*.").

[201] 405 U.S. 727 (1972).

[202] *Bhatt*, Writ Petition (PIL) No. 43 of 2014, at 34–35; *see also* CASS R. SUNSTEIN, *Can Animals Sue?*, *in* ANIMAL RIGHTS: CURRENT DEBATES AND NEW DIRECTIONS 251–62 (Cass R. Sunstein & Martha C. Nussbaum eds., 2004) (arguing that animals should be authorized to bring suit, with human representation, to vindicate their rights for violations of current law).

5

Rights of Nature

US and Foreign Domestic Perspectives

Chapter 5 shifts the focus to natural resources, the third and final category of the voiceless, and examines the legal initiatives that have sought to protect the rights of nature. Natural resources have been the subject of robust protection in constitutional provisions and legislative enactments in the United States and many other countries. The rights of nature movement has exploded within the past decade and has started to gain traction as a possible tool to combat climate change impacts. One prominent example is the recent effort in Australia that seeks to confer legal personhood to the Great Barrier Reef to help address the impacts of ocean acidification that are decimating this national and international treasure.

This chapter first explores rights of nature protections through case studies in the United States where legislative protections have enjoyed success at the local level in many states. The chapter then reviews leading foreign domestic jurisdictions in which rights of nature protections have been enshrined in constitutions or statutes. It also addresses leading court decisions in these countries that have recognized and enforced rights of nature protections. Australia is the only country addressed in which rights of nature protections have been sought but have not yet been achieved. The chapter concludes with a review of select cases before the innovative International Rights of Nature Tribunal.

I US DEVELOPMENTS

Laws granting rights to nature have proliferated in recent years at local, state, and national levels.[1] In the United States, approximately two hundred municipalities have passed ordinances granting nature rights in some manner.[2] Ecuador's

[1] Kyle Pietari, *Ecuador's Constitutional Rights of Nature: Implementation, Impacts, and Lessons Learned*, 5 WILLAMETTE ENVTL L.J. 37, 38 (2016).
[2] *Id.*

2008 Constitution inspired and propelled this movement.[3] This section summarizes examples of some of the most significant of these developments.

The rights of nature movement began in the United States in an inauspicious small town in rural Pennsylvania. The Tamaqua borough of Schuylkill County, Pennsylvania, passed a sewage sludge ordinance in 2006 that recognizes natural communities and ecosystems within the borough as a legal person for the purposes of enforcing the borough's civil rights.[4] Through this initiative, the Tamaqua borough became the first government in the world to legally recognize nature's rights.[5] The ordinance provides that the borough or any of its residents may file a lawsuit on behalf of an ecosystem to recover compensatory or punitive damages for harm done by land application of sewage, and the damages must be paid to the borough as a way to restore the ecosystem and natural communities.[6] Thomas Linzey, a lawyer for the Community Environmental Legal Defense Fund who assisted with the Tamaqua borough's ordinance, commented: "Coming after more than 150 years of judicially sanctioned expansion of the legal powers of corporations in the U.S., this ordinance is more than extraordinary – it is revolutionary."[7]

Rights of nature protections soon migrated west from Pennsylvania into neighboring Ohio. In Ohio, communities are governed by constitutional and statutory laws rather than having the right to local self-government.[8] However, in 2012, Yellow Springs and Broadview Heights became the first communities in the state to challenge the denials of self-government[9] by adopting a Community Bill of Rights that declares the community's right to clean air and water, the rights of nature, and their right to local self-governance.[10] In 2013, Oberlin residents adopted a similar initiative, followed by the city of Athens in 2014.[11] In November 2013, the Ohio Community Rights Network (OHCRN) was launched.[12] Many Ohio communities and counties are now involved in community rights campaigns to protect citizens and local ecosystems from fracking, disposal of waste, and pipelines.[13]

---

[3] *Id.*

[4] Cormac Cullinan, *If Nature Had Rights, What Would People Need to Give Up?*, ORION MAGAZINE (Jan./Feb. 2008), https://therightsofnature.org/wp-content/uploads/pdfs/If-Nature-Had-Rights.pdf.

[5] Press release: *First Rights of Nature Easement Established in Hawaii*, CMTY. ENVTL. LEGAL DEF. FUND (Dec. 20, 2017), https://celdf.org/2017/12/press-release-first-rights-nature-easement-established-hawaii.

[6] Cullinan, *supra* note 4.

[7] *Id.*

[8] *Ohio Community Rights Network*, CMTY. ENVTL. LEGAL DEF. FUND, https://celdf.org/join-the-movement/where-we-work/state-national-networks/ohio-community-rights-network (last updated Feb. 27, 2018).

[9] *Id.*

[10] *Id.*

[11] *Id.*

[12] *Id.*

[13] *Id.*

On March 12, 2013, Santa Monica, California adopted a Sustainability Rights Ordinance.[14] The ordinance codifies commitments made in the city's existing model "Sustainable City Plan," which sets out specific sustainable actions and goals.[15] The Ordinance recognizes the fundamental and inalienable rights of natural communities and ecosystems with the rights to exist and flourish in the city.[16] It also allows residents to assert rights on behalf of the environment.[17] Some of the rights enumerated in this ordinance are: "clean water from sustainable sources; marine waters safe for active and passive recreation; clean indoor and outdoor air; a sustainable food system that provides healthy, locally grown food; a sustainable climate that supports thriving human life and a flourishing biodiverse environment; comprehensive waste disposal systems that do not degrade the environment; and a sustainable energy future based on renewable energy sources."[18]

On April 9, 2013, Santa Monica also adopted the state's first Bill of Rights for Sustainability.[19] The Bill recognizes the rights of people, natural communities, and ecosystems to exist, regenerate, and flourish.[20] This Bill is one of the few initiatives prompted by concerns about the health of nature in general and its inherent rights rather than a specific issue, such as fracking.

In 2017, Lafayette, Colorado, enacted the first Climate Bill of Rights, recognizing the rights of humans and nature to a healthy climate, and banning fossil fuel extraction as a violation of those rights.[21] The City of Boulder is also working to get rights of nature established as law.[22] Boulder County is working on the Sustainable Rights of Nature Ordinance, which recognizes the importance of the rights of nature, the legal rights of natural beings and ecosystems, and provides for enforcement of those rights.[23]

---

[14] *An Ordinance of the City Council of the City of Santa Monica Establishing Sustainability Rights*, CITY OF SANTA MONICA (Mar. 12, 2013), https://www.smgov.net/departments/council/agendas/2013/20130312/s2013031207-C-1.htm.

[15] *Rights of Nature on the Santa Monica City Council Agenda*, GLOBAL ALLIANCE FOR THE RIGHTS OF NATURE (Mar. 8, 2013), http://therightsofnature.org/rights-of-nature-on-the-santa-monica-city-council-agenda/.

[16] *Id.*

[17] *Id.*

[18] *Id.*

[19] *Legalizing Sustainability? Santa Monica Recognizes Rights of Nature*, GLOBAL. EXCHANGE. (Apr. 11, 2013), https://globalexchange.org/2013/04/11/legalizing-sustainability-santa-monica-recognizes-rights-of-nature/.

[20] *Id.*

[21] *PR: Lafayette, CO, Residents Introduce Climate Change Bill of Rights and Protections*, CMTY. ENVTL. LEGAL DEF. FUND (Dec. 29, 2016), https://celdf.org/2016/12/pr-lafayette-co-residents-introduce-climate-bill-rights-protections.

[22] *Sustainable Rights of Nature Ordinance*, BOULDER RIGHTS OF NATURE (Apr. 25, 2013), http://boulderrightsofnature.org/wp-content/uploads/RON_Ordinance_4-25-13_Without_Per_Se_Violations.pdf.

[23] *Id.*

On September 25, 2017, *Colorado River* v. *State of Colorado* was filed in US federal court.[24] This suit was the first in the nation where a natural resource sought recognition of its legal rights.[25] The Colorado River was the plaintiff and sought judicial recognition of itself as a "person" with rights to exist and flourish.[26] Deep Green Resistance, an international organization committed to protecting the planet through direct action, filed suit as a "next friend"[27] on behalf of the river.[28]

Civil rights lawyer Jason Flores-Williams represented both the Colorado River and Deep Green Resistance.[29] The complaint sought recognition of the Colorado River ecosystem's rights to exist, flourish, regenerate, and restore, and recognition that the state of Colorado should be held liable for violating those rights in its future actions.[30] On November 28, 2017, the Colorado Attorney General threatened sanctions against Flores-Williams if he did not voluntarily withdraw the complaint.[31] On December 4, 2017, the federal court dismissed the case as Flores-Williams withdrew the complaint.[32]

The author interviewed Jason Flores-Williams for his impressions in working on this case. In response to a question regarding why this case failed where similar cases outside the United States prevailed, attorney Flores-Williams offered: "[D]ifferent countries have different cultures and traditions from us. The United States is a capitalistic society and bases its decisions on profits. We have a transactional culture that is dominated by corporate power, thus there is no equal playing field between nature and corporations."[33] Regarding his motivation in bringing this lawsuit, Flores-Williams reflected: "I brought the Colorado River lawsuit to raise public awareness of the personhood status for nature and to get people active in the cause. I wanted the courts to have to respond and move forward in the interest of justice."[34] Regarding how best to move forward with these cases in the United States, Flores-Williams proposed: "For a lawsuit to succeed in securing personhood status for nature, public pressure must increase and a light must be shined on the courts to

---

[24] Complaint for Declaratory Relief, Col. River Ecosystem v. Colorado, No. 1:17-cv-02316-NYW (D. Col. Sept. 25, 2017), 2017 WL 4284548; *First-in-the-Nation Lawsuit Seeks Recognition of Rights for the Colorado River*, Deep Green Resistance News Serv. (Sept. 21, 2017), https://dgrnewsservice.org/resistance/indirect/lobbying/first-nation-lawsuit-seeks-recognition-rights-col orado-river/ [hereinafter "First-in-the-Nation Lawsuit"].

[25] *Id.*

[26] *Id.*

[27] For a detailed discussion of "next friend" status as a tool to facilitate protection of voiceless communities, see *infra* Chapter 6.

[28] *First-in-the-Nation Lawsuit*, *supra* note 24.

[29] *Id.*

[30] Complaint for Declaratory Relief, Col. River Ecosystem v. Colorado, *supra* note 24.

[31] *First-in-the-Nation Lawsuit*, *supra* note 24.

[32] Lindsay Fendt, *Colo. River "Personhood" Case Pulled by Proponents*, Aspen Times (Dec. 4, 2017), https://www.aspentimes.com/news/colo-river-personhood-case-pulled-by-proponents/.

[33] Interview with Jason Flores-Williams, Lead Attorney, The Law Office of Jason Flores-Williams (Sept. 19, 2018).

[34] *Id.*

expand the definition of rights. We must pack the courthouses so judges can see for themselves that there is real-world consequence to denying this movement."[35]

The Ponca Nation of Oklahoma has suffered years of earthquakes, poisonous water, and serious health issues due to fracking and injection wells on and near its reservation.[36] There were 448 earthquakes reported in and around the Ponca reservation in 2017 alone.[37] Tribal members have experienced diseases, and the wells on the reserve are too toxic to use or drink from.[38]

On October 20, 2017, the Ponca Nation of Oklahoma voted to pass a statute recognizing the rights of nature[39] and became the first Native American tribe to recognize rights of nature into law in the United States.[40] The statute aligned "human law with natural law, to ban fracking and protect both people and the environment."[41]

In July of 2018, Todd Township, Pennsylvania approved an ordinance for a community bill of rights.[42] The bill opposed a proposed swine-concentrated animal feeding operation (CAFO).[43] The purpose of the ordinance is to prevent and regulate the negative impacts of industrial farming on landowners' property.[44] The ban within the ordinance will help alleviate many problems created by industrial farming, such as the threat to drinking water supplies, inhumane treatment of livestock, and severely low quality of life for community members.[45] Members of the community describe this ordinance as pro-farming because it protects family farms from the harm that comes from industrial farms.[46]

The ordinance draws support from the progressive language in Article 1, Section 27 of Pennsylvania's constitution, which states: "The people have a right to clean air, pure water, and to the preservation of the natural, scenic, historic and esthetic values of the environment."[47] During the public comment portion of the meeting in which the council agreed that the ordinance and community bill of rights should proceed,

---

[35] *Id.*

[36] Movement Rights, *Ponca Nation of Oklahoma to Recognize the Rights of Nature to Ban Fracking*, GLOBAL ALLIANCE FOR THE RIGHTS OF NATURE (Jan. 29, 2018), http://therightsofnature.org/ponca-rights-of-nature/.

[37] *Id.*

[38] *Id.*

[39] *Id.*

[40] First Tribe in the U.S. Recognizes Rights of Nature into Law, Indigenous Again (Jan. 23, 2018), http://indigenousagain.com/first-tribe-u-s-recognizes-rights-nature-law/.

[41] *Id.*

[42] Michael Kane, *The Daily News: Residents Rally to Stop Pig Farm*, CMTY. ENVTL. LEGAL DEF. FUND (July 10, 2018), https://celdf.org/2018/07/the-daily-news-residents-rally-to-halt-pig-farm.

[43] *Id.*

[44] *Id.*

[45] Press Release, *Pennsylvania Township Bans Corporate Industrial Farming*, CMTY. ENVTL. LEGAL DEF. FUND (July 10, 2018), https://celdf.org/2018/07/press-release-pennsylvania-township-bans-corporate-industrial-farming (last accessed Feb. 25, 2019).

[46] *Id.*

[47] PA. CONST. art. I, § 27.

it was said that "Pennsylvania's public resources are the common property of all the people, including generations yet to come. As trustees of these resources, the commonwealth shall preserve and maintain them for the benefit of all the people."[48]

This sampling of inspiring local initiatives throughout the United States reflects the growing recognition of rights of nature protections in various contexts. While there is much work to be done before the rights of nature paradigm is embraced in state legislatures and Congress, and in state and federal courts, these developments nonetheless are a promising first step on this path.

II FOREIGN DOMESTIC DEVELOPMENTS

This section provides an overview of rights of nature developments in the leading countries outside the United States that have adopted rights of nature protection mandates in their constitutions, legislation, and court decisions.[49]

A *Latin America: Ecuador, Bolivia, and Colombia*

1 Ecuador

In 2008, Ecuador amended its constitution to become the first country to recognize rights of nature with an article in its constitution, which begins: "Nature, or Pacha Mama, where life is reproduced and occurs, has the right to integral respect for its existence and for the maintenance and regeneration of its life cycle, structure, functions, and evolutionary processes."[50] Ecuador then ratified the constitution by referendum in September 2008.[51] This new constitution includes a chapter titled "Rights for Nature."[52] The articles therein acknowledge that nature, in all of its life

---

[48] Kane, *supra* note 42.

[49] For a helpful summary of these foreign domestic developments in securing rights of nature protections, see DAVID R. BOYD, THE RIGHTS OF NATURE: A LEGAL REVOLUTION THAT COULD SAVE THE WORLD (2017); Mihnea Tanasescu, *When a River Is a Person: From Ecuador to New Zealand, Nature Gets Its Day in Court*, 8 OPEN RIVERS: RETHINKING WATER, PLACE & CMTY. 127 (Fall 2017), http://editions.lib.umn.edu/openrivers/wp-content/uploads/sites/9/2017/11/9_tanasescu_perspectives_fall17.pdf.

[50] CONST. OF THE REPUBLIC OF ECUADOR, pmbl., http://pdba.georgetown.edu/Constitutions/Ecuador/english08.html (English translation) (last updated Jan. 31, 2011); Kevin Stark, *How Community-Led "Rights of Nature" Initiatives Are Protecting Ecosystems*, SHAREABLE (Aug. 31, 2017), https://www.shareable.net/blog/how-community-led-rights-of-nature-initiatives-are-protecting-ecosystems.

[51] *Ecuador Adopts Rights of Nature in Constitution*, GLOB. ALL. FOR THE RIGHTS OF NATURE, http://therightsofnature.org/ecuador-rights/ (last accessed Mar. 3, 2019).

[52] Article 71 of the 2008 Constitution acknowledges that nature has the "right to exist, persist, maintain and regenerate its vital cycles, structure, functions and evolutionary process." CONST. OF THE REPUBLIC OF ECUADOR, art. 71, http://pdba.georgetown.edu/Constitutions/Ecuador/english08.html (English translation) (last updated Jan. 31, 2011). The remaining articles address

forms, has the right to exist, persist, maintain, and regenerate its vital cycles, rather than being treated as property under the law.[53]

One of those rights of nature under Ecuador's Constitution is the right to be restored.[54] Ecuador's approach to rights of nature protection is pioneering in two respects: "First, it grants nature positive rights – that is, rights to something specific (e.g., restoration, regeneration, respect). It also resolves the issue of legal standing in the most comprehensive way possible: by granting it to everyone. In Ecuador, anyone – regardless of their relationship to a particular parcel of land – can go to court to protect it."[55]

Ecuador is one of the most environmentally rich places in the world. Protecting the biodiversity from development and industry was one reason why Ecuador enshrined the rights of nature protections in its constitution.[56] While Ecuadorian environmentalists have successfully enforced the rights of nature,[57] communities must continue to be vigilant in protecting places like the Yasuní National Park and Biosphere Reserve, which remain threatened by oil extraction.[58] Many commentators have analyzed the effectiveness of enforcement of the rights of nature protections in Ecuador.[59] While important strides have been made in enforcing these

the right to restoration (Art. 72); the state's authority to apply preventive and restrictive measures in all activities that could lead to the extinction of species, destruction of ecosystems or permanent alteration of natural cycles (Art. 73); and any individual having the right to bring legal action on behalf of nature (Art. 74). *Id.* arts. 10, 71–74.

[53] *Ecuador Adopts Rights of Nature in Constitution, supra* note 51.

[54] CONST. OF THE REPUBLIC OF ECUADOR, art. 72, http://pdba.georgetown.edu/Constitutions/Ecuador/english08.html (English translation) (last updated Jan. 31, 2011).

[55] Mihnea Tanasescu, *Rivers Get Human Rights: They Can Sue to Protect Themselves*, SCI. AM. (June 19, 2017), www.scientificamerican.com/article/rivers-get-human-rights-they-can-sue-to-protect-themselves/.

[56] Stark, *supra* note 50.

[57] For one example of this success, see R. F. Wheeler v. Director de la Procuraduria General Del Estado de Loja, Judgment No. 11121-2011-0010 (Loja Provincial Court of Justice Mar. 20, 2011), http://therightsofnature.org/wp-content/uploads/pdfs/Espanol/Sentencia%20Corte%20Provincial%20Loja_marzo_2011.pdf (in Spanish) (victory applying rights of nature protections in Ecuador's constitution to Vilcabamba River); *see also* Natalia Greene, *The First Successful Case of the Rights of Nature Implementation in Ecuador*, GLOBAL ALLIANCE FOR THE RIGHTS OF NATURE, http://therightsofnature.org/first-ron-case-ecuador/ (last accessed Mar. 3, 2019); Erin Daly, *Ecuadorian Court Recognizes Constitutional Right to Nature*, WIDENER ENVT'L L. CTR. BLOG (July 12, 2011), http://blogs.law.widener.edu/envirolawblog/2011/07/12/ecuadorian-court-recognizes-constitutional-right-to-nature/.

[58] Stark, *supra* note 50. For a discussion of the Ecuadorian government's resistance to these efforts, *see CELDF Partner in Rights of Nature Work, Fundacion Pachamama, Shut Down by Ecuadorian Government*, CMTY. ENVTL. LEGAL DEF. FUND (Dec. 6, 2013), https://celdf.org/2013/12/celdf-partner-in-rights-of-nature-work-fundacion-pachamama-shut-down-by-ecuadorian-government.

[59] *See generally* David R. Boyd, *Recognizing the Rights of Nature: Lofty Rhetoric or Legal Revolution?*, 32 NAT. RES. & ENV'T 13 (Spr. 2018); Louis J. Kotze & Paola Villavicencio Calzadilla, *Somewhere between Rhetoric and Reality: Environmental Constitutionalism and the Rights of Nature in Ecuador*, 6 TRANSNAT'L ENVTL. L. 401 (Nov. 2017); Craig M. Kauffman & Pamela L. Martin, *Testing Ecuador's Rights of Nature: Why Some Lawsuits Succeed and*

mandates, much work needs to be done to ensure that the ambitious rights of nature language in Ecuador's Constitution translates into meaningful protections on the ground.[60]

2 Bolivia

Like Ecuador, Bolivia has made a significant contribution to the rights of nature movement. This section reviews constitutional and legislative developments on rights of nature protections in Bolivia. To date, there have not been any cases directly regarding the rights of nature in the Bolivian court system.[61]

After the disappointment in the wake of the Conference of the Parties in Copenhagen in 2009, Bolivia hosted the first World People's Conference on Climate Change and the Rights of Mother Earth in 2010, which drew more than thirty thousand attendees from one hundred nations.[62] The Universal Declaration of the Rights of Mother Earth[63] was drafted and adopted at this event. This declaration recognizes "Mother Earth" as a living being and establishes its inherent rights, acknowledges that capitalist activities have contributed to the destruction of nature, recognizes that "every human being is responsible for respecting and living in harmony with Mother Earth," and establishes the obligations of human beings.[64] While some viewed this effort as a purely political maneuver that would attract little support, others recognized it as a first and necessary step in extending legal protections to the rest of the natural world.[65]

In the years following this landmark event in 2010, Bolivia continued to pass legal initiatives that embrace the indigenous conception of nature as a sacred home.[66]

Others Fail, EARTH LAW CENTER (Mar. 18, 2016), https://earthlawcenter.squarespace.com/s/ Kauffman-Martin-16-Testing-Ecuadors-RoN-Laws.pdf; Pietari, *supra* note 1; Mary Elizabeth Whittemore, *The Problem of Enforcing Nature's Rights under Ecuador's Constitution: Why the 2008 Environmental Amendments Have No Bite*, 20 PAC. RIM L. & POL'Y J. 659 (2011).

[60] Some of this language has been tested with positive results in the International Rights of Nature Tribunal. For a discussion of those cases, *see infra* Part III.

[61] *See infra* Part III for discussion of a case has been brought to the International Rights of Nature Tribunal on behalf of a national park in Bolivia.

[62] Michelle Maloney, *Finally Being Heard: The Great Barrier Reef and the International Rights of Nature Tribunal*, 3 GRIFFITH J. L. & HUMAN DIGNITY 40, 42 (2015).

[63] World People's Conference on Climate Change and the Rights of Mother Earth Cochabamba, Bolivia, *Universal Declaration of the Rights of Mother Earth*, GLOB. ALL. FOR THE RIGHTS OF NATURE (Apr. 22, 2010), http://therightsofnature.org/universal-declaration/ [hereinafter "Universal Declaration"].

[64] *Id.*

[65] Brandon Keim, *Nature to Get Legal Rights in Bolivia*, WIRED (Apr. 18, 2011), https://www .wired.com/2011/04/legal-rights-nature-bolivia/; Peter Neill, *Law of Mother Earth: A Vision from Bolivia*, HUFFINGTON POST, https://www.huffingtonpost.com/peter-neill/law-of-mother-earth-a-vis_b_6180446.html (last updated Jan. 18, 2015).

[66] Nick Buxton, *The Law of Mother Earth: Behind Bolivia's Historic Bill*, GLOBAL ALLIANCE FOR THE RIGHTS OF NATURE, http://therightsofnature.org/bolivia-law-of-mother-earth/ (last accessed Mar. 3, 2019).

These efforts represent some of the most ambitious environmental protection initiatives in the world. Bolivia has made significant progress in addressing rights of nature protections in its constitution and two national laws. Unfortunately, very little progress has been made in enforcement or interpretation of rights of nature protections in its courts.[67]

The Bolivian Constitution defines its understanding of Pachamama ("Mother Earth") as a legal subject, and outlines civil society's and state's obligations towards it.[68] As provided in Article 3, Mother Earth is "the dynamic living system made up of the indivisible community of all life systems and living beings, inter-related, interdependent, and complementary, which share a common destiny. Mother Earth is considered sacred from the perspective of the cosmologies of original indigenous peasant nations and peoples."[69] Ensuring that nature is sacred in national law secures Mother Earth and her components, including all human communities, as holders of all the historically informed rights established in this law.[70] Additionally, Bolivia's new constitution considers a wider array of both human and nonhuman perspectives, and a deeper understanding of temporality; one which extends both into the past and into the future.[71]

The Bolivian Constitution was implemented in February 2009 after receiving approval in a parliamentary referendum.[72] The new constitution prominently featured Mother Earth. While enforceable rights of nature are not explicitly granted as they were in the Ecuadorian Constitution of 2008, the Bolivian Constitution recognizes the concept of Pachamama and creates new avenues for citizen participation and consultation on decisions that affect the environment.[73] Respect for, and harmony with, Pachamama are adopted as ethical and moral principles.[74] The values of plurinationalism and respect for Mother Nature underscore how the Bolivian state's values are deeply rooted in indigenous thought and reflect a desire to depart from "the colonial, republican and neoliberal State in the past."[75]

---

[67] For an assessment of the effectiveness of the rights of nature protections in Bolivia, *see generally* Paola Villavicencio Calzadilla & Louis J. Kotzé, *Living in Harmony with Nature? A Critical Appraisal of the Rights of Mother Earth in Bolivia,* 7 Transnat'l Envtl. L. 397 (2018).

[68] Martin Premoli, *Reflections on Various Cases of the Legal Rights of Nature,* Penn Program in Envtl. Humanities (June 17, 2017), https://ppeh.sas.upenn.edu/field-notes/reflections-various-cases-legal-rights-nature.

[69] *Id.*; *see Law of the Rights of Mother Earth,* Law No. 071 *(Ley de Derechos de la Madre Tierra,* Ley No. 71), art. 3 (Dec. 7, 2010) (Bol.) [hereinafter "Law No. 071"].

[70] *Id.*

[71] *Id.*

[72] Simon Romero, *Bolivians Ratify New Constitution,* N.Y. Times (Jan. 25, 2009), www.nytimes.com/2009/01/26/world/americas/26bolivia.html.

[73] *Bolivia Adopts New Pro-Environment Constitution,* Access Initiative (July 2009), https://accessinitiative.org/creating-change/bolivia-adopts-new-pro-environment-constitution.

[74] Const. of Bolivia, art. 8 §1.

[75] *Id.* pmbl.

In other sections of the constitution, however, there is an emphasis on economic development and national control of natural resources.[76]

The preamble to the constitution makes multiple references to plurality, as in "the plurality that exists in all things and in our diversity as human beings and cultures,"[77] which suggests an equal valuation of entities other than human beings in the application of the principles to follow. The preamble also states that "We found Bolivia anew, fulfilling the mandate of our people, with the strength of our Pachamama"[78] reflecting the notion that the future fulfillment of Bolivia's political and national goals is predicated on the preservation of Pachamama's health. As such, the language of the preamble promotes conditions for alternative forms of decision making and considerations of rights.

The adoption of the principles of Vivir Bien, which translates directly to "Living Well," a Bolivian version of the same principle known as Buen Vivir in Ecuador, is first set out in the preamble. It mentions that Bolivia is "A State based ... on principles of sovereignty, dignity, interdependence, solidarity, harmony, and equity in the distribution and redistribution of the social wealth, where the search for a good life predominates."[79]

The definition of Vivir Bien as used by the Bolivian state is only found in the Framework Law of Mother Earth ratified in 2012. Vivir Bien, otherwise known as Sumaj Kamana, Sumaj Kausay, or Yaiko Kavi Päve, is defined as:

> [A] civilizational and cultural horizon that is alternative to capitalism and modernity that is born from the cosmovisions of Indigenous peasant, intercultural and afrobolivian nations and peoples, and is conceived in the context of interculturality. It is achieved in a collective, complementary and solidary manner, integrating in its practical realization, social, cultural, political, economic, ecological, and the affective, among other dimensions, to permit the harmonious meeting among the set of beings, components and resources of Mother Earth. Earth and societies, in equality and solidarity and eliminating inequality and mechanisms of domination. It is Living Well among us, Living Well with what surrounds us and Living Well with oneself.[80]

A key aspect of Vivir Bien is that humans are treated as inherently communal beings and that ecosystems are considered an inherent part of these social communities that are necessary for life. In Quechua and Aymara traditions, this approach is based on the notion of the *ayllu*, the traditional form of community, wherein the

[76] Fernando Cabrera Diaz, *Bolivian Voters Approve New Constitution as Government Continues to Nationalize Oil Assets*, INVESTMENT TREATY NEWS (Feb. 4, 2009), www.iisd.org/itn/2009/02/04/bolivian-voters-approve-new-constitution-as-government-continues-to-nationalize-oil-assets/.

[77] CONST. OF BOLIVIA, pmbl.

[78] *Id.*

[79] *Id.*

[80] The Mother Earth Law and Integral Development to Live Well Law No. 300, 2012 (Bol.) [hereinafter "Law 300"].

well-being of the community encompasses all entities in the community, including humans and nonhumans and the modern nature-culture dualism disappears. As such, the well-being of the individual is predicated on the well-being of the holistic community. Though the constitution itself does not explicitly enumerate these various aspects of the cosmovisions, their inclusion as "ethical, moral principles" suggests that it will be used to guide future decision making.

Under Chapter V on Social and Economic Rights, the section on Environmental Rights guarantees the right to a "healthy, protected, and balanced environment. The exercise of this right must be granted to individuals and collectives of present and future generations, as well as to other living things, so they may develop in a normal and permanent way"[81] and "any person, in his own right or on behalf of a collective, is authorized to take legal action in defense of environmental rights, without prejudice to the obligation of public institutions to act on their own in the face of attacks on the environment."[82] Here, nonhuman entities are granted the right to be "healthy, protected and balanced ... so they may develop in a normal and permanent way."

While this language lacks the same breadth of rights granted to human beings, it nevertheless provides a certain level of enforcement as Article 34 encourages and authorizes human individuals to pursue legal actions based on violations of these rights "in his own right or on behalf of a collective."[83] If a collective is taken here to signify its meaning in philosophies of Vivir Bien, it follows that cases may be pursued on behalf of natural, nonhuman beings. Moreover, Article 135, operationalized in Article 136, states that "The Popular Action (la Accion Popular) shall proceed against any act or omission by the authorities or individuals or collectives that violates or threatens to violate rights and collective interests related to public patrimony, space, security and health, the environment and other rights of a similar nature that are recognized by this Constitution."[84] This language reaffirms the ability of groups to pursue legal action in relation to violations of any rights enumerated in the Constitution. These articles suggest that it is within humans' responsibility to act on behalf of Mother Nature, even when it opposes the actions of the State. Despite the symbolic achievements embodied in these rights of nature provisions in the Bolivian Constitution, critics have noted that the provisions authorizing the state's right to develop natural resources for the benefit of economic development, as well as other economic aspects that entail exploitation of nature, are much more numerous and detailed. This disparity suggests a lack of commitment to the enforcement of such rights, insofar as there are limited legal procedures available to pursue such actions.[85]

[81] CONST. OF BOLIVIA, art. 33.
[82] *Id.* at art. 34.
[83] *Id.*
[84] *Id.* at arts. 135, 136.
[85] *See* Villavicencio Calzadilla & Kotzé, *supra* note 67.

Bolivia's most notable achievement regarding environmental rights came in the form of legislative protections introduced after the ratification of the 2009 Constitution. Bolivia recognizes nature's rights through two national laws. In December 2010, in response to climate change impacts on the nation's community and economic health, the National Congress voted to support a law to protect the well-being of its people by protecting the natural world, its sustainability, resources, and value, as vital to the common good. The law requires that people "uphold and respect the rights of Mother Earth."[86] This law, Law 71 of 2010 on the rights of Mother Earth, was a historic moment for Bolivia and the rest of the world. The act is the first statutory law in the world that formally recognizes and defines the rights of Nature, establishing eleven new rights for it, and granting it the same rights afforded to humans.[87]

The binding principles that govern this law include:

1) Harmony: Human activities, within the framework of plurality and diversity, should achieve a dynamic balance with the cycles and processes inherent in Mother Earth;

2) Collective Good: The interests of society, within the framework of the rights of Mother Earth, prevail in all human activities and any acquired right;

3) Guarantee of Regeneration: The state, at its various levels, and society, in harmony with the common interest, must ensure the necessary conditions in order that the diverse living systems of Mother Earth may absorb damage, adapt to shocks, and regenerate without significantly altering their structural and functional characteristics, recognizing that living systems are limited in their ability to regenerate, and that humans are limited in their ability to undo their actions;

4) Respect and defend the rights of Mother Earth: The state and any individual or collective person must respect, protect, and guarantee the rights of Mother Earth for the well-being of current and future generations;

5) No Commercialism: Neither living systems nor processes that sustain them may be commercialized, nor serve anyone's private property;

6) Multiculturalism: The exercise of the rights of Mother Earth requires the recognition, recovery, respect, protection, and dialogue of the diversity of feelings, values, knowledge, skills, practices, transcendence, science, technology, and standards of all the culture of the world who seek to live in harmony with nature.[88]

---

[86] *Law 071, supra* note 69 at art. 9, ¶ 1, www.worldfuturefund.org/Projects/Indicators/motherearth bolivia.html.

[87] *Bolivia: Fighting the Climate Wars*, GLOBAL ALLIANCE FOR THE RIGHTS OF NATURE, http://therightsofnature.org/bolivia-fighting-climate-wars/ (last accessed Mar. 4, 2019).

[88] *Law 071, supra* note 69 at art. 2.

Bolivian President Evo Morales supported the act and implemented over 2,900 conservation programs and antipollution projects in all 327 municipalities, endorsing the practical application of the law.[89]

The majority of principles in this law reflect a biocentric reorientation of human activity. Obligations extend to the state level to defend Mother Nature from over-exploitation and commodification of living systems or processes,[90] and even to the individual level, whereby individuals are required to ensure the sustainable use of Mother Nature's components and to denounce any violation of Mother Nature's rights, life systems or components.[91]

Mother Earth is defined as a "dynamic living system comprising an indivisible community of all living systems and living organisms, interrelated, interdependent and complementary, which share a common destiny" that is considered sacred[92] and humans are reconceptualized as a component of this system.[93] It takes on the status of a "collective public interest" and "all its components, including human communities, are entitled to all the inherent rights recognized in this Law."[94] Article 7 enumerates a wide range of rights of Mother Earth:

1. To life: The right to maintain the integrity of living systems and natural processes that sustain them, and capacities and conditions for regeneration.

2. To the diversity of life: It is the right to preservation of differentiation and variety of beings that make up Mother Earth, without being genetically altered or structurally modified in an artificial way, so that their existence, functioning or future potential would be threatened.

3. To water: The right to preserve the functionality of the water cycle, its existence in the quantity and quality needed to sustain living systems, and its protection from pollution for the reproduction of the life of Mother Earth and all its components.

4. To clean air: The right to preserve the quality and composition of air for sustaining living systems and its protection from pollution, for the reproduction of the life of Mother Earth and all its components.

5. To equilibrium: The right to maintenance or restoration of the interrelationship, interdependence, complementarity and functionality of the components of Mother Earth in a balanced way for the continuation of their cycles and reproduction of their vital processes.

6. To restoration: The right to timely and effective restoration of living systems affected by human activities directly or indirectly.

---

[89] Stephan Lefebvre & Jeannette Bonifaz, *Lessons from Bolivia: Renationalizing the Hydrocarbon Industry*, OPEN DEMOCRACY UK (Nov. 24, 2014), www.opendemocracy.net/ourkingdom/ste phan-lefebvre-jeanette-bonifaz/lessons-from-bolivia-renationalising-hydrocarbon-indust.

[90] *Law 071, supra* note 69 at art. 8.3.

[91] *Id.* at arts. 9e and 9f.

[92] *Id.* at art. 3.

[93] *Id.* at art 5.

[94] *Id.*

7. To pollution-free living: The right to the preservation of any of Mother Earth's components from contamination, as well as toxic and radioactive waste generated by human activities.[95]

The obligations of the state, enumerated in Article 8, include the duties: to develop policies that prevent the destruction of nature or livelihoods dependent on it; to create "balanced" approaches to development that enable Vivir Bien; to protect Mother Earth from exploitation and commodification; to ensure energy sovereignty and the "gradual" incorporation of clean energy; to promote peace, and to advance the recognition of Mother Earth's rights beyond the nation.[96] The duties of the Bolivian people are to undertake actions to uphold these enumerated rights, and, notably to "Report any act that violates the rights of Mother Earth, living systems, and/or their components"[97] and "Attend the convention of competent authorities or organized civil society to implement measures aimed at preserving and/or protecting Mother Earth."[98] Article 10 requires the establishment of an Office of Mother Earth to guarantee compliance with the rights enumerated in the Act, the structure, function, and attributes of which would be established in a separate law.[99]

In 2012, Law 300, the Framework Law of Mother Earth and Integral Development for Living Well, which was a more developed version of its 2010 predecessor, was passed in Bolivia.[100] The objective of this law, as stated in Article 1,[101] is to link the practical concepts of rights of nature, holistic development, and Vivir Bien.[102] The goals of the law are

(i) to determine the principles guiding access to the components and living systems of Mother Earth; (ii) to establish the objectives of integral development that orient the creation of conditions for transitioning to Living Well in harmony and balance with Mother Earth; (iii) to guide specific legislation, policies, regulations, strategies, plans and programmes ... to achieve Vivir Bien through integral development ... and (iv) to define the institutional framework for promoting and implementing integral development in harmony and balance with Mother Earth for Vivir Bien.[103]

---

[95] *Id.* at art. 7.
[96] *Id.* at art. 8.
[97] *Id.* at art. 9.6.
[98] *Id.* at art. 9.7.
[99] *Id.* at art. 10.
[100] *Law 300, supra* note 80, www.lse.ac.uk/GranthamInstitute/law/the-mother-earth-law-and-integral-development-to-live-well-law-no-300/.
[101] *Id.* at art. 1.
[102] Bolivia, Earth Law Center (Aug. 16, 2016), www.earthlawcenter.org/international-law/2016/8/bolivia.
[103] *Law 300, supra* note 80, at art. 3.

Integral development for Vivir Bien is defined as:

> "The continual process of generation and implementation of social, communal, citizen, and public actions and means for the creation, provision and strengthening of conditions, capacities and material, social and spiritual means, in the framework of practices and cultural actions that are adequate and appropriate that promote solidary relations of mutual cooperation and support, of complementarity and strengthening of communal and collective edifying links to achieve Vivir Bien in harmony with Mother Earth. This is not a goal, but rather an intermediate phase to achieve Vivir Bien as a new civilizational and cultural horizon."[104]

Key principles in Article 4 include the compatibility and complementarity of rights and obligations,[105] the non-mercantilization of the functions of Mother Earth,[106] precaution,[107] solidarity between human beings,[108] and climate justice.[109] The rights, responsibilities, and duties presented in Chapter 3 are largely the same as those delineated in the 2010 law. The implementation of the law is required at all levels of government[110] and can be defended in any relevant thematic jurisdiction.[111] All entities are required to denounce any violation of the rights enumerated in this Law before the competent authorities.[112] Administrative sanctions, civil liability[113] as well as criminal liability[114] can arise as a result of violations against the rights of Mother Earth. The act requires the creation of several new institutions to regulate implementation and compliance with the law. Article 39 authorizes the creation of a Mother Earth Ombudsman's Office similar to the Human Rights Ombudsman's Office.[115] As of this writing, however, this office has yet to be created.[116]

Law 300 made significant progress in formalizing the rights enshrined in Law 71. Nonetheless, some contradictions remain that indicate a low likelihood of full compliance with the core principles of both laws. First, while the principle of non-commercialization of Mother Earth's functions and natural processes is enshrined in Article 4,[117] the continued promotion of "sustainable" mining and exploitation of hydrocarbons[118] points to a subtle but important distinction between commercializing

---

[104] *Id.* at art. 5.3.
[105] *Id.* at art. 4.1.
[106] *Id.* at art 4.2.
[107] *Id.* at art. 4.4.
[108] *Id.* at art. 4.11.
[109] *Id.* at art 4.14.
[110] *Id.* at art. 35.
[111] *Id.* at art. 36.
[112] *Id.* at art. 39.
[113] *Id.* at art. 96.
[114] *Id.* at art. 97.
[115] *Id.* at art. 39.
[116] *Bolivia – National Rights of Nature Legislation*, AUSTRALIAN EARTH LAW ALLIANCE, www .earthlaws.org.au/what-is-earth-jurisprudence/rights-of-nature/bolivia/.
[117] *Law 300, supra* note 80 at art. 4.2.
[118] *Id.* at art. 26.

nature's systems and nature's products. In addition, while Vivir Bien is positioned in the law as an alternative to capitalism,[119] Article 10 places the need for the state to create the conditions for sustenance and growth of the state itself before all other state responsibilities.[120] Additional provisions, such as the duty to promote investment and equitable wealth distribution to achieve social justice and poverty reduction[121] as well as the principle of interhuman solidarity,[122] prioritize human beings over other living things.[123]

3 Colombia

In November 2016, Colombia's Constitutional Court declared that the Atrato River basin[124] possesses rights to "protection, conservation, maintenance, and restoration."[125] The case was filed to address the Atrato River basin's significant degradation from mining, impacting both nature and indigenous peoples.[126] For the first time in its jurisprudence, the Constitutional Court in Colombia recognized that a natural resource, in this case, a river and its watershed, are subjects and holders of rights alone, and it is the State's duty to protect it.[127] The Court concluded that "the defendant state authorities are responsible for violating fundamental rights to life, health, water, food security, the healthy environment, culture and territory of the local ethnic communities."[128]

While water is not considered a fundamental right in the National Constitution of Colombia, in this case, the Constitutional Court considered it "indispensable for guaranteeing the right to life, as well as essential for the environment and the life of multiple species that inhabit the planet."[129] The Court stated that "only an attitude

[119] *Id.* at art. 5.2.
[120] *Id.* at art. 10.1.
[121] *Id.* at arts. 18 and 19.
[122] *Id.* at art. 4.11.
[123] For a discussion of Bolivia's rights of nature protection efforts and implementation obstacles, see generally Peter Neill, *Law of Mother Earth: A Vision from Bolivia*, HUFFPOST (Nov. 18, 2014), www.huffpost.com/entry/law-of-mother-earth-a-vis_b_6180446; Franz Chavez, *Bolivia's Mother Earth Law Hard to Implement*, IPS NEWS (May 19, 2014), www.ipsnews.net/2014/05/bolivias-mother-earth-law-hard-implement/; John Vidal, *Bolivia Enshrines Natural World's Rights with Equal Status for Mother Earth*, THE GUARDIAN (Apr. 10, 2011), www.theguardian.com/environment/2011/apr/10/bolivia-enshrines-natural-worlds-rights.
[124] The Atrato River is one of the most biodiverse wildlife ecosystems in the world. Laura Villa, *The Importance of the Atrato River in Colombia Gaining Legal Rights*, EARTH LAW CENTER (May 5, 2017), www.earthlawcenter.org/international-law/2017/5/colombia. It is also home to indigenous groups and other minorities, is one of Colombia's poorest areas, and has been decimated by gold mining since Spanish colonial times. *Id.*
[125] Mari Margil, *Colombia Constitutional Court Finds Atrato River Possesses Rights*, THE RIGHTS OF NATURE (May 4, 2017), http://therightsofnature.org/colombia-constitutional-court-finds-atrato-river-possesses-rights/.
[126] *Id.*
[127] Villa, *supra* note 124.
[128] *Id.*
[129] *Id.*

of profound respect and humility with nature and its beings makes it possible for us to relate with them in just and equitable terms, leaving aside every utilitary, economic or efficient concept."[130]

To enforce this significant judgment, communities will have to create a commission of guardians with two delegates to follow up on the restoration and protection the State must provide for the river.[131] The World Wildlife Fund and the Humboldt Institute will advise this commission.[132] The Colombian public supports the Constitutional Court's judgment but is skeptical about its accomplishment.[133] This skepticism arises due to human rights legislation: though the laws and the constitution aim to protect human rights and individual freedom, journalists and indigenous leaders are still targets of killings and death threats.[134] The questions posed are "If the [S]tate cannot guarantee the traditional law in cities and municipalities where there is institutional presence, how will it fare in guaranteeing the protection and restoration of the Atrato River, located in a jungle – where the minimum living standards such as food security, fresh water, energy, health[,] and education are not available? How will the thousands of people that depend on illegal mining in the Atrato River replace their livelihoods?"[135]

Affirming that the River has rights comes after thousands of years of nature being treated as "property" or "right-less" under the law.[136] Much like indigenous peoples, women, and slaves have been treated as property under the law, legal systems treat nature the same way today.[137] Under this system, environmental laws regulate human *use* of nature, resulting in the global decline of ecosystems and species and the acceleration of climate change.[138]

The plaintiff, Centro de Estudios para la Justicia Social ("Tierra Digna"), filed a *tutela* proceeding[139] on behalf of various community councils of the Atrato region in the Colombian Pacific against the presidency of the republic and other government agencies.[140] The plaintiff alleged that the contamination of the river is a threat to the health of the communities that use the river as a source of work, recreation, and sustenance. The plaintiff requested that the court enjoin the intensive and large-scale use of illegal extraction methods of minerals such as gold and platinum, which have been intensifying for several years and are causing harmful and irreversible

---

[130] *Id.*
[131] *Id.*
[132] *Id.*
[133] *Id.*
[134] *Id.*
[135] *Id.*
[136] Margil, *supra* note 125.
[137] *Id.*
[138] *Id.*
[139] Colombian Constitution of 1991, art. 86 (a "tutela" action is a constitutional mechanism that addresses protection of fundamental rights).
[140] Sentencia T622/2016, www.corteconstitucional.gov.co/relatoria/2016/t-622-16.htm.

consequences on the environment, and impacting the fundamental rights of the neighboring communities and the natural balance of the territories they inhabit.[141] The lower courts denied this *tutela* action, concluding that the plaintiff sought the protection of collective rights, rather than fundamental rights. Therefore, this constitutional mechanism was not appropriate.

The Constitutional Court ruled that the case raised several complex constitutional legal issues related to illegal mining, which may have some repercussions on the content, scope, and limitations of the Colombian state mining energy policy. The main issue for the Court to determine was whether, due to illegal mining activities in the Atrato River basin, and the omission of the state authorities sued, there was a violation of the fundamental rights to life, health, water, food security, the healthy environment, culture, and territory of the neighboring ethnic communities. The Court held that a *tutela* action is designed to respond to complex problems like the ones at issue in this case and determined that it was the appropriate mechanism for the protection of the fundamental rights of the ethnic communities of the Atrato River basin.[142]

The Court proceeded to the merits of the case and concluded that the right to water was a fundamental right, as it is a necessary component of the right to a dignified life, and it is essential for many organisms that inhabit the planet to be able to survive.[143] The Court cited previous decisions of the Supreme Court of Justice that stated that "nature is not only conceived as the environment and environment of human beings, but also as a subject with its own rights, which, as such, must be protected and guaranteed."[144] In this sense, ecosystem compensation involves a type of restitution applied exclusively to nature.[145] Likewise, the Court relied on its ruling from 2015, which indicated that "the constitutional jurisprudence has attended the ancestral knowledge and the alternate currents of thought, coming to sustain that nature is not conceived only as the environment and environment of human beings, but also as a subject with its own rights, which, as such, must be protected and guaranteed."[146]

Based on this precedent, the Court found a need to establish an attitude of deep respect for nature, departing from notions of engagement with nature that are limited to mere utilitarian, economically efficient choices.[147] In compelling language, the Court acknowledged that:

> [T]he greatest challenge of contemporary constitutionalism in environmental matters is to achieve the safeguarding and effective protection of nature, the

---

[141] *Id.*
[142] *Id.* at 2.8.
[143] *Id.* at 3.8.
[144] *Id.* at 5.9 (citing Sentencia C-632 of 2011, 88).
[145] *Id.* (citing Sentencia C-632 of 2011, 87).
[146] *Id.* (citing Sentencia T-080 of 2015, 88).
[147] *Id.* at 5.10 (citing Sentencia C-449 of 2015).

cultures and life forms associated with it and biodiversity, not by the simple material, genetic or productive utility that these may represent for the human being, but because being a living entity composed of other multiple forms of life and cultural representations, they are subjects of individualizable rights, which makes them a new imperative of comprehensive protection and respect on the part of States and societies.[148]

In this respect, both the Constitution and the Constitutional Court decisions, in harmony with international agreements, offer protection of the environment and biodiversity for the benefit of present and future generations. They establish a series of principles and measures directed to the protection and preservation of such legal assets, objectives that must be achieved not only through concrete actions of the state, but with the participation of individuals, civil society, and other social and economic sectors of the country.[149] In this sense, the Court recognized, on one hand, the protection of the environment as a constitutional right intimately linked with life, health and physical, spiritual and cultural integrity. On the other hand, the Court recognized the protection of the environment is a duty, inasmuch as it demands the state and local authorities and private actors to guarantee the protections for which they are responsible.[150]

The Court's reasoning is premised on the notion of bioculturality and biocultural rights, based on "the relationship of profound unity between nature and human species." This relationship is expressed in other complementary elements such as: (1) the multiple ways of life, expressed as cultural diversity, which are inextricably linked to the diversity of ecosystems and territories; (2) the richness expressed in the diversity of cultures, practices, beliefs, and languages, a product of the coevolutionary interrelation of human communities with their environments that constitutes an adaptive response to environmental changes; (3) the relationships of different ancestral cultures with plants, animals, microorganisms, and the environment that actively contribute to biodiversity; (4) the spiritual and cultural meanings of nature to indigenous peoples and local communities as an integral part of biocultural diversity; and (5) how the preservation of cultural diversity leads to the conservation of biological diversity so that the design of policy, legislation, and jurisprudence should be focused on the conservation of bioculturality. The Court considered these elements very relevant and stated that "from now on, [these elements] should be taken into account as parameters for the protection of the rights of the environment and nature, from a biocultural perspective."

The Court crafted a new approach toward protecting natural resources in holding that the Atrato River is subject to rights that imply its protection, conservation, and maintenance. In an unusual approach, the Court instructed the national

[148] *Id.*
[149] *Id.*
[150] *Id.*

government to be the guardian and to exercise legal representation of the river through the president or a representative of the president, along with the ethnic communities that inhabit the basin of the river.[151] Thus, it guarantees the Atrato River is represented by a member of these communities and a delegate of the Colombian government. This decision is a landmark victory not only because of its groundbreaking ecocentric outcome to advance the rights of nature, but also because the Court fashioned this outcome on its own accord in dispensing justice on the merits of this case. The legal personhood status for the Atrato River was not a form of relief that the plaintiffs had requested in filing the case, but the Court exceeded the plaintiffs' expectations and assigned legal personhood status to the river.[152]

B *Oceania*

This section describes a tale of two experiences in rights of nature protections. New Zealand has been a global leader on these issues, whereas Australia's laudable efforts to secure rights of nature protections have been hampered by setbacks and resistance.

1 New Zealand

The Whanganui River runs for 290 kilometers from the center of New Zealand's North Island to the Tasman Sea on the North Island's lower west coast.[153] For over six hundred years, Māori, the indigenous peoples of New Zealand, have lived along the Whanganui, building villages, cultivating sheltered river terraces, and living in harmony with the forests.[154] Today, the river is still home to many descendants of the original inhabitants.[155] Following European settlement in the 1800s, the river

---

[151] *Id.*

[152] For a discussion of the practical and legal impacts of the Atrato River case, *see generally* Nick Mount, *Can a River Have Legal Rights? A Different Approach to Protecting the Environment*, INDEPENDENT (Oct. 13, 2017), www.independent.co.uk/environment/river-legal-rights-colombia-environment-pacific-rainforest-atrato-river-rio-quito-a7991061.html; Susan Bird, *Colombia Grants Legal Rights to the Polluted Atrato River*, TRUTHOUT (June 3, 2017), https://truthout.org/articles/colombia-grants-legal-rights-to-the-polluted-atrato-river/; Bram Ebus, *Colombia's Constitutional Court Grants Rights to the Atrato River and Orders the Government to Clean Up Its Waters*, MONGABAY (May 22, 2017), https://news.mongabay.com/2017/05/colombias-constitutional-court-grants-rights-to-the-atrato-river-and-orders-the-government-to-clean-up-its-waters/; Villa, *supra* note 124.

[153] Erin O'Donnell & Julia Talbot-Jones, *Creating Legal Rights for Rivers: Lessons from Australia, New Zealand, and India*, 23 ECOLOGY & SOC'Y 7 (2018).

[154] New Zealand Government, Department of Conservation, *History and Culture*, www.doc.govt.nz/parks-and-recreation/places-to-go/manawatu-whanganui/places/whanganui-national-park/history-and-culture [hereinafter "New Zealand Government, Department of Conservation"].

[155] *Whanganui River*, VISIT WHANGANUI, www.visitwhanganui.nz/whanganui-river.

became a major attraction, with visitors enjoying leisurely riverboat cruises. The Whanganui River became internationally known as the Rhine of New Zealand.[156] Today, the Whanganui River continues to provide Māori peoples with resources for customary use, including plants and animals for food and medicine,[157] and is a major tourist attraction.

Māori oral tradition conveys the Māori cultural relationship with the natural resources of water, land, and wind, personifying them as sisters, brothers, and ancestors.[158] The Whanganui River "is still seen as both an ancestor and a source of material and spiritual sustenance."[159] This sense of connection is reflected in how the Māori consider themselves and the Whanganui "as an indivisible whole, expressed in the common saying: 'I am the river, and the river is me.'"[160]

For more than a century, the Whanganui River has been the focus of a struggle between the New Zealand government and the Māori over its treatment.[161] In 1840, British crown representatives and five hundred Māori chiefs signed the Treaty of Waitangi.[162] This Treaty granted the Māori exclusive rights over forests, lands, estates, fisheries, and other properties, while giving Great Britain the exclusive right to trade with their population.[163] However, soon after the treaty was signed, the Whanganui River was sold in a contested purchase, which led to "the longest-running legal case in New Zealand history," and finally concluding with the settlement granting the river legal personhood.[164]

As part of settling these ongoing disputes, the Te Awa Tupua (Whanganui River Claims Settlement) Act 2017 ("the Settlement Act") was passed in March 2017 as a Treaty of Waitangi settlement agreement after eight years of negotiation by Whanganui Iwi (tribe) and the New Zealand government.[165] The Settlement Act grants legal personality to the Whanganui River and its catchment and creates a new governance framework for the river. Under the Act, the Whanganui River and ecosystem have legal standing in their own right and are guaranteed "health and

[156] *Id.*
[157] *New Zealand Government, Department of Conservation, supra* note 154.
[158] Caitlin Flannery, *Is It Time We Gave Mother Nature Human Rights? New Zealand Says Yes,* Blue Ocean Network (2017), https://blueocean.net/is-it-time-we-gave-mother-nature-human-rights-new-zealand-says-yes/.
[159] *Id.*
[160] Ashish Kothari et al., *Now Rivers Have the Same Legal Status as People, We Must Uphold Their Rights,* The Guardian (Apr. 21, 2017), www.theguardian.com/global-development-professionals-network/2017/apr/21/rivers-legal-human-rights-ganges-whanganui.
[161] *Id.*
[162] Flannery, *supra* note 158.
[163] *Id.*
[164] *Id.*
[165] O'Donnell & Talbot-Jones, *supra* note 153, at 7.

well-being."[166] The Whanganui River is the first river in the world to hold the same legal rights, liabilities, and responsibilities as a human person.[167] New Zealand's law defines the river's representatives as a committee of indigenous community members that fought for these rights, as well as representatives of the Crown, as New Zealand is part of the British Commonwealth.[168] Thus, the Whanganui tribe and the government must work together and speak on behalf of the river.[169] They are responsible for taking action to court when required and presenting their arguments for the well-being and health of the river.[170] This settlement can also be read as a colonizing nation making reparations for its cultural imposition.[171]

In addition to the complexities that this settlement creates, the government also agreed to pay NZ$80 million dollars (US$56 million dollars) as compensation to the Māori for past abuses and establish a fund of NZ$30 million dollars to enhance the "health and well-being" of the river.[172] This settlement diverges significantly from Ecuador and Bolivia's model by naming specific guardians and not granting positive rights.[173]

Granting legal personhood to the Whanganui River has been the result of an ongoing and extensive dispute between the Whanganui Iwi and the New Zealand Government since the 1870s.[174] Following European settlement of New Zealand, a number of Māori chiefs sought recognition of their trade relationship with Britain, protection from invasion of other countries, and an end of the lawlessness of British people in their country. In order for the British government to formalize the colony, it commenced negotiations with the Māori. The Treaty of Waitangi was drafted in English and translated into Māori before execution on February 6, 1840 by forty-three chiefs, and eventually by over five hundred chiefs across New Zealand.[175]

The treaty has been central in framing the political relationship between the Crown and Māori but has triggered disputes arising from translation disagreements. In particular, the term *tino rangatiratanga* was used in the Māori treaty text to describe what the Māori gained from signing. *Tino rangatiratanga* has been

---

[166] Kothari et al., *supra* note 160.
[167] David Korten, *A New Zealand River Has Human Rights. Now Will Modern Law Come to Its Senses?*, YES! MAGAZINE (July 7, 2017), www.yesmagazine.org/people-power/a-new-zealand-river-has-human-rights-now-will-modern-law-come-to-its-senses-20170707.
[168] *Id.*
[169] Kathleen Calderwood, *Why New Zealand Is Granting a River the Same Rights as a Citizen*, ABC RADIO NAT'L (Sept. 6, 2016), www.abc.net.au/radionational/programs/sundayextra/new-zealand-granting-rivers-and-forests-same-rights-as-citizens/7816456.
[170] *Id.*
[171] Flannery, *supra* note 158.
[172] *Id.*
[173] *Id.*
[174] DAVID YOUNG, WOVEN BY WATER: HISTORIES FROM THE WHANGANUI RIVER 113 (1998).
[175] New Zealand Government, Ministry for Culture and Heritage, *Treaty of Waitangi*, https://mch.govt.nz/treatyofwaitangi.

translated as "the full chieftainship of their lands, their settlements, and all their property"[176] – in other words, sovereignty.[177] The Crown, on the other hand, gained *kāwanatanga*, the right to form government.[178] In 1975, the Waitangi Tribunal was established as a forum to rectify breaches of the Treaty, but also to settle disputes arising out of its translation. Importantly, in 1983, the Waitangi Tribunal defined *kāwanatanga* as "something less than" absolute sovereignty,[179] and in 2014 held that the relevant iwi "did not cede their sovereignty to Britain."[180] The Treaty of Waitangi "inherently contained two understandings of sovereignty and the relationship between the Crown and iwi,"[181] and history has shown the difficulty that this controversy has created.

The turning point in the Whanganui River dispute was the enactment of the Treaty of Waitangi Amendment Act 1985, which created the Waitangi Tribunal and empowered it to hear historic claims dating back to 1840.[182] This legislation caused the relationship between Whanganui Iwi and the Crown to enter a new phase.[183] Further establishing the foundations on which the Whanganui River settlement was possible, in 1988 the Whanganui River Māori Trust Board Act 1988 established a Trust Board comprised of nine members appointed by the Minister of Māori Affairs to represent the iwi in future negotiation and litigation against the Crown.[184]

The Trust Board submitted its claim to the Waitangi Tribunal in 1990, and public hearings began in 1994. The Waitangi Tribunal finalized the Wanganui River Report in 1999, which formed the basis of future negotiations.[185]

On August 30, 2012, Whanganui Iwi and the Crown signed an agreement, Tūtohu Whakatupua, which recorded the key elements of the agreed framework for the Whanganui River.[186] The Deed of Settlement was signed and ratified by Whanganui Iwi members and the Crown on August 5, 2014.[187] The Deed of Settlement consists of two documents. The first is Ruruku Whakatupua – Te Mana

---

[176] VINCENT O'MALLEY, BRUCE STIRLING & WALLY PENETITO, EDS., THE TREATY OF WAITANGI COMPANION: MAORI AND PAKEHA FROM TASMAN TO TODAY 41 (2014).

[177] Claudia Orange, The Treaty of Waitangi 154 (2011).

[178] STEPHANIE WARREN, WHANGANUI RIVER AND TE UREWERA TREATY SETTLEMENTS: INNOVATIVE DEVELOPMENTS FOR THE PRACTICE OF RANGATIRATANGA IN RESOURCE MANAGEMENT 13 (Master's thesis, Victoria University of Wellington, 2016).

[179] Waitangi Tribunal, *Report of the Waitangi Tribunal on the Motunui-Waitara Claim* 66 (1983).

[180] Waitangi Tribunal, *Te Urewera Pre-publication, Part Five* WAI 894, 529 (2014).

[181] WARREN, *supra* note 178, at 14.

[182] Treaty of Waitangi Amendment Act 1985, § 3.

[183] WARREN, *supra* note 178, at 36.

[184] Waitangi Tribunal, *The Whanganui River Report* 246 (1999).

[185] *Id.*

[186] New Zealand Government, *Whanganui Iwi (Whanganui River) Deed of Settlement: Background*, www.govt.nz/treaty-settlement-documents/whanganui-iwi/whanganui-iwi-whanganui-river-deed-of-settlement-summary-5-aug-2014/background/.

[187] Office of Treaty Settlements, *Ruruku Whakatupua – Whanganui River Deed of Settlement between the Crown and Whanganui Iwi* 3 (2012) [hereinafter "Ruruku Whakatupua"].

o Te Awa Tupua, which is directed at the formation of a new legal framework.[188] It includes recognition of the Whanganui River as a legal person with all the corresponding rights, duties, and liabilities of a legal person and that the river is Te Awa Tupua, a living being and an indivisible entity incorporating all its physical and metaphysical elements.[189] The second is Ruruku Whakatupua – Te Mana o Te Iwi o Whanganui, which is directed at the Whanganui Iwi and sets out further development of their relationship with the Whanganui River through both cultural and financial redress.[190] The second document contains an iwi narrative and an agreed historical account of the river. A particularly important component of this settlement is the Crown's acknowledgment of its past acts and omissions relating to the Whanganui River and its apology for failing to protect the interests of Whanganui Iwi and causing adverse effects and prejudice to Whanganui Iwi.[191]

The Deed of Settlement sets out a set of intrinsic values that represent the essence of Te Awa Tupua. These are:[192]

(a) *Ko te Awa te mātāpuna o te ora* (**The River is the source of spiritual and physical sustenance**)
Te Awa Tupua is a spiritual and physical entity that supports and sustains both the life and natural resources within the Whanganui River and the health and well-being of the iwi, hapū and other communities of the River.

(b) *E rere kau mai te Awa nui mai te Kahui Maunga ki Tangaroa* (**The great River flows from the mountains to the sea**)
Te Awa Tupua is an indivisible and living whole from the mountains to the sea, incorporating the Whanganui River and all of its physical and metaphysical elements.

(c) *Ko au te Awa, ko te Awa ko au* (**I am the River, and the River is me**)
The iwi and hapū of the Whanganui River have an inalienable interconnection with, and responsibility to, Te Awa Tupua and its health and well-being.

(d) *Ngā manga iti, ngā manga nui e honohono kau ana, ka tupu hei Awa Tupua* (**The small and large streams that flow into one another and form one River**)
Te Awa Tupua is a singular entity composed of many elements and communities, working collaboratively to fulfill the common purpose of the health and well-being of Te Awa Tupua.

---

[188] *Id.* at 2.
[189] *Id.* at 6.
[190] *Ruruku Whakatupua, supra* note 187, at 3.
[191] *Id.*
[192] *Id.* at 2.

The financial redress included in the settlement package will total NZ$81 million dollars, plus interest accrued since the Deed of Settlement was signed.[193] NZ$30 million dollars was dedicated to the establishment of Te Korotete (a fund to support the health and well-being of the river), granting NZ$200,000 per year for twenty years for Te Pou Tupua (the comanagement position, which means "the human face of the River" and is jointly appointed by the iwi of Te Awa Tupua and the Crown) to develop the Te Awa Tupua strategy, and NZ$430,000 for the establishment of Te Heke Ngahuru (the strategy that will identify issues relating to environmental, social, cultural and economic health of the River and make recommendations on how to address those issues).[194] Ngā Tāngata Tiaki o Whanganui was also established as the Post Settlement Governance Entity, which replaced the Whanganui River Māori Trust Board and receives the financial redress on behalf of Whanganui Iwi.[195]

On March 20, 2017, royal assent was granted to the Settlement Act, the legislation that gives legal effect to the Whanganui River settlement. Section 14 is the operative provision creating Te Awa Tupua, and the Whanganui River as a legal person with all accompanying rights, powers, duties, and liabilities.

Section 3 of the Settlement Act defines its purpose as:

(a) to record the acknowledgments and apology given by the Crown to Whanganui Iwi in Ruruku Whakatupua – Te Mana o Te Iwi o Whanganui (the second document in the Deed of Settlement); and

(b) to give effect to the provisions of the deed of settlement that establish Te Pā Auroa nā Te Awa Tupua (the River as an indivisible legal entity); and

(c) to give effect to the provisions of the deed of settlement that settle the historical claims of Whanganui Iwi as those claims relate to the Whanganui River.

To achieve this purpose, the Settlement Act creates a number of regulatory bodies and functions. Section 18 establishes Te Pou Tupua, an office to act as the human face of the River and act in its name.[196] Section 20 provides the process for appointments to Te Pou Tupua and stipulates that the office must be comprised of two people, a representative of the Crown and a representative of Whanganui Iwi. Section 14(2) states that Te Pou Tupua must exercise or perform the rights, powers,

---

[193] *Id.* at 4.
[194] Linda Te Aho, *Ruruku Whakatupua Te Mana o te Awa Tupua – Upholding the Mana of the Whanganui River*, Maori L. Rev. (May 2014), http://maorilawreview.co.nz/2014/05/ruruku-whakatupua-te-mana-o-te-awa-tupua-upholding-the-mana-of-the-whanganui-river/; *Ruruku Whakatupua, supra* note 187, at 4.
[195] Ngā Tāngata Tiaki, *About Us*, www.ngatangatatiaki.co.nz/?page_id=515.
[196] Te Awa Tupua (Whanganui River Claims Settlement) Act 2017, § 18 [hereinafter "Whanganui River Claims Settlement"].

and duties of the river, and that Te Pou Tupua will be responsible for the river's liabilities. These duties include acting and speaking on behalf of the river and promoting and protecting its health.[197] The Settlement Act also provides for administrative matters related to Te Pou Tupua, including tax and audit requirements.[198] Section 27 establishes Te Karewao, an advisory group to provide advice and support to Te Pou Tupua in performing its functions.

Section 29 establishes Te Kōpuka, a permanent strategy committee for the river made up of no more than seventeen members with a vested interest in the river.[199] This may include iwi, environmental groups, local authorities, state departments, recreational users, and commercial users.[200] The primary function of Te Kōpuka is to develop a strategy for the management of the river and to provide a forum for discussion regarding its health and well-being.[201]

With respect to property rights, section 40 provides that on the settlement date any Crown-owned part of the river bed ceased to be a conservation area, Crown land, a national park, or a reserve for the purposes of the relevant legislation.[202] Instead, section 41 states that, on the settlement date, the fee simple estate in the Crown-owned parts of the Whanganui River bed vested in Te Awa Tupua (the legal person). The entire river is not vested in Te Awa Tupua; only the river bed. Section 46 provides that the vesting of Crown-owned parts of the river bed does not include a proprietary interest in the water, wildlife, fish, aquatic life, seaweeds, or plants (unless the plants are attached to the river bed). Section 46 also stipulates that certain matters are not affected by the vesting of Crown land, including public use of, and access to, and across the river, any private property rights, certain fishing rights, and any statutory functions and powers of local authorities, which are all preserved.

Prior to this groundbreaking legislation granting legal personhood to the Whanganui River, a former New Zealand national park also was granted personhood.[203] Up until 2014, Te Urewera was an 821-square-mile national park, but once the Te Urewera Act[204] took effect, "the government gave up formal ownership, and the land became a legal entity with 'all the rights, powers, duties and liabilities of a legal person'."[205]

---

[197] *Id.* § 14(2).

[198] *Id.* §§ 21–25.

[199] *Id.* §§ 32(1).

[200] *Id.* § 29(2).

[201] *Id.*

[202] The relevant legislation is the Conservation Act 1987, Land Act 1948, National Parks Act 1980, and Reserves Act 1977.

[203] Bryant Rousseau, *In New Zealand, Lands and Rivers Can Be People (Legally Speaking)*, N.Y. Times (July 13, 2016), www.nytimes.com/2016/07/14/world/what-in-the-world/in-new-zealand-lands-and-rivers-can-be-people-legally-speaking.html.

[204] Env't Guide, *Te Urewera Act*, Environment Guide (Nov. 17, 2017), www.environmentguide .org.nz/regional/te-urewera-act/.

[205] Rousseau, *supra* note 203.

In 2014, the New Zealand government enacted legislation granting legal person-
ality to Te Urewera,[206] a 12,127 square–kilometer forest forming the ancestral land of
Tūhoe Māori, the largest area of native forest remaining on the North Island and
home to nearly all species of New Zealand's native birds.[207] Under the Te Urewera
Act 2014, Te Urewera National Park became a legal entity and its management
responsibilities were transferred from the Department of Conservation to a new Te
Urewera Board.[208] The Te Urewera Act provides that for the first three years, the Te
Urewera Board is comprised of equal membership of Crown and Tūhoe, each with
four appointed representatives. After three years, the Board is to be made up of nine
members, of which six will be Tūhoe appointed and three will be appointed by the
Minister for Conservation.[209]

An important legal distinction between the settlements of the Whanganui River
and the Te Urewera National Park is that the Tūhoe Māori never signed the Treaty
of Waitangi, instead seeking to maintain sovereignty over their lands.[210] This is
significant as it demonstrates the New Zealand Government's willingness to grant
legal personality to resources where claims arise from varying historical contexts.
Another distinction lies in the fact that the Te Urewera Act contains an exception
that allows future mining activities within the National Park by treating Te Urewera
land as Crown land for the purposes of the Crown Minerals Act 1991.[211] This allows
mining to be undertaken within Te Urewera under the Crown's authority without
the authorization of the Te Urewera Board, which suggests that the Whanganui
River Settlement Act provides a more protective form of legal personhood than is
provided for Te Urewera.

The granting of legal personhood to Te Urewera and the Whanganui River is not
only reflective of postcolonial legal redress for New Zealand's indigenous people,
but also recognizes the Māori's spiritual connection to the land and understanding
of humanity's place in the world. Following the Whanganui River settlement,
Gerrard Albert, the lead negotiator for the Whanganui Iwi said:[212]

> We have fought to find an approximation in law so that all others can understand
> that from our perspective treating the river as a living entity is the correct way to

---

[206] New Zealand Legislation, *Te Urewera Act 2014*, § 11, Parliamentary Council Office (July 27, 2014), www.legislation.govt.nz/act/public/2014/0051/latest/DLM6183601.html [hereinafter "Te Urewera Act 2014"].

[207] New Zealand, *Te Urewera*, www.newzealand.com/au/feature/te-urewera/.

[208] Te Urewera Act 2014, § 12.

[209] *Id.* § 21.

[210] Environmental Justice Atlas, *Māori Resistance Results in Te Urewera Gaining Legal Personality, New Zealand*, https://ejatlas.org/conflict/rights-of-nature-māori-resistance-results-in-te-urewera-former-national-park-gaining-legal-personality.

[211] Crown Minerals Act 1991, § 614.

[212] Eleanor Ainge Roy, *New Zealand River Granted Same Legal Rights as Human Being*, THE GUARDIAN (Mar. 16, 2017), www.theguardian.com/world/2017/mar/16/new-zealand-river-granted-same-legal-rights-as-human-being.

approach it, as an indivisible whole, instead of the traditional model for the last 100 years of treating it from a perspective of ownership and management ... We can trace our genealogy to the origins of the universe and therefore rather than us being masters of the natural world, we are part of it. We want to live like that as our starting point. And that is not an anti-development, or anti-economic use of the river but to begin with the view that it is a living being, and then consider its future from that central belief.

These two New Zealand examples demonstrate that the concept of legal personhood is capable of granting varying levels of protection to natural features, arising from varying circumstances. The Whanganui River Settlement Act appears to be more proscriptive. Not only does it explicitly state that Te Awa Tupua is a legal person and has all the rights, powers, duties, and liabilities of a legal person, but it also establishes a complex governance mechanism for the long-term maintenance of the entire ecosystem and community. With respect to standing, the Whanganui River Settlement Act establishes the "face of the river" to represent it – the river's two guardians, one from the Crown and one from the Whanganui Iwi – and makes reference to "Whanganui Iwi standing" in Part 3, Subpart 2.[213]

The Whanganui River Settlement Act specifies that, for the purposes of the Resources Management Act of 1991, the trustees "are entitled to lodge submissions on a matter ... affecting the Whanganui River" and are "recognized as having an interest ... greater than any interest in common with the public generally."[214] Decision makers exercising regulatory functions under environmental legislation set out in Schedule 2, Part 1 of the Whanganui River Settlement Act must "recognise and provide for" the Te Awa Tupua status and Tupua Te Kawa in their decision making. This applies to the most important environmental governance measures in New Zealand and is intended to ensure that the unique status of the Te Awa Tupua is reflected in plans and project governance under, *inter alia*, the National Parks Act 1980, Local Government Acts 1974 and 2002, the River Boards Act 1908, the Walking Access Act 2008, the Reserves Act 1977, and the Resource Management Act 1991.[215]

Nevertheless, there is some concern that the status of *Te Heke Ngahuru* (the river strategy) is relatively weak, because those exercising powers or duties under any of the environmental management instruments referred to in the Whanganui River Settlement Act are only required to have a "particular regard" to *Te Heke Ngahuru*.[216] With its implementation under the Resources Management Act, there is a risk that this could be another example of cultural and ecological interests being

---

[213] Lidia Cano Pecharroman, *Rights of Nature: Rivers That Can Stand in Court*, 7 RESOURCES 13 (2018).

[214] *Whanganui River Claims Settlement, supra* note 196, pt. 3, subpt. 2.

[215] *See* Christopher Rodgers, *A New Approach to Protecting Ecosystems: The Te Awa Tupua (Whanganui River Claims Settlement) Act 2017*, 19 ENVTL. L. REV. 226 (2017).

[216] *Whanganui River Claims Settlement, supra* note 196, § 37.

outweighed by economic ones, which may result in few new outcomes under the Whanganui River Settlement Act, if any.[217]

The Te Urewera Act also grants legal personality as a separate legal entity.[218] It establishes the structure for governance and management of the entity[219] to recognize the forest's "intrinsic values ... by putting it beyond human owner-ship."[220] The implementation of the Te Urewera Act is described in section 5, which requires all persons performing or exercising functions under the part of the Act relating to the legal entity of to act in accordance with those principles.[221] However, the Crown's authority to allow and undertake mining activities within Te Urewera without the authorization of the Te Urewera Board is a significant limitation of the Te Urewera legislation.

Given the novelty of these instruments, only time will tell how these norms will be applied to practical matters,[222] such as future developments or industrial projects. While the practical realities of the future management of resources under the new legislation are still being assessed, the enactment of these two news laws is significant in its shift towards an appreciation and recognition of the rights of nature. Additionally, it shows a willingness on the part of the New Zealand community to honor both its indigenous and colonial histories, while forging new norms to protect its environment.[223]

2 Australia

Australia's Great Barrier Reef (GBR) is the world's largest coral reef stretching twenty-three hundred kilometers along the Queensland coastline and covering an area of 344,400 square kilometers, making it the largest living structure on the planet. It is the size of Japan, bigger than the United Kingdom, Switzerland, and the Netherlands combined, and can be seen from space.[224] The GBR is a unique ecosystem, home to 1,625 species of fish, over 600 types of hard and soft coral, and 30 species of whales and dolphins.[225] One of the seven natural wonders of the world and a UNESCO World Heritage Site, it contributes an estimated AU$6.4 billion to

---

[217] See Tyson Hullena, *Te Awa Tupua (Whanganui River Claims Settlement) Act 2017 and Lex Aotearoa*, MAORI L. REV. (Feb. 2017), http://maorilawreview.co.nz/2017/02/sir-edward-taiha kurei-durie-student-essay-competition-2016-te-awa-tupua-whanganui-river-claims-settlement-act-2017-and-lex-aotearoa/.

[218] *Te Urewera Act 2014, supra* note 205, § 11.

[219] *Id.* pt. 2.

[220] *Te Urewera-Tūhoe Bill 2013* (146-1) (explanatory note).

[221] *Te Urewera Act 2014, supra* note 205, § 5.

[222] Pecharroman, *supra* note 213.

[223] See Liz Charpleix, *The Whanganui River as Te Awa Tupua: Place-Based Law in a Legally Pluralistic Society*, 184 GEOGRAPHIC J. 19 (2018).

[224] Deloitte, *At What Price? The Economic, Social and Icon Value of the Great Barrier Reef* (Report, 2018), 3, www2.deloitte.com/content/dam/Deloitte/au/Documents/Economics/deloitte-au-econom ics-great-barrier-reef-230617.pdf.

[225] *The Facts*, GREAT BARRIER REEF FOUNDATION, www.barrierreef.org/the-reef/the-facts.

the Australian economy each year and supports sixty-four thousand jobs.[226] Sir David Attenborough described the GBR as "one of the greatest, and most splendid treasures that the world possesses."[227]

In 2012, the Australian Institute of Marine Science and the University of Wollongong found that the GBR had lost half its coral in the preceding twenty-seven years due to increased tropical cyclones (48 percent), coral predation by the crown-of-thorns starfish (42 percent), and coral bleaching due to warmer waters (10 percent).[228]

In 2004, a report was filed with the World Heritage Committee requesting the GBR to be added to the List of World Heritage in Danger, which the World Heritage Committee addressed as a petition. The petition argued that by 2100 the GBR site might be without coral due to climate change and that Australia needed to dramatically reduce its greenhouse gas emissions. The petition also called for Australia to include in its periodic reporting to the General Conference of UNESCO "information and documentation concerning the development of Australia's climate change policy and an assessment of the extent to which the integrity of the [GBR World Heritage Area] has been impaired by the effects of climate change."[229]

In 2015, the Australian and Queensland Governments released the Reef 2050 Long-Term Sustainability Plan ("Reef 2050"), a blueprint for protecting the GBR in partnership with governments, scientists, Traditional Owners, community, and industry. Reef 2050 contains concrete targets, actions, objectives, and outcomes along with defined areas of responsibility to comprehensively preserve the GBR's health and resilience while allowing ecologically sustainable use. Projected investment in the coming decade for research and management activities on the GBR and in the adjoining catchments along the Queensland coast is more than AU$2 billion.[230]

In 2017, UNESCO's World Heritage Committee recognized Australia's efforts to improve the health and status of the reef by deciding against placing the GBR on its "in danger" list. Such a listing would require the World Heritage Committee to develop and adopt, in consultation with the Australian government, a program for corrective measures, and subsequently to monitor the situation of the site. Following

---

[226] Deloitte, *supra* note 224.

[227] *Id.*

[228] Australian Institute of Marine Science, *The Great Barrier Reef Has Lost Half of Its Coral in the Last 27 Years* (2012), www.aims.gov.au/docs/media/latest-releases/-/asset_publisher/8Kfw/content/2-october-2012-the-great-barrier-reef-has-lost-half-of-its-coral-in-the-last-27-years.

[229] Keely Boom, *Climate Justice for Future Generations: A Case Study in the Great Barrier Reef World Heritage Site of Australia,* in CLIMATE JUSTICE: CASE STUDIES IN GLOBAL AND REGIONAL GOVERNANCE CHALLENGES 611 (Randall S. Abate ed., 2016).

[230] Australia Department of the Environment and Energy, *Highlights of the Reef 2050 Long-Term Sustainability Plan* (2015), www.environment.gov.au/marine/gbr/publications/highlights-long-term-sustainability-plan.

a site's listing on the UNESCO List of World Heritage In Danger,[231] all efforts must be made to restore the site's values in order to enable its removal from the list as soon as possible.[232] A listing would have been potentially disastrous for the GBR tourism industry, which has always been a significant motivation for government action to protect the reef, rather than a focus on sustainable environmental practice or protection.

The Environmental Protection and Biodiversity Conservation Act 1999 (Cth) (EPBC Act) is the principal regulatory framework governing decisions affecting the environment in Australia. It applies to any action that has, will have, or is likely to have a "significant impact" on a matter of national environmental significance, including World Heritage Sites such as the GBR.[233] The EPBC Act aims are to promote a "co-operative approach to the protection and management of the environment involving governments, the community, land-holders and indigenous peoples"; "co-operative implementation of Australia's international environmental responsibilities"; and "a partnership approach to environmental protection and biodiversity conservation."[234]

There are two provisions of the EPBC Act that are particularly relevant to the GBR. Section 322(2) states that the federal government must take all reasonable steps to ensure it exercises its powers and performs its functions in relation to the property in a way that is consistent with the World Heritage Convention.[235] In addition, section 137 provides that:

> [I]n deciding whether or not to approve ... the taking of an action and what conditions to attach to such an approval, the Minister must not act inconsistently with:
>   (a) Australia's obligations under the World Heritage Convention; or
>   (b) the Australian World Heritage management principles; or
>   (c) a plan that has been prepared for the management of a declared World Heritage property under section 316 or 321.[236]

The GBR is currently afforded a limited form of legal standing under the EPBC Act. Individuals and organizations can commence a proceeding or an appeal, for the purposes of judicial review under the EPBC Act, if they can show: (a) Australian citizenship, residency or, in the case of an unnatural person, establishment; and (b) environmental protection, conservation, or research activities within the previous

---

[231] United Nations Educational, Scientific and Cultural Organization, List of World Heritage in Danger, https://whc.unesco.org/en/danger/.
[232] Id.
[233] Environmental Protection and Biodiversity Conservation Act 1999 (Cth), § 12.
[234] Id. § 3(1).
[235] Id. § 322.
[236] Id. § 137.

two years.[237] The only caveat is that the action must be related to a decision made, the failure to make a decision, or conduct engaged in for the purpose of making a decision, under the EPBC Act.[238] Standing under the EPBC Act does not apply exclusively to the GBR, but to all decisions made under the instrument in relation to, for example, matters of national environmental significance and the conservation of Australian biodiversity.

In recent years, momentum has been building in the Australian civil society community to achieve greater protection of the GBR so that one of the country's greatest assets is not lost. One such effort has been the push to have the GBR granted legal personhood.[239] Current environmental law in Australia is based on principles of short-term economic gain rather than long-term sustainability.[240] Where legislation establishes restrictions on potentially detrimental impacts to the World Heritage value of the GBR, it also carves out exceptions to this protection, enabling harm of any magnitude to be approved by the relevant minister.[241]

The Environmental Defenders Office of Northern Queensland (EDONQ), the primary entity seeking legal personhood for the reef, has expressed its concern that the federal government has the power to undertake environmental restoration itself, or oblige others to do so, but there are currently no compulsory obligations on either government or the persons causing harm to undertake such measures.[242] Legal personhood would grant the GBR representation to have its interests pursued in major decisions, ensuring that relevant federal and state government departments and agencies perform their environmental protection functions consistently and effectively. EDONQ envisioned that trustees would also have power to legally enforce the GBR's rights if the government disregards these rights.[243] In its campaign, EDONQ noted that granting legal personhood to the GBR would have little effect on day-to-day management of the GBR. The Great Barrier Reef Marine Park Authority would still oversee everyday activities on the reef, tourist operators would continue their business as usual, and tourists would continue to enjoy the beauty of the GBR.

In its efforts to achieve legal personhood for the GBR, EDONQ relied on the global movement that has begun to secure recognition of the rights of nature to exist and flourish. Using Ecuador, Bolivia, and India as examples, EDONQ argued that giving the GBR the right to exist and flourish would enable the reef, through a board

[237] *Id.* § 487.
[238] *Id.*
[239] Legal personhood is referred to as "legal personality" in Australia; however, these terms are interchangeable.
[240] Peter Burdon, *Earth Jurisprudence and the Murray Darling*, 32 ALTERNATIVE LAW J. 82 (2012); Environmental Defenders Office of Northern Queensland, *Legal Personality for the Great Barrier Reef – What Does It Mean?* 2 (Discussion Paper, Mar. 10, 2014).
[241] Environmental Protection and Biodiversity Conservation Act 1999 (Cth) §§ 12 and 15A; *Id.*
[242] *Id.* at 3.
[243] *Id.*

of trustees acting on its behalf, to protect these rights where government and industry actions and inactions jeopardize the sustainability of the GBR.[244]

EDONQ maintains that if the GBR were granted legal personality to enforce these fundamental rights, it would not mean that activities likely to impede these rights or that all human interaction with the reef would be stopped because rights are never absolute. The GBR's rights may not always prevail. The result of such rights would mean that during consideration of a project proposal that may harm the GBR, the rights of the reef would need to be balanced against the benefits of the prospective project.[245]

The right of people to a healthy reef and the needs of future generations were essential components of the argument of legal personality for the GBR. Drawing on experience in India, EDONQ referenced the National Ganga Rights Act, which includes provisions establishing "the rights of people, as well as other ecosystems and natural communities, to a healthy river basin."[246] Another important right EDONQ envisioned being granted to the GBR included a right to restoration,[247] modeling the right on Ecuador's constitution and Bolivia's Charter for Mother Earth.[248]

On February 20, 2014, EDONQ launched its campaign to obtain legal personhood for the GBR. The timing of EDONQ's campaign was critical. Around this time, the Environmental Defenders Office Queensland (EDOQ) took action on behalf of the North Queensland Conservation Council, with the support of protest group GetUp Australia, in the Administrative Appeals Tribunal to overturn the government decision to dump three million cubic meters of dredge spoil inside the GBR World Heritage area.[249]

EDONQ argued that there were many ways that the GBR could be granted legal personhood. "Trustees could be appointed to look after the natural ecosystem and act on behalf of the entity" and the trustees would be "respected groups (or people) who are devoted to the protection of the natural environment, or another simple way is for all people to have standing to protect the interest of the Reef."[250] EDONQ called on parties interested in protecting the GBR World Heritage area to form a working group to draft a bill to define the rights sought for the GBR through the

---

[244] *Id.* at 6.

[245] *Id.* at 6.

[246] *Id.*

[247] *Id.*

[248] CONST. OF ECUADOR (2008), art 72; Peter Burdon, *The Rights of Nature: Reconsidered*, 49 AUSTL. HUMANITIES REV. 69, 76 (2011).

[249] Denise Carter Kimberly Vlasic, *Environmental Defenders Office NQ Set to Launch Push to Make Great Barrier Reef Its Own Legal Identity*, CAIRNS POST (Feb. 4, 2014), www.cairnspost .com.au/news/cairns/environmental-defenders-office-nq-set-to-launch-push-to-make-great-bar rier-reef-its-own-legal-identity/news-story/495f0e464a6791c2fda50028b80da3e6.

[250] *Id.*

conferral of legal personhood.[251] However, unlike efforts in other countries to have legal personhood granted to natural features, the campaign to have the GBR afforded legal rights has so far struggled to gain traction.

Australian Earth Laws Alliance (AELA) has also created a set of draft laws that focus on granting rights for the GBR, aimed at three levels of government in Australia: state, local, and constitutional.[252] The State draft laws recognize the GBR as a living entity with a right to exist, thrive, and evolve and a right to a healthy climate. The laws also recognize the rights of First Nations peoples and community members to defend the rights of the reef and calls for similar federal legislation.[253] The draft model local law is ambitious in the Australian context as it rejects the current convention that state laws preempt local laws. It seeks to support greater democracy and greater custodianship of the living world, allowing local communities to have more meaningful input in how the reef is managed.[254] Finally, AELA's draft constitutional amendment seeks recognition of the rights of nature and the GBR at the federal level, similar to the approach in Ecuador.[255]

There is precedent in Australia for the GBR to have its legal rights recognized, but not to the extent of legal personhood. Water resource management in Australia is regulated at a state level, with Victoria taking a novel approach to its water laws and leading the way in a rights-based approach to protecting natural features. The Victorian Environmental Water Reserve (EWR) is an independent statutory body responsible for holding and managing Victoria's environmental water entitlements. Its purpose is to provide and maintain the necessary river flows to support the health of rivers, wetlands, and estuaries throughout Victoria.[256] During a period of extreme drought in Victoria, it became apparent that the regulatory framework was placing environmental water management decisions under unnecessary political pressure.[257] In 2010, ownership of the water entitlements component of the EWR was granted to the Victorian Environmental Water Holder (VEWH), a newly established entity empowered with the responsibility for holding and managing water rights for the purpose of maintaining and improving the health of the aquatic environment. The VEWH is statutorily bound to make annual determinations regarding how its water rights will be exercised.

---

[251] *Environmental Defenders Office of Northern Queensland, supra* note 240, at 14.

[252] Australian Earth Laws Alliance, *Draft Laws Recognising the Rights of the Reef*, https://right sofnature.org.au/gbr-campaign/draft-laws-for-the-gbr/.

[253] Australian Earth Laws Alliance, *Draft Legal Rights of the Great Barrier Reef Bill 2018*, https:// rightsofnature.org.au/wp-content/uploads/2018/08/Draft-State-Law_Rights-of-the-GBR.pdf.

[254] Australian Earth Laws Alliance, *Draft Local Law (Rights of the Great Barrier Reef)* 2018, https:// rightsofnature.org.au/wp-content/uploads/2018/08/Draft-Local-Law_Rights-of-the-Great-Bar rier-Reef.pdf.

[255] Australian Earth Laws Alliance, *supra* note 253.

[256] Erin O'Donnell & Julia Talbot-Jones, *Creating Legal Rights for Rivers: Lessons from Australia, New Zealand, and India*, 32 ECOLOGY & SOC'Y 7, 7 (2018).

[257] Erin O'Donnell, *Institutional Reform in Environmental Water Management: The New Victorian Environmental Water Holder*, 22 J. WATER L. 73, 79 (2012).

Victoria's Yarra River has been granted an especially high level of protection in the enactment of the Yarra River Protection (Wilip-gin Birrarung murron) Act 2017 (Vic) ("Yarra River Act"), which is Australia's first legislative recognition of a Rights of Nature approach. Additionally, the use of Woi-wurrung, the language of the Wurundjeri people, represents the first time language of Traditional Owners has appeared in the title of an Act of Victorian Parliament.[258] *Wilip-gin Birrarung murron* is translated to "keep the Yarra alive."[259] Section 1 states that the purposes of the Yarra River Act are to provide for the protection of the river as "one living and integrated natural entity," to establish the Birrarung Council to provide advice to the minister in relation to the river and surrounding land in terms of development, and to establish principles to which public entities must adhere when performing duties or exercising powers in relation to the Yarra River.[260] The Birrarung Council, established under Part 5 of the Yarra River Act, does not consist of any government representatives.

Part 2 of the Yarra River Act provides for the Yarra Protection Principles on which decisions concerning the river should be based. These are divided into general principles, environmental principles, social principles, recreational principles, cultural principles, and management principles.[261] Notable principles include that each generation should ensure that the environmental, social, and cultural benefits that have been acquired are maintained or enhanced for the benefit of future generations, and environmental practices and procedures should ensure that biodiversity and ecological integrity is maintained or enhanced in ways that are proportionate to the significance of the environmental risks and consequences being addressed.[262]

To achieve its purpose, Part 4 of the Yarra River Act provides for the development of a strategic plan for the protection and management of the Yarra, to be informed by the Yarra Protection Principles.[263] Although the Yarra River Act recognizes the river as a living and integrated entity, it does not explicitly establish the river as a legal person. Instead it uses language to affirm the intrinsic and human values of the river.[264] Rather than focusing on the river as a separate legal person, the legislation seeks to recognize the cultural and social significance of the Yarra River

---

[258] State Government of Victoria Department of Planning, *Yarra River Protection* (2018), www.planning.vic.gov.au/policy-and-strategy/waterways-planning/yarra-river-protection.

[259] Katie O'Bryan, *New Law Finally Gives Voice to the Yarra River's Traditional Owners*, SBS NEWS (Sept. 27, 2017), www.sbs.com.au/nitv/article/2017/09/27/new-law-finally-gives-voice-yarra-rivers-traditional-owners.

[260] Yarra River Protection (Wilip-gin Birrarung murron) Act 2017 (Vic.), § 1.

[261] *Id.* §§ 7–13.

[262] *Id.* §§ 8(4), 9(2).

[263] *Id.* pt. 4.

[264] Environmental Justice Australia, *New Ways for Law to Protect Nature: Victoria's Yarra Act Part of a Gradual Shift* (2018), www.envirojustice.org.au/projects/new-ways-for-law-to-protect-nature-victorias-yarra-act-part-of-a-gradual-shift/.

to the Victorian Traditional Owners and the various communities who live along-side and connect to the river.[265] Although the legislation has many of the same characteristics of the instruments that grant legal personhood to natural features in other countries, such as in New Zealand, the Parliament of Victoria has focused on the river's relationship with the people who have a connection to it rather than on establishing it as a legal person itself. A critical feature that distinguishes the developments under the Yarra River Act from legal personhood is that the Birrarung Council is established to advocate for the protection and preservation of the Yarra River, but the council is not the embodiment of the river advocating for itself.

The author interviewed Dr. Michelle Maloney, Co-Founder and National Convenor of the Australian Earth Laws Alliance (AELA), to solicit her reflections on her efforts with AELA to show how legal rights could be created for the Great Barrier Reef.[266]

ABATE: How does AELA's campaign to obtain legal recognition of the Great Barrier Reef's rights relate to the concept of legal personhood? Is legal personhood a goal of the campaign?

MALONEY: We started promoting the model laws only a month ago to build the profile of what nature laws can look like. Legal personhood to us is a linked but slightly different issue. When we explain to people about the rights of nature movement, we tend to differentiate between the laws created by the Ecuadorian Constitution, the Bolivian National Law (the Act for Mother Earth), and the US approach to enacting local ordinances for the rights of nature. Those three approaches all assert positive rights for nature, and they assert open standing for anybody in the community. They don't talk about legal personhood and they don't limit who can speak for nature. We have been watching for many years the developments under the Treaty of Waitangi for New Zealand's Māori people who have used compensation agreements under the Treaty of Waitangi process to seek access to, ownership of, or compensation for the loss of their tribal or traditional lands. Under that arrangement – from all the research and the discussions we've had with the locals there – the legal personhood structure, particularly for the first instance,

[265] Commissioner for Environmental Sustainability Victoria, *Discussing the State of the Yarra at the Victorian Catchments Summit* (2018); Government of Victoria, www.ces.vic.gov.au/articles/discussing-state-yarra-victorian-catchments-summit.
[266] Interview with Dr. Michelle Maloney, Co-Founder and National Convenor, Australian Earth Laws Alliance (Sept. 14, 2018), www.earthlaws.org.au/.

for the Whanganui River, was really reached as a convenient construct because the government would not let the Māori own it and the Māori people would not give it up and sign onto a compensation agreement until they got greater access to their traditional lands. The legal personhood construct in that country represents to us a really important but unique aspect of their colonial legacy. You have Māori people advocating for access as custodians and guardians of their traditional lands, which are particular ecosystems, which is a very different approach to what we see as a much broader "rights of nature" movement. And then we watched Courts in India and Colombia make decisions locally about legal personhood, while referring directly to the New Zealand situation. So we are now seeing a really interesting discussion and debate amongst lawyers about legal personhood, guardianship, etc., but "rights of nature" as a concept is receiving less legal scrutiny. So what we did with the Great Barrier Reef was articulate a vision similar to that which we call a rights of nature framework, articulating that the Great Barrier Reef is a living entity with its own legal rights but opening it up so that we did not articulate those legal rights as legal personhood or guardianship. Our model laws set out positive rights and open standing to anyone in the community to defend the rights of the reef. We articulate what the Reef's rights are in the draft legislation. I remember you asked me what the barriers were to having legal rights for the Reef, and I would say we have a lot of political resistance to putting constraints on industry activity and also, awe have a very conservative legal system in Australia. While other countries may change their constitutions more regularly, we have one of the oldest continuous modern constitutions in the world and in our legal system it's often hard to change core elements of how the law works, especially regarding environmental protection. Our legal system is not going to leap forward into recognizing the rights of nature just yet, so what we are doing is working on projects that can articulate what that looks like and still put First Nations people front and center. In our draft laws, which are really designed to open up conversations, you will see that we have included a provision setting out that First Nations peoples should have the right to defend their ancestral lands and if, for example, any other non-Indigenous entities started any kind of legal action under that kind of law, then First Nations peoples would have the right to be a part of that action or to be involved in it.

ABATE: You mentioned the idea of the conservative legal system influencing the way this movement has developed in Australia. Do you think that there are any other factors that are unique to Australia that will perhaps inform the rights of nature movement going forward?

MALONEY: It is so hard to tell. These ideas are still quite new for many people over here. The biggest issue we have is how to develop rights of nature concepts here without repeating the mistakes of colonization, i.e., without disrespecting the First Nations peoples here. In Australia, one of the most important and difficult contexts we deal with is being a colonial jurisdiction. We have a unique situation where we are one of the only, I think, colonized jurisdictions that has no treaty with its First Nations people at all. For more than two hundred years, since the British colonization of the continent in 1788, we have had a legal lie, a horrible legal insult called "terra nullius", where the British pretended that the country was uninhabited or "empty land," so that they could take control, without any kind of treaty, of the land and also take control of one of the oldest continuing cultures on earth. To recognize the rights of nature in Australia, we're going to have to grapple with whether rights of nature is just a western legal construct, just another colonial construct overriding First Nations peoples' laws, or whether we can take "rights of nature" laws and modify them for this country, in a way that supports or is compatible with ancient first laws of Aboriginal people. I cannot speak for what will happen in the future. Change happens in strange ways, but AELA is keenly aware of the profound difficulties of working in a colonial nation, and we are working with First Nations colleagues to explore these issues. I'm working on a book with Mary Graham, a Kombumerri elder, and we are looking at different projects together so that we can explore how the legal status of the living world can be part of a program of action for the future that challenges colonial legal systems. I do not pretend to have many answers, but we will be pushing forward with rights of nature ideas because they are starting to gain a bit of traction; we see them as exciting and positive and if nothing else, a "bridge" to a more earth-centered governance system among non-Indigenous Australians. The only thing I can say with surety is that AELA is very interested in what we think of as "the local law-making approach," spearheaded by Community

Environmental Legal Defense Fund (CELDF), which is an organization run by Thomas Linzey and Mari Margil in the United States, and which helps local communities assert their community and nature rights regardless of the fact that the state and federal government law can most of the time override the local laws. It is a way of articulating Earth Democracy. In Australia, we have powerful fossil fuel interests, and other industry groups who have a huge influence over the current government. We are working with a range of communities around Australia, and using the Australian People's Tribunal for Community and Nature's Rights as a way of promoting a different way of thinking about how it all works. We are moving into the next phase as an organization, which is going to be looking at how grassroots groups can take on some of these ideas, working in partnership with local Indigenous communities, and seeing what they can push for. What we are seeing here is the ongoing legacy of the laws that arrived in 1788 and how that excludes not only First Nations peoples but also other local communities, from any decision making about the living world. So that is why Earth jurisprudence and the work of Thomas Berry, is the framework that we work with because it advocates for earth democracy rather than just using western legal constructs to fiddle around the edges. Honestly, that is why personally I am not hugely fond of legal personhood as a concept, but I think for some people it is just easier to understand and it is easier than just a blanket rights of nature approach.

However, to me legal personhood can be seen as, and others have written about this, another anthropocentric structure that we are trying to jam nature into. It all came undone in my humble view when India's courts said something about "these rivers should have all the rights and liabilities of a legal person" and everyone said "well hang on, what liabilities? Can we sue the river when it floods?" This is what happens when we don't think through the arguments or we try, as usual in the Western way, to squish nature into constructs that were designed by Western law for something completely different from environmental care. That is why AELA will be pushing for rights of nature rather than legal personhood. That said, if groups in Australia want to focus more on legal personhood, then we will support it because it means something new and something that might offer greater protection for the environment. But if it is just left to us, we will be pushing for the broader rights of nature approach. When people don't understand it we just say, "well you know how human rights spring from just the sheer act of being a human? Earth rights or rights of nature come from life itself." People seem to get that and it is not so difficult to understand.

ABATE: What legal strategies do you think offer the most promise to secure legal rights for the Great Barrier Reef?

MALONEY: We'd love to see popular support for recognizing the rights of the Reef. But for us, the ultimate end game is not actually just new laws. It's cultural change as well. For us in AELA, we're more interested in First Nations' Peoples' understanding of what law is. And by that, I mean, law is not just something made on high by someone far away in a city. It is your daily behaviors, your daily practice, and your daily *ethics*. Similarly, AELA has a focus on earth ethics and the cultural change advocated for by Earth jurisprudence. The ultimate goal is "earth-centered everything" so that people literally wake up every morning and they are aware of their obligations to the local Earth community, to life around them. We want to change the whole legal and economic system so that this is easier to achieve. We have a long way to go but we have some frameworks developing. Rights of nature is a really exciting area of *law* but it's also an effective spearhead communication tool and, if nothing else, it's something new that stimulates questions and conversations. When you talk about it, people ask: "What does it mean? What is it all about?" And you get people engaged a bit more. You can explain how the current legal system treats nature merely as human property, and for many people, this is a paradigm shift. There seems to be a lot of excitement about it now. There wasn't as much excitement when we started talking about it five years ago, when people didn't understand it.

Despite my concerns about the impacts of focusing on "legal personhood" for nature instead of rights of nature, one of the good things about the New Zealand laws and the Indian and Colombian courtdecisions is that it captured people's imagination. They seemed to be able to understand how and why local communities wanted to make their local ecosystems have rights.

> Someone at a recent symposium said, "But what do we do, do we
> give every river legal rights and then what if something is outside
> the catchment? Or what if rivers have to compete with each
> other to have their rights recognized?" Exactly.
>
> We are far more interested in the jurisdictional approach to rights of
> nature, where the entire system of life has to be looked at differently.
> For us, rights of nature laws are just a means to an end. We are really
> interested in Earth-centered governance – cultural change, an
> ethical framework, actually planning an ecologically based societal
> framework, and understanding what its limits look like in a particular
> ecosystem or bioregion. That is our master plan and everything else,
> including the rights of nature concept, weaves into it.

It is important to reflect on why efforts in Australia to secure rights of nature or legal personhood protections have not been successful to date, standing in stark contrast to the successful efforts in Ecuador, Bolivia, Colombia, and New Zealand. Australia's resistance to addressing climate change is well documented.[267] In August 2018,[268] Malcolm Turnbull was the third Australian prime minister to lose his position over a climate dispute within the last decade.[269] The "energy wars" escalated after Turnbull introduced an energy bill that placed limits on greenhouse gas emissions and met opposition by conservatives in his own party.[270] Eventually, Turnbull abandoned the energy bill, but this animosity increased talks of a leadership change that resulted in Turnbull's ouster and replacement by Scott Morrison.[271]

Policy experts point to many reasons for the internal disputes in Australia, from partisanship to personality conflicts, but some have speculated that much of the climate change resistance comes from issues arising from the land itself.[272] Since 1797, when coal was discovered in New South Wales, Australia has become the largest coal exporter in the world, accounting for about 37 percent of global exports.[273] As a result, mining companies have significant influence in Australian politics.[274]

---

[267] Damien Cave, *Australia Wilts from Climate Change. Why Can't Its Politicians Act?* N.Y. TIMES (Aug. 21, 2018), www.nytimes.com/2018/08/21/world/australia/australia-climate-change-malcolm-turnbull.html.

[268] Jen Kirby, *What the Hell Is Happening with Australia's Prime Minister, Explained*, VOX (Aug. 24, 2018), www.vox.com/2018/8/24/17777112/australia-prime-minister-malcolm-turnbull-scott-morrison.

[269] Cave, *supra* note 267.

[270] *Id.*

[271] *Id.*

[272] *Id.*

[273] *Id.*

[274] *Id.*

Campaign contributions are difficult to track in Australia due to a lack of relevant transparency laws, but coal lobbyists supplied an estimated US$3.6 million in campaigns last year.[275] By comparison, four of the country's leading environmental groups, including Greenpeace, World Wildlife Fund, Environment Victoria, and the Sunrise Project, only contributed about US$135,000 combined.[276] For all of these reasons, assigning legal personhood to resources like the GBR poses a threat to the prevailing pro-extractivist sentiment in Australia's federal government. As long as coal mine development remains a priority in the country, which is likely to remain true for the foreseeable future, progress on assigning legal personhood to natural resources will advance at a glacial pace.[277]

The author obtained additional insights on Australia's challenges in seeking personhood for the GBR in an interview with EDONQ's current principal solicitor, Kirstiana Ward. Ward observed that Australia's difficulty in this area is largely due to the lack of a unified voice advocating on behalf of the reef and the jurisdictional issue of whose responsibility it is to advocate on behalf of an entity that is so large.[278] In other countries, like New Zealand, there has often been one indigenous group connected to the natural feature in question.[279] Ms. Ward noted that "the different indigenous groups associated with the different areas of the reef are vast and [do] not have that one singular voice."[280] In addition to indigenous groups, there are many governmental and nongovernmental organizations that have a vested interest in the GBR and are currently responsible for its management, including the Great Barrier Reef Marine Park Authority, Queensland Parks and Wildlife Service, the federal and Queensland governments, and the Association of Marine Park Tourism Operators. She concluded by noting that while "those jurisdictional issues are not necessarily an absolute impediment, they do raise the question of who is going to manage and administer [the reef]" if legal personality were to be achieved.[281]

C India

Two weeks after the Whanganui River was granted legal personhood, the High Court in the State of Uttarakhand in northern India issued a ruling declaring the

---

[275] *Id.*

[276] *Id.*

[277] For an encouraging exception to this prevailing sentiment, see *infra* Chapter 6 for a discussion of a recent court decision in Australia that prevented a proposed coal mine project from proceeding on the basis of its projected impacts on climate change.

[278] Interview with Kirstiana Ward, Principal Solicitor, Environmental Defenders Office of Northern Queensland (Aug. 7, 2018).

[279] *Id.*

[280] *Id.*

[281] *Id.*

Yumana River and the Ganga River to be "juristic/legal persons/living entities."[282]
Citing to the New Zealand law as precedent, the High Court's decision was the
culmination of several court rulings finding that while the rivers are "central to the
existence of half of the Indian population and their health and well-being," they are
extremely polluted, with their very existence in question.[283] The High Court
declared that throughout India's history, it has been necessary to declare certain
"entities, living inanimate, objects or things" as a "juristic person."[284] With the
Yumana and Ganga, the court explained that it is time to recognize them as legal
persons "in order to preserve and conserve" the rivers.[285]

CELDF joined India-based NGOs to recognize fundamental rights of the Ganga
River and the entire river basin.[286] In collaboration with the Ganga Action Parivar
and the Global WASH Alliance-India, CELDF drafted the proposed National
Ganga River Rights Act.[287] The Act recognizes the Ganga's fundamental rights to
exist, be restored, flourish, and evolve, and the right of the people of India to a
healthy river ecosystem.[288]

The High Court's February 2016 ruling called for significant legal change, noting
the need for comprehensive legislation at the national level focusing exclusively on
the Ganga. The Court further stated that "[a]ll the rivers have the basic right to
maintain their purity and to maintain free and natural flow."[289] It is not clear
whether the court includes these rights within the scope of its recent "personhood"
declaration, or whether courts will expand on the rights recognized from this
ruling.[290]

In the National Ganga River Rights Act (Proposed, 2016), CELDF is partnering
with Ganga Action Parivar and the Global Interfaith WASH Alliance to develop the
National Ganga River Rights Act[291] to present to India Prime Minister Narendra
Modi's government.[292] Today, the Ganges River basin is managed under environmental regulatory laws that are similar to conventional environmental laws found
around the world; however, this structure of environmental law does not effectively

[282] *A First in India: Uttarakhand High Court Declares Ganga, Yamuna Rivers as Living Legal Entities*,
http://vrindavanactnow.com/documents/first-india-uttarakhand-hc-declares-ganga-yamuna-rivers-
living-legal-entities-read-judgment/.
[283] Press Release, *India Court Declares Personhood for Ganga and Yumana Rivers*, GLOBAL
ALLIANCE FOR THE RIGHTS OF NATURE, http://therightsofnature.org/india-court-personhood-
ganga-and-yumana-rivers/.
[284] *Id.*
[285] *Id.*
[286] *Id.*
[287] *Id.*
[288] *Id.*
[289] *Id.*
[290] *Id.*
[291] *A Campaign to Establish Rights of the Ganges River*, CELDF, (Sept. 13, 2016), https://celdf.org/
2016/09/blog-gangas-rights-rights/.
[292] *Id.*

mitigate environmental harms.[293] This structure legalizes environmental harms by regulating how much pollution or environmental destruction is allowed under law.[294] By shifting the paradigm to legal personhood, the National Ganga River Rights Act would recognize the rights of the Ganges, prohibit any activity that interferes with the River's rights, and empower civil society and the government to protect the River for future generations.[295]

In addition to these developments, India's international leadership on environmental protection and conservation issues is reflected in other developments and initiatives.[296] One example is the draft National Forest Policy (Proposed, 2018). The current National Forest Policy 1988 (NFP-1988)[297] was announced thirty years ago. The Ministry of Environment, Forest and Climate Change (MoEFCC), the country's principal administrative body for environmental regulation and protection, published the new Draft National Forest Policy 2018 (DNFP-2018).[298] The new draft policy's overall goal is to "safeguard the ecological and livelihood security of people, of the present and future generations, based on sustainable management of the forests for the flow of ecosystem services."[299] The draft policy also aims to maintain at least one-third of India's total land area under forest and tree cover. In the hills and mountainous regions, the policy's goal is to maintain two-thirds of the area under forest and tree cover to both "prevent soil erosion and land degradation and also to ensure the stability of the fragile ecosystems."[300]

The National Green Tribunal Act, 2010 (NGT ACT) is another hallmark of India's forward-thinking environmental protection efforts. The NGT ACT was enacted on October 18, 2010 to establish the National Green Tribunal (NGT) to adjudicate all environmental laws relating to air and water pollution, India's Environmental Protection Act, the Forest Conservation Act, and the Biodiversity Act.[301] The NGT Act established the NGT to oversee the effective and expedient disposal of cases relating to environmental protection and conservation, and enforce legal rights relating to the environment.[302] The NGT also provides relief and compensation for damages to persons and property.[303]

---

[293] *Id.*

[294] *Id.*

[295] *Id.*

[296] Vinay Vaish, *India: Environmental Laws in India*, Mondaq (Aug. 31, 2017), www.mondaq .com/india/x/624836/Waste+Management/Environment+Laws+In+India.

[297] Ministry of Environment, Forest and Climate Change, Government of India, http://envfor.nic .in/division/fp-important-links.

[298] S. Gopikrishna Warrier, *India's New Forest Policy Draft Draws Criticism for Emphasis on Industrial Timber*, Mongabay (Apr. 12, 2018), https://news.mongabay.com/2018/04/indias-new-forest-policy-draft-draws-criticism-for-emphasis-on-industrial-timber/.

[299] *Id.*

[300] *Id.*

[301] Vinay Vaish, *supra* note 296.

[302] *Id.*

[303] *Id.*

In *Bhatt* v. *Union of India*, the petitioner filed a *pro bono publico* petition, seeking restrictions on movement of horse carts/tongas between Nepal and provisions for vaccination and medical checkup of the horses involved for suspected infections. It was alleged that there is no check-on fare charged from passengers; ailing, infirm, and old horses are abandoned by owners; infected horses are hazardous to humans; and the tongas are overloaded, which causes cruelty to animals.[304] The petitioner argued that according to an Indo-Nepal trade treaty signed in 1991 and revised in 2009, "the contracting party may impose restrictions for ... protecting human, animal and plant life ... ." and it was within the Government of India's right to regulate fare and freight.[305] He alleged that the treatment of the animals violated the Prevention of Cruelty to Animals Act (1960), the Prevention and Control of Infections and Contagious Diseases in Animals Act (2009), and the Transport of Animals Rules (1978).[306]

The High Court explained that declaring the animal kingdom as possessing rights was necessary "in order to protect and promote greater welfare of animals including avian and aquatic."[307] The Court also decided that the growing environmental crises across the globe is evidence that "there are gaps in laws" that should be addressed in order to protect the environment.[308] The Court concluded that the laws that treat nature, including animals, as property without legal rights should change.[309] This ruling by the High Court builds on the momentum from the Court's decision declaring legal personhood rights of the Ganges River.[310]

Like the promising developments in New Zealand, the movement in India to recognize rights of ecosystems is important in the growing movement to depart from legal systems that treat nature as property under the law.[311] Yet Ecuador and Bolivia went further still by amending their respective constitutions to grant equal rights to nature. All of these developments offer promise as a foundation for enhanced action on climate change by providing mechanisms to enjoin activities that may violate the rights of these resources to sustain themselves.

III INTERNATIONAL RIGHTS OF NATURE TRIBUNAL CASE STUDIES

Developed as an alternative to traditional courts and tribunals at the international and domestic levels, the International Rights of Nature Tribunal seeks to offer

---

[304] Bhatt v. Union of India, 2018 SCC OnLine Utt 645, 2 § 7 (Apr. 7, 2018).

[305] *Id.* at 3 § 12.

[306] *Id.*

[307] Mari Margil, *India Court Declares Legal Rights of "Entire Animal Kingdom,"* CELDF (Jul. 6, 2019), https://celdf.org/2018/07/press-release-india-court-declares-legal-rights-of-entire-animal-kingdom/.

[308] *Id.*

[309] *Id.*

[310] *Id.*

[311] *Id.*

nonbinding alternative solutions to environmental protection challenges by using a rights of nature framework.[312] The tribunal convenes once a year. During the adjudication process, after legal analysis of the issues is presented, the tribunal issues recommendations of actions to repair, mitigate, restore, and prevent harm. The Secretariat of the Global Alliance for the RoN oversees regular proceedings of the tribunal. Ten judges are selected from around the world, at least one of whom is chosen as the spokesperson for each case. They first decide to admit cases and then adjudicate them, either in the present court or in a following year. A prosecutor for the Earth is also present.

The tribunals do not have any formal legal authority, but the process "generates sophisticated legal analysis of diverse cases; recommends mitigation based on rights of nature, educates governments, advocacy groups, and the interested public on the tenets of the rights of nature and how they can be applied; [and] enables others to develop legal structures that recognize the inherent rights of nature."[313] As other people's tribunals have done in the past, it can still address issues of justice that are beyond the reach of traditional courts and evolve into formal, legal tribunals over time. By applying the legal frameworks of rights of nature, it seeks to expand knowledge of these frameworks such that they can gain global acclaim and legitimacy. In many ways, decisions from the International Rights of Nature Tribunal parallels the development of international environmental law generally. First, today's "soft" law (such as nonbinding declarations and resolutions) often evolves into tomorrow's "hard" (i.e., binding) law. Second, even though the decisions of the International Court of Justice and other international courts and tribunals typically do not bind parties and issues that are not before the court in that proceeding, the legal reasoning in these decisions (and even in their advisory opinions) often becomes the foundation for future binding principles of law in treaties and international customary law.

Australia

In 2014, in *Great Barrier Reef vs. Australia Federal and State Governments*,[314] Michelle Maloney of the Australian Earth Laws Alliance (AELA) presented the case. AELA argued that, in breach of the Universal Declaration on the Rights of Mother Earth,[315] human activities are disrupting the GBR's ability to continue its

---

[312] Global Alliance for the Rights of Nature, *What Is an International Rights of Nature Tribunal?* http://therightsofnature.org/rights-of-nature-tribunal/.

[313] Earth Law Center, *Rights of Nature Tribunals*, https://www.earthlawcenter.org/rights-of-nature-tribunals/.

[314] *Rights of Nature Tribunal: Case Overview*, GLOBAL ALLIANCE FOR THE RIGHTS OF NATURE, http://therightsofnature.org/great-barrier-reef-australia/.

[315] Global Alliance for the Rights of Nature, *Universal Declaration of Rights of Mother Earth*, http://therightsofnature.org/universal-declaration/.

vital cycles and processes. AELA further alleged that "the Queensland and Australian Governments must: (i) be held to account for allowing the volume of industrial
development that is now occurring on the Queensland coast and threatening the
Reef; and (ii) set limits on human developments and ensure the Great Barrier Reef
can continue its vital cycles and processes and continue its evolutionary journey."[316]
In addition to presenting written and oral evidence to the Tribunal, Dr. Maloney
used the unique and innovative framework of the Tribunal to speak "on behalf of
the GBR, as a member of the Earth community."[317] Dr. Maloney has since written
that perhaps the greatest potential strength of the Tribunal "is the ability to use a
formal structure, present evidence about environmental harm, argue for new legal
frameworks, but also to then break free of the usual 'fact based' focus of western style
law to speak from the heart, as a member of the Earth community, concerned about
other members of the Earth community."

Environmental attorney Cormac Cullinan accepted the case on the grounds that
parties are responsible for establishing precautionary and restrictive measures to
protect rights, and that there was evidence of specific rights violations, including
the right to exist free of contamination, the rights to integral health and well-being,
and potentially the right to regenerate freely. Further, they did not find that there
were sufficient conditions that justified the expansion of future destructive activities
on the part of governments or the private sector. Interestingly, he noted that this case
raised questions with future global implications, specifically: "if the amount of
greenhouse gases in the air is already so great that it is causing significant climate
change, is any significant increase in the rate of production of hydrocarbons, such as
coal mining, automatically a violation of the RoN and of Mother Earth?"[318]

After the acceptance of the case, hearings in an Australian Regional Chamber of
the Tribunal in Queensland were conducted to obtain testimonies from local
witnesses for the case.[319] The case was presented with this additional evidence in
Lima, Peru, with the additional argument that AELA did not think that the "black
letter of the law" alone should be used to adjudicate this case, since that law allowed
for such developments within Australia, but rather that the argument of permanent
and irreversible damage to such an important resource should be considered.

Tantoo Cardinal, an Aboriginal actress and performer from Canada, presented
the final judgment on the case, which was deliberated by the jury as a whole. They
found that "Deliberate human activities are directly and indirectly violating the right

[316] Michelle Maloney, *Finally Being Heard: The Great Barrier Reef and the International Rights of Nature Tribunal*, 3 GRIFFITH J.L. & HUM. DIGNITY 40, 47-48 (2015), https://www.earthlaws.org .au/wp-content/uploads/2015/07/Maloney_Finally-Being-Heard_Griffith-Journal-of-Law-and-Human-Dignity-2015.pdf.

[317] *Id.* at 48.

[318] *Cormac Cullinan Judges Ruling on Great Barrier Reef Case*, GLOBAL ALLIANCE FOR THE RIGHTS OF NATURE, http://therightsofnature.org/cormac-cullinan-great-barrier-reef-case/.

[319] *Great Barrier Reef Judgement Paris Tribunal*, GLOBAL ALLIANCE FOR THE RIGHTS OF NATURE, http://therightsofnature.org/great-barrier-reef-judgement-paris-tribunal/.

of the Great Barrier Reef community to integral health (article 2(1)(g)) and its related rights to well-being (article 2(3)); to continue its vital cycles and processes free from human disruptions (article 2(1)(c)); to be free from contamination, pollution and toxic or radioactive waste; (article 2(1)(h)); to play its role in Mother Earth for her harmonious functioning (article 2(2)); and ultimately to exist (article 2(1)(a))."[320]

The Tribunal resolved to demand that the Queensland State authorities and federal government control human activities in the area, condemning the governments for violations of the rights of the reef to maintain its vital cycles and fulfill its natural potential, and requesting that they reduce land-based pollution from human activities, ensure the sensitivity of tourism to the health of the reef, refrain from expanding the presence of ports, prohibit shipping through sensitive areas of the reef, commit to the complete restoration of the reef, and comply fully with UNESCO's recommendations. Finally, they characterized the current condition and threats to the reef as an emergency requiring urgent and global action.

The Tribunal ruled in favor of the GBR, finding that the Rights of Nature are being violated and will continue to be violated in breach of the Universal Declaration on the Rights of Nature.[321] The next stage of the case was held in Brisbane, Queensland with judges presiding to represent scientists, Indigenous community leaders, ethicists, and youth representatives. Evidence was heard from EDOQ, EDOFNQ, a marine biologist, and AELA, represented by Dr. Maloney. Ultimately the Tribunal again found in favor of the reef and made a series of recommendations. These recommendations included a finding that cessation of further industrial development along the coastline adjacent to the reef would support the restoration of the GBR and that the state and federal governments must bear responsibility for such an action. The Tribunal also found that a new ethical and legal framework is required to give legal expression to the rights of nature.[322]

Building on the jurisdiction of the Tribunal for the Rights of Nature, in 2016 AELA created a permanent Rights of Nature Australia (RONA) Peoples Tribunal. On October 22, 2016, the Rights of Nature Tribunal recognized the legal rights of the GBR.[323] While this recognition is significant, decisions of the Rights of Nature Tribunal do not have *legal* effect in the traditional sense in Australia and are not binding or enforceable. The Rights of Nature Tribunal, and its Australian presence, aims to create a forum for people from all around the world to give a voice to protest the destruction of the earth, to make recommendations about the earth's protection and restoration, and build a new, unconventional jurisprudence for the

---

[320] *Id.*

[321] Michelle Maloney, *Building an Alternative Jurisprudence for the Earth: The International Rights of Nature Tribunal*, 41 VT. L. REV. 129 (2016).

[322] *Id.*

[323] Australian Earth Laws Alliance, *Rights of Nature* (2018), https://www.earthlaws.org.au/what-is-earth-jurisprudence/rights-of-nature/.

earth and the rights of nature.[324] The RONA Tribunal is a distinctive forum for ecological and social justice in Australia.[325] It was established to enable the sharing of "concerns about the destruction of the environment, [to] articulate ... vision[s] for ecological justice and law reform, and [to] work collectively to develop ... ideas for building an [Earth-centered] society."[326]

The RONA Peoples Tribunal is not a government-endorsed activity, but hears ecological justice cases, brought on behalf of fauna, flora, ecosystems, bioregions, and local communities around Australia, and holds public inquiries.[327] As a "'citizen's tribunal', a Tribunal Panel consisting of First Nations Peoples, lawyers, community representatives[,] and eminent scientists, hear[s] Inquiries and Cases, and make[s] recommendations for restorative justice, innovative law reform[,] and socio-political reforms that will Care for Country and protect the Rights of Nature."[328]

The Tribunal is a reaction to the current legal system's failure to protect the natural world.[329] While there have been some admirable initiatives in environmental law, Australia's legal, political, and economic system supports unsustainable, human-centered development and limitless growth.[330] Very few serious alternative approaches have been proposed to create a new, distinctive legal approach to protecting the integrity of nature in Australia.[331]

Ecuador

In Ecuador, Julio Prieto of Frente de Defensa de la Amazonía presented the *Amazon vs. Chevron/Texaco* case to the International Tribunal on the RoN.[332] In the mid-twentieth century, the Ecuadorean government sold a concession of 1,431,430 acres to the Gulf Texaco Consortium to explore and extract oil from the Amazon, with Texaco in charge of all technical operations until 1992. The concession was provided with the condition that Texaco would utilize less harmful technology to conduct its operations, which Ecuadorean companies would be unable to do. Texaco did not fulfill this requirement and there was a massive

---

[324] Australian Earth Laws Alliance, *The Great Barrier Reef Case – International Rights of Nature Tribunal*, https://www.earthlaws.org.au/what-is-earth-jurisprudence/rights-of-nature/world-ethics-tribunal-for-the-rights-of-nature-and-mother-earth/.

[325] Rights of Nature Australian Tribunal, *About*, AUSTRALIAN PEOPLES' TRIBUNAL (Oct. 27, 2018), https://www.ronatribunal.org.au/?page_id=54.

[326] *Id.*

[327] *Id.*

[328] *Id.*

[329] *Id.*

[330] *Id.*

[331] *Id.*

[332] *Chevron/Texaco Case*, GLOBAL ALLIANCE FOR THE RIGHTS OF NATURE, http://therightsofnature.org/chevron-texaco-case/.

spill in the sensitive ecosystem, in addition to other extensive environmental damages in the area.

Indigenous and environmental groups in the United States and Ecuador filed suits against Chevron (formerly Texaco) and, after ten years of litigation, prevailed in achieving a judgment against Chevron, requiring that it repair and compensate for the damages caused and publicly apologize. The company did not comply with the ruling and instead fought back vehemently and filed counterclaims against the groups who brought the case to court. The purpose of bringing the case to the International Tribunal was to obtain a ruling that would compel Chevron to be held to account for the additional and lasting damages it caused through its failure to comply with the original ruling, and acknowledge that the rights of nature to exist, regenerate, and maintain integral health are being violated by this lack of compliance.

Several parties were deemed responsible. The Ecuadorean state is responsible for neglecting areas of land affected by Chevron's activities, for allowing Texaco to operate in such an important ecosystem without complying with technological requirements, and for signing an agreement in which they were released of liabilities in 1995. Chevron itself is responsible for failing to use appropriate technology while knowing the possible risks, and for further impacting those already victimized by the environmental damages. The relief sought is that the Tribunal compels Chevron to take action to repair the violated RoN and comply with its responsibility to pay a financial penalty due to its lack of public apology. In addition, Frente de Defensa de la Amazonía want recognition of the purposeful violation of RoN caused by a lack of compliance with the prior ruling and that the Tribunal condemn Chevron, issue a warning to all countries in which it operates, declare it a fugitive from justice in Ecuador, and an enemy of the RoN and human rights worldwide.[333] Julio Cesar Trujillo announced the decision of the Tribunal to accept the case.[334]

At the Tribunal in Lima, more evidence was presented. The Tribunal condemned Chevron for its use of inadequate technology and ordered it to comply with the previous rulings of the courts to fully compensate the subject sites. They considered the CEO of Chevron responsible for violations of RoN due to his lack of compliance and the Ecuadorean state responsible for allowing the negligence during their original operations. The Tribunal's decision sought to submit a record of the case to the UN in efforts to disallow the impunity of transnational corporations and to the Court of Arbitration in the Hague to update the current case to reflect ecocide.[335] This case was reopened at the Tribunal in

---

[333] *Chevron Trial in Ecuador*, GLOBAL ALLIANCE FOR THE RIGHTS OF NATURE, http://therightsof nature.org/wp-content/uploads/Chevron_CaseEN.pdf.

[334] *Julio César Trujillo Judge's Ruling on Chevron/Texaco Case*, GLOBAL ALLIANCE FOR THE RIGHTS OF NATURE, http://therightsofnature.org/julio-cesar-trujillo-chevron/.

[335] *Final Verdict – Lima*, GLOBAL ALLIANCE FOR THE RIGHTS OF NATURE, http://therightsofnature. org/final-verdict-lima/.

Paris by Pablo Fajardo with the argument that, under the updates to the Rome Statute, Chevron's original dumping and spill, in addition to their purposeful refusal to remediate its impacts, represented a case of ecocide. This damage constituted a significant and durable harm to the Global Commons as defined in the ecocide amendments. Further, Humberto Piaguaje (of the Secoya people) explained how the remaining pollution was damaging a central part of his peoples' cosmovision – the waterways – and that this cosmovision in itself is a cultural service of spiritual enrichment that is also considered part of the Global Commons in the amendments.

Bolivia

After the passage of the 2009 Constitution establishing the Plurinational State of Bolivia, Evo Morales signed a US$415 million dollar contract with Brazilian construction company OAS to build a road through the Isidoro Sécure National Park and Indigenous Territory (TIPNIS).[336] Lowland Indigenous Peoples, who are organized under the regional Confederation of Indigenous Peoples of the East, and who had support from other Indigenous organizations in the country, vehemently opposed the project.[337]

In 2011, they organized the Eighth Indigenous March in Defence of TIPNIS from the capital of Beni to La Paz. They were stopped in Chaparina, where the armed forces of Bolivia violently quelled the protest. This incident was later known as the "Chaparina Massacre."[338] In response, Morales approved Law 180 that declared the territory encompassed by TIPNIS as inviolable and untouchable, therefore precluding the construction of the road.

One year later, in 2012, Law 222 was passed, establishing a process of renewed consultation with TIPNIS communities to determine whether the road could be built. That year, they organized the ninth march to reject Law 222 and protect Law 180, but Morales did not receive them to discuss the demands when they arrived in La Paz. He went forth with conducting a process of consultation within TIPNIS in late 2012, but the communities alleged that international standards of free, prior, and informed consent of Indigenous peoples were not met. A commission representing the Catholic Church, the Permanent Assembly of Human Rights in Bolivia, and the Inter-American Federation of Human Rights conducted a survey in the TIPNIS finding that thirty of thirty-six communities rejected the road, three accepted it under certain conditions and amendments, and three accepted it outright, which

---

[336] Ana Carolina Delgado, *The TIPNIS Conflict in Bolivia*, 39 CONTEXTO INTERNACIONAL (May/ Aug. 2017), www.scielo.br/scielo.php?script=sci_arttext&pid=S0102-85292017000200373; Nick Buxton, *The Law of Mother Earth: Behind Bolivia's Historic Bill*, http://therightsofnature.org/ bolivia-law-of-mother-earth/.

[337] *Id.*

[338] *Id.*; Buxton, *supra* note 336.

directly contradicted the findings of the government that 80 percent of the sixty-nine communities included in their consultation supported the road.[339]

Nonetheless, based on the findings of its "consultation," the government concluded that the majority of communities were not interested in maintaining the intangibility of the park and would rather access the benefits that would come from the development of the road.[340] Several years later, in 2017, after there was substantial turnover in the leadership of TIPNIS, the government approved Law 929 that eliminated the intangibility of TIPNIS and enabled the continued construction of the road.[341] Concerns about the impacts of road construction include disruption of Indigenous communities' livelihoods; disturbance and destruction of biodiversity; deforestation; and expansion of coca cultivation.[342] The Program of Strategic Research in Bolivia prepared a report that concluded that 64.5% of the forest would be lost over eighteen years if the road were built, and a Strategic Environmental Evaluation of the TIPNIS by the National State Office of Protected Areas warned that there would be substantial impacts on Indigenous peoples lives.[343]

In late 2017, the Indigenous leaders of the TIPNIS presented a case against the State of Bolivia to the International Rights of Nature Tribunal arguing that the passage of Law 969 violated the Universal Declaration of the Rights of Mother Earth as well as Bolivian national legislative and constitutional protections. They argued that it would constitute a violation in particular of article 2(a), right to life and to exist; 2(b), right to be respected; 2(c), the right to regenerate its biocapacity and to continue vital cycles and processes free from human disruptions; and 2(g), right to integral health in the Universal Declaration. In the Law 71 of Rights of Mother Earth, it would be in direct conflict with Article 7, which enumerates the Rights of Mother Earth, and Article 8, which enumerates the obligation of the state to "develop public policies and systematic actions to prevent, warn against, protect, and establish precautions against human activities that lead to the extinction of populations of beings and the alteration of the cycles and processes that guarantee their life."[344] They also argued that it violated Article 385 of the Constitution, which stated that "protected areas constitute a common good, and they form part of the natural and cultural patrimony of the

[339] Emily Achtenberg, *Why Is Evo Morales Reviving Bolivia's Controversial TIPNIS Road?*, 2017, NACLA, https://nacla.org/blog/2017/08/22/why-evo-morales-reviving-bolivia%E2%80%99s-con troversial-tipnis-road.

[340] Pablo Solon, *TIPNIS: The Saga for the Rights of Nature and Indigenous People*, COUNTER- PUNCH (Dec. 8, 2017), https://www.counterpunch.org/2017/12/08/tipnis-the-saga-for-the-rights- of-nature-and-indigenous-people.

[341] Buxton, *supra* note 336.

[342] *Id.*

[343] *Id.*

[344] Law 71, Rights of Mother Earth; http://therightsofnature.org/wp-content/uploads/2018/03/ BONN-2018-TIPNIS-English.pdf.

country," and wherever there is an overlapping of "protected areas and indigenous territories, the shared management shall be undertaken, subject to the norms and procedures of the indigenous nations and peoples, and respect for the goal for which these areas were created."[345] It also violated the Indigenous and Tribal Peoples Convention, 1989 (No. 169) and the UN Declaration on the Rights of Indigenous Peoples, which were both legally adopted in Bolivia.[346]

The Tribunal accepted the case and expressed "great concern particularly because the Universal Declaration of the Rights of Mother Earth was proclaimed in Bolivia in 2010, and Bolivia has championed rights of Nature internationally."[347] The Tribunal decided to gather more evidence, called on the government to respond to the accusations under article 3(2) of the Universal Declaration of the Rights of Mother Earth, and requested that the state place a moratorium on construction of the road and other exploratory activities in or near TIPNIS until the investigation was complete.[348] The International Rights of Nature Tribunal planned a trip to investigate the reality of TIPNIS on the ground in August 2018 that would last eleven days.[349] By early 2019, no decision was reached on this decision.[350]

Though there have been national and internal legislative changes surrounding the TIPNIS case in Bolivia, there were no judicial decisions made explicitly regarding the Rights of Nature in the country, or utilizing the Ombudsman's Office, which has yet to be formalized. The decision not to use the national system could be a reflection of the lack of robust infrastructure to handle such complaints or the perception that it would not be handled fairly, considering the state-led interests at stake.

Bolivia faces various obstacles to the full implementation of its laws on Mother Nature, stemming from the reality that the country is structurally dependent on extractive industries and that major enterprises representing industry interests continue to hold sway over decision making.[351] While the law on the rights of nature remains the same, other environmental laws have been weakened.[352] Some have argued that the Framework Law serves to legitimize the existing Bolivian economic model by making it "eco-friendly" instead of requiring a complete restructuring that would move away from extractivism.[353]

---

[345] CONST. OF BOLIVIA, art. 385.
[346] Maloney, *supra* note 321, at 129–42.
[347] Buxton, *supra* note 336.
[348] *Id.*
[349] *Id.*
[350] *Commission of International Rights of Nature Tribunal Examines the Controversial Road Project in the Heart of TIPNIS*, MOVEMENT RIGHTS (Sept. 4, 2018), www.movementrights .org/commission-of-international-rights-of-nature-tribunal-examines-the-controversial-road-pro ject-in-the-heart-of-tipnis/.
[351] Buxton, *supra* note 336.
[352] *See* Boyd, *supra* note 59.
[353] Emily Actenberg, *Earth First? Bolivia's Mother Earth Meets the Neo-Extractivist Economy*, NORTH AMERICAN CONGRESS OF LATIN AMERICA (Nov. 16, 2012) https://nacla.org/blog/2012/11/ 16/earth-first-bolivia%25E2%2580%2599s-mother-earth-law-meets-neo-extractivist-economy.

6

Proposal for Enhanced Stewardship and Rights-Based Protections for the Voiceless

Chapter 6 proposes a framework to enhance protection of the voiceless in the Anthropocene era. It proposes a substantive standard based on sustainable development, catalyzed by the climate change crisis, and accompanying procedural mechanisms to enforce that standard. Enforcement of the sustainable development standard can be achieved through plaintiffs asserting a procedural and/or informational injury from a government's breach of duties toward future generations, wildlife, and/or natural resources. These protections can be patterned after US federal environmental laws like the National Environmental Policy Act (NEPA), which reflects ecocentric thinking, whereby an agency's failure to undertake procedures or provide information designed to fulfill stewardship duties toward the voiceless community would enable humans to sue on behalf of those protected entities to compel the performance of the duty.

This chapter addresses three steps to facilitate the transition from an Anthropocentric to an ecocentric regulatory framework to enhance protection of the voiceless. It is premised on helping the sustainable development paradigm move from aspirational rhetoric to enforceable substantive mandates. The Brundtland Commission's definition of sustainable development – "development that meets the needs of the present without compromising the ability of future generations to meet their own needs"[1] – addresses the common plight of the voiceless who require effective stewardship to ensure their ability to inherit a habitable planet.

First, new regulatory bodies and courts and tribunals need to be established that focus on protection of the voiceless. Future generations commissions already exist in several countries, and these bodies need to develop mandates that implement sustainable development goals in a binding and enforceable manner. Similarly, although rights of nature tribunals exist and have issued many nonbinding decisions

---

[1] World Comm'n on Env't and Dev., *Our Common Future*, ch. 2 ¶ 1, U.N. Doc. A/42/427, annex (Aug. 4, 1987) [hereinafter "The Brundtland Report"].

in the past few years, these tribunals need to operate from a mandate that enforces sustainable development principles rather than nonbinding rhetoric in what are treated as simply advisory opinions. A similar regulatory body and/or court needs to address wildlife protection through a sustainable development paradigm in lieu of the existing approach of permitted consumption and exploitation.

The second step is to integrate the urgency of the climate change crisis into the sustainable development mandate. Sustainable development embraces all three categories of the voiceless, but needs a common foundation to serve all of them in a unified manner. Climate change threatens all three categories in a common way that can be addressed through a sustainable development mandate. Climate change and the sustainable development mandate have already been addressed effectively in NEPA cases in the United States and environmental impact assessments cases in Australia and Canada, which will be addressed in this chapter.

The third step is to implement stewardship responsibilities and rights-based protections. This goal can be attained by building on accountability theories in climate change litigation and imposing stewardship responsibilities on governmental entities and, in the long term, also on private sector entities. This strategy can be enhanced by drawing on the urgency of the climate change science, as in *Urgenda Foundation v. State of the Netherlands*, to help raise the ambition of the stewardship responsibilities. Enhanced stewardship responsibilities alone are insufficient, however, regardless of their level of ambition. Those duties need to be held in check by establishing rights-based protections for the voiceless community to hold government and private sector entities accountable. A final step in implementing rights-based protections is to establish procedural and informational harms as actionable injuries, which in turn can be enforceable by guardian-oriented plaintiffs. This approach combines success under NEPA on enforceable procedural and informational injuries, and breaks new ground in seeking legal personhood protection for the voiceless as well as use of the "next friend" mechanism for guardianship-based vindication of rights.

I SUBSTANTIVE STANDARD

Sustainable development should be the standard for stewardship of future generations, wildlife, and natural resources. This paradigm is on its way to reaching the level of a customary international law norm. Its scope and meaning are not yet self-evident and clear, but neither is the meaning of freedom of speech or freedom of religion in the United States, even though US courts have been interpreting the meaning of these constitutional rights and vigorously defending them for more than two centuries. Simply because the goal of shaping sustainable development into a substantive mandate is a long, slow, and difficult journey does not mean that it is not worth pursuing. As discussed in this chapter, the transition is already underway and is happening quickly. Vice-President Christopher Weeramantry of the International Court of Justice recognized in his separate opinion in the *Gabčíkovo-Nagymaros* case that just because it is hard to strike that balance between economic development and environmental protection – and that the global community is still learning how to strike that balance – does not mean that the sustainable development norm does not exist as a governing principle that states embrace and abide by in domestic and global engagement on development and environmental protection.[2]

In the tight carbon budget years of the Anthropocene era, sustainable development must take on a more aggressive environmental protection focus as the foundation for any economic and social benefits that may ensue. A substantive mandate based on this "greener" version of sustainable development is necessary to enjoin or restrict proposed actions that threaten significant projected climate change impacts to ensure adequate protection of the voiceless while working against the clock of the Anthropocene era.

There are three stages of the role of environmental protection in development decisions. The first wave that accompanied the industrial revolution was to develop without regard for the environment. The second wave was that sustainable development requires consideration of environmental concerns in an aspirational manner. The third wave has just begun. In this period, the Anthropocene era requires mandatory application of the sustainable development principle to ensure the viability of future generations and to promote resilience for wildlife and natural resources to resist the current and imminent future severe disruptions from climate change.

A Sustainable Development as the Governing Mandate

This section reviews the treatment of sustainable development as a standard that is approaching the status of customary international law. Sustainable development supports the proposal in this chapter in two ways. First, sustainable development is a de facto norm in humanity's interface with the voiceless in the Anthropocene era. Humans should have an interest in maintaining resources and wildlife because humans' continued unsustainable consumption will ensure elimination of those resources in the future. All human and nonhuman resources are threatened with extinction in the next century to varying degrees and climate change serves as a threat multiplier to that existing threat. The only way for domestic and international law to govern this new era of precarious ecological imbalance is to require that the sustainable development standard serve as a legally required check on many forms of human consumption.

Although commentators are critical of the vague and imprecise references to sustainable development in aspirational rather than mandatory language in treaties and declarations, the principle's increasingly widespread use as a goal supports its

---

[2] Case Concerning the Gabcíkovo-Nagymaros Project (Hungary v. Slovakia), 1997 I.C.J. 7, 90, 1997 WL 1168556 (Sept. 25, 1997) (separate opinion of Vice President Weeramantry).

role as a general principle of customary law. Provisions relating to sustainable development may be too soft to impose an obligation on states to develop sustainably, but they still impose an obligation on states to "strive to achieve" or "promote" sustainable development. As such, it is likely that sustainable development, at least to the extent it obligates states to enact policies to develop sustainably, could attain the status of customary law through its increasing use in agreements and treaties, and widespread recognition in judicial decisions. It is only a matter of time before this transition manifests, but the Anthropocene era's clock does not permit the luxury of delay.

Nonbinding international law instruments – declarations, resolutions, programs of action, and codes of conduct – increasingly recognize and support the concept of sustainable development.[3] The principle of sustainable development can be traced to the 1987 *Report of the World Commission on Environment and Development: Our Common Future*, commonly known as the Brundtland Report.[4] The Brundtland Report defined sustainable development as "development that meets the needs of the present without compromising the ability of future generations to meet their own needs."[5]

The Rio Declaration, adopted at the 1992 United Nations Conference on Environment and Development in Rio de Janeiro, Brazil, recognized that "[h]uman beings are at the centre of concerns for sustainable development. They are entitled to a healthy and productive life in harmony with nature."[6] The Declaration affirms that the "right to development must be fulfilled so as to equitably meet the developmental and environmental needs of present and future generations."[7] It provides that "[i]n order to achieve sustainable development, environmental protection shall constitute an integral part of the development process and cannot be considered in isolation from it."[8]

Agenda 21, adopted at that same conference, represents a commitment by nations to take actions to advance sustainable development.[9] Although nonbinding, Agenda 21 presents an action plan for the international community to integrate

---

[3] Virginie Barral, *Sustainable Development in International Law: Nature and Operation of an Evolutive Legal Norm*, 23 EUR. J. INT'L L. 377, 383–84 (2012).

[4] The Brundtland Report, *supra* note 1; Michelle Biddulph & Dwight Newman, *A Contextualized Account of General Principles of International Law*, 26 PACE INT'L L. REV. 286, 311–13 (2014); Alhaji B.M. Marong, *From Rio to Johannesburg: Reflections on the Role of International Legal Norms in Sustainable Development*, 16 GEO. INT'L ENVTL. L. REV. 21, 22–23, 28 (2003).

[5] The Brundtland Report, *supra* note 1.

[6] Rep. of the United Nations Conf. on Env't and Dev., *Rio Declaration on Environment and Development*, U.N. Doc. A/CONF.151/26 (Vol. I), Annex I, Pr. 1 (Aug. 12, 1992), http://www.un .org/documents/ga/conf151/aconf15126-1.

[7] *Id.* at Pr. 3.

[8] *Id.* at Pr. 4.

[9] *Id.* at Annex II.

environmental and development concerns for a sustainable future.[10] In coordination with the United Nations, other international, regional, and subregional organizations, nongovernmental organizations, and the public, governments are responsible for implementing sustainable development principles in Agenda 21.[11]

In April 2002, at the 70th Conference of the International Law Association in New Delhi, India, the Committee on the Legal Aspects of Sustainable Development released its New Delhi ILA Declaration on Principles of International Law Relating to Sustainable Development.[12] The Declaration outlines principles of international law on sustainable development including integrated policy assessment, environmental sustainability, intergenerational equity, robust political participation, and intergenerational responsibility.[13] The Declaration's principles could be used to help interpret the concept of sustainable development under binding treaty obligations and domestic law, as well as in the absence of binding treaties and enabling domestic law, particularly in local adjudications.

The United Nations' June 2002 World Summit on Sustainable Development in Johannesburg, South Africa resulted in the Johannesburg Declaration on Sustainable Development and a Johannesburg Plan of Implementation.[14] The Johannesburg Declaration provides a political commitment to sustainable development where states "assume[d] a collective responsibility to advance and strengthen the interdependent and mutually reinforcing pillars of sustainable development – economic development, social development and environmental protection – at the local, national, regional and global levels."[15] The Plan of Implementation provides a framework for action to implement the commitments originally adopted at Rio.[16] Additionally, the Summit resulted in sustainable development partnerships to achieve a set of measurable objectives and results on implementing sustainable development in specific areas.[17]

---

[10] *Id.*

[11] *Id.*

[12] International Law Association, New Delhi, India, Apr. 2-6, 2002, *ILA New Delhi Declaration of Principles of International Law Relating to Sustainable Development*, U.N. Doc. A/CONF. 199/8 (Aug. 9, 2002), http://www.un.org/ga/search/view_doc.asp?symbol=A/CONF.199/8&Lang=E.

[13] *Id.*; Abbey Stemler, *Paris, Panels, and Protectionism: Matching U.S. Rhetoric with Reality to Save the Planet*, 19 VAND. J. ENT. & TECH. L. 545, 552 (2017).

[14] *Plan of Implementation of the World Summit on Sustainable Development*, U.N. Doc. A/Conf.199/20, annex 1 (Sept. 4, 2002), http://www.un-documents.net/aconf199-20.pdf; *Johannesburg Declaration on Sustainable Development*, U.N. Doc. A/Conf.199/20, ¶ 5 (Sept. 4, 2002), http://www.un-documents.net/aconf199-20.pdf, ch. I.

[15] *Johannesburg Declaration on Sustainable Development, supra* note 14.

[16] *Plan of Implementation of the World Summit on Sustainable Development, supra* note 14, at ch. XI.

[17] Marie-Claire Cordonier Segger, *The Role of International Forums in the Advancement of Sustainable Development*, 10 SUSTAINABLE DEV. L. & POL'Y 4, 6 (2009). Sustainable development has also been committed to in development goals. The Millennium Declaration, adopted in 2000 in New York, reaffirmed support for the principle of sustainable development and Agenda 21. *United Nations Millennium Declaration*, G.A Res. 55/2, U.N. Doc. A/res/55/2

The UN Conference on Sustainable Development held in June 2012 (Rio+20) established an intergovernmental working group, the Open Development Group, to formulate the Sustainable Development Goals (SDGs).[18] In September 2015, the United Nations adopted the Sustainable Development Goals, when 193 states committed to achieve 17 goals by 2030.[19] This sustainable development agenda includes 17 global goals and 169 targets focused on advancing the three pillars of sustainable development: economic growth, social inclusion, and environmental protection.[20]

These declarations, resolutions, and goals are usually described as soft law, and not considered legally binding.[21] But they may give rise to legitimate expectations in that states might be precluded from deliberately violating agreements or commitments contained in soft law without notice, or at least may be assumed to be acting in accordance with such commitments.[22] These soft-law agreements can also provide evidence of emerging customary norms.[23]

Sustainable development is also referenced in binding treaties and conventions.[24] Specifically, it is expressed in over three hundred conventions, and the location of the proposition relating to sustainable development, and the function attributed to it, is often found in operative, or binding, clauses of those documents – not just in the nonbinding preambles.[25] References to sustainable development can also be found in 112 multilateral treaties. This proliferation of references reflects an evolving consensus in the international community concerning the relevance of sustainable development for international law.[26] Sustainable development is mostly referred to as an objective for the parties to strive to achieve, and occasionally, the agreements describe the types of measures to be undertaken to fulfill that objective.[27]

(Sept. 18, 2000), http://www.un.org/millennium/declaration/ares552e.pdf. The 2001 Millennium Development Goals then codified "the Declaration's development related objectives," including Goal 7, "Ensure Environmental Sustainability." Imrana Iqbal & Charles Pierson, *A North-South Struggle: Political and Economic Obstacles to Sustainable Development*, 16 Sustainable Dev. L. & Pol'y 16, 18 (2016).

[18] United Nations Environment Programme, *Proceedings of the Governing Council/Global Ministerial Environment Forum at Its First Universal Session*, ¶ 28, U.N. Doc. UNEP/GC.27/17 (Mar. 12, 2013), http://undocs.org/UNEP/GC.27/17.

[19] *United Nations, General Assembly, Resolution Adopted by the General Assembly on 25 September 2015: Transforming Our World: The 2030 Agenda for Sustainable Development*, G.A. Res. 70/1 (Oct. 21, 2015), http://www.un.org/en/development/desa/population/migration/general assembly/docs/globalcompact/A_RES_70_1_E.pdf.

[20] *Id.* at pmbl.

[21] Cordonier Segger, *supra* note 17, at 6.

[22] *Id.*

[23] *Id.*

[24] Barral, *supra* note 3, at 384.

[25] *Id.*

[26] *Id.*

[27] *Id.*

Several binding international environmental instruments contain sustainable development provisions. For example, the United Nations Framework Convention on Climate Change[28] seeks to promote sustainable development for the protection of current and future generations.[29] The promotion and achievement of sustainable development, including methods of doing so, also appears throughout the Kyoto Protocol of 1997.[30] Parties have also accepted responsibility to promote sustainable development and use resources sustainably in other binding documents, such as the Convention on Biological Diversity,[31] the Cartagena Protocol on Biosafety,[32] and the Convention to Combat Desertification in those Countries Experiencing Serious Drought and/or Desertification.[33]

Regional agreements have done the same. For example, the Charter of Fundamental Rights for the European Union, adopted in 2000 and then made binding in the European Union in 2009, provides: "[a] high level of environmental protection and the improvement of the quality of the environment must be integrated into the policies of the Union and ensured in accordance with the principle of sustainable development."[34]

The wording in these documents around sustainable development can be vague, and the provisions often provide an incentive for action rather than compelling or constraining parties.[35] But these provisions can still impose an obligation on states to "strive to achieve" or "promote" sustainable development. This obligation is not deprived of normative character, but rather a norm with a different object: one that is implemented to try to achieve that result.[36] Such conventional provisions can confer normative status to sustainable development and help it rise to the status of customary international law.

---

[28] United Nations Framework Convention on Climate Change, U.N. Doc. A/AC.237/18 (Part II)/ Add.1, 31 I.L.M. 849, annex I (May 9, 1992), www.un.org/documents/ga/ac237/ac237-18pt2addi.

[29] *Id.* at art. 3.

[30] *See, e.g., Adoption of the Kyoto Protocol to the United Nations Framework Convention on Climate Change* (Dec. 11, 1997), U.N. Doc. FCCC/CP/1997/7/Add.1, art. 2(1)(a)(iii) (promotion of sustainable agricultural practices) and art. 2(1)(a)(iv) (research and promotion of renewable energy and carbon dioxide sequestration technology), 37 I.L.M. 22 (Mar. 25, 1998), https://unfccc.int/resource/docs/cop3/07a01.pdf.

[31] *United Nations Conference on Environment and Development: Convention on Biological Diversity*, 1760 U.N.T.S. 79, 31 I.L.M. 818 (June 5, 1992).

[32] *Cartagena Protocol on Biosafety to the Convention on Biological Diversity*, U.N. Doc. UNEP/ CBD/ExCOP/1/3, 39 I.L.M. 1027 (Jan. 29, 2000).

[33] *United Nations: Convention to Combat Desertification in Those Countries Experiencing Serious Drought and/or Desertification, Particularly in Africa*, U.N. Doc. A/AC.241/15/Rev.7, 33 I.L.M. 1328 (June 17, 1994).

[34] Charter of Fundamental Rights of the European Union, 2007 O.J. (C 303) article 37; Treaty of Lisbon, Amending the Treaty on European Union and the Treaty Establishing the European Community, Dec. 13, 2007, 2007 O.J. (C 306); Luis E. Rodríguez-Rivera, *The Human Right to Environment in the 21st Century: A Case for Its Recognition and Comments on the Systemic Barriers It Encounters*, 34 Am. U. Int'l L. Rev. 143, 179 (2018).

[35] Barral, *supra* note 3, at 384.

[36] *Id.*

International tribunals also are relying on the principle of sustainable development as an aid to judicial reasoning.[37] For example, the International Court of Justice (ICJ) recognized the significance of sustainable development independently of its inclusion in a treaty in the *Gabčíkovo-Nagymaros* case.[38] The Court decided that an economic treaty between Hungary and Slovakia was still in force.[39] But the court concluded that current norms of international environmental law had to be taken into consideration because of the need to reconcile economic development with environmental protection, which the Court thought was "aptly expressed in the concept of sustainable development."[40] The Court stated:

> Throughout the ages, mankind has, for economic and other reasons, constantly interfered with nature. In the past, this was often done without consideration of the effects upon the environment. Owing to new scientific insights and to a growing awareness of the risks for mankind – for present and future generations – of pursuit of such interventions at an unconsidered and unabated pace, new norms and standards have been developed, set forth in a great number of instruments during the last two decades. Such new norms have to be taken into consideration, and such new standards given proper weight, not only when States contemplate new activities but also when continuing with activities begun in the past. This need to reconcile economic development with protection of the environment is aptly expressed in the concept of sustainable development.[41]

In a separate opinion, Vice-President Weeramantry elaborated on sustainable development as more than a mere concept – he viewed it as a "principle with normative value" crucial to the disposition of the case.[42] Vice-President Weeramantry noted that both parties to the case had endorsed sustainable development as a principle of international law, with its main function as reconciling the goals of economic development and environmental protection.[43] He concluded that the principle's normative authority is rooted in its endorsement in multilateral treaties, international declarations, documents of international organizations, regional declarations, state practice, and the practices of cultures and states for millennia.[44]

Only procedural requirements were imposed on the parties in connection with a concept of sustainable development.[45] But the Court ordered the parties to balance environmental protection with their development interests and to "look afresh at the effects on the environment" and "find a satisfactory solution."[46] The majority

---

[37] Cordonier Segger, *supra* note 17, at 14.
[38] *Case Concerning the Gabčíkovo-Nagymaros Project (Hungary v. Slovakia)*, *supra* note 2.
[39] *Id.* at ¶ 132.
[40] *Id.* at 77–78, ¶ 140.
[41] *Id.*
[42] *Id.* at 88–90 (separate opinion of Vice President Weeramantry).
[43] *Id.* at 93.
[44] *Id.* at 93–94.
[45] *Id.* at 77–78, ¶ 140.
[46] *Id.*

opinion, and Vice President Weeramantry's separate opinion, set the stage for the incorporation of sustainable development as a principle of customary international law.

The World Trade Organization came close to recognizing sustainable development's customary nature in the *Shrimp-Turtle* case, which ultimately concluded that the United States had violated the General Agreement on Tariffs and Trade 1994.[47] The dispute involved US measures barring imports of shrimp and shrimp products from WTO members who had not adopted and enforced national programs for the protection of sea turtles from bycatch during shrimp harvesting.[48] At the panel stage of the dispute, the United States argued that sustainable development is a principle of international law, in particular of WTO law, and the rules of trade must promote trade in a manner that respects the principle of sustainable development and protects and preserves the environment.[49] This argument was based in part on the preamble of the WTO Agreement, which allows "for the optimal use of the world's resources in accordance with the objective of sustainable development . . . ."[50]

The panel concluded that "the Preamble endorses the fact that environmental policies must be designed taking into account the situation of each Member, both in terms of its actual needs and in terms of its economic means."[51] The panel highlighted a quote from the 1992 Rio Declaration, recognizing that countries could design their own environmental policy and that international cooperation rather than unilateral measures are needed for sustainable development.[52]

The Appellate Body also recognized the relevance of sustainable development for resolving the dispute, and drew legal consequences from it, but fell short of recognizing sustainable development as customary international law.[53] The Appellate Body acknowledged the "objective of sustainable development" as informing all of WTO law, based on the preamble of the 1994 WTO Agreement.[54] The Appellate

---

[47] WTO Report of the Appellate Body, *United States – Import Prohibition of Certain Shrimp and Shrimp Products*, WT/DS58/AB/R (Oct. 12, 1998), https://www.wto.org/english/tratop_e/dispu_e/58abr.pdf.

[48] Tomer Broude, *Principles of Normative Integration and the Allocation of International Authority: The WTO, the Vienna Convention on the Law of Treaties, and the Rio Declaration*, 6 LOY. U. CHI. INT'L L. REV. 173, 204–06 (2008).

[49] WTO Report of the Panel, *United States – Import Prohibition of Certain Shrimp and Shrimp Products*, WT/DS58/R, at 73 ¶ 3.146 (May 15, 1998); Cordonier Segger, *supra* note 17, at 17.

[50] Agreement Establishing the World Trade Organization, pmbl., 1867 U.N.T.S. 3 (Apr. 15, 1994), http://treaties.un.org/doc/Publication/UNTS/Volume%201867/volume-1867-I-31874-English.pdf.

[51] Broude, *supra* note 48, at 204–6. WTO Report of the Panel, *supra* note 49, at 294 ¶ 7.52; Cordonier Segger, *supra* note 17, at 17.

[52] *Id.*

[53] WTO Report of the Appellate Body, *United States – Import Prohibition of Certain Shrimp and Shrimp Products*, WT/DS58/AB/R (Oct. 12, 1998), https://www.wto.org/english/tratop_e/dispu_e/58abr.pdf.

[54] *Id.*

Body explained that "[t]his concept has been generally accepted as integrating economic and social development and environmental protection."[55]

The *Shrimp-Turtle* report also considered the mandate of the WTO Committee on Trade and the Environment as indicative of the balance to be struck between free trade and environmental protection.[56] The Appellate Body turned to the WTO Ministerial Decision on Trade and the Environment, the preamble of which provides:

> *Considering* that there should not be, nor need be, any policy contradiction between upholding and safeguarding an open, non-discriminatory and equitable multilateral trading system on the one hand, and acting for the protection of the environment, and the promotion of sustainable development on the other.[57]

This dispute, which resulted in four Panel and Appellate Body Reports, provided a clearer expression of the meaning of state commitments on sustainable development in the WTO Agreements, concluded that it is considered to be an objective of the WTO, and recognized the need to integrate all elements of sustainable development.

Regional human rights law and foreign domestic law offer even more conclusive references to the centrality of sustainable development as a governing mandate. Connecting the role of sustainable development to government stewardship duties, the African Commission on Human and Peoples' Rights decided the *Ogoniland* case, enforcing the human right to environment as provided for in the 1981 African Charter on Human and Peoples' Rights.[58] The Commission stated:

> The right to a general satisfactory environment, as guaranteed under Article 24 of the African Charter or the right to a healthy environment, as it is widely known, therefore imposes clear obligations upon a government. It requires the state to take reasonable and other measures to prevent pollution and ecological degradation, to promote conservation, and to secure an ecologically sustainable development and use of natural resources.[59]

This language connecting sustainable development to government stewardship responsibilities raises a need for clarification on how and to what degree

---

[55] *Id.* at ¶ 129, n.107.

[56] *Id.* at ¶ 154.

[57] *Id.* (quoting World Trade Organization, Ministerial Decision on Trade and the Environment, Annex II, WT/MTN.TNC/45(MIN) (Apr. 14, 1994), 33 I.L.M. 1267, 1267 (1994)); Broude, *supra* note 48, at 204–06.

[58] Soc. & Econ. Rights Action Ctr. v. Nigeria, Comm. No. 155/96, African Commission on Human and Peoples Rights (Oct. 27, 2001), http://www1.umn.edu/humanrts/africa/comcases/155-96.html.

[59] *Id.* at ¶ 52 (citing African Charter on Human and Peoples' Rights art. 24, *adopted* June 27, 1981, 21 I.L.M. 58, http://www.achpr.org/files/instruments/achpr/banjul_charter.pdf ["All peoples shall have the right to a general satisfactory environment favorable to their development."]); *see also* Rodríguez-Rivera, *supra* note 34, at 179.

governments are required to act to implement the sustainable development mandate in their decisions.

Two decisions in New South Wales, Australia reached opposite conclusions in applying the concept of ecological sustainable development (ESD) as a stewardship responsibility for governments. In *Taralga Landscape Guardians Inc. v. Minister for Planning*,[60] the Land and Environment Court of New South Wales upheld a proposal for a wind farm, noting that the overall public benefits outweighed any private burdens.[61] A community organization challenged the proposal, citing negative impacts on their village and the surrounding countryside.[62] The Court held that the concept of ecologically sustainable development, specifically intergenerational equity, is central to any decision-making process concerning the development of new energy resources.[63] In this case, it is reasonable to substitute an energy source that results in lower greenhouse gas emissions for energy sources that result in more greenhouse gas (GHG) emissions.[64]

Conversely, in *Walker v. Minister for Planning*,[65] the Minister for Planning approved a residential development project, and the respondent challenged the approval in the Land and Environment Court. The lower court found that the Minister erred in failing to apply ESD principles when approving the project.[66] The court held that the agency had an obligation under the Environmental Planning and Assessment Act 1979 to take into account the principle of ESD and the impact of the proposal upon the environment, including whether the flooding impacts of the project would be compounded by climate change.[67] On appeal, the New South Wales Court of Appeal overturned the lower court's decision, holding that while the Environmental Planning and Assessment Act 1979 required the Minister to take into account the "public interest," the Minister was under no obligation to consider ESD principles.[68]

The principle of sustainable development is now recognized by states and tribunals across the world.[69] Despite judicial confirmation, however, these two decisions from New South Wales are one example among many regarding how it remains unclear to what extent sustainable development, as an objective, already constitutes

---

[60] Taralga Landscape Guardians Inc. v. Minister for Planning (Land and Environment Court of New South Wales, 2007).

[61] *Id.* at ¶ 3(13).

[62] *Id.* at ¶ 7 (44).

[63] *Id.* at ¶ 2 (1).

[64] *Id.* at ¶ 12 (74); http://www.lse.ac.uk/GranthamInstitute/litigation/taralga-landscape-guardians-inc-v-minister-for-planning-land-and-environment-court-of-new-south-wales-2007/.

[65] Walker v. Minister for Planning (Court of Appeal of the Supreme Court of New South Wales, 2008).

[66] *Id.* at ¶¶ 21(33–34).

[67] *Id.*

[68] Taralga Landscape Guardians, *supra* note 60.

[69] *See also* Martha Fitzgerald, *Prison or Precaution: Unilateral, State-Mandated Geoengineering Under Principles of International Environmental Law*, 24 N.Y.U. ENVTL. L.J. 256, 276 (2016).

a principle of customary law. Sustainable development has widespread state recognition, even if state practice does not always conform to that recognition.[70] It has been applied in cases resolving international disputes, indicating that it has some binding force. Although the ICJ has yet to issue a definitive pronouncement on the legal status of sustainable development, it has nevertheless occasionally referred to it and alluded to its component principles. Other judicial bodies have done the same. Based on its inclusion in a significant number of binding and nonbinding documents, as well as judicial bodies' reliance on it, a strong case can be made for sustainable development's emerging recognition as customary international law.

Three decades after its pronouncement in the Brundtland Commission report in 1987, sustainable development today remains largely aspirational and not legally required, though some scholars and jurists have suggested that it is on its way to becoming binding customary international law. A case in India traced the evolutionary steps of sustainable development as a governing principle and concluded that sustainable development has already arrived as a customary international law norm.

In *Vellore Citizens Welfare Forum v. Union of India*,[71] the Supreme Court observed that sustainable development has come to be accepted as a viable concept to eradicate poverty and improve the quality of human life while living within the carrying capacity of the supporting ecosystem.[72] The Supreme Court of India ordered the government to address pollution from tanneries. The court explained that "[t]he traditional concept that development and ecology are opposed to each other, is no longer acceptable. Sustainable Development is the answer."[73] The court examined the Brundtland Report and Agenda 21, among other legal instruments, to determine the contours of sustainable development.[74] In decisive language that will likely soon be replicated in other domestic and international courts and tribunals around the world, the court concluded: "We have no hesitation in holding that 'Sustainable Development' as a balancing concept between ecology and development has been accepted as a part of the Customary International Law though its salient features have yet to be finalised by the International Law Jurists."[75]

At its session in September 2016, the World Conservation Congress issued a resolution calling on the General Assembly of the United Nations to request an advisory opinion from the ICJ on the legal status and content of the principle of sustainable development.[76] While the progress report for this resolution noted an intention to prepare a communication for the General Assembly Debate in

---

[70] *Id.*

[71] Vellore Citizens Welfare Forum v. Union of India, 5 S.C.C. 647 (Aug. 28, 1996), https://indiankanoon.org/doc/1934103/.

[72] *Id.*

[73] *Id.* at 9.

[74] *Id.*

[75] *Id.*

[76] Int'l Union for Conservation of Nature, *Request for an Advisory Opinion of the International Court of Justice on the Principles of Sustainable Development in View of the Needs of Future*

September 2018,[77] no additional progress has been made as of this writing. Although nonbinding, should the ICJ ultimately issue an advisory opinion on this topic, it would carry significant legal and moral influence and could clarify that sustainable development has achieved the status of customary international law.

B *Administrative Bodies to Enforce the Mandate*

Several countries either have or had administrative bodies charged with stewardship responsibilities for future generations. For example, Israel had the Commission for Future Generations from 2001 to 2006. The commissioner was authorized to examine any parliamentary bill and secondary legislation where it judged potential harm on future generations, and to express opinions during legislative committee deliberations or as an attachment to bills. According to the first (and only) commissioner, its mission was "enhancing long-term and sustainable thinking among policymakers and in the state of Israel at large and ensuring that these considerations are included in primary and secondary legislation." While the Commission had extensive rights to information and participation in the workings of the Knesset, perhaps the most significant power it possessed was of delay: "the right to be given enough time to prepare an opinion on a bill." As the first commissioner noted: "The commissioner can introduce uncomfortable delays ... on issues he deems critical – but in doing so, he risks drawing antagonism from all sides. Thus, this authority was rarely invoked.[78]

Drawing guidance from the concept of sustainable development, Israel's Commission for Future Generations was able to engage on any subject on the parliament's agenda, but aimed to select issues where it would have the most opportunity for impact, including education, health, environment, economy and budget, and science and technology. The Commission was abolished because of "the cost of its operations and [the perception from other administrative bodies] that the Commission received too much authority to interfere in their work."[79]

Like Israel, Hungary also eliminated an administrative body that was authorized to protect future generations' interests. Unlike Israel, however, this commission in Hungary was replaced by a new administrative body that protects future generations' interests in a manner similar to the now-disbanded commission in Israel.

Generations, WCC-2016-Res-079-EN (Sept. 10, 2016), https://portals.iucn.org/library/sites/library/files/resrecfiles/WCC_2016_RES_079_EN.pdf.

[77] Int'l Union for Conservation of Nature, *Request for an Advisory Opinion of the International Court of Justice on the Principles of Sustainable Development in View of the Needs of Future Generations*, WCC-2016-Res-079 – Progress Report (2017), https://portals.iucn.org/library/node/47458.

[78] *Knesset Commission for Future Generations*, FOUND. FOR DEMOCRACY AND SUSTAINABLE DEV., http://www.fdsd.org/ideas/knesset-commission-future-generations/.

[79] *Id.*

The Commissioner for Fundamental Rights in Hungary[80] is responsible particularly for the rights of children, vulnerable social groups, and the interests of future generations. He or she has deputy commissioners, elected by the Hungarian Parliament, one of whom was responsible for the protection of the interests of future generations and is known as the Ombudsman for Future Generations.[81] The Commissioner and relevant deputy are authorized to provide an opinion on draft laws that affect future generations, and on "plans and concepts otherwise directly affecting the quality of life of future generations." They can be petitioned by people who feel that public bodies are infringing fundamental rights, with the potential for review of legal rules in the Constitutional Court.[82]

This approach to future generations arose out of the 2011 new constitution, which includes responsibility to descendants and protection of the living conditions of future generations and common heritage. It places stewardship obligations on government, states, and people. Another role is to ensure the provision of strong scientific information to parliament.[83] Prior to 2011, the Office of the Parliamentary Commissioner for Future Generations[84] was operating with what was more commonly called the Ombudsman for Future Generations, who could stop environmentally damaging legislation through a constitutional mandate for the right to a healthy environment.[85]

Switzerland, Germany, and Wales also have established administrative bodies to safeguard the interests of future generations. Institutions for long-term shaping and safeguarding of the rights of future generations have been created in Switzerland;[86] however, their effectiveness in practice is still evolving. In the revised Swiss federal constitution in 1999, the responsibility toward future generations is mentioned in the preamble.[87] Moreover, since 2009, the Swiss government is obliged by parliamentary law to review every matter that it brings to parliament for the potential consequences on future generations "as far as substantial information can be provided."[88] Reference to future generations can be found in only 37 of the 560 matters brought

---

[80] The Office of the Commissioner for Fundamental Rights, http://www.ajbh.hu/en/web/ajbh-en/main_page.

[81] *Hungarian Parliament's Deputy Commissioner for Fundamental Rights, the Ombudsman for Future Generations*, FOUND. FOR DEMOCRACY AND SUSTAINABLE DEV., http://www.fdsd.org/ideas/the-hungarian-parliaments-ombudsman-for-future-generations/.

[82] *Id.*

[83] *Id.*

[84] The Office of the Commissioner for Fundamental Rights, *supra* note 80.

[85] *Id.* The Ombudsman for Future Generations was discontinued pursuant to Act 111 (2011) of the Hungarian Commissioner for Fundamental Rights. Effective January 1, 2012, its tasks were assumed by its legal successor, the Office of the Commissioner for Fundamental Rights.

[86] Paula Tiihonen ed., *For the Next Generations: Report of the International Seminar in the Finnish Parliament*, PUBLICATIONS OF THE COMMITTEE FOR THE FUTURE 85 (June 7–8, 2016), https://www.eduskunta.fi/FI/tietoaeduskunnasta/julkaisut/Documents/tuvj_5+2016.pdf.

[87] Bundesverfassung [BV] [Constitution] Apr. 18, 1999, SR 101, pmbl. (Switz.).

[88] Tiihonen, *supra* note 86.

to parliament by government between 2009 and spring 2016, and mostly in very general terms without any substantial information and reflection. As such, an intention to take into account the consequences for future generations exists in Switzerland, but a regular practice of it has not yet been implemented.[89]

Germany's approach shows much more promise. The Parliamentary Advisory Council on Sustainable Development (PACSD) is a special body of the German Parliament. Operating as a de facto parliamentary advisory body, its activities are partly concerned with legislative acts discussed in the German Parliament, and partly with other issues unrelated to the former.[90] One of the most important tasks of the PACSD is related to the national strategy for sustainable development adopted by the German Council for Sustainable Development. PACSD monitors sustainability in four areas, namely, in the fields of intergenerational equity, social cohesion, quality of life, and international responsibility. It maintains constructive dialogue with other parliamentary bodies within the European Union and promotes the participation of social actors in decision making, thus facilitating the wider public debate of sustainability related parliamentary initiatives and questions and the establishment of civil dialogue.[91] Although the German Parliament is not bound by rules requiring the participation of the Parliamentary Advisory Council in the legislative process, this special body, weighing and monitoring the long-term effects of issues debated in the parliament on future generations, is a major means of intra-parliamentary control.[92]

In 2015, the Welsh Assembly passed the Well-being of Future Generations (Wales) Act, making it the first legislature in the world to enshrine in law a duty, falling on public bodies, to safeguard the well-being of future generations. The well-being duty is based on the principle of sustainable development and encompasses economic, social, environmental and cultural factors.[93] This Act creates a duty for specified public bodies to meet well-being goals[94] while observing the sustainable development principle. It also establishes a Future Generations Commissioner for Wales, who will advocate for future generations and advise and support public bodies to carry out their duties under the Act.[95] This Act is the first that protects the welfare of stakeholders who do not yet exist and, as such, requires a guardian in the form of the

---

[89] *Id.*

[90] *Id.*

[91] *Id.*

[92] *Id.*

[93] See Haydn Davies, *The Well-Being of Future Generations (Wales) Act 2015: Duties or aspirations?* 18 ENVTL. L. REV. 41 (2016).

[94] Well-being goals: "A globally responsible Wales, a prosperous Wales, a resilient Wales, a healthier Wales, a more equal Wales, a Wales of cohesive communities, a Wales of vibrant culture and thriving Welsh Language."

[95] *The Well-Being of Future Generations (Wales) Act Places a Duty on Public Bodies to Sustainably Meet Defined Wellbeing Goals*, FOUND. FOR DEMOCRACY AND SUSTAINABLE DEV., http://www.fdsd.org/ideas/well-being-of-future-generations-bill-wales (last accessed Mar. 11, 2019).

Future Generations Commissioner.[96] The Well-being of Future Generations (Wales) Act has the potential to be an exemplary approach to the protection of future generations. Its success in safeguarding the interests of future generations will depend heavily on harnessing the requisite political will to support the implementation efforts of those tasked with holding public bodies accountable.[97]

II PROCEDURAL MECHANISM

As sustainable development continues to work its way toward the status of customary international law, there are informational and procedural safeguards that can be implemented as a check on activities that threaten future generations' rights to inherit a habitable planet and the viability of wildlife populations and natural resources. Activities that pose an undue threat of exacerbating global climate change and where less impactful alternatives are available is one context in which those unsustainable practices could be held in check through the procedural and informational mechanisms of an environmental impact assessment analysis.

A Procedural and Informational Accountability with Environmental Impact Assessment in the United States and Abroad

The United States, South Africa, Canada, and Australia have already embraced this approach regarding environmental impact assessment and climate change to varying degrees in recent cases involving proposed projects with significant climate change impacts. In the United States, NEPA[98] is an indirect tool to address climate change. Although NEPA does not include a climate mitigation mandate (or any substantive mandate for that matter), it can be a potent tool for restricting proposed federal agency actions that threaten to contribute significantly to global climate change. As such, these cases involving NEPA and climate change provide some measure of protection for the voiceless in requiring consideration of climate change impacts on ecosystem resilience and future generations' needs.

This section first addresses NEPA cases involving climate change impacts. In each case, federal agencies were required to reevaluate proposed projects and consider the project's impacts on climate change. The section then explores environmental impact assessment cases outside of the United States involving climate change impacts. It examines recent landmark decisions from South Africa, Canada, and Australia.

NEPA is recognized as the "Magna Carta" of US environmental law.[99] If the approval of a major federal action has the potential to cause significant impact on

---

[96] *See* Davies, *supra* note 93.
[97] *Id.*
[98] 42 U.S.C. §§ 4321–37 (2018).
[99] Richard Lazarus, *The National Environmental Policy Act in the U.S. Supreme Court: A Reappraisal and a Peek Behind the Curtains*, 100 GEO. L.J. 1507, 1509 (2012).

the environment, NEPA requires the federal agency to prepare an environmental impact statement (EIS) providing a detailed analysis of the proposed action's environmental impacts.[100] NEPA can play a critical role in promoting sustainable development as it has the potential to force federal agencies to "become more environmentally conscious and accountable for their decisions."[101] Although a NEPA challenge may not ultimately prevent a federal agency from proceeding on a proposed project, NEPA cases offer the opportunity to delay and generate negative publicity for some proposed federal agency actions. This delay not only provides community groups more time to develop an effective response, but the cost of delay for the federal agency may ultimately cause the project to lose funding in a transition between presidential administrations, or at the very least, force it to make a greater effort to reduce the project's environmental impacts.[102]

In *Mid States Coalition for Progress v. Surface Transportation Board*,[103] the Eighth Circuit vacated and remanded the Surface Transportation Board's (STB's) decision to approve a proposal to extend and expand rail lines to coal mines in Wyoming's Powder River basin.[104] The EIS submitted by the Board's Section of Environmental Analysis (SEA) violated NEPA by failing to provide full disclosure on how these new train lines would affect increased traffic, vibration, and sound and air pollution in

---

[100] *See* Marissa Tripolsky, *A New NEPA to Take a Bite out of Environmental Injustice*, 23 B.U. Pub. Int'l L.J. 313 (2014) (explaining what an EIS must include under NEPA and how it requires federal agencies to take a "hard look" at the environmental consequences of their actions); *see also* Melinda Harm Benson & Ahjond S. Garmestani, *Embracing Panarchy, Building Resilience and Integrating Adaptive Management through a Rebirth of the National Environmental Policy Act*, 92 J. Envtl. Mgmt. 1420, 1423 (2011) (providing a detailed and helpful flowchart outlining when NEPA would apply to an federal action); *see generally* Rachael E. Salcido, *Reviving the Environmental Justice Agenda*, 91 Chi.-Kent L. Rev. 115 (2016) (describing how NEPA is triggered and applied, and explaining that two main goals of NEPA focus on "engaging the public and its function of providing a measure of government transparency.").

[101] Jeff Todd, *Trade Treaties, Citizen Submissions, and Environmental Justice*, 44 Ecology L.Q. 89, 106 (2017).

[102] *See* Tripolsky *supra* note 100, at 331 (discussing the important impact NEPA challenges can have because the "cumulative effects of these environmental justice suits have the power to force corporations to change their practices from pollution control to pollution prevention."); *see generally* Lazarus, *supra* note 99 (stating that even unsuccessful NEPA challenges can have an important impact on the future of climate change litigation because "the significance of a Court opinion turns on the particular wording of its reasoning far more than on whether it ends with an "affirmed" or "reversed.").

[103] 345 F.3d 520 (8th Cir. 2003).

[104] *Id.* at 532, 550 (8th Cir. 2003). The STB noted that "in both size and scope, this project is undoubtedly one of the largest ever to have come before the Board." *See generally* Elizabeth Gross & Paul Stretesky, *Environmental Justice in the Courts*, in Failed Promises: Evaluating the Federal Government's Response to Environmental Justice, 205–32 (David M. Konisky ed., 2015) (referring to *Mid States* Coalition for Progress v. Surface Transportation Board as an important and successful environmental justice case).

the city of Rochester.[105] The SEA also failed to provide proper reasons for concluding that sound and air pollution mitigation was unwarranted.[106] The SEA relied on statutory emissions caps mandated in the 1990 Clean Air Act Amendments to conclude that any emissions resulting from the proposed project "will definitely fall to the mandated level, producing whatever effect the emissions will have on global warming."[107] However, the court noted that although the "SEA's 'assumption' may be true for those pollutants that the amendments have capped . . . it tells the decision-maker nothing about how this project will affect pollutants not subject to the statutory cap."[108] Such pollutants not capped by the 1990 Clean Air Act Amendments include nitrous oxide, carbon dioxide, particulates, and mercury.[109] Thus, the court concluded that "the proposed project will increase the long-term demand for coal and any adverse effects that result from burning coal."[110]

The court in *Montana Envtl. Info. Ctr. v. United States Office of Surface Mining*[111] applied similar reasoning. The court granted, in part, the plaintiff's claim challenging the Office of Surface Mining Reclamation and Enforcement's (OSMRE's) approval of a mining plan modification for an underground coal mine located in the Bull Mountains. The Enforcement Office decided not to prepare an EIS based on its Finding of No Significant Impact (FONSI) report's conclusion.[112] The court concluded that the environmental effects of the project were "'highly' uncertain" and, therefore, the decision not to prepare an EIS violated NEPA because it failed to effectively assess foreseeable GHGs and any associated "indirect and cumulative effects of coal transportation and coal combustion."[113] OSMRE explained that precise calculations of the mining modification plan's GHG emissions would be too speculative.[114] However, the court concluded that the Social Cost of Carbon Protocol was an existing tool that could have been used to assist in making these calculations.[115] The court held that OSMRE "acted arbitrarily and capriciously by quantifying the benefits of the mine expansion while failing to

---

[105] *Id.* at 557. Emphasizing the importance of reasonable foreseeability, Justice Arnold stated "we believe that it would be irresponsible for the Board to approve a project of this scope without first examining the effects that may occur as a result of the reasonably foreseeable increase in coal consumption." *Id.* at 550.

[106] *Id.* at 535–36.

[107] *Id.* at 550.

[108] *Id.*

[109] *Id.* at 548.

[110] *Id.* at 549 (stating that "when the nature of the effect is reasonably foreseeable but its extent is not . . . the agency may not simply ignore the effect.").

[111] 274 F. Supp. 3d 1074 (D. Mont. 2017).

[112] *Id.* at 1081.

[113] *Id.* at 1081, 1091. Such indirect effects may include the "health, economic, and environmental impacts of diesel emissions, noise, vibrations, rail congestion, and coal dust."

[114] *Id.*

[115] *Id.* at 1094.

account for the costs, even though a tool was available to do so."[116] The court remitted the matter to OSMRE for further consideration,[117] noting that "although this Order does not mandate the preparation of an EIS, an EIS may be required under NEPA."[118]

In the most significant victory for consideration of climate change impacts in a NEPA analysis, the Tenth Circuit in *WildEarth Guardians v. United States Bureau of Land Management*[119] held that Bureau of Land Management's (BLM's) decision to approve four coal leases in Wyoming's Powder River basin region was "arbitrary and capricious."[120] The court reversed the district court's decision to uphold the leases, and remanded "with instructions to enter an order requiring the BLM to revise its Environmental Impact Statements and Records of Decision."[121] Although BLM agreed that "carbon dioxide emissions from coal use cause climate change,"[122] the court disagreed with BLM's Draft Environment Impact Statement, which concluded that "issuing the leases would not result in higher national carbon dioxide emissions than would declining to issue them."[123] This assumption, also understood as "perfect substitution," is a common argument that federal agencies have made when faced with a NEPA challenge.[124] This argument "posits that the extraction of fossil fuels will not actually cause an increase in consumption, because the same quantity of the fuel would be produced elsewhere and eventually transported and consumed, even if the agency did not approve the proposal at issue."[125] The court rejected this argument and ruled that by failing to consider and compare adequate alternatives, BLM's "perfect substitution" assumption "defeated NEPA's purpose,"[126] and its carbon emissions analysis "underestimate[d] the effect on climate change."[127] The court concluded that BLM's assertion that

---

[116] *Id.*

[117] *Id.* at 1104.

[118] *Id.; see generally* Lowell J. Chandler, *Montana Environmental Information Center v. U.S. Office of Surface Mining*, 0 Pub. Land & Resources L. Rev. 1 (2018) (analyzing the elements of this case and noting that this was "a major decision that affects how federal agencies must evaluate the environmental impacts of future carbon-intensive projects.").

[119] 870 F.3d 1222 (10th Cir. 2017).

[120] *Id.* at 235 (10th Cir. 2017). The court acknowledged that "The Powder River Basin region is the largest single contributor to United States' domestic coal production" *Id.* at 1227.

[121] *Id.* at 1240.

[122] *Id.*

[123] *Id.* at 1226.

[124] *See generally* Michael Burger & Jessica Wentz, *Downstream and Upstream Greenhouse Gas Emissions: The Proper Scope of NEPA Review*, 41 Harv. Envtl. L. Rev. 109, 148 (2017) (analyzing the "perfect substitution" argument that federal agencies assert in NEPA challenges and discussing why courts often reject this argument).

[125] *Id.* at 150.

[126] *WildEarth Guardians*, 870 F.3d at 237. Justice Briscoe noted that BLM's failure to consider alternatives was "more than a mere flyspeck."

[127] *Id.* at 1236.

there was no difference between acting and not acting was a "blanket assertion ... unsupported by hard data."[128]

Two decisions in 2018 involving NEPA and climate change impacts confirm that the mandate of sustainable development applied to proposed agency actions involving significant climate change impacts is gaining traction. In *AquAlliance v. United States Bureau of Reclamation*,[129] the plaintiff challenged a ten-year water transfer program that sought to "'move water from sellers located upstream of the Sacramento/San Joaquin Delta ('Delta') to willing buyers south of the Delta.'"[130] The US District Court for the Eastern District of California granted the plaintiff's motion for summary judgment because the climate change analysis in the project's Final Long-Term Water Transfers Environmental Impact Statement/Environmental Impact Report (FEIS/R) lacked record evidence to support its conclusions, thus violating NEPA.[131] The FEIS/R concluded that "inflow to key reservoirs in California will not be substantially different from historic patterns."[132]

The federal defendants argued that because greenhouse gas emissions are a global phenomenon, their distribution cannot solely be traced to California's localized emissions.[133] Therefore, they stated that since the FEIS/R concludes that California's emissions are declining and the project would be short term, the project's impact on climate change would "be less than significant" in the long run.[134] The court ruled that the "FEIS/R fails to address or otherwise explain how this information about the potential impacts of climate change can be reconciled with the ultimate conclusion that climate change impacts to the Project will be less than significant."[135]

The US District Court for the District of Colorado in *High Country Conservation Advocates v. United States Forest Service*[136] applied similar reasoning. The plaintiff challenged interrelated agency actions that authorized on-the-ground mining exploration in the North Fork Valley, a protected area of twenty thousand acres.[137]

---

[128] *Id.* For a discussion of the need to administratively mandate the outcomes achieved in these cases, *see generally* Taylor Ann Whittemore, *WildEarth Guardians v. Jewell: The Need for Regulations Directing Agencies to Consider the Impact of Their Decisions on Global Climate Change*, 42 ECOLOGY L.Q. 565 (2015).

[129] 287 F. Supp. 3d 969, 984 (E.D. Cal. 2018).

[130] *Id.* at 984.

[131] *Id.* at 1028, 1030, 1032; *see generally* Taylor Wetzel, *AquAlliance v. United States Bureau of Reclamation: The Impact of Withholding Information from the Public*, 44 ECOLOGY L.Q. 565 (2017) (discussing the importance of public consultation).

[132] *Id.* at 1029; *see also id.* at 1031 (acknowledging that although "courts must give deference to an expert agency on highly scientific or technical questions ... a voluminous and technical record does not insulate a decision from judicial review under that deferential standard.").

[133] *Id.* at 1030.

[134] *Id.* at 1023.

[135] *Id.* at 1032.

[136] 52 F. Supp. 3d 1174 (D. Colo. 2014).

[137] *Id.; see* Kathryn S. Ore, *High Country Conservation Advocates v. United States Forest Service*, 52 F. Supp. 3d 1174 (D. Colo. 2014), 0 PUB. LAND & RESOURCES L. REV. 1, 6 (2015).

The court held that the agency's FEIS for mining lease modifications violated NEPA because it "failed to disclose the social, environmental, and economic impacts of GHG emissions resulting from the lease modifications."[138] The agency instead focused on the economic benefits of these modifications and stated that any attempt to predict GHG emissions' "degree of impact" would be too speculative.[139]

The court reasoned that it was "arbitrary and capricious to quantify the *benefits* of the lease modifications and then explain that a similar analysis of the *costs* was impossible."[140] The court noted that the agency could have used the Social Cost of Carbon Protocol to assist them in calculating GHG's impacts.[141] However, the agency failed to utilize this tool and failed to provide reasons for not doing so in its FIES.[142] The court also concluded that the FIES for the North Fork mining area exemption to the Colorado Roadless Rule violated NEPA by failing to disclose relevant information related to the impact of reasonably foreseeable GHG emissions that would result from mining operations and coal combustion.[143] The agency also neglected to "address, acknowledge, or respond to an expert report criticizing the [a]gencies' assumptions about GHG pollution."[144] As a result, the court instructed the parties "to confer and attempt in good faith to reach agreement as to remedies."[145] Parties, could not, however, reach a mutual agreement. For this reason, the court vacated the mining lease modifications and the Colorado Roadless Rule and the North Fork exemption.[146]

This line of successful challenges in NEPA cases involving climate change impacts is highly significant for three reasons. First, the decisions chastise federal agencies' "business as usual" approach to treating the environment as an unlimited bounty of resources available for human use and consumption. Second, these decisions show how an informational mandate can achieve substantive outcomes in thwarting proposed agency projects that threaten serious climate change impacts. Third, the courts' reasoning in these cases offers exceptional promise to develop an ecocentric approach to apply to agencies' decisions that threaten unsustainable use of resources with corresponding impacts on global climate change. This approach is necessary to make meaningful progress in protecting the voiceless communities.

---

[138] Ore, *supra* note 137, at 5.
[139] *High Country Conservation Advocates*, 333 F. Supp. 3d at 1198.
[140] *Id.* at 1191.
[141] *Id.* at 1190. The court recognized that "one of the foreseeable effects of the Lease Modification approval is the likely release of methane gas from the expanded mining operations"; *see also* Ore, *supra* note 137, at 6 (explaining the purpose of the Social Cost of Carbon Protocol.)
[142] *High Country Conservation Advocates*, 333 F. Supp. 3d at 1193.
[143] *Id.* at 1196; *see also* Ore, *supra* note 137, at 10 (explaining the Colorado Roadless Rule and the North Fork exemption).
[144] Ore, *supra* note 137, at 6.
[145] *High Country Conservation Advocates*, 333 F. Supp. 3d at 1200.
[146] Ore, *supra* note 137, at 7.

Environmental impact assessment case law in South Africa, Canada, and Australia is equally promising as a tool to constrain proposed projects with significant climate change impacts. Heralded as "South Africa's first climate change-related judicial decision," the North Gauteng High Court in *Earthlife Africa Johannesburg v. Minister of Environmental Affairs*[147] held that the Department of Environmental Affairs' (DEA's) decision to authorize Thabametsi Power Company to construct a coal-fired power station in the Limpopo Province failed to comply with section 24 of the National Environmental Management Act (NEMA).[148] Thabametsi's application for environmental authorization neglected to consider the climate change impacts of the proposed power station, yet the Chief Director of the DEA (Chief Director) granted the authorization.[149] Earthlife appealed this approval to the DEA Minister, contending that the Chief Director "failed to take into account the state's international and national obligations to mitigate and take positive steps against climate change."[150] Although the DEA Minister acknowledged that the Chief Director's decision lacked climate change considerations, she nonetheless dismissed Earthlife's appeal and upheld the Chief Director's authorization.[151]

In this judicial review of the DEA's decisions, the Court ruled that both the Chief Director and the DEA Minister failed to comply with section 24(1) of NEMA because they neglected to consider the climate change impacts of the proposed

---

[147] Case No. 65662/16 (South Africa High Court 2017); *see generally* Tracy-Lynn Humby, *The Thabametsi Case: Case No 65662/16 Earthlife Africa Johannesburg v Minister of Environmental Affairs*, 30 J. ENVTL L. 145 (2018) (describing this case as "South Africa's first climate change-related judicial decision" and analyzing the significant contribution it may have on climate change litigation in South Africa); Jean-Claude N. Ashukem, *Setting the Scene for Climate Change Litigation in South Africa: Earthlife Africa Johannesburg v Minister of Environmental Affairs and Others*, 13 LAW ENV'T & DEV. J. (2017) (analyzing the significant impact this decision may have by setting a precedent that will hold the DEA accountable for its actions).

[148] *Id.* at ¶ 5.

[149] *Id.* Section 24 (1) of NEMA states that proposed projects that have potential to affect the environment are required to apply for an environmental authorization before proceeding. In this case, the Chief Director of the DEA was the appropriate authority to decide on environmental authorizations. Once an environmental authorization is granted, § 43(1) of NEMA permits affected parties to appeal such environmental authorization grants. These appeals are decided by the Minister of DEA.

[150] *Id.* at ¶ 53. Earthlife refers to the government's National Climate Change Response White Paper (CCR White Paper), which is considered a key national policy instrument outlining the governmental duty to consider long-term adaptation and mitigation strategies to address climate change; *see generally* Anel de Plessis & Louis J. Kotze, *The Heat Is On: Local Government and Climate Governance in South Africa*, 58 J. AFR. L. 145 (2014) (providing a detailed description of the CRR White Paper, which is recognized as "the most authoritative national climate change policy in the country ... [and is] the first statement of official national policy delineating the roles of the different organs of state and other institutional arrangements with respect to climate change.").

[151] Case No. 65662/16 (South Africa High Court 2017), at ¶ 107.

power station.[152] The court acknowledged the country's heavy reliance on coal-generated power, as well as its particular vulnerability to the impacts of climate change and GHG emissions.[153] Under these circumstances, the court recognized that a delicate balance must be struck when granting authorizations and evaluating climate change impact assessments.[154] The court determined that once the DEA Minister recognized that the Chief Director's authorization lacked a proper climate change impact assessment, a logical step would have been to refer the matter back to the Chief Director for reevaluation, or adjourn Earthlife's appeal and instruct Thabametsi to conduct a proper EIA.[155] Consequently, the court set aside the DEA Minister's appeal decision and ordered the matter to be remitted back to the DEA Minister with instructions to consider relevant EIA reports and related material to ensure that a proper climate change analysis is conducted.[156] This decision is highly significant because it may encourage future challenges to coal-fired power station construction projects in an effort to minimize future climate change impacts.[157]

In Canada, challenges to environmental impact assessments prepared under the Canadian Environmental Assessment Act produced two favorable outcomes in seeking to address projected climate change impacts from major federal agency projects. In *Pembina Institute v. Canada (A. G.)*,[158] the Federal Court held that a Joint Review Panel (Panel) established by the Alberta Energy Utilities Board and the Government of Canada erred in its recommendation to authorize construction of the Imperial Oil's Kearl Oil Sands Project (Project), an oil sands mine located in northern Alberta.[159] Imperial Oil's environmental impact assessment described projected annual GHG emissions during the Project's operation period and proposed mitigation measures.[160] The Panel concluded that based on these mitigation measures, any adverse environmental effects of annual GHG emissions

---

[152] *Id.* at ¶¶ 107, 124; *see generally* de Plessis & Kotze, *supra* note 150 (discussing the elements of NEMA and various other national climate change policy documents, and noting that "South Africa has no specific national law exclusively dedicated to climate change.").

[153] *Earthlife Africa Johannesburg*, Case No. 65662/16 (South Africa High Court 2017), at ¶ 35.

[154] *See id.* at ¶ 34.

[155] *Id.*

[156] *Id.* at ¶ 126.

[157] Ashukem, *supra* note 147, at 43.

[158] 323 F.T.R. 297 (FC) (2008).

[159] *Id.* at ¶ 79. The Panel was created through an agreement between the Government of Canada and the Government of Alberta to "render a project approval decision on behalf of Alberta authorities and make an approval recommendation to the responsible federal authority," which, in this case, was the Minister of the Department of Fisheries and Oceans (DFO). In 2006, the DFO proposed to the Minister of the Environment "that the Kearl Project be referred to a review panel due to the potential for the proposed project to cause significant adverse environmental effects." *Id.* at ¶ 8.

[160] *Id.* at ¶ 71.

released during the Project's operation period would be reduced to "a level of insignificance."[161]

The court held that the Panel failed "to provide a cogent rationale for [this] conclusion,"[162] and thus failed to comply with the two-step decision making process in the Canadian Environmental Assessment Act (CEAA).[163] The court stated that the Panel was "tasked with conducting a science and fact-based assessment of the potential adverse environmental effects of a proposed project" and determined that there was no evidence that such an informed assessment took place.[164] Therefore, the court ordered the matter to be referred back to the Panel to provide a reasoned basis for the its conclusions.[165]

Six years later, in *Greenpeace Canada* v. *Canada (A.G.)*,[166] another successful challenge under the CEAA was secured. The Federal Court concluded that the Panel's environmental assessment seeking approval for the construction of a new nuclear power generation station (Project) in Bowmanville, Ontario failed to comply with the CEAA because the Panel "did not reasonably address the issue of the long-term management and disposal of used nuclear fuel"[167] and failed to provide a "'qualitative' assessment of hazardous substance releases."[168] The court

---

[161] *Id.* at ¶ 78.

[162] *Id.* at ¶ 70.

[163] *Id.* at ¶ 79. The court referrred to § 34(c)(i) of the Canadian Environmental Assessment Act, S.C. 1992, c.37 (now § 43(d)(i) of the Canadian Environmental Assessment Act, S.C. 2012, c. 19, s. 52), which mandates that an informed rationale must be provided when any conclusions and recommendations are made regarding the authorization of proposed projects; *see generally* Martin Z. P. Olszynski, *Environmental Assessment as Planning and Disclosure Tool: Greenpeace Canada v. Canada (A.G.)*, 38 DALHOUSIE L.J. 207 (2015) (discussing the developments of the CEAA and comparing the differences between CEAA 1992 and CEAA 2012).

[164] *Id.* at ¶ 72. Justice Tremblay-Lamer recognized that deference should be given to the Panel's expertise since it had the opportunity to review the relevant materials, which would aid in arriving at a conclusion. However, she noted that "this deference to expertise is only triggered when those conclusions are articulated."

[165] *Id.* at ¶ 80; *see also* Nathalie J. Chalifour, *Case Comment: A (Pre)Cautionary Tale about the Kearl Oil Sands Decision, the Significance of Pembina Institute for Appropriate Development et al. v. Canada (Attorney-General) for the Future of Environmental Assessment*, 5 McGILL INT'L J. SUSTAINABLE DEV. & POL'Y 251, 255 (2009) (noting that [this] decision was significant "because it is the first case to offer judicial interpretation of the [precautionary] principle's application in environmental assessment since its inclusion in the CEAA."); *accord* Toby Kruger, *The Canadian Environmental Assessment Act and Global Climate Change: Rethinking Significance*, 47 ALTA. L. REV. 161, 162 (2009) (observing that "[this] is the first time a Canadian court has held that "unmitigated GHG emissions from a proposed project could be significant.'"); *see generally* Geoffrey H. Salomons & George Hoberg, *Setting Boundaries of Participation in Environmental Impact Assessment*, 45 ENVTL. IMPACT ASSESSMENT REV. 69 (2014) (examining amendments to the CEAA that limit the public participation process and discussing potential consequences of these changes).

[166] F.C.J. No. 515 (2014).

[167] *Id.* at ¶¶ 318, 282.

[168] *Id.* at ¶ 10.

rejected the environmental assessment report's conclusion, which stated that "the Project is not likely to cause significant adverse environmental effects."[169] This conclusion was based on "to-be-determined mitigation measures" and failed to provide relevant information related to the Project's construction and implementation plan.[170] Therefore, the court ordered that the environmental assessment report be remitted to the Panel for reconsideration.[171] The court further ordered that during this reconsideration period, federal agencies "have no jurisdiction to issue any authorizations or take any other actions which would enable the Project to proceed" [and] "shall not issue any licenses, permits, certificates, or statutory authorizations which would permit the Project to be carried out."[172]

Courts in Australia have similarly embraced environmental impact review as an indirect mechanism through which to address projected climate change impacts. In *Gray* v. *Minister for Planning and Ors.*,[173] an Australian federal court rejected an environmental impact assessment prepared as part of a development approval process for a large open-cut coal mine at Anvil Hill.[174] Coal from the proposed mine was destined for use in coal-fired power stations in Australia and overseas.[175] The proponents of the project failed to consider the GHG emissions from the burning of coal by third parties.[176] The court held that for projects with the potential to directly or indirectly contribute to GHG emissions, the climate change impacts of the proposal should be properly considered and assessed under the Environmental Planning and Assessment Act 1979.[177] The court held that "The fact there are many contributors globally does not mean the contribution from a single large source such as the Anvil Hill Project in the context of NSW should be ignored in the environmental assessment process. The coal intended to be mined is clearly a potential major single contributor to GHG emissions deriving from NSW given the large size of the proposed mine."[178]

On February 8, 2019, the New South Wales Land and Environment Court delivered a landmark decision on environmental impact assessment and climate

---

[169] *Id.* at ¶ 44.
[170] *Id.* Applicants argued "what the [Panel] purported to assess was a plan – a proposed or tentative course of future action – rather than a 'project' within the meaning of the CEAA." Applicants also argued that by basing the environmental assessment solely on certain future action, failing to assess foreseeable emissions, and then concluding that this action was unlikely to cause significant adverse environmental effects is contrary to the precautionary principle set out in the CEAA.
[171] *Id.* at ¶ 431.
[172] *Id.*
[173] (2006) NSWLEC 720, http://blogs2.law.columbia.edu/climate-change-litigation/wp-content/uploads/sites/16/non-us-case-documents/2006/20061127_5283_decision.pdf.
[174] *Id.* at ¶100.
[175] *Id.* at ¶ 99.
[176] *Id.* at ¶¶ 98–99.
[177] *Id.* at ¶99.
[178] *Id.* at ¶ 98.

change that has already attracted significant international attention. In *Gloucester Resources Limited* v. *Minister for Planning*,[179] Gloucester Resources Limited (GRL) proposed an open-cut coal mine near the small country town of Gloucester in New South Wales. Named the Rocky Hill Coal Project, the mine was intended to produce twenty-one million tons of coal over a period of sixteen years.[180] Of the submissions on the amended development application, 90 percent of the respondents opposed the mine.[181] Many were "concerned about the noise and dust impacts of the mine, the adverse impacts on the visual amenity and rural and scenic character of the valley, and the social impacts on the community" and that "the opening of a new coal mine will contribute to climate change."[182]

GRL's application to the Minister for Planning for development approval for the Project was denied. On appeal, the court exercised the function of the Minister as the consent authority to review the development application.[183] The Environmental Defenders Office of New South Wales secured approval from the Court to join the case, arguing on behalf of its client Groundswell Gloucester that the mine's detrimental impact on climate change and on the social fabric of the town must be considered.[184] The court considered the potential impacts of the mine, including the visual impacts on the surrounding community,[185] the amenity impacts such as exposure to noise and dust,[186] the social impacts such as the effects on culture and health,[187] and the economic and public benefits of the mine.[188] The court also discussed in great detail the potential direct and indirect impacts of the mine on climate change,[189] relying on expert evidence from the applicant and the respondents.

Detailed expert analysis was provided on the potential impacts of the Project in the context of the United Nations Framework Convention on Climate Change, the 2015 Paris Agreement, and the most recent climate change reports from the IPCC. One expert, Professor Will Steffen of the Australia National University Climate Change Institute, stated that "no new fossil fuel development is consistent with meeting the Paris accord climate targets"[190] Professor Steffen also offered that the

---

[179] [2019] NSWLEC 7, http://blogs2.law.columbia.edu/climate-change-litigation/wp-content/uploads/sites/16/non-us-case-documents/2019/20190208_2019-NSWLEC-7_decision-1.pdf.

[180] *Id.* at ¶4.

[181] *Id.* at ¶6.

[182] *Id.* at ¶ 6.

[183] *Id.* at ¶ 7.

[184] Peter Hannam, *"We Won": Landmark Climate Ruling as NSW Court Rejects Coal Mine*, SYDNEY MORNING HERALD (Feb. 8, 2019), https://www.smh.com.au/environment/climate-change/we-won-landmark-climate-ruling-as-nsw-court-rejects-coal-mine-20190207-p50wer.html.

[185] Gloucester Resources Limited, (2006) NSWLEC 720, at ¶¶ 90–222.

[186] *Id.* at ¶¶ 223–69.

[187] *Id.* at ¶¶ 270–421.

[188] *Id.* at ¶¶ 557–685.

[189] *Id.* at ¶¶ 422–556.

[190] *Id.* at ¶ 447.

refusal to permit the Project to proceed is justified "regardless of the fact that the total GHG emissions of the Project would be a small fraction of total global emissions."[191]

GRL argued that the "Commonwealth and State laws do not specify how Australia's [nationally determined contributions] emission reductions need to be achieved and, in particular, do not specify that no new coal mines can be approved."[192] GRL also asserted that reductions in other sources of GHG emissions (such as electricity generation) could offset the GHG emissions associated with the mine, and therefore the Project would not necessarily cause the carbon budget to be exceeded.[193] The court rejected this argument as "speculative and hypothetical."[194]

The court's opinion endorsed the "carbon budget" approach that Professor Steffen raised to measure compliance with and progress towards achieving the 2°C temperature target in the Paris Agreement.[195] The approach is "based on the approximately linear relationship between the cumulative amount of CO_2 emitted from all human sources since the beginning of industrialisation (often taken as 1870) and the increase in global average surface temperature." Following the carbon budget methodology, "most fossil fuel reserves will need to remain in the ground unburned."[196] This is "the first time climate change has been addressed this way in an Australian court using the concept of a carbon budget as its basis,"[197] and it may be significant for future cases considering the climate change impacts of a development, both in Australia and internationally.

The court further noted that "emissions over the life of the Project will be at least 37.8Mt CO_2-e," which was described as "a sizeable individual source of GHG emissions."[198] The court recognized that the state of New South Wales government has endorsed the Paris Agreement and has set for itself the goal of achieving zero net emissions by 2050.[199] As such, the court reasoned that "the exploitation and burning of a new fossil fuel reserve, which will increase GHG emissions, cannot assist in achieving the rapid and deep reductions in GHG emissions that are necessary in order to achieve a balance between anthropogenic emissions by sources and removals by sinks of greenhouse gases in the second half of this century" or "the long term temperature goal of limiting the increase in global average

---

[191] *Id.* at ¶ 450.
[192] *Id.* at ¶ 452.
[193] *Id.* at ¶ 529.
[194] *Id.* at ¶ 530.
[195] *See, e.g., id.* at ¶¶ 550–54.
[196] *Id.* at ¶ 550.
[197] Environmental Defenders Office of New South Wales, *Landmark Legal Win for Climate and Community*, (Feb. 8, 2019), https://www.edonsw.org.au/gloucester_climate_win (last accessed Mar. 9, 2019).
[198] *Id.* at ¶ 515.
[199] *Id.* at ¶ 526.

temperature to between 1.5°C and 2°C above pre-industrial levels," in compliance with the Paris Agreement.[200]

Another significant aspect of the decision is the court's rejection of GRL's argument that the Project should be approved because the GHG emissions will occur regardless of the Project because of carbon leakage. The argument was that GHG emissions would increase if coal mining were to be moved from Australia to other countries, given that Australian coal mines operate to some of the highest environmental and emissions standards in the world.[201] The court rejected this argument, stating that GRL failed to substantiate that "the risk of such leakage would actually occur if approval for the Project was not granted."[202] Similar carbon leakage arguments have also been rejected in other jurisdictions, including by the Hague Court of Appeal in the *Urgenda* case.[203] The court also rejected GRL's market substitution argument, that coal mining investment will occur elsewhere if not in the present mine.[204] The court based its conclusion on the evidence of coal demand experts to the effect that there were other coking coal mines, both existing and approved, in Australia that could meet current and likely future demand for coking coal.[205]

The court rejected the development application for the Project, ruling that "The costs of this open cut coal mine, exploiting the coal resource at this location in a scenic valley close to town, exceed the benefits of the mine, which are primarily economic and social."[206] The substantial proportion of the judgment devoted to consideration of the climate change impacts of the mine, and the emphasis they received in the opinion, is ground-breaking in Australia.

The *Gloucester Resources Limited* case is very encouraging as a platform for protecting the voiceless for several reasons. First, it addresses intergenerational equity in conjunction with the sustainable development focus in evaluating the impacts of the proposed project. Second, the "carbon budget" approach helps enshrine a new way of thinking about development. The "no development" option can now be more regularly considered and determined to be appropriate when fossil fuel-intensive projects are proposed in the face of the urgent climate change crisis in the Anthropocene era. Third, the decision represents a massive pendulum swing away from supporting carbon-intensive development in a business-as-usual manner. Our climate has "tipping points," beyond which emission reduction efforts will have no effect. Perhaps most importantly, this case may represent recognition of a similar "tipping point" in carbon-intensive development in that we may have reached a

---

[200] *Id.* at ¶ 527.
[201] *Id.* at ¶¶ 534–35.
[202] *Id.* at ¶ 536.
[203] *Id.*
[204] *Id.* at ¶ 534.
[205] *Id.* at ¶ 536.
[206] *Id.* at 8.

point where there's no more room in our atmosphere to tolerate these destructive carbon-intensive activities. Consistent with this evolving new ethic, Germany announced in January 2019 that it will close all eighty-four of its coal-fired power plants and rely primarily on renewable energy.[207]

The landmark decision in *Gloucester Resources Limited* sparked a deluge of commentary. One source observed that the case is "the first time an Australian court has heard evidence of a global budget of greenhouse gas emissions to avoid dangerous climate change to justify the refusal of a new coal mine"[208] and "the first time an Australian court has highlighted a mine's contribution to total global greenhouse gas emissions . . . as a key reason to reject its approval."[209] The Environmental Defenders Office of New South Wales also emphasized the significance of the decision:

> The judgment presents a foundational question for all decision makers. It is this: given that, if we are to remain within the global carbon budget, only a finite amount of additional carbon can be burned, and that existing approvals already exhaust that budget, why should this particular project be prioritised over any other, or displace an existing approval? That is 'the wrong time' test and will prove an insurmountable barrier for many projects going forward.[210]

The Environmental Defenders Office further observed that "[t]his was a once in a generation case: the first hearing of its kind since the historic Paris Agreement, in which a superior jurisdiction Australian court heard expert testimony about climate change, the carbon budget and the impacts of burning fossil fuels."[211]

Brendan Sydes, the chief executive of Environmental Justice Australia, said that the case was "dramatically different in the sense that every argument that has been successfully put forward by mining companies in the past has been completely considered, discredited and rejected."[212] The same article stated that activists and residents fighting against another proposed coal mine in central New South Wales are hoping the judgment in *Gloucester Resources Limited v. Minister for Planning* will sway the state's Independent Planning Commission to reject the project.[213]

---

[207] Erik Kirschbaum, *Germany to Close All 84 of Its Coal-Fired Power Plants, Will Rely Primarily on Renewable Energy*, L.A. TIMES (Jan. 26, 2019), https://www.latimes.com/world/europe/la-fg-germany-coal-power-20190126-story.html.

[208] Hannam, *supra* note 184.

[209] *Id.*

[210] Environmental Defenders Office of New South Wales, *supra* note 197.

[211] *Id.*

[212] Lisa Cox, *Hunter Valley Coalmine Ruling Buoys Other Anti-Mine Campaigners*, THE GUARDIAN (Feb. 11, 2019), https://www.theguardian.com/australia-news/2019/feb/11/hunter-valley-coal mine-ruling-buoys-other-anti-mine-campaigners.

[213] *Id.*

B *"Next Friend" Mechanism to Vindicate Injuries to the Voiceless*

Once a substantive duty is established pursuant to the sustainable development standard, and a procedural mechanism[214] to fulfill that duty is established to protect the voiceless, there must be a mechanism in place that would enable humans to sue to enforce violations of that duty caused by government action or inaction. This section considers case studies in the Philippines and the United States that illustrate the need for the "next friend" mechanism to be adopted as the means by which humans can represent voiceless communities to vindicate violations of the standards designed to protect them.

A case in the Philippines, *Resident Marine Mammals of the Protected Seascape Tañon Strait* v. *Reyes*,[215] is a case study in the need for an effective standard to enforce procedural and informational duties to protect the voiceless. On November 6, 2007, JAPEX commenced offshore oil and gas exploration and began to drill exploratory wells in Tañon Strait.[216] In response, both sets of petitioners[217] under G. R. No. 180771[218] and G. R. No. 181527[219] filed petitions with the Supreme Court of the Philippines on December 17, 2007.[220] The petitions sought to enjoin the respondents from implementing the governmental contract, SC-46, which authorized the oil exploration.[221] On April 8, 2008, the Court consolidated the G. R. No. 180771 and G. R. No. 181527 proceedings.[222] In 2010, the Supreme

---

[214] This procedural mechanism would be patterned after the line of environmental impact assessment victories described in the previous section. The plaintiffs would be authorized to sue to hold government actors accountable when they pursue projects that potentially violate a prescribed standard of sustainable development in a given context, such as approval of coal mining projects.

[215] Resident Marine Mammals of the Protected Seascape Tañon Strait v. Secretary Angelo Reyes, G.R. No. 180771/G.R. No. 181527, 5 (S.C., Apr. 21, 2015) (Phil.) (citing *Rollo* (G.R. No. 181527), Vol. I, pp. 62–66). The drilling at issue continued until February 8, 2008. *Id.*

[216] *Id.*

[217] G.R. No. 180771 petitioners were the "Resident Marine Mammals of the Protected Seascape Tañon Strait, e.g., Toothed Whales, Dolphins, Porpoises, and Other Cetacean Species," and Gloria Estenzo Ramos and Rose-Liza Eisma-Osorio, "In Their Capacity as Legal Guardians of the Lesser Life-Forms and as Responsible Stewards of God's Creations." G.R. 181527 petitioners were the "Central Visayas Fisherfolk Development Center (FIDEC), Cerilo D. Engarcial, Ramon Yanong, Francisco Labid, in their personal capacity and as representatives of Subsistence Fisherfolk of the Municipalities of Aloguinsan and Pinamungajan, Cebu, and Their Families, and the Present and Future Generations of Filipinos Whose Rights Are Similarly Affected." *Id.* at 1.

[218] Resident Marine Mammals and Gloria Estenzo Ramos and Rose-Liza Eisma-Osorio." Id.

[219] FIDEC as representatives of the subsistence fisherfolk, their families, and present and future generations. *Id.*

[220] *Id.* at 6.

[221] *Id.* at 3.

[222] *Id.*

Court adopted the Rules of Procedure for Environmental Cases.[223] Those rules authorize citizen suits and allow any Filipino citizen to file suits for violations of environmental laws in the Philippines.[224] In March 2012, JAPEX Philippines contended that the case was moot because the oil exploration had ceased in February 2008.[225]

The Court acknowledged that while conferring standing to animals was not unusual in the animal rights and environmental law fields, it was unprecedented in the Supreme Court of the Philippines.[226] The Resident Marine Mammal petitioners cited *Minors Oposa* v. *Factoran*[227] as precedent for their standing. The respondents challenged "the applicability of *Minors Oposa*, pointing out that petitioners therein were all natural persons, albeit some of them were still unborn."[228]

The Court considered several cases in reaching its decision. First, the Court looked to the US Supreme Court's decision in *Sierra Club* v. *Morton*.[229] Specifically, the Court cited a portion of Justice Douglas's famous dissent, which stated:

> The critical question of "standing" would be simplified and also put neatly in focus if we fashioned a federal rule that allowed environmental issues to be litigated before federal agencies or federal courts in the name of the inanimate object about to be despoiled, defaced, or invaded by roads and bulldozers and where injury is the subject of public outrage. . . . Inanimate objects are sometimes parties in litigation. A ship has a legal personality, a fiction found useful for maritime purposes. . . . The ordinary corporation is a "person" for purposes of the adjudicatory processes, whether it represents proprietary, spiritual, aesthetic, or charitable causes.
>
> So it should be as respects valleys, alpine meadows, rivers, lakes, estuaries, beaches, ridges, groves of trees, swampland, or even air that feels the destructive pressures of modern technology and modern life. The river, for example, is the living symbol of all the life it sustains or nourishes – fish, aquatic insects, water ouzels, otter, fisher, deer, elk, bear, and all other animals, including man, who are dependent on it or who enjoy it for its sight, its sound, or its life. The river as plaintiff speaks for the ecological unit of life that is part of it. Those people who have a meaningful relation to that body of water – whether it be a fisherman, a canoeist, a zoologist, or a logger – must be able to speak for the values which the river represents and which are threatened with destruction.[230]

---

[223] *Resident Marine Mammals*, G.R. No. 180771/G.R. No. 181527 at 15 (citing A.M. No. 09-6-8-SC, effective Apr. 29, 2010).

[224] *Id.*; *see also* id. at 16 (discussing how the Rules of Procedure for Environmental Cases were retroactively applicable to the case at bar). Ultimately, the Court used these rules to support its decision to deny the Resident Marine Mammals their own legal standing.

[225] *Id.* at 79.

[226] *Id.* at 13–14.

[227] G.R. No. 101083, July 30, 1993, 224 SCRA 792.

[228] *Resident Marine Mammals*, G.R. No. 180771/G.R. No. 181527 at 12–13.

[229] *Id.* at 14 (citing Sierra Club v. Morton, 405 U.S. 727 (1972)).

[230] *Id.* (citing Sierra Club, 405 U.S. at 647).

Noting that the "developments in Philippine legal theory and jurisprudence have not progressed as far as Justice Douglas's paradigm of legal standing for inanimate objects," the Court nonetheless acknowledged a trend in Filipino jurisprudence towards enhanced court access for environmental cases in the Philippines.[231]

Second, the Court looked to the Rules of Procedure for Environmental Cases, which provide that "any Filipino citizen in representation of others, including minors or generations yet unborn, may file an action to enforce rights or obligations under environmental laws."[232] The official annotation to the rule explains that the rule is meant to "liberalize standing for all cases filed enforcing environmental laws ... on the principle that humans are stewards of nature." The annotation also mentions that the rule is intended to "reflect[] the doctrine first enunciated in *Minors Oposa* insofar as it refers to minors and generations yet unborn."[233]

Third, the Court explained the precedent supporting its retroactive application of the Rules of Environmental Procedure – promulgated in 2010 – to the case at bar, which was filed in 2007.[234] Finally, the Court looked to the seminal case of *Minors Oposa* v. *Factoran*[235] as support for the proposition that the Court had previously "taken a permissive position on the issue of locus standi in environmental cases" when it allowed *Minors Oposa* to be brought in representation of future generations based on "intergenerational responsibility ... as the right to a balanced and healthful ecology."[236]

The consolidated petition involved three different sets of petitioners: (1) the Resident Marine Mammals; (2) the Stewards of Nature, Ramos and Eisma-Osorio; and (3) FIDEC as representatives for subsistence fisherfolk and their future generations.[237] The court granted standing to petitioners FIDEC, in their capacity as representatives of the subsistence fisherfolk and their present and future generations, without discussion.

---

[231] *Id.* at 15.

[232] *Id.* at 15 (citing A.M. No. 09-6-8-SC, effective Apr. 29, 2010).

[233] *Id.* at 16 (citing Annotations to Rules of Procedure for Environmental Cases, p. 111) (citations omitted)).

[234] *Id.* ("Remedial statutes or statutes relating to remedies or modes of procedure, which do not create new or take away vested rights, but only operate in furtherance of the remedy or confirmation of rights already existing, do not come within the legal conception of a retroactive law, or the general rule against retroactive operation of statutes. Statutes regulating the procedure of the courts will be construed as applicable to actions pending and undetermined at the time of their passage. Procedural laws are retroactive in that sense and to that extent.").

[235] Minors Oposa v. Factoran, G.R. No. 101083, 33 I.L.M. 173 (S.C., July 30, 1993) (Phil.)).

[236] *Resident Marine Mammals*, G.R. No. 180771/G.R. No. 181527 at 16.; *see also* Hilario G. Davide Jr. (ret. Chief Justice), *The Environment as Life Sources and the Writ of Kalikasan in the Philippines*, 29 PACE ENVTL. L. REV. 592 (2012) (discussing the unique writs and rules of procedure utilized by the Supreme Court of the Philippines in adjudicating environmental cases).

[237] *Id.* at 1.

The Resident Marine Mammals brought suit to represent their own interests and claimed standing because they "assert their right to sue for the faithful performance of international and municipal environmental laws created in their favor and for their benefit."[238] Ultimately, the Court held that because of the Rules of Environmental Procedure, the standing for animals is no longer necessary, since humans, as stewards of nature, can file actions "to enforce rights or obligations under environmental laws."[239] The wording of the petition reflects that the petitioners ideally wanted standing granted to the Resident Marine Mammals for their own sake. However, the Court denied standing to the dolphins on the basis that humans, as stewards of nature, can bring actions on nature's behalf to enforce laws, which indicated that the Court is embracing a more anthropocentric view of the role of "stewards of nature."

The Stewards of Nature, Ramos[240] and Eisma-Osorio, claimed standing because they have a "right to represent the Resident Marine Mammals" and serve as "forerunners of a campaign to build awareness among the affected residents of Tañon Strait and as stewards of the environment since the primary steward, the Government, had failed in its duty to protect the environment pursuant to the public trust doctrine."[241] In denying the Resident Marine Mammals' standing, but granting Ramos and Eisma-Osorio standing, the Court emphasized that not only are Ramos and Eisma-Osorio representing the marine mammals, but they were also "real parties in the Petition."[242] Because they were real parties, and because they had sufficiently alleged violations of laws related to the Resident Marine Mammals' habitat, the Court held they had legal standing.[243] The theory of "stewards of nature" was being granted for conservational reasons based on the violation of environmental laws, and thus is more of an anthropocentric view.

Concurring in part and dissenting in part, Justice Leonen would have dismissed the Resident Marine Mammals petition entirely. While he agreed that the Resident Marine Mammals did not have legal standing, he disagreed with the holding that

---

[238] *Id.* at 12; *see also* Hope M. Babcock, *A Brook with Legal Rights: The Rights of Nature in Court,* 43 ECOLOGY L.Q. 1 (2016) (discussing why legal personhood should be assigned to nature).

[239] *Id.* at 16–17.

[240] Numerous other articles on environmental and political issues written by Gloria Ramos can be found on Cebu Daily News: https://cebudailynews.inquirer.net/byline/atty-gloria-estenzo-ramos; *see also* Gloria Estenzo Ramos, *The Right to Public Participation in Decision-Making in the Implementation of Fisheries and Other Environmental Laws in the Philippines* (2015), http://greenaccess.law.osaka-u.ac.jp/wp-content/uploads/2015/03/4-4-13f_ramos.pdf); Gloria Estenzo Ramos, *Innovative Procedural Rules on Environmental Cases in the Philippines: Ushering in a Golden Era for Environmental Rights Protection,* 2011 IUCN ACAD. J. ENVT'L L. 187, http://www2.ecolex.org/server2neu.php/libcat/docs/LI/MON-085570.pdf.

[241] *Id.* at 12–13. This language supports a significant theme in this chapter: when the government fails in its stewardship duties, humans should be able to sue on behalf of the voiceless as guardians of their interests.

[242] *Id.* at 17.

[243] *Id.*

Petitioners Ramos and Eisma-Osorio had legal standing on behalf of the mammals.[244] To Justice Leonen, the rules for standing in environmental cases were already sufficiently liberal, and to widen the scope of the rules as requested by Petitioners would only create "occasion[s] for abuse."[245] In his opinion, the majority view was not anthropocentric enough; he viewed the "feign[ed] representation on behalf of animals," as a "betray[al] of a very anthropocentric view of environmental advocacy."[246] The responsibility of ensuring a healthy ecology is up to humans entirely to "ensur[e] a viable ecology *for themselves.*"[247]

> Animals play an important role in households, communities, and the environment. While we, as humans, may feel the need to nurture and protect them, we cannot go as far as saying we represent their best interests and can, therefore, speak for them before the courts. As humans, we cannot be so arrogant as to argue that we know the suffering of animals and that we know what remedy they need in the face of an injury . . .
>
> Finally, we honor every living creature when we take care of our environment. As sentient species, we do not lack in the wisdom or sensitivity to realize that we only borrow the resources that we use to survive and to thrive. We are not incapable of mitigating the greed that is slowly causing the demise of our planet. Thus, there is no need for us to feign representation of any other species or some imagined unborn generation in filing any action in our courts of law to claim any of our fundamental rights to a healthful ecology. In this way and with candor and courage, we fully shoulder the responsibility deserving of the grace and power endowed on our species.[248]

Therefore, even though the majority opinion denied standing for mammals and was, in language and viewpoint, an anthropocentric approach, Justice Leonen's opinion indicates that the court was not strict enough in applying anthropocentrism. He would have only granted standing to Petitioners FIDEC under G. R. 181527, because of the demonstrated "actual, direct, and material damage" SC-46 had on their livelihood, as well as the "potential long-term effects [of SC-46 on] transcending generations."[249]

As evidenced in the *Resident Marine Mammals* case, there is a need for more liberal standing jurisprudence to protect the voiceless. This is true even in the Philippines, which is one of the most progressive jurisdictions in the world on environmental protection. The next friend provision in the Federal Rules of Civil Procedure provides that "[a] minor or an incompetent person who does not have a

---

[244] *Resident Marine Mammals*, 22 (Leonen, J., concurring), http://sc.judiciary.gov.ph/pdf/web/viewer.html?file=/jurisprudence/2015/april2015/180771_leonen.pdf).

[245] *Id.* at 3.

[246] *Id.* at 9.

[247] *Id.* at 8 (emphasis added).

[248] *Id.* at 7, 22.

[249] *Id.* at 11–12.

duly appointed representative may sue by a next friend or a guardian ad litem."[250] For this standard to apply to the voiceless communities, future generations, wildlife, and natural resources would need to be deemed "incompetent persons" for purposes of this rule. As described in this book, legal personhood has been ascribed to all three communities of the voiceless in various countries to varying degrees. Being considered an "incompetent" person follows from assigning legal personhood to the voiceless communities because these entities cannot speak for themselves in legal proceedings.

Several cases have applied the next friend standard to cases within and outside the voiceless communities addressed in this book. In *Ad Hoc Committee of Concerned Teachers on behalf of Minor & Under-Age Students* v. *Greenburgh #11 Union Free School District*,[251] Greenburgh Eleven Union Free School District is a public school district whose purpose is to educate students of minority backgrounds at a private social house known as Children's Village. A small number of the children live with their families. In an effort to stop the school district's alleged racially discriminatory employment practices, a group of white and black teachers formed a committee, which took the position: "[s]ince the students 'reside separate and apart from their own families, the Committee asserts that it alone is in a position to represent [the Children's] right to and interest in a discrimination free environment of public education.'"[252]

The Second Circuit concluded that this unique situation should permit the committee to represent the children's interests in protecting their constitutional rights pursuant to Federal Rule of Civil Procedure 17 (c) (the next friend provision), but noted that the rule is permissive rather than mandatory. The US District Court for the Southern District of New York has allowed next friends of institutionalized children where parents were not ideal guardians. The court identified three reasons to allow the committee to represent the children as next friend: 1) "the committee represents teachers who are intimately involved with the children's education and possess first hand knowledge of their needs," 2) "those teachers appear to have instituted this suit in good faith and out of genuine concern for the children's development," and 3) "the Committee is the only group of adults likely to seek vindication of the children's constitutional rights to a learning environment free of any racially discriminatory practices."[253] The court reviewed the committee's finances for its ability to prosecute the action because it did not want to sanction any attempt to assert the legitimate rights of the children as an ulterior motive for political or economic aims.

---

[250] Fed. R. Civ. P. 17(c)(2).
[251] 873 F.2d 25 (2d Cir. 1989).
[252] *Id.*
[253] *Id.*

As a counter example, courts have not permitted use of the next friend provision when the party in need of protection does not lack access to the courts on his or her own behalf, and when the party seeking next friend status may not be acting in the best interest of the party in question. In *Al-Aulaqi v. Obama*,[254] the father of a US citizen with alleged terrorist ties and reportedly targeted for assassination by the US government lacked standing to bring constitutional claims as his son's next friend. There are two prerequisites to establish third-party standing under the next friend provision: 1) "the putative 'next friend' must provide an adequate explanation – such as inaccessibility, mental incompetence, or other disability – why the real party in interest cannot appear on his own behalf to prosecute action" [and] 2) "have some significant relationship with the real party in interest."[255]

The plaintiff father stated that his son could not file suit on his own behalf because he is hiding under threat of death. The US government asserted that the son could have peacefully presented himself in the US Embassy in Yemen, which would have prevented, by law, lethal force. The court was also unsure whether the father as next friend represented the best interests of his son because the father stated that the lack of his son's express disavowal of the suit was confirmation that this was his son's wishes. The court rejected this argument, stating "the burden is on the 'next friend' clearly to establish the propriety of his status and thereby justify the jurisdiction of the court."[256] This case is important for the proposition that even a significant relationship such as the parent-child bond is not enough by itself to establish next friend status.

A leading case on next friend status is the US Supreme Court's decision in *Whitmore v. Arkansas*.[257] In *Whitmore*, a death row inmate stated under oath that he did not want an appellate court review and wished that no one would interfere with his death sentence. A priest sought to intervene as the prisoner's next friend. The Court concluded that the priest lacked standing to proceed as the inmate's next friend, reasoning that "one necessary condition for such standing is a showing by the proposed 'next friend' that the real party in interest is unable to litigate his . . . own case due to mental incapacity, lack of access to court, or other similar disability, and there was no reason . . . to disturb the judgment below that the individual was competent to waive his right to appeal."[258]

The *Whitmore* decision is a sensible interpretation of next friend status. This status was not meant to be conferred to third parties as a means to second-guess the

---

[254] 727 F. Supp. 2d 1 (D.D.C. 2010).

[255] *Id.*

[256] *Id.; see also* Coalition of Clergy, Lawyers, and Professors v. Bush, 310 F.3d 1153 (9th Cir. 2002) (rejecting "next friend" habeas corpus claim submitted by coalition of clergy on behalf of detainees at Guantanamo Naval Base on grounds that "permit[ing] petitioners to seek writ of habeas corpus would invite well-meaning proponents of numerous assorted 'causes' to bring lawsuits on behalf of unwitting strangers.").

[257] 495 U.S. 149 (1990).

[258] *Id.*

judgment of a competent party. The decision did, however, appear to leave the door open for a next friend claim on behalf of a nonhuman plaintiff because the Court did not define what it means for a party to have "mental incapacity, lack of access to court, or other similar disability."[259] In 2018, next friend status was tested in the animal protection context in the widely publicized "monkey selfie" case, *Naruto v. Slater*.[260]

In this case, Naruto was a crested macaque, living in Indonesia, who took a "selfie" with David Slater's unattended camera. Slater published the photos in a book, which identifies him and his company as the copyright owners of the photos. Slater admitted that Naruto took the photographs. People for the Ethical Treatment of Animals (PETA) and Dr. Antje Engelhardt filed a complaint for copyright infringement against Slater as next friends on behalf of Naruto. The complaint stated that Dr. Engelhardt has studied macaques in the area extensively, but did not allege any relationship between PETA and Naruto. PETA had failed to show any significant relationship with Naruto (between next friend and real party in interest). PETA did not claim to have any more significant relationship with Naruto as compared to any other animal.

The court held that "an animal cannot be represented, under our laws, by a 'next friend'." The court reasoned that "however worthy and high minded the motives of next friends may be, they inevitably run the risk of making the actual [party] a pawn to be manipulated on a chessboard larger than his own case."[261] In other words, PETA only had a generalized interest in Naruto and used it for their own personal gains. Federal Rule of Civil Procedure 17 obligates the court to consider the case or controversy regardless of a next friend or guardian. The court has broad discretion to determine if the party can be adequately protected; a court can find that a lawyer can adequately protect the party. In this case, the court concluded that next friend status is intended to represent incompetent or incarcerated persons – not animals.[262]

The court held that Naruto's Article III standing was not dependent on PETA's sufficiency as a next friend, and proceeded to address the standing analysis. In *Cetacean Community* v. *Bush*, the court focused on the statutory interpretation issue that if Congress wanted to have animals to have statutory standing, then it would have plainly stated that intention. The court made the cetaceans the "sole

---

[259] *Id.*

[260] 888 F.3d 418 (9th Cir. 2018).

[261] *Id.* Judge Smith commented disapprovingly of PETA's tactics: "Puzzlingly, while representing to the world that 'animals are not ours to eat, wear, experiment on, use for entertainment, or abuse in any other way,' PETA seems to employ Naruto as an unwitting pawn in its ideological goals." *Id.* at 427; *see also* Sarah Jeong, *Appeals Court Blasts PETA for Using Selfie Monkey as "an Unwitting Pawn*," THE VERGE (Apr. 24, 2018), https://www.theverge.com/2018/4/24/17271410/monkey-selfie-naruto-slater-copyright-peta.

[262] Naruto v. Slater, 888 F.3d at 430–31; *see also* Scott Graham, *No Standing for Monkey to Bring Selfie Copyright Suit*, THE RECORDER (Apr. 23, 2018), https://www.law.com/therecorder/2018/04/23/no-standing-for-monkey-to-bring-selfie-copyright-suit.

plaintiff in the case" and did not discuss next friend or third-party standing. The court determined that the cetaceans lacked standing under any environmental statutes because the statutes did not specifically allow animals to have standing.[263] In *Naruto*, the court held that the Copyright Act also did not authorize statutory standing for animals, so the monkey lacked statutory standing to sue.[264]

III LESSONS TO HELP IMPLEMENT THE PROPOSAL

Developments protecting the voiceless have occurred in legislatures and courts throughout the world. This section explores how victories and mechanisms within and outside the United States can be leveraged to advance protection of the voiceless in the United States and abroad.

On July 4, 2018, in *Bhatt v. Union of India*,[265] the Uttarakhand High Court granted the entire animal kingdom legal personhood status within the state to promote improved animal welfare within its borders. Humans were declared to be persons in loco parentis – the party responsible for upholding the court's decision – and serve as guardians of all aquatic and avian animals.[266] The case did not begin as litigation to secure legal personhood status for animals in India; instead, it was filed as public interest litigation seeking to regulate horse-drawn carriages that traveled from India to Nepal.[267]

The welfare activism began in the form of Writ Petition No. 43 in 2014, when Narayan Dutt Bhatt sought to regulate the horse cart/tonga route between India and Nepal. The route runs over fourteen kilometers and is only 3.5 meters wide at most parts.[268] The concerns outlined in the petition were characterized in the following manner:

> The horse dung is polluting the river water. The ailing, infirm and old horses are abandoned by the owners in the Indian Territory. The infected horses are hazardous to the human beings. The horse carts/tongas stay overnight and are being parked on the roadside. The tongas are overloaded. It causes cruelty to the horses. There is no record of the persons or their identity plying the horse carts/tongas with the Indian Territory. The record of horse carts/tongas is required to be maintained.[269]

---

[263] Cetacean Community v. Bush, 386 F.3d 1169 (9th Cir. 2004).

[264] Although PETA lost on the "next friend" argument in the case, PETA was pleased that, pursuant to a settlement, Slater agreed to donate 25 percent of the proceeds from the selfie photos to a fund to protect Naruto's habitat.

[265] Writ Petition (PIL) No. 43 of 2014, Bhatt v. Union of India (Apr. 7, 2018), http://files.harmony withnatureun.org/uploads/upload706.pdf.

[266] *Id.* at ¶ 50.

[267] Mrinalini Shinde, *Here's the Problem with Declaring Animals as Legal Beings in India*, THE QUINT (Nov. 7, 2018), https://www.thequint.com/voices/opinion/uttarakhand-high-court-declares-animals-legal-beings-questions. This development offers an interesting parallel to the Atrato River case in Colombia, where the litigants similarly were not seeking personhood recognition, but the court granted such protection on its own initiative in that case.

[268] Writ Petition (PIL) No. 43 of 2014, Bhatt v. Union of India (Apr. 7, 2018), at 1.

[269] *Id.* at ¶ 7.

The petition also alleged enforcement failures of the Prevention of Cruelty to Animals Act, 1960 and the provisions of the Prevention and Control of Infectious and Contagious Diseases in Animals Act, 2009. In the Prevention of Cruelty to Animals Act, the Indian Supreme Court relied on the decision of *Animal Welfare Board of India* v. *Nagaraja* in which the Court recognized freedom from hunger, suffering, physical discomfort, injury, and freedom to express ordinary behavioral patterns. Based on the Court's decision in the *Nagaraja* case, the petition in the *Bhatt* case was expanded to include animal welfare.[270]

In an unusually broad decision supporting animal protection, the Court concluded that all animals, when considered legal persons, have the same rights as humans.[271] The Court held that "[t]he entire animal kingdom including avian and aquatic are declared as legal entities having a distinct *persona* with corresponding rights, duties and liabilities of a living person" and stated that "[a]ll the citizens throughout the State of Uttarakhand are hereby declared persons in loco parentis as the human face for the welfare/protection of animals."[272] The Court further determined that "there are gaps in laws" that need to be addressed to protect wildlife and the environment and that "[a]nimals cannot be treated merely as property" for human use.[273] Under Indian law, there are two types of legal persons: (1) sentient human beings and (2) "juristic persons" such as minors, companies, trusts, or people with mental incapacities.[274] This ruling puts animals in the "juristic persons" category of legal persons.[275]

The Court also held that the state government must enforce the Prevention of Cruelty to Animals Act and the provisions of the Prevention and Control of Infectious and Contagious Diseases in Animals Act when regulating horse cart/tonga routes.[276] These enforcement mandates include requirements that the state appoint veterinarians to treat and eradicate diseases among cart-drawing animals.[277]

---

[270] George Divorsky, *India and New Zealand Were Wrong to Recognize Rivers as Persons*, GIZMODO (Mar. 24, 2017), https://gizmodo.com/india-and-new-zealand-were-wrong-to-recog nize-rivers-as-1793612698.

[271] Saptarshi Ray, *Animals Accorded Same Rights as Humans in Indian State*, THE TELEGRAPH (July 5, 2018), https://www.telegraph.co.uk/news/2018/07/05/animals-accorded-rights-humans-indian-national-park/.

[272] Bhatt v. Union of India & Others, in the High Court of Uttarakhand at Nainital, Writ Petition (PIL) No. 43 of 2014, 50 (July 7, 2018), http://lobis.nic.in/ddir/uhc/RS/judgement/07-07-2018/RS04072018WPPIL432014.pdf.

[273] *Id.* at 34–35.

[274] *Id.* at 19; Ray, *supra* note 271.

[275] Ray, *supra* note 271.

[276] Vineet Upadhyay, *Animals Have Equal Rights as Humans, Says Uttarakhand High Court*, THE TIMES OF INDIA (July 5, 2018), https://timesofindia.indiatimes.com/city/dehradun/members-of-animal-kingdom-to-be-treated-as-legal-entities-ukhand-hc/articleshow/64860996.cms.

[277] Writ Petition (PIL) No. 43 of 2014, Bhatt v. Union of India (Apr. 7, 2018), at ¶ 99, http://files .harmonywithnatureun.org/uploads/upload706.pdf.

Although progressive compared to the rest of the world, the strides that India has made in animal welfare are not surprising in light of earlier litigation in the same High Court. In March 2017, the Uttarakhand High Court declared the Ganga and Yamuna Rivers, and all of their tributaries and streams, as living entities.[278] This decision granted these bodies of water legal personhood with the same rights and corresponding duties as people of the state. The court appointed the Director of NAMAMI Gange, the Chief Secretary of the State of Uttarakhand, and the Advocate General of the State of Uttarakhand as persons in loco parentis to protect the rivers and their tributaries.[279] The decision protecting the Ganga and Yamuna Rivers served as a platform for the Uttarakhand High Court to make similar decisions regarding animal welfare. In granting legal personhood status to natural resources and wildlife, India followed a path established earlier in Ecuador, Bolivia, and New Zealand.

The Uttarakhand High Court's decisions have been called into question, however. First, the High Court relied on precedent from the Supreme Court, which cited Article 21 of the Constitution that addresses the right to life. The Supreme Court interpreted "life" as all forms of life, including animals, and stated that if animals were included in the community of legal persons, humanity should be able to value them, rather than objectify them.[280] While the principles underlying this decision are sound, critics have drawn attention to the hypocrisy of the Indian government's equality claims. India is the world's second-largest beef exporter, with USD $4.3 billion in annual revenues.[281] Cows are considered sacred to the Hindu religion, which approximately 80 percent of the Indian population claims to practice.[282] The cow is worshipped as Gautama, and represents selfless giving and embodies anti-violence. Yet cows, along with buffalo, are being slaughtered and exported for capital gain. There are nongovernmental organizations working to ban the slaughter of all cattle, with little to no success. Thus, cattle (both sacred and non-sacred) are still recognized as legal property under the Indian Constitution, primarily because of their economic value.[283] If animal welfare activism in India seeks to be equitable, the nation must not prioritize and excuse exploitation for capital gain. For animals to truly have the same rights as people, humanity would have to

---

[278] Writ Petition (PIL) No. 126 of 2014, Salim v. State of Uttarakhand, at ¶ 19; https://www.elaw .org/salim-v-state-uttarakhand-writ-petition-pil-no126-2014-december-5-2016-and-march-20-2017; *see also* https://www.livelaw.in/first-india-uttarakhand-hc-declares-ganga-yamuna-rivers-living-legal-entities/.

[279] Writ Petition (PIL) No. 126 of 2014, Salim v. State of Uttarakhand, at ¶ 19, https://www.elaw .org/salim-v-state-uttarakhand-writ-petition-pil-no126-2014-december-5-2016-and-march-20-2017.

[280] Shinde, *supra* note 267.

[281] Virginia Harrison, *Holy Cow! India Is the Largest Beef Exporter*, CNN BUSINESS (Aug. 5, 2015), https://money.cnn.com/2015/08/05/news/economy/india-beef-exports-buffalo/index.html.

[282] Sena Desai Gopal, *Selling the Sacred Cow*, THE ATLANTIC (Feb. 12, 2015), https://www .theatlantic.com/business/archive/2015/02/selling-the-sacred-cow-indias-contentious-beef-industry/385359/.

[283] Shinde, *supra* note 267.

eliminate all forms of animal labor and terminate the use of animal bodies for agricultural, medicinal, dietary, and recreational needs.[284]

Another criticism of the Uttarakhand High Court's decisions is that granting "personhood" to things that are not humans diminishes the status and value of human rights.[285] For example, rivers do not deal with the same issues of bodily autonomy, nor can they vote in elections. On the other hand, many animal species like great apes, whales, dolphins, and elephants have similar cognitive, emotional, and psychological attributes to humans. Foundations like the Institute for Ethics and Emerging Technologies (IEET) have started programs advocating for the rights of these nonhuman persons, and have excluded "inanimate objects" like rivers and forests. Members of the program describe persons as "self-aware, emotional creatures with a sense of the past and the future. And perhaps most importantly, they can suffer."[286] Many consider that granting legal personhood to rivers undermines the importance of granting personhood to living entities. Nevertheless, legal personhood must not be confused with status as humans. Legal personhood only addresses what entities "matter" under the law. It is entirely consistent for the law to determine that wildlife and rivers "matter" under the law and deserve legal personhood protection. Such recognition poses no threat to the recognition and protection of human rights.

Despite the imperfections of the Indian animal rights movement, it offers foundational concepts that have the potential to make headway in US animal rights litigation. The United States offers limited federal protection of animal welfare with the Twenty-Eight Hour Law in 1873,[287] the Humane Methods of Slaughter Act of 1958,[288] and Animal Welfare Act of 1966 (AWA).[289] In addition to these limited federal animal welfare measures, all fifty states also have misdemeanor and felony anti-cruelty protections.[290]

To enhance this bare minimum level of animal welfare protection in the United States, creative litigation initiatives have developed to secure enhanced protection of animals and preserve necessary natural resources. Indian progressivism can serve as a

---

[284] *Id.*

[285] Divorsky, *supra* note 270.

[286] *Id.*

[287] The Twenty-Eight Hour Law requires that stops be made every twenty-eight hours to provide food, water, and rest for animals in transit. 49 U.S.C. § 80605 (2018).

[288] The Humane Methods of Slaughter Act was implemented so that livestock (excluding poultry) had to be stunned before they were killed, to reduce the amount of pain they would feel. Religious (ritual) slaughters are exempt. 7 U.S.C. §§ 1901–7 (2018).

[289] The AWA regulates the treatment of animals involved in commercial enterprises, more specifically for purposes of research, exhibition, or companionship. The Act excludes several classes of animals from the Act's protections including agricultural animals, animals in entertainment, fish, crustaceans, horses not being used for research, cold-blooded reptiles, and some birds. 7 U.S.C. §§ 2131–59 (2018).

[290] The National Humane Education Society, *Felony Anti-cruelty Laws in All 50 States*, https://nhes.org/felony-animal-cruelty-laws-in-all-50-states/ (last accessed Mar. 10, 2019).

potential roadmap for the US initiatives. In the US, animals and resources are reduced to property status, whereas in India, rivers and animals have the same rights of freedom and existence as humans. Some cases in the US have sought to establish these rights for animals[291] and resources,[292] but have faced daunting obstacles in the courts. Nevertheless, the publicity associated with these efforts has helped advance these initiatives.

In a creative effort to employ the next friend mechanism to be the voice for captive wildlife, PETA and individual human plaintiffs filed suit against SeaWorld, acting as the orca plaintiffs' next friends.[293] The plaintiffs consisted of five orca whales: Tilikum, Katina, Corky, Kasatka, and Ulises. Since PETA and the individuals sued as next friends, only the five orcas, not PETA, were the actual plaintiffs in the case. Next friends commenced this action by filing a complaint for declaratory and injunctive relief, seeking a declaration that the named wild-captured orcas were being "held by the Defendants in violation of Section One of the Thirteenth Amendment to the Constitution of the United States, which prohibits slavery and involuntary servitude."[294]

Jeffrey Kerr, PETA's general counsel, noted that the Thirteen Amendment prohibits the *condition* of slavery without reference to "person" or any particular class of victim. "Slavery is slavery, and it does not depend on the species of the slave any more than it depends on gender, race, or religion."[295] Next friends alleged that the confinement of the orcas in barren concrete tanks[296] negatively impacts them in many ways, including the suppression of "Plaintiffs' cultural traditions and deprives them of the ability to make conscious choices and of the environmental enrichment required to stimulate Plaintiffs mentally and physically for their well-being."[297]

Next friends also alleged that these orcas "were born free and lived in their natural environment until they were captured and torn from their families."[298] While in captivity, the orcas often suffer severe distress.[299] The unnatural conditions under which the orcas are held in captivity "[d]eprived of liberty, forced to live in grotesquely unnatural conditions and perform tricks,"[300] resulted in "extreme

---

[291] *See supra* Chapter 4.

[292] *See supra* Chapter 5.

[293] Tilikum v. Sea World Parks & Entm't, Inc., 842 F. Supp. 2d 1259 (S.D. Cal. 2012).

[294] Complaint for Declaratory and Injunctive Relief, Tilikum v. Sea World Parks & Entm't, Inc., No. 11-cv-2476 JM WMC, ¶ 1 (U.S. Dist. Ct. S.D. Cal., Oct. 26, 2011).

[295] People for the Ethical Treatment of Animals, *PETA Sues SeaWorld for Violation of Orcas' Constitutional Rights*, (Oct. 25, 2011), https://www.peta.org/blog/peta-sues-seaworld-violating-orcas-constitutional-rights/ (last accessed Mar. 11, 2019).

[296] These orcas lived in concrete tanks approximately eighty-six feet by fifty-one feet, which is comparable to a six-foot-tall man living his entire life within the confines of one half of a volleyball court. Compl., *supra* note 294, at ¶ 37.

[297] *Id.* at ¶ 19.

[298] *Id.* at ¶ 31.

[299] *Id.* at ¶¶ 32–66.

[300] *Id.* at ¶ 55.

physiological and mental stress and suffering while, at the same time, Defendants and their predecessors have reaped millions of dollars in profits from their slavery and involuntary servitude."[301]

Next friends contended that the orcas are being held as slaves because they are (1) held physically and psychologically captive; (2) without the means of escape; (3) separated from their homes and families; (4) unable to engage in natural behaviors and determine their own course of action or way of life; (5) subjugated to the will and desires of SeaWorld; (6) confined in unnatural, stressful and inadequate conditions; and (7) subject to artificial insemination or sperm collection for the purposes of involuntary breeding.[302] SeaWorld argued that plaintiffs lacked Article III standing to bring this action and, alternatively, next friends lacked capacity to bring this action Pursuant to Rule 17 of the Federal Rules of Civil Procedure.[303] On this issue, Judge Miller stated, "In the absence of an applicable statute authorizing Plaintiffs to bring a private right of action, whether Plaintiffs suffer a cognizable constitutional injury turns on whether the Thirteenth Amendment affords any legal protection to Plaintiffs."[304]

On February 8, 2012, the Court ruled that the Thirteenth Amendment only applies to humans and therefore the case lacks subject matter jurisdiction. The Court supported this conclusion by looking to the Constitution for Framers' intent. Enacted in 1865, the Thirteenth Amendment provides: (1) Neither slavery nor involuntary servitude, except as a punishment for crime, whereof the party shall have been duly convicted, shall exist within the United States or any place subject to their jurisdiction. (2) Congress shall have power to enforce this article by appropriate legislation.[305] In 1864, slavery was understood to apply only to human beings.[306] As further support, the *Tilikum* court noted that President Abraham Lincoln's Emancipation Proclamation declared freedom for people held as slaves.[307] The *Tilikum* court then concluded that the Thirteenth Amendment cannot apply to nonhumans because the text of the Amendment includes the phrase "whereof the party shall have been duly convicted,"[308] and only people can be subject to criminal convictions.[309]

Ultimately, the court held that "[t]he only reasonable interpretation of the Thirteenth Amendment's plain language is that it applies to persons, and not to non-persons such as orcas."[310] Although PETA argued that constitutional rights have expanded over time, the court held that the Thirteenth Amendment, unlike the

---

[301] *Id.* at ¶¶ 46, 55, 62, 66.
[302] *Id.* at ¶106.
[303] *Tilikum*, 842 F. Supp. 2d at 1261–62.
[304] *Id.* at 1262.
[305] US CONST. amend. XIII.
[306] *Tilikum*, 842 F. Supp. 2d at 1263.
[307] *Id.*
[308] US CONST. amend. XIII, § 1.
[309] *Tilikum*, 842 F. Supp. 2d at 1263.
[310] *Id.*

Fourteenth Amendment, is inflexible and incapable of expanding protection to nonhumans.[311] Thus, the case was dismissed.[312] Interestingly, though, the *Tilikum* opinion noted that the Fourteenth Amendment, as opposed to the Thirteenth Amendment, may be a more effective legal claim in future animal rights-based cases.

The court did not have to, and ultimately decided not to, engage in an analysis of the viability of next friends' standing in the case. The next friend approach used to represent the orcas against SeaWorld could have been successful, and the orcas could have been represented in loco parentis. A habeas corpus petition to seek the release of the orcas to a sanctuary to ensure more favorable living conditions also could have been pursued, comparable to termination of the inhumane condition of the horses pulling carriages in India.[313]

The Ganga and Yamuna River case in India may have served as the motivation behind *Colorado River Ecosystem v. State of Colorado*.[314] Attorney Jason Flores-Williams represented an environmental advocacy group known as Deep Green Resistance in a case in 2017 to attempt to gain personhood for the Colorado River. Parts of the Colorado River contain high amounts of selenium and mercury, both of which create unsuitable habitats for inhabitants and can cause health issues for surrounding people and ecosystems.[315] Unfortunately, the case did not have the same successful outcome as the case in India. The state of Colorado threatened to file sanctions against Flores-Williams for "frivolous" arguments, which forced him into filing for a case dismissal to preserve his legal career.

The Colorado River case is premised on the notion that human beings depend on natural resources for their livelihood and traditional environmental law has failed because it treats resources as property and only regulates the rate at which they are exploited. The complaint alleged that the river provides water for forty million people and irrigates four million acres of American and Mexican croplands. In addition, thirty-four Native American reservations exist in the basin. The river's ability to continue to provide sustenance for human and nonhuman communities is in danger.

Deep Green Resistance (DGR) is next friend for and guardian of the river. DGR has a history of protecting ecosystems. Its members live in the basin in

---

[311] *Id.* at 1264.

[312] *Id.*

[313] Shinde, *supra* note 267.

[314] *See* Chris Walker, *The State of Colorado Is Being Sued by . . . the Colorado River?*, WESTWORD (Sept. 22, 2017), https://www.westword.com/news/jason-flores-williams-to-sue-colorad-on-behalf-of-the-colorado-river-9512116.

[315] Cole Mellino, *Grand Canyon Stretch of the Colorado River Threatened by Mercury Contamination*, ECOWATCH (Aug. 25, 2015), https://www.ecowatch.com/grand-canyon-stretch-of-the-colorado-river-threatened-by-mercury-pollu-1882089088.html.

communities that depend on the river. The complaint sought judicial recognition that the river has rights similar to that of a person: rights to exist, flourish, regenerate, and naturally evolve. DGR sought a declaration that the river is a legal person capable of exercising rights and to allow DGR to be guardian of that person. The complaint also alleged that the government has duties with respect to the river's rights and the government's issuance of permits has violated the river's rights, including permitting water pollution from mine wastewater and laws regulating the sharing of water that allocate too much water and contribute to reduction in the river's flow.

The Colorado River case is another example of losing the battle but creating potential to win the war, similar to the outcome of *Tilikum* v. *Sea World*, because of the useful awareness raising that is associated with the case.[316] The case generated extensive publicity for the rights of nature movement and has prompted the public to consider the need for more stringent preservation tactics like granting legal personhood to resources. If the Colorado River were granted legal personhood, it would open the door for other polluted rivers and resources, and likely force statutes like the Clean Water Act to become more stringent in determining permit conditions and enforcement. Future legislation may favor giving rights to nature because of the foundation established with rights of corporations, but also due to the possible judicial acceptance of the atmospheric trust theory in *Juliana* v. *United States*, which represents a considerable expansion of the common law foundation of the public trust doctrine and imposes considerably higher stewardship responsibilities on the federal and state governments.

Drafted in Paris in 1978, the Universal Declaration of Animal Rights (UDAR)[317] includes fourteen articles, some of which assert that animals are entitled to respect under all circumstances. Article 9 states that animals used in the food industry should be used without the infliction of pain or suffering,[318] while Article 4 provides that animals have the right to freedom, and deprivation of that right is considered infringement.[319] If the United States can incorporate some of India's progress on these issues in future policy formulation in the US, the welfare of animals and preservation of resources could be greatly improved for future generations.

Many aspects of animal welfare progressivism occur in a hypocritical context. As progressive as India has been, the use of cows in exports and labor despite legal protection and religious sacredness remains a problematic and recurring issue. In the UDAR, articles contradict one another by claiming animals have the right

---

[316] Lindsay Fendt, *Colorado River "Personhood" Case Pulled by Proponents*, ASPEN JOURNALISM (Dec. 5, 2017), https://www.aspenjournalism.org/2017/12/05/colorado-river-personhood-case-pulled-by-proponents/.

[317] Universal Declaration of Animal Rights (Oct. 15, 1978), https://constitutii.files.wordpress.com/2016/06/file-id-607.pdf.

[318] *Id.* at art. 9

[319] *Id.* at art. 4.

to freedom, yet are still explicitly utilized for agricultural purposes. True equality among animals, resources, and humans may never be achieved, but India presents exportable concepts to improve the life of animals and the status of resources in the United States.

Professor David Cassuto at Pace University's Elisabeth Haub School of Law has proposed the creation of an independent federal agency – the Animal Welfare Agency (AWA) – to regulate the safety and welfare of all animals.[320] The agency would be devoted exclusively to the conditions of animals, which would owe no allegiance to the agricultural industry.[321] It would be an independent impartial agency unaffiliated with or nested within any existing agency, which would help alleviate pressure from the agricultural lobby and the prioritizing of profits over animal welfare.[322]

The proposed AWA would be authorized to protect all animals from cruelty from birth to death. The agency could review current farming practices to determine if the industry's chosen methods cause needless suffering – prioritizing the animal's experience; enabling improved prosecutorial capability; and encouraging public involvement, i.e., welcoming and encouraging evidence.[323] The agency can play a key role in providing expertise, investigation, and information that would more objectively design or contribute to the industry's operation in a way that protects animals from mistreatment.[324] Such an agency would advance protection of the voiceless in much the same way that the future generations commissions referenced earlier in this chapter would protect the interests of the unborn through an enforceable and substantive mandate based on sustainable development.

In a 2019 book chapter, Professor Catherine Iorns Magallanes of Victoria University of Wellington in New Zealand has effectively categorized types of efforts to protect the rights of nature.[325] She explained that where legal personhood has been adopted, it has been framed not as a matter of rights, but of responsibility.[326] She articulated a continuum of mechanisms through which nature can be protected. These protections range from legal personhood requiring human guardianship (least desirable) to rights of nature with government stewardship

---

[320] *Id.* at 4. While Cassuto's article focuses on the welfare of agricultural animals, his proposal is aimed at all animals present within the jurisdiction of a state or under the territorial sovereignty of a state.

[321] *Id.* at 34.

[322] *Id.*

[323] *Id.* at 41–42.

[324] *Id.* at 42.

[325] Catherine Iorns, *From Rights to Responsibilities Using Legal Personhood and Guardianship for Rivers, in* Responsability: Law and Governance for Living Well with the Earth 216–39 (Betsan Martin, Linda Te Aho & Maria Humphries-Kil eds., 2019), https://papers.ssrn .com/sol3/papers.cfm?abstract_id=3270391.

[326] *Id.* at 1.

responsibilities (more desirable) to the approach for protecting the Whanganui River in New Zealand, which is most effective.

Iorns described how ideas of legal personhood and rights for nature arose from Christopher Stone's foundational work in 1972, *Should Trees Have Standing?*, in which Stone argued that legal personhood should be conferred to all natural objects to enable nature to have rights that could be enforced.[327] This "legal person" is not property; other persons would be necessary to uphold the rights of the natural object/person.[328] Nature would need a guardian, which could be appointed by a court or through legislation, like a trustee, and the guardian would be able to speak on behalf of the natural object.[329] Rights to prevent damage to nature itself could be enforced, as opposed to now, where only damage to other persons' property interests can be claimed. Under this approach, the natural object would hold its own rights, which would require procedural safeguards.[330]

Iorns distinguished the legal personhood concept in Stone's approach from the rights of nature established in the United States through the efforts of the Community Environmental Legal Defense Fund (CELDF). She explained that these initiatives were designed to enable communities to exercise more democratic control over local environmental decision making,[331] which is consistent with, but distinguishable from, Stone's idea of legal standing. CELDF's efforts focused on drafting ordinances to enable communities to ban particular activities of corporations in a municipality,[332] ordinances that refused to acknowledge any constitutional personhood rights of corporations in a municipality,[333] and ordinances that included rights for nature, so citizens could exercise these rights on behalf of nature in question.[334]

Iorns argued that these examples do not establish a separate legal personality for nature; rather, those rights can be protected by humans on nature's behalf – it assumes someone will step in to protect them.[335] Iorns articulated an important distinction in this regard concerning rights and responsibilities in protecting the voiceless. This establishment of rights in CELDF's rights of nature protections are mechanisms that mandate the exercise of government stewardship, rather than mandating that responsibility or protection actually be exercised by humans on behalf of nature.[336] These protections offer a strong statement of responsibility in

---

[327] *Id.* at 2.
[328] *Id.*
[329] *Id.*
[330] *Id.*
[331] *Id.* at 3.
[332] *Id.*
[333] *Id.*
[334] *Id.* For a detailed discussion of some of CELDF's ordinances in the United States, *see supra* Chapter 5.
[335] *Id.* at 3.
[336] *Id.*

which a right of standing on behalf of these resources is not required to ensure action – government responsibility is implied and does not require legal personhood.

Iorns also addressed the 2008 Ecuador Constitution, which is even more ambitious than CELDF's rights of nature protections in the United States because it explicitly identifies the parameters of human responsibility.[337] Like CELDF's approach in the United States, the Ecuadorian approach emphasizes rights more than responsibilities and emphasizes standing before a court as a method to uphold them. The Ecuadorian Constitution goes one step further than a statement of rights by including a statement of state duties to adopt measures of protection, but does not establish structures or authorities to compel fulfillment of those duties, except with actions in court.[338]

According to Iorns, the most effective approach to granting rights to nature is in New Zealand, where the parliament made a river a legal person[339] and give it the name Te Awa Tupua, which is a legal person that has all the rights, powers, duties, and liabilities of a legal person.[340] Iorns highlighted the differences between this approach from the previously discussed examples as including: (1) the vesting of ownership of the riverbed to itself, (2) the creation of statutory guardians to uphold the interests of the river, and (3) recognition of the river's own intrinsic value. The New Zealand approach focuses on responsibility rather than rights and seeks to uphold indigenous rights and an indigenous concept of kinship with and responsibility for the river.[341] The Act recognizes the indivisible connection between the Whanganui Iwi people and the Whanganui River, and the river's metaphysical status as a living being. Thus, this personhood enables the river to have legal standing in its own right.

The implementation of this conceptual framework further promotes its effectiveness. Legal guardians must be appointed to uphold and protect the interests of the Whanganui River. Two persons "of high standing," one from the Crown and one collectively chosen, are the river's guardians and must act in the name of Te Awa Tupua.[342] The Act provides a "Whole of River Strategy" that addresses and advances the health and well-being of the river and establishes a "River Fund" of NZD $30 million.[343]

Iorns discussed cases in India and Colombia where rivers were granted legal personhood protections by courts.[344] In March 2017, the Ganges River and the

---

[337] *Id.* at 4. For a detailed discussion of the Constitution of Ecuador's rights of nature provisions, *see supra* Chapter 5.

[338] *Id.* at 6.

[339] *Id.* at 8. For a detailed discussion of two significant rights of nature protections in New Zealand, *see supra* Chapter 5.

[340] *Id.* at 6.

[341] *Id.* at 7.

[342] *Id.* at 9.

[343] *Id.*

[344] For a detailed discussion of these decisions protecting rivers in Colombia and India, *see supra* Chapter 5.

linked Yamuna River were declared by an Indian court to be legal persons.[345] The court directed that (1) mining the beds of the rivers should be banned and the respondents evicted, and that the central government set up a Ganga management board to better manage the river, and most importantly that the rivers become legal entities in their own right;[346] (2) the Director of Namami Gange, the Chief Secretary of the State of Uttarakhand, and the Advocate General of the State of Uttarakhand be persons in loco parentis to protect, conserve, and preserve the rivers and their tributaries, binding them to uphold the status of the rivers and promote the health and well-being of these rivers;[347] and (3) the Advocate General represent at all legal proceedings to protect the interests of the Ganges and Yamuna Rivers. The court's reasoning for conferring legal personhood had three components: (1) negligence of the state in failing to comply with previous court orders;[348] (2) constitutional argument that it was necessary to grant the river legal status in order to give effect to the Constitution;[349] and (3) finding that it was consistent with Hindu teaching that the river be a legal person and that the Court was prepared to incorporate that conclusion into the interpretations of Indian common law.[350]

In Colombia, a similar effort to confer legal personhood to protect an important and dangerously polluted river through the courts succeeded in the case of the Atrato River. In November 2016, the Colombian Constitutional Court heard an action filed by community groups living in the Atrato River basin contesting the considerable number of illegal mines in operation along its banks, and argued that the state had an obligation to remove these mining operations.[351] The Constitutional Court made the orders requested and, on its own accord, recognized the river as a legal person with its own rights that needed protecting.[352]

The Court offered three reasons for granting legal personhood to the rivers: individual rights, community rights, and "biocultural" rights, which led the Court to recognize the river as a legal entity with its own environmental rights.[353] The river was not at the center of its decision; rather it was a way of reinforcing the duties owed to the indigenous communities of the region and protecting their rights, which from this flow the sources of obligations on the state to protect the environment.[354] The Court order pronounced the Atrato River as a legal subject with specific rights regarding its protection, conservation, maintenance, and rehabilitation. It required the government to establish a commission of guardians to safeguard the river

[345] *Id.* at 9.
[346] *Id.* at 11.
[347] *Id.*
[348] *Id.*
[349] *Id.* at 11–12.
[350] *Id.* at 12.
[351] *Id.* at 14.
[352] *Id.* at 14–15.
[353] *Id.* at 15–16.
[354] *Id.* at 17.

(two designated guardians – one local community and one government, plus an "advisory team"), and a separate panel of experts to ensure the court orders are fulfilled. Iorns noted that although the Court made no specific orders outlining what personhood would look like, the ruling was more than symbolic in seeking to ensure rights are respected and clean-up measures adopted and implemented.[355]

In assessing these different approaches to granting rights to nature, Iorns noted important differences in methods of creating legal protections for nature and methods to ensure responsibility is upheld. She observed that the enactment of a statute, ordinance, or constitution can establish parameters of legal personality or define its relevant rights more comprehensively and effectively than a court hearing. Statutory recognition reflects a democratic mandate that can provide more enduring protection.[356] With respect to the methods of ensuring compliance, Iorns explained that while Ecuador and the United States leave it to the courts, New Zealand, India, and Colombia required the creation of a guardian entity that is designed to ensure that activities affecting the river are monitored and the interests of the river are upheld.[357]

IV ADDRESSING CHALLENGES AND LIMITATIONS OF THE PROPOSAL

As is true of all valuable new approaches to regulation in society, the process of gaining public support and securing the political will to implement them can be a slow and difficult process. There are two significant challenges in this regard: establishing and sustaining the political will to both regulate climate change and protect the three categories of the voiceless more ambitiously. As discussed in this chapter and throughout this book, significant progress has been made on both fronts, especially outside the United States. While it may seem counterintuitive to promote two ambitious agendas simultaneously instead of addressing one at a time, this book's thesis is that that these two ambitious and important agendas are better pursued simultaneously because successes in each domain facilitate success in the other. For example, enhanced regulation of climate change protects the voiceless communities, and enhanced protection of the voiceless communities helps promote ecosystem resilience necessary in the fight against climate change.

The most encouraging evidence of the synergies between considering climate change and sustainable development regulation is reflected in the 2019 UN High-Level Meeting on Climate Protection for All.[358] This meeting is intended to bridge the Katowice Climate Change Conference and the in-depth review of Sustainable

---

[355] *Id.* at 17–18.
[356] *Id.* at 19–20.
[357] *Id.* at 19.
[358] IISD, High-Level Meeting: Climate Protection for All, http://sdg.iisd.org/events/high-level-meeting-climate-protection-for-all/ (last accessed Mar. 12, 2019).

Development Goal 13 on Climate Action. It is taking place as part of the July 2019 session of the UN High-Level Political Forum on Sustainable Development (HLPF) and the UN Climate Action Summit being convened by the UN Secretary-General and the HLPF session taking place under the UN General Assembly's auspices in September 2019. According to the concept note for this event,[359] the meeting will focus on the following themes: synergies between the climate and sustainable development agendas; long-term planning and the consideration of future generations in implementation; and means of implementation such as financing, capacity building, and low-carbon technologies. This agenda is very much in line with the advocacy contained in this book.[360]

The most difficult challenge that the proposal in this book faces is the need for regulatory bodies to embrace the sustainable development paradigm as a substantive mandate. There is growing evidence of how sustainable development is rising to the level of customary international law. There are also increasing examples globally of regulatory bodies that have been established with this mandate in mind, but without clear guidelines for how to implement the sustainable development mandate. There has also been very encouraging progress in the courts worldwide regarding how proposed development projects that threaten to exacerbate climate change and further marginalize the voiceless populations need to be held in check by a substantive standard grounded in sustainable development.

Implementing legislation will be challenging in developed nations because this is new regulatory territory and it will be perceived by many as having a potentially crippling effect on economic progress. But the transition from a fossil fuel–based economy to a clean and renewable energy economy poses the same perceived and unsubstantiated threat. There is significant momentum from the climate justice movement in the United States to move toward renewable energy development, propelled both by efforts in the courts, as reflected in the *Juliana* case, and in Congress, as reflected in the Green New Deal. This momentum is also due to the evolving science on "carbon budget" and the global efforts to reel in destructive, carbon-intensive projects in countries like Australia and Canada, as was seen in the *Gloucester Resources Limited* case in Australia in 2019.

Developing countries have generally been much more receptive to the concept of adhering to the sustainable development paradigm. The primary challenges that

---

[359] IISD, Concept Note, High-level Meeting: Climate Protection for All, https://www.un.org/pga/73/wp-content/uploads/sites/53/2018/12/18-LPGA-0193_HLMGlobalClimatePRs_5Dec2018.pdf (last accessed Mar. 12, 2019).

[360] These developments take the intergenerational equity discussion out of the more general framework of sustainable development and connect it to climate change, which is a very positive step forward. An earlier approach just six years ago did not consider climate change as an essential piece of the intergenerational equity discussion. *See generally* UN General Assembly, Report of the Secretary General, Intergenerational Solidarity and the Needs of Future Generations (Aug. 5, 2013), https://sustainabledevelopment.un.org/content/documents/2006future.pdf.

they face are in securing adequate funding and effective enforcement for such mandates to be effectively implemented on the ground. A good example of this "great idea, but will it work?" reality is in Colombia where two landmark decisions in protecting the voiceless were issued within the past few years, but the challenge will be in how effectively these mandates are enforced regarding the zero deforestation goal secured in Dejusticia's youth climate justice case and the legal personhood protections for the Atrato River, which predated the victory in Dejusticia's case. Both decisions involved remarkable and visionary language from the courts regarding how these protections are necessary. Only time will tell regarding whether those ambitious objectives will be implemented effectively.

Both developed and developing countries face a similar challenge in translating the sustainable development paradigm into concrete legal standards. Two examples could be borrowed from legal standards in other legal contexts. For example, in the Anthropocene era, development should not proceed without an evaluation of its potential impact on exacerbating climate change. Every effort to develop has some impact on climate change. But a standard could be adopted in applying sustainable development to climate change that parallels the approach in evaluating whether there has been an unconstitutional infringement of a woman's right to seek an abortion in the United States. The law now asks whether a state law imposes an undue burden that places a substantial obstacle in the path of exercising her right.[361] Similarly, a standard could be established regarding whether a development proposal imposes an undue burden on the sustainability interests of future generations, wildlife, and natural resources such that their continued viability is unreasonably impaired. Another potential approach could parallel the Animal Welfare Amendment Act in New Zealand,[362] which requires assessment of the suitability of non-sentient or nonliving alternatives before proceeding with testing on animals in any context. This type of regulatory standard could be applied on a grander scale to protect the voiceless and promote sustainability. In addition to this standard of sustainable development protection, future generations would have a positive constitutional right to inherit a stable climate as future climate stewards, which would be accompanied by corresponding duties.

Courts need to continue to lead the way in this rights-based revolution and not abrogate their essential role in finding new ways to protect the voiceless through interpretation issue of the common law. Cases like *Juliana* v. *United States* show great promise in laying a foundation for subsequent implementation of government stewardship duties on regulating climate change and/or constitutionally enshrined rights-based protections to a stable climate at the federal or state government levels.

---

[361] *See* Planned Parenthood v. Casey, 505 U.S. 833 (1992).
[362] Katie Pevreall, *NZ Introduce 46 New Regulations to Protect Animals against Human Cruelty*, LIVE KINDLY (July 27, 2017), https://www.livekindly.co/new-zealand-introduces-more-animal-welfare-regulations/.

Regardless of its ultimate success in the courts, the *Juliana* case has inspired a climate justice movement that will continue to propel much-needed elevated ambitions in regulating climate change, much like the unsuccessful Inuit Petition in 2005 ignited a subsequent global climate change and human rights movement.

Constitutional and statutory protection of voiceless populations have been much more common in developing rather than developed countries, yet they face enforcement limitations. Constitutional protections are much less likely in countries like the United States, Canada, and Australia, but the courts are leading the way in developing policy concepts that can be subsequently implemented into law at the national and subnational levels. The Green New Deal[363] is an example of how judicial developments regarding the urgency of the climate change crisis can inspire legislative response, albeit ones that will be very difficult to implement, at least initially.

Despite several recent victories in the United States and abroad, problems of jurisdiction and standing will continue to present a potential obstacle in protection of all three categories of the voiceless. US courts frequently rely on the political question doctrine to evade jurisdiction to establish groundbreaking new precedent opportunities, as the US Circuit Court for the Ninth Circuit did in the *Kivalina* case. The doctrine enables the courts to defer to the legislative or the executive branch on the basis that courts lack standards to make such determinations and/or that the legislative or executive branch is the constitutionally designated forum for the issue. Yet courts must not abrogate their essential role in this rights-based revolution. Waiting for federal legislative action, especially in the United States, will be too little and too late. State and local initiatives have made some progress, but courts can facilitate the movement's impact on a broader scale, as reflected in *Juliana* and the NhRP cases in the wildlife protection domain.

Standing has been a vexing obstacle in protection of all three categories of the voiceless. There are three types of standing for animals. The first is the US view, which requires that human plaintiffs must experience harm themselves in connection with harm in nonhuman entities to be able to sue to protect the interests of nonhuman entities. The second is the "Stewards of Nature" view in the Philippines, whereby humans can protect animals and natural resources from an Anthropocentric perspective, like a private attorney general stepping into the shoes of a government steward to enforce environmental laws. Third, and most effective, is standing for the voiceless entities themselves, pursuant to which humans would serve as guardians to represent the best interests of the voiceless. The next friend mechanism offers promise for humans to serve on behalf of voiceless entities' interests in US courts.

---

[363] Recognizing the duty of the Federal Government to create a Green New Deal, H. Res. 109, 116th Cong. (Feb. 7, 2019), https://www.congress.gov/bill/116th-congress/house-resolution/109/text.

Regardless of which approach to standing for the voiceless is ultimately embraced, critics have expressed concerns regarding possible frivolous litigation and congestion of the court system. An effective solution to address this concern is to require the human guardian in each case to establish a relationship to the voiceless entity to ensure that the guardian is representing the voiceless entities' best interests. This approach parallels mechanisms already in place for approving class actions and guardian ad litem representatives in family law matters. There are also slippery slope concerns about how protections for the voiceless could create unwelcome scenarios that threaten to disrupt the very fabric of our society by empowering those entities who were previously considered property and without rights.[364] These concerns are merely a function of how new developments in the law take time to be accepted in society, much like the long process in conferring legal rights to slaves, women, racial and ethnic minority populations, and the LGBTQ community in the United States over the past two centuries. These legal revolutions did not occur overnight. The legal revolution to protect the voiceless will face similar challenges of societal resistance in the immediate future.

This book has addressed an ambitious task of advocating for two revolutions to proceed simultaneously because of their synergistic relationship – more ambitious climate change regulation and more ambitious protections of the voiceless communities. The eloquent Judge Weeramantry, quoted previously in this book, captures the challenge at hand, and the shared plight of the voiceless, in characteristically compelling and poetic language:

> Justice Douglas thought in terms of giving standing to natural objects, like streams and rivers. Why cannot this principle be extended to human beings? To deny this is to foreclose to future generations their rights to the basic fundamentals of civilized existence. Can any legal system allow this, particularly when the violator is fully aware that this will be the result of his or her action? ... Article 8 of the Universal Declaration ... gives the right to everyone to an effective remedy for acts violating the fundamental rights granted to him or her. Would not members of future generations have this right? Can we deprive them of it with impunity merely because they are not yet in existence?[365]

In 2008, Judge Weeramantry could have only speculated regarding how true his sentiment would be in 2019. His reference to "when the violator is fully aware that this will be the result of his or her action" has prescient relevance in 2019 in light of advances in climate science and the notion of the planet's carbon budget.

---

[364] For a discussion of some of these concerns, *see generally* Shinde, *supra* note 267; Madeleine Lovelle, *Entering Unchartered Waters: Awarding Legal Rights to Rivers*, FUTURE DIRECTIONS INT'L (Sept. 11, 2018), http://www.futuredirections.org.au/publication/entering-unchartered-waters-awarding-legal-rights-to-rivers/.

[365] Judge C. G. Weeramantry, *Commentary on Securing the Rights of Future Generations in International Law* (2008), http://futureroundtable.org/documents/2238847/0/Judge+C.+G.+Weeramantry.pdf/efe49509-32fc-49ad-bb19-64083877d08b.

Governments and private sector actors that act in disregard of these new sources of information regarding the urgency of the climate change crisis are knowingly stealing the future from the unborn and trampling the sustainability of voiceless populations struggling to survive on the planet. The questions that remain are whether the global community will rise to address this daunting regulatory challenge and, if so, whether the response will occur soon enough to save the most vulnerable present and future inhabitants of our planet.

Subject Index

Cases Index

Made in the USA
Las Vegas, NV
14 January 2021

15914418R00144